Modern Political Economy
and Latin America

D1240374

Modern Political Economy and Latin America

Theory and Policy

edited by

Jeffry Frieden, Manuel Pastor Jr., and Michael Tomz

A Member of the Perseus Books Group

All rights reserved. Printed in the United States of America. No part of this publication may be reproduced or transmitted in any form or by any means, electronic or mechanical, including photocopy,
recording, or any information storage and retrieval system, without permission in writing from the
publisher.

Copyright © 2000 by Westview Press, A Member of the Perseus Books Group

Published in 2000 in the United States of America by Westview Press, 5500 Central Avenue, Boulder,
Colorado 80301-2877, and in the United Kingdom by Westview Press, 12 Hid's Copse Road, Cumnor
Hill, Oxford OX2 9JJ

Find us on the World Wide Web at www.westviewpress.com

A CIP catalog record for this book is available from the Library of Congress.
ISBN 0-8133-2417-3 (hc)—0-8133-2418-1 (pb)

The paper used in this publication meets the requirements of the American National Standard for
Permanence of Paper for Printed Library Materials Z39.48-1984.

10   9   8   7   6   5   4   3

Contents

PART ONE
Theoretical Perspectives

PART TWO
Applications

Acronyms

ABEIP	Argentine-Brazilian Economic Integration Program
AD	Democratic Action Party (Venezuela)
ADR	American Depository Receipt
APA	Administrative Procedures Act
CACM	Central American Common Market
CANACINTRA	National Chamber of Manufacturing Industry (Mexico)
CITES	Convention on International Trade in Endangered Species
CONCAMIN	Confederation of Chambers of Industry (Mexico)
CONCANACO	Confederation of National Chambers of Commerce (Mexico)
COPARMEX	Confederation of Employers of the Mexican Republic
COPEI	Social Christian Party (Venezuela)
CPI	Consumer Price Index
DASP	Administrative Department of Public Service (Brazil)
EAI	Enterprise of the Americas Initiative
EBRD	European Bank for Reconstruction and Development
ECLA(CEPAL)	Economic Commission for Latin America
EOI	Export-oriented Industrialization
ERP	Effective Rate of Protection
FDI	Foreign Direct Investment
FMLN	Farabundo Martí National Liberation Front (El Salvador)
GATT	General Agreement on Tariffs and Trade
IDB	Inter-American Development Bank
IMF	International Monetary Fund
ISI	Import Substituting [Substitution] Industrialization
IUCN	International Union for the Conservation of Nature
LAFTA	Latin American Free Trade Association
LDC	Less Developed Country
LIBOR	London Interbank Offer Rate
MERCOSUR	Common Market of the South
MNC	Multinational Corporation
NAFTA	North American Free Trade Agreement
NBER	National Bureau of Economic Research
NGO	Non-Governmental Organization
NIC	Newly Industrialized Country
NIE	Newly Industrializing Economy
OECD	Organization for Economic Cooperation and Development
OPEC	Organization of Petroleum Exporting Countries
PRD	Democratic Revolutionary Party (Mexico)
PRI	Institutionalized Revolutionary Party (Mexico)

PSD	Social Democratic Party (Brazil)
PTB	Brazilian Labor Party
SEWA	Self-employed Women's Association
TNC	Transnational Corporation
UDN	National Democratic Union Party (Brazil)
UNCED	United Nations Conference on Environment and Development
UNCTAD	United Nations Conference on Trade and Development
USAID	United States Agency for International Development
VAT	Value-added Tax
WWF	World Wildlife Fund

Introduction

Modern Political Economy and the Policy Revolution in Latin America

During the final two decades of the twentieth century, Latin America experienced an extraordinary shift in economic policy. After many years of large-scale government intervention in economic affairs, countries throughout the region increased their reliance on the free market and integrated tightly with the world economy. Barriers to foreign trade fell, state-owned enterprises shifted to private hands, public revenues began to approximate expenditures, and leaders abolished many traditional regulations on economic activity.

For both scholars and policymakers, this dramatic transformation raises a series of fascinating questions. Why were the reforms adopted, particularly given a long suspicion of market-friendly strategies in Latin America? Why did the reforms persist, even as financial crises in Mexico (1994), Brazil (1998), and elsewhere seemed to threaten the viability of liberalization? And how did the sea change occur in the midst of democratization, which, by the lights of many observers, should have unleashed populist opposition to the painful reforms?

Increasingly, analysts have viewed this striking period of Latin American reform through the prism of *modern political economy*. Although this approach has many variants, we believe there are three fundamental underpinnings. First, modern political economy distinguishes normative considerations from positive ones. Some practitioners of modern political economy debate the proper level of government involvement in economic affairs, but most simply attempt to explain the choices that governments actually make. After all, it is possible and often desirable to account for government policies without judging them as good or bad. Second, modern political economy takes economics seriously. It understands microeconomic and macroeconomic constraints, recognizes that governments can ignore markets only at great cost, and assumes that actors—even politicians and bureaucrats—rationally seek to maximize their interests. Third, modern political economy takes politics seriously. It acknowledges the power of voters and interest groups, and it pays special attention to inequality and other social pressures that not only emerge from but also affect public policy and economic performance.

This book introduces readers to modern political economy in the Latin American context. The project grew from our frustration with traditional classes and literature on the region. Many books devoted inadequate attention to the interaction between economics and politics or analyzed reforms from a purely normative perspective, with some authors celebrating the triumph of market reason and others decrying the distributional damage. As we struggled to fill the gap in our own courses, we built collections of reserve articles and sent students on endless trips to the library. Noting the wear and tear on copy machines and shoe leather, we recognized the existence of a potential market and, as rational actors, sought to fill it.

Modern Political Economy: Setting the Stage

For decades, most discussions of economic and political development in Latin America reflected the clash between modernization and dependency theories. Proponents of both theories recognized that Latin America was underdeveloped relative to the United States and other industrialized nations, but they disagreed about the roots of the problem and the appropriate solution. According to modernization theory, Latin American countries were following a development trajectory similar to the one that Western Europe and North America had traveled long ago. By simply letting the free market work, governments in Latin America could allegedly speed the development process. Dependency theorists, in contrast, argued that global imperialism and declining terms of international trade were impeding economic performance. Inward-oriented economic policies and extensive government regulation could help even the development odds.

Each perspective had strengths and weaknesses. The *dependistas* correctly noted that the progress of a country depends partly on its foreign relations, but their pessimism seemed misplaced in light of the Asian "economic miracle." By integrating with the world economy instead of erecting barriers to trade, East Asia managed to industrialize and achieve rapid but equitable economic growth. The modernization school, for its part, rightly emphasized that local and national leaders could spoil development by adopting ill-conceived economic policies. Nevertheless, modernizationists could not explain why the more advanced countries of Latin America fell into dictatorship during the 1960s and 1970s, since economic and political progress were supposed to go hand in hand.

The debate between these contending perspectives waned in the 1980s, when a series of events seemed to demonstrate the superiority of free-market policies. Most Latin American economies stagnated or regressed during this period, such that per capita income throughout the region was lower at the end of the decade than when it began. The debt crisis both symbolized and exacerbated the economic malaise. Beginning with Mexico in 1982, nearly every Latin American country fell into arrears on its foreign debts and rescheduled its obligations to international banks. Scholars and policymakers traced the troubles to a bloated public sector and inefficient industries, which were allegedly the by-products of heavy government involvement in the economy.

Outside the region, the fall of the Berlin Wall and the subsequent disintegration of the socialist bloc reinforced skepticism of the government as an effective economic manager. Dependency theories fell into disarray, much like the interventionist strategies they once justified, and it appeared that there were no serious alternatives to the free market as a vehicle for development. With the discussion narrowed to refinements of the laissez-faire model, technocratic details became the order of the day: which markets to liberalize first, how best to privatize state-owned enterprises, and what institutional rules would prevent government spending from rising to its formerly excessive levels.

Yet even as free-market thinking rose to dominate policy in Latin America, it came under the scrutiny of economists and political scientists. Some repeated the old refrain that markets perpetuate inequality, a critique that continued to resonate with much of the Latin American public. At the same time a new wave of thinkers, working within and elaborating upon what we have termed modern political economy, questioned whether markets always produce the most efficient outcomes in the absence of government involvement. These scholars identified a host of "market failures" that governments might seek to correct.

Market Failures

Market failures occur when free exchanges among private buyers and sellers create situations that are undesirable for society as a whole. For instance, individuals and firms may fail to produce goods at the ideal level. Left to their own devices, private actors may generate excessive levels of unwanted outputs (like air pollution) while failing to meet the social demand for more desirable goods (like advanced education). Even when markets do succeed in producing at the optimal level, a second problem could arise: The invisible hand may fail to *distribute* goods to people who need or want them most desperately. In some cases, government could make society better off by redistributing goods in ways that enhance the well-being of some consumers without seriously compromising the welfare of others.

Market failures can arise from many sources, but scholars have focused special attention on problems of *asymmetric information*, in which doubts about the reliability of economic partners can lead to undesirable outcomes. Consider the credit market. A borrower may choose to spend the proceeds of the loan on a highly risky investment. Lenders cannot know the intentions of the borrower in advance—therein lies the asymmetry of information, but they do understand the folly of raising interest rates without limit to compensate for the risk of default. Expensive credit would attract "lemons" with the highest probability of default while discouraging more reliable borrowers who would feel reluctant to borrow at exorbitant rates that they could never repay with earnings from their conservative investments. Moreover, higher interest rates could encourage reckless behavior and make default even more likely. To avoid selecting lemons and promoting irresponsibility, creditors may keep interest rates below the market-clearing level and refuse loans to small or unproven borrowers, about whom there is little information. In this way, markets may fail to meet the demand for credit. This analysis may explain why so many seemingly strong but small enterprises in Latin America have trouble finding the credit to expand and modernize.

Similar problems hamper the labor market. Firms employ workers, but no supervisor can monitor all workers all the time, and it is nearly impossible to infer the effort of an individual employee from the output of the entire workforce. In many instances, only the employees themselves truly know how hard they work on the job. Given this asymmetry of information, price (the major informational signal used in markets) may be a poor indicator: Those willing to work for the lowest wage might also be likeliest to shirk, perhaps because of frustration with a low wage! To avoid attracting the wrong workers, firms may choose to pay higher wages. As a result, wages could rise above the point at which demand equals supply, causing persistent unemployment, which is clearly undesirable from a societal perspective. This incomplete-information approach may explain why the informal sector, which exists in the netherworld between wages that maximize effort and wages that clear markets, has persisted and grown in Latin America.

Even in the presence of symmetric information, though, a gap between supply and demand can arise due to monopolies, externalities (spillover effects), and other sources of market failure. For example, the effluent from a factory could contaminate the water and air used by thousands of people. In the absence of government regulation, managers of the factory may not fully consider the public costs of their actions, resulting in more pollution than is socially optimal. Of course, spillover effects could also be positive: Education not only benefits those who undertake schooling but also raises the productivity of the entire economy. Without government efforts to encourage education, this valuable good may be under-provided. In Latin America and other regions of the world, these kinds of spillovers are pervasive and may call for government intervention.

One lesson is common to all these examples: Rational individuals and firms may find themselves stuck in situations where supply does not match demand and in which the invisible hand does not allocate resources in the most efficient way. The existence of market failures does not negate the general conclusion that competition is good for economic performance, but it does make clear that government policy can contribute to social welfare in some circumstances. For this reason, many political economists have turned their attention to explaining the policies that governments actually adopt. Why are certain governments more interventionist than others, and why do leaders sometimes fail to adopt policies that would enhance the well-being of society as a whole?

Government Failures

Although governments can promote efficiency by intervening in selected markets, the words "efficient" and "government" do not always go together in Latin America. Whatever the range of market failures, the region is also replete with *government failures:* state policies that undermine social welfare. The "lost decade" of the 1980s, partly the result of a previous era of stifling regulations, excessive foreign debts, and bloated state enterprises, illustrates how far public policy can deviate from the economic ideal.

For a time, observers blamed government failures on the errors of misinformed or incompetent bureaucrats. Key decisionmakers exacerbated problems of production and distribution because presumably they did not know any better. This condescending view of the state, however, seems inconsistent with standard models of the economy as a collection of rational individuals and firms that seek to maximize their interests. Why would social actors who are rational in their roles as consumers and producers suddenly become irrational and prone to foolish mistakes when they cross the line from the private to the public sector?

Fortunately, a more plausible explanation is available: Politicians and bureaucrats are sensible, but some prefer to serve the narrow interests of lobby groups or individuals rather than society as a whole. Modern political economy takes precisely this perspective. The authors whose works are included in this volume assume that policymakers are as rational as the economic actors—workers, firms, and consumers—that they regulate. To some extent, these policymakers pursue their own vision of how extensively the state should be involved in the economy. At the same time, policymakers must respond to the demands of key constituents, including private individuals and groups that determine who will hold political office.

It is also useful to presume that economic actors behave rationally in their interactions with politicians. These actors understand that governments can shape the economy, and they demand policies that will enhance the value of their own assets. Of course, some actors are highly sensitive to government policy and strongly motivated to press their case, whereas others are relatively insulated from government interference and more likely to remain aloof from the political process. In any case, the clout of economic actors depends on how effectively they are organized, how many resources lie at their disposal, and how political and social institutions channel their demands into government policy.

By taking the political process seriously, we can appreciate why government policies often fail to reflect the recommendations of economists. Self-evidently bad policies, such as cripplingly high barriers to foreign trade, can provoke economists to throw up their hands in puzzlement and disapproval: Why are leaders forsaking a policy that would improve the welfare of society as a whole? Modern political economy brings us closer to the answer. Excessive trade barriers and other seemingly wasteful policies emerge from the interaction of rational economic and political agents who are striving to advance their own goals. Rather than "mistakes" arising from misinformation or incompetence, their decisions represent conscious attempts to promote their own goals, however narrowly or broadly defined. In some cases, the interests of a few politicians and lobby groups may prevail over the more utilitarian objectives of society. Modern political economy, with its emphasis on the clash of interests, can help account for these lopsided outcomes.

What's Modern About
Modern Political Economy?

Of course, political economy is not an entirely new phenomenon. Many of history's most significant economic thinkers—Adam Smith, David Ricardo, John Stuart Mill, and Karl Marx—blended political and economic concerns into their work. Only in the late nineteenth century did the two fields begin to diverge, with economics increasingly focusing on the structure of the firm and general equilibria between supply and demand, whereas political science concentrated on legislative organizations, electoral rules, and the partisan affiliations of voters.

In the long night of separation, two schools of thought seemed to keep the flames of political and economic interaction ablaze. The first was the Marxist school, sometimes called *radical political economy*, which viewed the state as a tool of capitalists and argued that most political and economic struggles pitted workers against the bourgeoisie. The second was the public choice framework, sometimes called *new political economy*, which developed the notion of rent-seeking and regarded most government policy as parasitic or misguided.

Each school has strengths, but modern political economy represents a new and different synthesis. Many authors in this volume acknowledge the Marxist insight that class conflict pervades economic and political life. Nevertheless, class-based cleavages do not always predominate in Latin America, and government policy does not always serve the wealthy. For instance, the trade protection associated with Import Substituting Industrialization benefited both workers *and* firms in targeted industries, thereby encouraging a cross-class alliance against proletarians and capitalists in the export sector. Moreover, the recent turn toward freer trade has not unambiguously benefited the rich. Instead, laissez-faire policies have disciplined capitalists by curtailing the power of the least productive and, hence, most exploitative and wasteful firms. Modern political economy augments the central lessons of Marxism by considering economic sectors as well as classes, and it refines the analysis by allowing for inter-class alliances and government policies that hurt the rich.

Modern political economy also borrows many attractive elements of the public choice approach while avoiding some of its shortcomings. Like Marxists, public choice theorists contend that interest groups can twist government policy to serve narrow goals, although they tend to blame nonmoneyed actors, like labor, for socially undesirable results. This view resonates with many proponents of modern political economy who have supplemented the public choice perspective by considering how foreign pressure and domestic institutions mix with interest groups to influence economic policy. Public choice and modern political economy differ not only in scope but also in their attitude toward government intervention in the economy. Most public choice theorists harbor a visceral distaste for government, causing them to overlook important market failures that could warrant a more active state. Modern political economy, in contrast, seeks to identify ways in which the government could intervene to minimize rent-seeking.

The modernity of modern political economy stems not only from its synthesis of earlier perspectives but also from the advanced tools that it deploys. The leading scholars use meticulous logic and, in some cases, mathematical models to derive their hypotheses. Then, they deploy econometric techniques and qualitative case studies to test their arguments as thoroughly as possible. Throughout this process, they devote considerable attention to specifying the dependent variable and its likely causes. In the interests of accessibility, this book eschews much of the mathematical material that now appears in the professional literature. Nevertheless, the articles in this volume should make clear how the new premium on logical and empirical rigor has enriched our understanding of politics and economics in Latin America.

The Structure of the Book

This volume introduces students to modern political economy and shows how scholars have used the approach to analyze Latin American issues. We selected thirty-five readings, organized them thematically, and included a series of synthetic introductions to guide readers through the material. In the interest of saving space, we shortened many articles without—we hope—obscuring the central message and analytical rigor of the original pieces. As a consequence, this volume contains pithy synopses of work by some of the most distinguished researchers in the field.

The book is divided into two parts. Part One covers the leading theoretical approaches to political economy in the Latin American context. We begin by reviewing the central dilemmas of market failure and government failure. The readings identify many scenarios that could justify government intervention, but they also caution about the risks of state action. With this panorama of economic and political pitfalls in mind, we offer a framework for explaining the policies that governments actually adopt. Why does the degree of government involvement in economic affairs vary across countries and over time? The readings suggest how politicians and bureaucrats, interest groups and firms, voters, ideas, social institutions, and foreign pressures combine to produce the policies we observe.

Part Two applies the theoretical apparatus to specific problems in Latin America. The readings consider how the interplay of economics and politics affects economic growth, foreign trade, and macroeconomic decisionmaking in the region. Of course, political institutions play a special role in all these areas, so we include a series of readings that probe the causes and consequences of independent central banks, democratic decisionmaking processes, and other prominent institutions that affect economic policy. The book concludes with new thinking about social issues, including gender inequality, environmental degradation, and the distribution of income.

Many of the readings in Parts One and Two probe the bidirectional relationship between economics and politics: how the economy structures political power and social opportunity, and how political coalitions and popular frustrations influence the economy. The authors show how markets constrain the choices of political leaders and why government policy sometimes falls short of its potential. At the same time, they explain why a "second-best" policy that enjoys broad political support might be better than a "first-best" policy that is popular with professional economists but doomed at the ballot box. All the readings exhibit a rich understanding of the interaction between economics and politics, which will prove increasingly important as Latin America enters a second, and perhaps more difficult, phase of reform.

Political Economy and the Future of Latin America

Although there remain exceptions to, and laggards in, the process of economic reform and restructuring, most of Latin America has changed in striking ways since the early 1980s. State firms have been privatized, trade barriers have fallen, and deficits have been tamed. Money flows freely to and from the capital markets of Mexico City, Buenos Aires, and São Paulo, subjecting Latin American economies to the discipline of the international financial system as well as the threat of exit by local investors. Despite imperfections, the political systems of the region are more democratic and competitive than in previous generations. Economic and political reform now seem like resilient features of the regional landscape in the same way that dictatorship and economic nationalism were once regarded as backdrops to all things Latin American.

Of course, the increasing consolidation of reform does not signal the arrival of nirvana. Results from the first wave of liberalization have appeared, and not all are positive. Some privatizations have resulted in monopoly or near-monopoly conditions for newly profit-maximizing firms. The resumption of growth, particularly after the early 1990s, has reduced poverty but done little to equalize the distribution of income. Elections now occur regularly but technocratic elites continue to make key decisions, particularly on economic policy, without much public input. To increase accountability, countries in the region must shift from the technocratic present as well as the authoritarian past.

In short, important political and economic challenges remain. As a result, a wide range of actors, from center-left parties and coalitions in Mexico, Argentina, and Chile to the International Monetary Fund and the InterAmerican Development Bank, are now calling for a second phase of reform. Even those most directly involved in organizing and implementing the first generation of changes acknowledge the need for another round of reforms—not necessarily as deep and paradigmatic as those in the desperate times of the early 1990s but profound nonetheless.

The blueprint for this second phase remains unclear, however. Some think that governments in Latin America should create institutions and regulations to overcome market failures in the newly liberalized economies (see Levy). Others believe the region must now remedy the inequality that the first wave of reform neglected, perhaps by improving education and finance for the poor (see IDB and UNCTAD readings). Still others insist that the second phase should focus on good governance: more transparent politics and lower levels of corruption (see Pradhan). To achieve this end, countries might strengthen their legal systems and include traditionally marginalized groups (the lower class, ethnic minorities, and indigenous peoples) in the policymaking process.

The Mexican bank controversy of 1998–1999 illustrates how challenging the second round of reforms can be. To prevent a meltdown of the domestic financial system after the 1994 peso crisis, the Mexican government absorbed the bad loans of private banks. International technocrats initially hailed the plan, in part because it protected depositors and prevented an even more desperate run on the banks. In this sense, the bailout achieved an important second-generation goal: overcoming market failures that were threatening the survival of the financial system. Controversy arose in 1998, however, when Mexican policymakers proposed to consolidate the bad loans as part of the national debt. This seemingly rational extension of the bailout program would have garnered kudos in the U.S. graduate programs in which many Mexican technocrats had trained, but it provoked an acrimonious debate about inequality and transparency.

Critics from the left and the right argued that the government was bailing out the rich at the expense of the poor. Meeting the interest and principal payments on unsecured loans, which were held by wealthy individuals, would have forced the government to cut spending in other areas, including social services for marginal groups. The plan seemed even more galling when several reports revealed that Mexican bank owners had abused the previous round of bank privatization by lending to themselves and in some cases, siphoning money to Swiss bank accounts, failing enterprises, and the campaign coffers of the government party. In a previous era of authoritarian politics, the government would have controlled the popular debate, but in the new age of political accountability, the opposition held congressional hearings and even organized a national plebiscite on the issue.

The government eventually triumphed in Congress, but only after providing more favorable treatment for small debtors and co-opting the more conservative wing of the opposition. In 1999, with costs of the bailout climbing up to nearly 20 percent of the gross domestic product, the banking issue once again raised its head by feeding popular resentment of the government. In summary, a strategy that had passed the technocratic test floundered because of distributional and governance concerns.

As the Mexican example makes clear, Latin America still faces many economic and political challenges. Modern political economy offers the tools to understand these challenges and identify possible solutions. By paying careful attention to the interactions among public officials and private markets, scholars and policymakers can explain the choices of governments and evaluate their effects on social welfare. The readings in this volume show how much we can learn by rigorously exploring the interplay of economics and politics in Latin America.

A note to the reader: This book contains abridged versions of previously published material. Complete references to the original sources appear in the Acknowledgments (pages 331–332) and at the end of each reading.

PART ONE
Theoretical Perspectives

Section I

Contending Perspectives
on Market Failure
and Government Failure

Scholars and observers of Latin America are often concerned with explaining the region's developmental progress and the variations among the countries of the region. Early attempts along these lines focused on more or less purely economic factors; more recently scholars have attempted to incorporate political economy considerations (see Section II: Explanations of Government Policy). But the purely economic issues provide an important baseline for understanding Latin American development.

Early on, the most common view of observers of Latin America was what has come to be known as the *modernization* perspective, which anticipated that economic development was only a matter of time. Eventually the region would pass through the various stages of economic growth characterized by the developed world—from agriculture to industry to services—and as it did so its income and wealth would rise accordingly. The region's underdevelopment was only a temporary condition that would be overcome with the passage of time and growth. It was easy to subscribe to this view between the 1860s and the 1920s, as the continent's major countries did in fact seem to be on a growth path not dissimilar to that of North America and Western Europe, only several decades behind them.

In the 1930s and 1940s, many scholars and others came to believe that Latin America's developmental difficulties were more than a passing phase and that they were rather the result of some deeper features of the structure of Latin American societies. The *structuralists* emphasized how the very organization of these economies might make development difficult (see Arndt, reading 1). For example, although increased foreign demand for a country's products would normally lead to increased production and income, the structuralists argued that many bottlenecks impeded such a response in Latin America. Inadequate information meant few knew about the opportunities, poor financial markets meant that even those who wanted to could not fund new investments, and weak infrastructure meant it was hard to get new products to market. In these circumstances, they argued, leaving development to the market was a formula for continued stagnation and backwardness. Purposive government action was called for to encourage industrialization: trade protection and subsidies for industries deemed to be of national importance, state control of banking, and government ownership of such basic industries as electricity, petroleum, and steel. Only this sort of conscious intervention—usually under the rubric of Import Substituting Industrialization (ISI)—could break the bottlenecks of structural insufficiencies. The emphasis was on government action to correct rampant market failures.

By the 1970s, many of the countries that had followed this path seemed to be in serious economic trouble, which was exacerbated by the debt crisis that started in 1982. In addition, a cohort of countries in East Asia that had eschewed some of the more interventionist features of Latin American ISI seemed to be doing extremely well. Although these nations were hardly paragons of laissez-faire, the more successful East Asian countries generally had lower levels of protection, subsidy, and government ownership than in Latin America. All this encouraged something of a reaction to structuralist views; those opposed pointed out that Latin American government interventions were often pernicious. The new economic reformers further countered the structuralist emphasis on the need to correct market failures by insisting that government failures were even more common and more damaging. Why, they argued, replace an imperfect market with an even more imperfect government policy?

Over the course of the 1980s and 1990s, a general consensus emerged that includes elements of all three views. Most analysts now agree that market forces are generally effective at encouraging economic growth and development. But most also agree that there are in fact areas in which measured and careful government involvement can improve the functioning of the market. What exactly these areas are, and what sorts of involvement are most desirable, remains the topic of much debate (see Williamson, reading 3; Levy, reading 4; and Pradhan, reading 5).

Nonetheless, there is probably more consensus on the prerequisites of economic development now than there has been for much of this century. Market forces should predominate, but they need the underpinnings of solid political institutions and stable economic policies. The fact that such consensual prescriptions are rarely followed leads to important questions about exactly what does in fact determine the course of political and economic organization in the nations of Latin America, questions that are raised in Section II.

1

The Origins of Structuralism

H. W. ARNDT

Introduction

In his recent book on economic development, I. M. D. Little distinguishes two broad categories of development economics. He calls them 'neoclassical economics' and 'structuralism'.

> The structuralist sees the world as inflexible. Change is inhibited by obstacles, bottlenecks and constraints. People find it hard to move or adapt, and resources tend to be stuck. In economic terms, the supply of most things is inelastic. Such general inflexibility was thought to apply particularly to LDCs. . . . Entrepreneurs were lacking; and communications were poor. . . . This alleged inflexibility was married to the evident fact that the production structure of developing countries was very different from that of developed countries. To achieve development, it had to be changed rapidly. . . . The structuralist view of the world provides a reason for distrusting the price mechanism and for trying to bring about change in other ways. If supplies and demands are very inelastic large price changes are needed to achieve small quantitative adjustments. Large price changes are disturbing, both directly and also because they result in changes in income distribution. . . . If the losers are powerful, they may . . . be able to resist the change through organised industrial or political action. . . . [Structuralism] primarily seeks to provide a reason for managing change by administrative action.

The purpose of this article is to explore further the origins of structuralism, both in the broader sense and in the more specific context of Latin American structuralist theories of inflation, and the links between them.

The Doctrine of Market Failure

In the nineteenth century and well into the twentieth, socialist and other critics of capitalism condemned it chiefly on two grounds. First, that it was unjust and exploitative. Secondly, that it was unstable, prone to crises and doomed to collapse. Rarely, if ever, was capitalism criticized on the ground that its quintessential mechanism of market forces operating through the price system fails to work. This third line of criticism, which may be called the doctrine of market failure, was developed, chiefly in Britain, in the 1930s and 1940s, though traces of it can of course be found earlier in many places.

The classical and neoclassical thesis according to which, in a perfectly competitive economy and in the absence of externalities, market forces operating through the price mechanism assure an optimum allocation of resources, statically and dynamically, was open to attack at three points. First, prices may give the wrong signals because they are distorted by monopoly or other influences. Secondly, labour and other factors of production may respond to price signals inadequately or even perversely. Thirdly, although ready to respond appropriately to correct price signals, factors of production may be immobile, unable to move quickly if at all. Let us call them the 'signalling', 'response' and 'mobility' components of the mechanism.

Structuralism in the broad sense of scepticism about the efficacy of the price mechanism and a conviction that government planning and controls must make up for 'market failure' was common to most, though not all, of the first generation of development economists. Some emphasized the inadequacy of prices as a guide to investment decisions. Others stressed what they believed to be the unacceptable social costs of the free play of market forces, especially its effects in aggravating inequality, nationally and internationally. All agreed that for various reasons all three components of the price mechanism work even less well in underdeveloped than in developed countries and that neoclassical economic theory was therefore largely inapplicable to LDCs.

What is the connection between structuralism in this broad sense and the Latin American 'structuralist' theory of inflation?

The Latin American Structuralist Theory of Inflation

Inflation had bedevilled economic policy in most Latin American countries for many years, and structuralist-type arguments had been put forward by opponents of liberal economic policies from time to time, in Brazil as early as 1949. But it was primarily the experience of Chile, the most conspicuous case of chronic inflation, that gave rise to the formulation of a structuralist theory of inflation. The Chilean peso had depreciated externally and domestically in all but 15 of the preceding 80 years, at annual rates which rose from around 20% in the 1940s to well over 50% in the mid–1950s. In the latter half of 1955, the Chilean Government decided on yet another effort at stabilization and employed a group of American consultants, the Klein-Saks Mission, to prepare a stabilization program. It was this, reinforced by broadly 'monetarist' stabilization policies recommended by the IMF in Argentina and Chile in 1958/9, that sparked off the monetarist–structuralist controversy.

Credit for the first formal statement of the structuralist theory of inflation is due to a Mexican economist, Juan Noyola Vazquez, who in an article published in a Mexican journal in 1956 argued that, especially in underdeveloped countries, inflation is not a monetary phenomenon but the result of interaction between two factors, 'basic inflationary pressures' due to structural rigidities and the 'propagating mechanism' of competing income claims accommodated by monetary expansion.

After this initial Mexican contribution, the structuralist theory of inflation was developed in Santiago, at ECLA (the UN Economic Commission for Latin America of which Prebisch was Executive Secretary) and at the Institute of Economics of the University of Chile. The chapter on Chile in the ECLA *Economic Survey of Latin America for 1957* contained a brief statement of the view that Chile's inflation was a structural phenomenon, but what has been called the *locus classicus* of the structuralist theory of inflation is an article, first published in Spanish in December 1958 by Osvaldo Sunkel. He stated the central proposition of structuralism concisely:

> *Basic Inflationary Pressures.* These are fundamentally governed by the structural limitations, rigidity or inflexibility of the economic system. In fact, the inelasticity of some productive sectors to adjust to changes in demand—or, in short, the lack of mobility of productive resources and the defective functioning of the price system—are chiefly responsible for structural inflationary disequilibria.

The intriguing fact is that both Sunkel and Noyola (to whom Sunkel expressed his indebtedness) cited, as the authority for their statements about structural factors, an article by Kalecki published in Mexico in 1955. Noyola referred to 'the analysis by Kalecki which stresses the importance of the rigidity of supply and the degree of monopoly in the economic system'. Sunkel cited both Kalecki's article and the UN *World Economic Survey 1956* written after Kalecki had ceased to be in charge of the surveys but no doubt still under his influence.

The chief point of Kalecki's article, based on lectures he gave in Mexico in 1953, was to stress that in LDCs 'the supply of food may be fairly rigid', and that the inelastic supply of food will, if aggregate demand increases and raises food prices, 'cause a fall in real wages and will generate an inflationary price-wage spiral'. The UN *World Economic Survey* spelled out the structuralist doctrine more fully:

> An additional key element in inflationary pressure in under-developed countries is the high degree of immobility of resources. . . , which prevents the structure of production from adapting itself sufficiently rapidly to the pattern of demand. . . . Thus, in under-developed countries with limited supplies of food and other essential consumer goods, severe inflationary pressures may be generated even in the absence of budget deficits and with relatively low rates of investment.

A year after the publication of Kalecki's article, in 1956, Kaldor visited Santiago as a consultant to ECLA, commissioned to undertake a study of Chile's economic problems. In his 1959 paper, which was also initially published in Mexico, Kaldor attributed many of Chile's problems to overregulation of the economy, but also restated Kalecki's argument more formally: if productivity rises in non-agricultural sectors, but not in agriculture, then, assuming that the demand for food depends purely on the level of real wages and is inelastic with respect to the relative prices of food and non-food items, an expansion of money supply in step with rising GDP would raise money wages and 'the rise in money wages would cause, by a series of steps, a sufficient rise in food prices (relative to both wages and non-food prices) as to offset entirely the increase in real earnings in terms of non-food items'.

A year later, the American economist, Hollis Chenery, was invited to Santiago to give the ECLA Lectures. His main concern was to stimulate interest in input–output analysis and linear programming for investment planning in developing countries. But he also made a spirited plea for structuralism:

> A central problem of development policy is the adequacy of free market forces in allocating investment resources. . . . The traditional view of economic policy in Western countries is derived from the classical theory of competitive equilibrium. . . . The main policy implication of this model is that, under static conditions of perfect competition, market forces will tend to bring about the best use of a country's resources.

He pointed out that the Keynesian revolution, while successfully challenging classical theory in relation to short-term fluctuations in income and employment, had left its conclusions on longer-term resource allocation virtually unaffected. He identified departures from competition, dynamic causes and equity considerations as the 'three kinds of defect in the free price-mechanism as an instrument for achieving the maximum social welfare' and listed, under the first heading, such obstacles as inadequate information, restrictions on entry into occupations and limited access to capital.

> These factors combine to produce a rigid market structure, prevalent monopoly positions, immobile labour and capital, and consequently great inequalities in the returns to labour and capital in different uses. . . . Serious structural disequilibrium in the use of labour, natural resources or foreign exchange represents one of the situations justifying state intervention in investment decisions.

Interest in the subject reached its climax with a monster conference on 'Inflation and Growth in Latin America' held in Rio de Janeiro in January 1963 and attended by 80 economists.

The structuralist theory of inflation did not emerge unscathed from the intensive discussion. Arthur Lewis, in his summing up, stressed the need to distinguish between the original cause and the spiral mechanism. The structuralist arguments about supply inelasticity related entirely to the former, but in this respect there was no difference between Chile and (say) India. Why then has inflation been so much more of a problem in Chile? 'The difference is that Chile is in the grip of the spiral process to a much greater degree than India.' Another participant, T. E. Davis, spelled this out. Inflation in Chile has been 'a conscious policy that constitutes a common second best' for powerful interest groups; conservatives that have the power to block direct taxation; Radicals and the Left that have sufficient power to block any attempts to reduce real wages; and large private firms that have sufficient power to insist that bank credit to the private sector expands *pari passu* with that to government. 'Stabilization programs are politically feasible only when it appears to these groups that inflation might conceivably "get out of hand"; but opposition reappears when the rate of inflation has been reduced to what historically seem to constitute "safe" levels.'

If this was the crux of the problem of inflation in Latin America, it had little if anything to do with all the arguments about inelastic supply, immobility of resources and the other alleged defects of the price mechanism. The problem of excess income claims by organized sectional interests had, after all, long been recognized as one form of 'cost push', although not always, it must be admitted, given its due by hard-line monetarists.

Oddly enough, the same conclusion was already implicit in the very first statement of the structuralist theory of inflation, by Noyola. While he attributed inflation in both Chile and Mexico fundamentally to structural factors—chiefly instability of export earnings and capacity to import in Chile and inelastic supply of food due to earlier land reform and government agricultural policies in Mexico—he explained the much more severe inflation in Chile by the fact that the 'propagating mechanism' was much weaker in Mexico because its huge labour surplus in agriculture depressed real wages and weakened the trade unions. It was the strong organization in Chile of the major social groups with their competing income claims, in other words the 'propagating mechanism' rather than the initiating 'structural factors', that accounted for Chile's much more serious inflation problem.

Conclusion

Criticism of the structuralist theory of inflation of course did not spell the end of structuralism as a broad anti-market ideology, either in developed or developing countries. In developed countries the doctrine of market failure has come under increasingly critical scrutiny, broadly on the ground, as H. G. Johnson once put it, that 'the possibility of market failure is not sufficient to prove the certainty of government success'. The price system, with all its acknowledged defects, may yet, on balance, be the lesser evil, compared with the operation in practice of bureaucratic planning and controls—controls which are often, as at least one contributor to the Latin American debate pointed out, a major source of the very rigidities which hamper the working of the price system.

H. W. Arndt, "The Origins of Structuralism," *World Development* 13, no. 2 (1985): 151–59.

2

Government Failures
in Development

ANNE O. KRUEGER

Early development economists recognized the role of government in providing "social overhead capital" or "infrastructure" to facilitate economic development. However, most analysis focussed on a second role: government should, they believed, undertake activities that would compensate for "market failures." These were regarded as being so much more extreme in developing countries as to make their economies different not only in degree but in kind from industrial countries. Market failures were thought to result from "structural rigidities," which were defined as a lack of responsiveness to price signals. It was therefore concluded that governments should take a leading role in the allocation of investment, control the "commanding heights" of the economy, and otherwise intervene to compensate for market failures. Indeed, some associated "development economics" with structuralist views and believed that development economics was different *because* markets did not function.

Whether this emphasis on market failures and the role of government only provided an ideological justification for what would have happened anyway, or whether governments assumed a central role in the economy because of these beliefs is not particularly relevant. The fact is that, by the 1970s and early 1980s, governments in most developing countries were mired down in economic policies that were manifestly unworkable. Whether market failures had been present or not, most knowledgeable observers concluded that there had been colossal government failures. In many countries, there could be little question but that government failure significantly outweighed market failure

There were many failures, both of omission and commission. Failures of commission included exceptionally high-cost public sector enterprises, engaged in a variety of manufacturing and other economic activities not traditionally associated with the public sector. Notable among these were: state marketing boards, which often served as a monopoly distribution network and frequently also provided inputs (erratically, and often heavily subsidized if not free) to farmers, state ownership of retail shops for the distribution of foods and other items deemed essential; state operation of mines and manufacturing activities, state enterprises accorded monopoly rights for importing a variety of commodities; nationalized banking and insurance operations; even luxury hotels are often found in the public sector. In addition, government investment programs were highly inefficient and wasteful; government controls over private sector activity were pervasive and costly; and government public sector deficits, fuelled by public sector enterprise deficits, excessive investment programs, and other government expenditures, led to high rates of inflation, with their attendant consequences for resource allocation, savings behavior, and the allocation of private investment.

Complementary to these phenomena were failures of omission: deterioration of transport and communications facilities, which raised costs for many private (and public) sector activities; maintenance of fixed nominal exchange rates in the face of rapid domestic inflation, buttressed by exchange controls and import licensing; insistence upon nominal rates of interest well below the rate of inflation with credit rationing so that governments could supervise credit allocation among competing claimants; and failure to maintain existing infrastructure facilities.

As by-products of these failures, large-scale and visible corruption often emerged. Further, evidence mounted that many of the programs and policies that had been adopted with the stated objective of helping the poor had in fact disproportionately benefitted the more affluent members of society. All of these phenomena took place in the context of pervasive government involvement in, and control over, economic activity.

"Market failure" has always been defined as being present when conditions for Pareto-optimality are not satisfied in ways in which an omniscient, selfless, social guardian government could costlessly correct. One of the lessons of experience with development is that governments are not omniscient, selfless, social guardians and corrections are not costless. If one takes as a rough-and-ready standard that a successful government will undertake policies that result in a satisfactory rate of growth of living standards relative to the available resources, there is some suggestive empirical evidence. First, there is no evidence that living standards fell in the now-developing countries prior to 1950, a time which many observers associate with a period of laissez-faire. In many African countries however, living standards have been falling—in some cases precipitously—since. The latter period has been one of active government intervention, and there is no other obvious reason for the difference in performance in the two periods.

It is also suggestive, but not conclusive, that savings rates in many developing countries rose sharply from the 1950s to the 1970s, while growth rates showed little change, or even fell. India's savings rate, for example, rose from 14 percent in 1960 to 22 percent of GNP in 1987, although the growth rate remained constant. Despite the increased price of oil and an increase in the savings rate from 12 to 20 percent, Nigeria experienced only a 1.1 percent annual rate of increase in per capita income over the same period. It is certainly plausible that higher rates of savings and investment should result in more rapid rates of growth: to the extent they did not do so, there is presumptive evidence that government policies were not growth-promoting.

This experience has naturally raised a large number of interrelated questions. They may broadly be grouped in four categories: 1) What is "the government"? 2) What is the comparative advantage of government? 3) What are the dynamics of government intervention? 4) Can a positive theory of political behavior be formulated that will help explain when and how alternative policies will evolve in the political arena?

What Is "The Government"?

In the 1940s and 1950s, most development economists believed that markets in developing countries functioned highly imperfectly, and concluded that there was therefore a strong case for government intervention. Implicitly, it was assumed that the government would behave as a benevolent social guardian, in the Fabian Socialist tradition. Economists would serve in government, calculating shadow prices and formulating planning models. Selfless bureaucrats would then carry out the plans. Coordination and administration of public sector activity was implicitly assumed to be costless. Moreover, as long as technocrats were in any event going to decide upon an investment and production plan, it was a logical next step to believe that the activities so determined should also be carried out in the public sector.

Experience with development over the past 40 years has led to considerable skepticism about this view. One must ask why economists were ever comfortable with the simultaneous beliefs that individuals in the private sector act in their self-interest and that individuals in the public sector are motivated by a Benthamite vision of social justice. In addition, one must ask why collective decisions are likely to be the result of the same utility calculus as individual decisions.

At a more practical level, however, other questions arose. Decisions regarding economic policy were not made by economists/technocrats, except in rare instances. Political pressures often shaped economic programs in ways that were not consistent with the ideal resource allocation goals initially envisaged. Pressure groups often exerted strong disproportionate influence over policy formulation, and policy execution was far from what had been intended. Corruption and favoritism surrounded bureaucratic allocations of investment licenses, import licenses, and the awarding of government contracts.

Although the infant industry argument was invoked as a basis for protecting domestic industry from foreign competition, for example, the scope and height of protection was usually far greater than could be defended on infant industry grounds. In Turkey, effective rates of protection (ERPs) of well over 200 percent were frequent 20 years after the start-up of infant industries, and Turkish protection was not regarded as unusually high. In India, one study found 39 industries (of a 76-industry classification) with ERPs in excess of 100 percent in 1968–69. One industry was estimated to have an ERP equal to 3,354 percent!

Not only was protection high, but it was conferred in ways which gave virtual monopoly power to domestic entrepreneurs. Efforts to remove this "temporary" protection were infrequent and, when they did occur, met with great resistance. In effect, the decision to grant some infant industry protection had several results: it resulted in pressure groups lobbying for continuation of the protection; it reduced the future power of the technocrats to formulate economic policy; and it created incentives which did not induce maximal efficiency of the enterprises.

The litany could go on and on. The question here, however, is what lessons may be learned from these experiences for economists concerned with analysis of economic policy alternatives. A starting point is to recognize that "the government" consists of a multitude of actors: politicians who must seek political support from various groups, bureaucrats, technocrats, and so on. There are often divisions within each of these groups, and it is rare that any individual or any group is unconstrained in its decision-making or implementation functions.

Although there are no doubt selfless civil servants and politicians concerned with the public good, not all individuals are selfless, and it may be more realistic to assume that individual actors within the public sector are as concerned with their self-interest as those in the private sector. Self-interest may be focussed on survival, on promotion, on re-election, or on other rewards. On occasion, these achievements are consistent with good technocratic analysis like carrying out an appropriate cost-benefit analysis and correctly sizing and placing a dam. But on other occasions, the decision-maker may well attempt to minimize the social cost of a given activity subject to winning reelection, or possibly to maintaining or at least avoiding diminution of chances for promotion.

Moreover, even when there are no conflicts of interest, administrative difficulties can be overwhelming, either because of a shortage of trained personnel or because of the enormous administrative difficulties of establishing and maintaining complex operations within the public sector. On occasion, as for example when a marketing board is supposed to purchase the harvest, lack of facilities can frustrate bureaucrats. On other occasions, however, poor administration—like siting collection points far away from farms and inability to pay farmers for months after harvest—of economic functions which require timely action is a major impediment. In still other instances, the political imperatives arising from the need to treat remote uneconomic areas equally with other regions, from the mandate to hire politically connected, rather than qualified, personnel, or from political pressures to underprice output can result in major problems.

From this it follows that an important question is that of institutional design: what sets of institutions and incentives are likely to be most conducive to achieving a least-cost outcome? Understanding of this question is at best very partial, but two examples may illustrate. First, in many developing countries, parastatal enterprises were established which legally were entitled to borrow from the central bank in the event of losses. This procedure can be changed so that some form of action, embarrassing or worse for enterprise managers, results when losses occur. One such procedure is to require approval of a high official such as a member of the Cabinet or the Prime Minister before borrowing is permitted. Another is to make those losses a line item in the government budget. A second example is the state marketing boards that were established and given monopoly power over distribution of inputs to farmers and marketing of specified farm products. Removal of monopoly power by itself has spurred increasing efficiency of the state enterprise.

What Is the Comparative Advantage of Government?

Most observers believe government should undertake a list of items—usually referred to as "infrastructure"—that has some aspects of a public good. Most infrastructure has many consumers, most of whom have little opportunity in their capacity as consumers to reward good providers or penalize poor ones; similarly, most infrastructure is fairly large scale. The two characteristics combined provide some basis for believing that the market may not function terribly well, and suggest that the disadvantages of large-scale organization and bureaucracy will be least in these instances.

Users of a road, for example, may not individually have sufficient incentive to monitor and hold accountable those providing road construction and maintenance services. This might imply that market provision of roads may not have an advantage over a political process that is somewhat responsive to citizens. This may be especially true at early stages of development, when the presence of indivisibilities may imply that provision of infrastructure might not be privately profitable in the short run.

Infrastructure activities are often large-scale, where administration and organization are important. Moreover, the nature of government is that services provided to some probably must be provided to most, if not all. Political pressures to provide rural postal service, agricultural extension services to all farmers, and similar examples come to mind. Under these circumstances, most governmental activities require a considerable amount of organization and administration—both activities utilizing individuals of significant educational attainments. Since the available supply of skilled manpower is limited in developing countries, and resources for education are scarce, employing highly educated persons in the public sector or educating more persons to increase the supply available to the public sector is far from costless.

Based on those propositions, two conclusions can be drawn. One is that undertaking any activity in the government sector is costly because it places an even greater drain on scarce administrative and organizational resources; not only will scarce talent be drained from the private sector, but administration of other governmental activities is likely to be weakened. The second is that an economically efficient division of economic activity between the public and private sector will be based in part on the administrative and organizational requirements of the two alternatives.

Government is a non-market organization, and it generally must do things on a large scale. It should follow that activities such as maintenance of law and order (including especially enforcement of contract), provision of information (such as agricultural research and extension) and provision of basic public services which are inherently large-scale in scope (such as roads and communications) are those in which the government is at no disadvantage in providing services on a large scale and where private agents may face a disadvantage in attempting to do so.

Although the theory seems clear, little work has been done on the comparative advantage of the public sector in these activities. What seems clear from experience is that focus on other activities (manufacturing, regulating credit and foreign exchange markets, investment licensing, and so on) has diverted governmental resources and efforts away from those areas of activity in which the government may have a comparative advantage. Government failure may have consisted as much in failing to provide the infrastructure in which government has a large comparative advantage as it has in providing poorly things in which it does not have a comparative advantage.

What Are the Dynamics of Government Intervention?

Disillusionment about the selflessness, benevolence, and costlessness of governments has led to a number of insights. Among them, three are important and worth mention here. First, when economic policies create something that is to be allocated at less than its value by any sort of government process, resources will be used in an effort to capture the rights to the items of value. Second, whenever a government policy has clearly identifiable beneficiaries and/or victims, those groups will tend to organize in support or opposition to the policies and then lobby for increasing the value of the gains or reducing the value of the losses from those policies. This is so regardless of whether the policy instruments themselves were adopted at the instigation of the beneficiaries or were initially the result of public interest decisions. Third, one may differentiate the interests of different groups and institutions within the government. "Spending ministries" will tend to become advocates of programs and policies falling within their domain. By contrast, finance ministries tend to be public interest agencies to a greater degree.

The first proposition, that people will spend resources to capture property rights from the government, is the proposition that rent-seeking behavior will occur. Whether rent-seeking takes the form of illegal activity or of legal activity is not usually relevant for economic analysis of its costs, although corruption and other forms of illegal activity do undermine the legitimacy of government, and hence reduce its capacity for maintaining law and contracts and providing other services that are essential for the smooth functioning of economic activity. What is relevant is that the economic costs of many policies—minimum wage legislation, import licensing under quantitative restrictions, credit rationing, and so on—are far greater when rent-seeking takes place than traditional welfare cost analysis would suggest. In some instances, policies that might otherwise appear desirable to meet noneconomic objectives, or even to correct "market failures," may result in a situation even less satisfactory than that prevailing before the policy was put in place.

The second proposition, that groups will spring up to defend their positions, has several implications. An initial political "equilibrium" may not be a long-term equilibrium, as newly formed pressure or interest groups lobby for increasingly favorable, or less unfavorable, treatment. For example, once a system of protection against imports is in place, protected producers will generally lobby for higher tariffs and/or lower quotas, using contrasts with other levels of protection and other arguments. Likewise, initially unprotected groups will begin lobbying for protection, on the grounds that their case is at least as strong as that of already-protected interests. More generally, there will be a tendency for increasing proliferation of categories and of policy instruments, as various groups assert conflicting and competing claims, and this proliferation should also be counted as a cost of the original policy.

One of the groups that normally springs up is the group administering the policies. Once a particular policy is regulated, either a group is established, or an existing unit of government is expanded, to fill the function. Either way, a part of the government will usually become an advocate for maintaining the functions involved and, in many cases, extending them. Those administering the policies necessarily believe that they are doing something important, and also know that discontinuance of the function would result in a loss of jobs for some and of bureaucratic power for others.

To make this tendency to bureaucratic advocacy even more costly, bureaucrats tend to interpret their own ineffectiveness as a consequence of insufficient resources and policy instruments at their command. When price controls are imposed on food crops, for example, farmers tend to shift to the production of other commodities. Frustrated bureaucrats are likely to advocate controlling prices of other commodities, and possibly nationalization of wholesaling. When these controls are less effective than anticipated because of smuggling or other reasons, still other policy instruments are sought.

The third proposition, that there are different interests within the government, is a direct corollary of the view that many of those within government are self-interested. Typically, each spending ministry will want to increase spending, believing it in the social interest that those activities within its particular domain are the most important. The finance ministry, by contrast, will be more concerned about raising revenues, and is therefore less likely to represent special interests.

In this regard, ideology becomes an important determinant of what is, and is not, generally acceptable. Clearly, in democratic societies, policy makers within governments have autonomy only insofar as the voters acquiesce in their activities, whether that permission is out of ignorance or out of sanction for their activity. At least to a degree, acquiescence is a result of the general "ethos" surrounding economic policy.

What Guidance for Policy Makers?

These considerations lead directly to the final question: based on what we know or suspect about government behavior, can any guidance be given to the policy maker? The answer is yes, although a great deal more needs to be learned.

First, and most obvious, is that action by government is not costless. *Any* policy affecting the allocation of resources, any economic activity undertaken in the public sector, and any regulation of private economic activity, can be undertaken only when there is a specified set of procedures or criteria for deciding what fits within the scope of the enunciated policy and also an administrative apparatus for implementing the policy. It is grossly insufficient for economists to assert that the existence of market failure implies that there is a case for government intervention. What is needed is the specification of a set of criteria, or rules, by which interventions will be administered, and an indication as to the process by which this will occur. Then, judgments may be made as to the administrative cost and feasibility of the activity, as well as the likelihood that political pressures will quickly alter the initially chosen process.

Second, even when it appears that government action would actually be effective, there is something of a presumption in favor of policies and programs requiring a minimum of administrative and bureaucratic input. This is both because policies, once in place, appear to have a life of their own and because they divert scarce administrative resources from those in which governmental comparative advantage is stronger.

Third, if alternative mechanisms and policies might be able to achieve a given social or political objective, a presumption exists in favor of choosing a mechanism which provides least scope for rent-seeking. For example, even though tariffs invite smuggling, underinvoicing, and lobbying to increase protection, they are probably less open to rent-seeking behavior than are quantitative restrictions on import licenses. Since at least some tariff revenue is likely to be turned in to the government, there are fewer rents to be sought than under equivalent quantitative restrictions. Likewise, despite the long-standing theorem that (capital flows aside) a tariff on imports and subsidy on exports is equivalent to devaluation, there is certainly nonequivalence when considering the political economy of the two alternatives: under the tariff-subsidy alternative, there remain incentives for smuggling imports, overinvoicing exports, and so on, which do not arise in the presence of a uniform exchange rate. These examples, in turn, suggest that policies directly controlling private economic activity are likely to be less efficacious in terms of achieving their objectives than policies that provide incentives for individuals to undertake the activities which are deemed desirable. This can often be achieved by finding ways which strengthen the functioning of markets.

Yet another implication is that it is preferable to choose policies and institutional arrangements that will force tradeoffs to be faced in the administration and execution of policy. On this reasoning, a tariff commission would tend to be more protectionist than would a ministry of trade; the latter would have a constituency of exporters as well as of protected industries. Similarly, requiring that government programs be funded out of government revenue, rather than financed off-budget, should result in more satisfactory outcomes.

Finally, there is a question of transparency. When the costs of a policy are obscure, special interests in the private sector and government have a greater opportunity to use those policies for their own advantage without incurring the disopprobrium of voters and other politicians. Thus, choosing the policy with lower information costs is usually preferable.

This essay has suggested some of the emerging lessons from the development literature. These answers are preliminary, and indeed rest on a less sound base than one could wish. The defense for putting them forth at all is merely that economists have demonstrated an incredible naivete with regard to government behavior.

Anne O. Krueger, "Government Failures in Development," *Journal of Economic Perspectives* 4, no. 3 (Summer 1990): 9–23.

3

What Washington Means
by Policy Reform

JOHN WILLIAMSON

No statement about how to deal with the debt crisis in Latin America would be complete without a call for the debtors to fulfill their part of the proposed bargain by "setting their houses in order," "undertaking policy reforms," or "submitting to strong conditionality." The question posed in this paper is what such phrases mean, and especially what they are generally interpreted as meaning in Washington. Thus the paper aims to set out what would be regarded in Washington as constituting a desirable set of economic policy reforms. An important purpose in doing this is to establish a baseline against which to measure the extent to which various countries have implemented the reforms being urged on them.

The paper identifies and discusses 10 policy instruments about whose proper deployment Washington can muster a reasonable degree of consensus. In each case an attempt is made to suggest the breadth of the consensus, and in some cases I suggest ways in which I would wish to see the consensus view modified. The Washington of this paper is both the political Washington of Congress and senior members of the administration and the technocratic Washington of the international financial institutions, the economic agencies of the US government, the Federal Reserve Board, and the think tanks.

The 10 topics around which the paper is organized deal with *policy instruments* rather than objectives or outcomes. They are economic policy instruments that I perceive "Washington" to think important, as well as on which some consensus exists. It is generally assumed, at least in technocratic Washington, that the standard economic objectives of growth, low inflation, a viable balance of payments, and an equitable income distribution should determine the disposition of such policy instruments.

Fiscal Deficits

There is very broad agreement in Washington that large and sustained fiscal deficits are a primary source of macroeconomic dislocation in the forms of inflation, payments deficits, and capital flight. They result not from any rational calculation of expected economic benefits, but from a lack of the political courage or honesty to match public expenditures and the resources available to finance them. Unless the excess is being used to finance productive infrastructure investment, an operational budget deficit in excess of around 1 to 2 percent of GNP is *prima facie* evidence of policy failure.

Public Expenditure Priorities

When a fiscal deficit needs to be cut, there are three major expenditure categories on which views are strongly held: subsidies, education and health, and public investment.

Subsidies, especially indiscriminate subsidies (including subsidies to cover the losses of state enterprises) are regarded as prime candidates for reduction or preferably elimination. Everyone has horror stories about countries where subsidized gasoline is cheaper than drinking water, or where subsidized bread is so cheap that it is fed to pigs, or where telephone calls cost a cent or so because someone forgot (or lacked the courage) to raise prices to keep pace with inflation, or where subsidized "agricultural credit" is designed to buy the support of powerful landowners, who promptly recycle the funds to buy government paper. The result is not just a drain on the budget but also much waste and resource misallocation, with little reason to expect any offset from systematically favorable effects on income distribution, at least where indiscriminate subsidies are concerned.

Education and health, in contrast, are regarded as quintessentially proper objects of government expenditure. They have the character of investment (in human capital) as well as consumption. Moreover, they tend to help the disadvantaged. Just how much help expenditures on education and health in fact provide to the disadvantaged depends on their composition as well as their level. Primary education is vastly more relevant than university education, and primary health care (especially preventive treatment) more beneficial to the poor than hospitals in the capital city stuffed with all the latest high-tech medical gadgets. This is not to say that there is no need for universities or state-of-the-art hospitals: developing countries need to train and retain an educated elite as well as to raise the standards of the masses and the poorest. But it is to assert that many in Washington believe that expenditures need to be redirected toward education and health in general, and most especially in a way that will benefit the disadvantaged.

The other area of public expenditure that Washington regards as productive is public infrastructure investment. There is of course a view that the public sector tends to be too large (see the section on privatization below). However, that view coexists with the view that spending on infrastructure that is properly within the public sector needs to be large (and also that an industry should not be starved of investment just because it is, however inadvisedly, within the public sector).

Policy reform with regard to public expenditure is thus perceived to consist of switching expenditure from subsidies toward education and health (especially to benefit the disadvantaged) and infrastructure investment.

Tax Reform

Increased tax revenues are the alternative to decreased public expenditures as a remedy for a fiscal deficit. Most of political Washington regards them as an inferior alternative. Much of technocratic Washington (with the exception of the right-wing think tanks) finds political Washington's aversion to tax increases irresponsible and incomprehensible.

Despite this contrast in attitudes toward the merits of increasing tax revenue, there is a very wide consensus about the most desirable method of raising whatever level of tax revenue is judged to be needed. The principle is that the tax base should be broad and marginal tax rates should be moderate.

Interest Rates

Two general principles about the level of interest rates would seem to command considerable support in Washington. One is that interest rates should be market-determined. The objective of this is to avoid the resource misallocation that results from bureaucrats rationing credit according to arbitrary criteria. The other principle is that real interest rates should be positive, so as to discourage capital flight and, according to some, increase savings.

The question obviously arises as to whether these two principles are mutually consistent. Under noncrisis conditions, I see little reason to anticipate a contradiction; one expects market-determined interest rates to be positive but moderate in real terms, although high international interest rates may make it difficult to hold rates quite as moderate as might be desired. Under the sort of crisis conditions that much of Latin America has experienced for most of the 1980s, however, it is all too easy to believe that market-determined interest rates may be extremely high. It is then of interest to examine whether either principle has been followed or what sort of compromise between the two may have been achieved.

The Exchange Rate

Like interest rates, exchange rates may be determined by market forces, or their appropriateness may be judged on the basis of whether their level seems consistent with macroeconomic objectives. Although there is some support in Washington for regarding the former principle as the more important (a view held in particular by those who deny the possibility of estimating equilibrium exchange rates), the dominant view is that achieving a "competitive" exchange rate is more important than how the rate is determined. In particular, there is relatively little support for the notion that liberalization of international capital flows is a priority objective for a country that should be a capital importer and ought to be retaining its own savings for domestic investment.

The test of whether an exchange rate is appropriate is whether it is consistent in the medium run with macroeconomic objectives. In the case of a developing country, the real exchange rate needs to be sufficiently competitive to promote a rate of export growth that will allow the economy to grow at the maximum rate permitted by its supply-side potential, while keeping the current account deficit to a size that can be financed on a sustainable basis. The exchange rate should not be more competitive than that, because that would produce unnecessary inflationary pressures and also limit the resources available for domestic investment, and hence curb the growth of supply-side potential. A competitive real exchange rate is the first essential element of an "outward-oriented" economic policy.

Trade Policy

The second element of an outward-oriented economic policy is import liberalization. A policy of protecting domestic industries against foreign competition is viewed as creating costly distortions that end up penalizing exports and impoverishing the domestic economy.

The worst form of protection is considered to be import licensing, with its massive potential for creating opportunities for corruption. To the extent that there has to be protection, let it be provided by tariffs, so that at least the public purse gets the rents. And keep distortions to a minimum by limiting tariff dispersion and exempting from tariffs imports of intermediate goods needed to produce exports.

The free trade ideal is generally (although perhaps not universally) conceded to be subject to two qualifications. The first concerns infant industries, which may merit substantial but strictly temporary protection. Furthermore, a moderate general tariff (in the range of 10 percent to 20 percent, with little dispersion) might be accepted as a mechanism to provide a bias toward diversifying the industrial base without threatening serious costs. The second qualification concerns timing. A highly protected economy is not expected to dismantle all protection overnight.

Foreign Direct Investment

As noted above, liberalization of foreign financial flows is not regarded as a high priority. In contrast, a restrictive attitude limiting the entry of foreign direct investment (FDI) is regarded as foolish. Such investment can bring needed capital, skills, and know-how, either producing goods needed for the domestic market or contributing new exports. The main motivation for restricting FDI is economic nationalism, which Washington disapproves of, at least when practiced by countries other than the United States.

Privatization

Privatization may help relieve the pressure on the government budget, both in the short run by the revenue produced by the sale of the enterprise and in the longer run inasmuch as investment need no longer be financed by the government.

However, the main rationale for privatization is the belief that private industry is managed more efficiently than state enterprises, because of the more direct incentives faced by a manager who either has a direct personal stake in the profits of an enterprise or else is accountable to those who do. At the very least, the threat of bankruptcy places a floor under the inefficiency of private enterprises, whereas many state enterprises seem to have unlimited access to subsidies. This belief in the superior efficiency of the private sector has long been an article of faith in Washington (though perhaps not held quite as fervently as in the rest of the United States), but it was only with the enunciation of the Baker Plan in 1985 that it became official US policy to promote foreign privatization. The IMF and the World Bank have duly encouraged privatization in Latin America and elsewhere since.

Deregulation

Another way of promoting competition is by deregulation. This was initiated within the United States by the Carter administration and carried forward by the Reagan administration. It is generally judged to have been successful within the United States, and it is generally assumed that it could bring similar benefits to other countries.

The potential payoff from deregulation would seem to be much greater in Latin America, to judge from the assessment of Balassa:

> Most of the larger Latin American countries are among the world's most regulated market economies, at least on paper. Among the most important economic regulatory mechanisms are controls on the establishment of firms and on new investments, restrictions on inflows of foreign investment and outflows of profit remittance, price controls, import barriers, discriminatory credit allocation, high corporate income tax rates combined with discretionary tax-reduction mechanisms, as well as limits on firing of employees. . . . In a number of Latin American countries, the web of regulation is administered by underpaid administrators. The potential for corruption is therefore great.
>
> Productive activity may be regulated by legislation, by government decrees, and case-by-case decision making. This latter practice is widespread and pernicious in Latin America as it creates considerable uncertainty and provides opportunities for corruption. It also discriminates against small and medium-sized businesses which, although important creators of employment, seldom have access to the higher reaches of the bureaucracy.

Property Rights

In the United States property rights are so well entrenched that their fundamental importance for the satisfactory operation of the capitalist system is easily overlooked. I suspect, however, that when Washington brings itself to think about the subject, there is general acceptance that property rights do indeed matter.

There is also a general perception that property rights are highly insecure in Latin America.

Concluding Remarks

The economic policies that Washington urges on the rest of the world may be summarized as prudent macroeconomic policies, outward orientation, and free-market capitalism. A striking fact about the list of policies on which Washington does have a collective view is that they all stem from classical mainstream economic theory, at least if one is allowed to count Keynes as a classic by now. None of the ideas spawned by the development literature—such as the big push, balanced or unbalanced growth, surplus labor, or even the two-gap model—plays any essential role in motivating the Washington consensus. This raises the question as to whether Washington is correct in its implicit dismissal of the development literature as a diversion from the harsh realities of the dismal science. Or is the Washington consensus, or my interpretation of it, missing something?

_____

John Williamson, "What Washington Means by Policy Reform," in *Latin American Adjustment: How Much Has Happened?* ed. John Williamson (Washington, DC: Institute for International Economics, 1990): 7–20.

4

How Can States Foster Markets?

BRIAN LEVY

Governments can encourage market development by clearly defining property rights, ensuring a sound regulatory framework, and pursuing industrial policies. But what they do in these areas should be determined by their institutional capability.

Property Rights

Markets cannot develop unless property rights—including the right to use an asset, to permit or exclude its use by others, to collect the income generated by the asset, and to sell the asset—are adequately defined. Property rights, in turn, rest on social arrangements, which include reasonable restraints on lawlessness (protection from theft, violence, and other acts of predation); protection from arbitrary government actions that disrupt business activity; and fair and predictable mechanisms for resolving disputes. But many countries lack even these basic social arrangements. In a survey of private firms in 69 countries, firms in 27 countries said that the triple curse of corruption, crime, and an unpredictable judiciary was a powerful deterrent to investment.

Once there is a modicum of order, development can begin, even in the absence of formal, state-sponsored institutions. In the early Middle Ages, European merchants devised their own sophisticated legal code to govern commercial transactions. A twentieth-century example of informal social enforcement mechanisms is provided by the extensive business networks of Chinese clans.

Informal arrangements are usually inadequate, however, when business transactions become more complex. Consider the example of nineteenth century mining investments in the "Wild West" state of Nevada in the United States. Initially, Nevada's few hundred miners were able to operate on the basis of unwritten, informal ownership agreements. But the discovery of rich lodes of gold and silver precipitated a flood of prospectors, making it necessary for miners to establish formal rules. As surface ore was exhausted and mining became a more expensive, capital-intensive undertaking, the miners pressed for full recourse to the US judicial system, and Nevada became a state. Once formal mechanisms have been put in place, economic development may accelerate.

The number of ways different aspects of the legal system can buttress property rights is vast—ranging from land titling and the collateralization of movable property to laws governing securities markets, the protection of intellectual property, and anti-monopoly legislation. However, sophisticated reforms in this area will not bear fruit in countries that lack strong institutional capabilities.

Information and Coordination

Even in countries with well-defined property rights, information and coordination problems can impede market and private sector development. Information problems occur because the "rules of the game" may not be spelled out clearly, and because knowledge and understanding are inevitably limited. For example, businesses or individuals may lack knowledge about the probity of potential partners or be unaware of potentially profitable opportunities. Coordination is difficult because self-interested people and firms generally are willing to share information only when they do not lose by doing so. The risk that other parties might renege on agreements makes it difficult for firms to take advantage of opportunities for mutual gain. However, states can alleviate information and coordination problems through regulation and industrial policy.

How much the state does in these areas should reflect its institutional capabilities in two regards: first, the ability of government officials and agencies to manage technical complexity; and, second, the extent to which the checks and balances in force in the country can restrain agencies, officials, and politicians from departing from their stated commitments and lapsing into arbitrary and unpredictable enforcement. In countries where institutional capabilities are strong, restraints can be accompanied by some flexibility, allowing officials to respond to unexpected events. Countries with weaker capabilities may need to do less and to proceed in ways that limit the risks of arbitrary behavior.

Regulation

Regulation, if well designed and implemented with care, makes it possible for societies to influence market outcomes for public purposes. It can be used to conserve the environment as well as to protect consumers and workers from some of the consequences of information asymmetries. It can also foster competition and innovation, and prevent the abuse of monopoly power. More broadly, it can help win social acceptance of market outcomes by establishing their legitimacy and ensuring their fairness. If badly designed, however, regulation can result in large costs for firms and society. It can undermine property rights, fuel corruption, and inhibit market entry. As countries proceed with economic liberalization, many areas of regulation are recognized as counterproductive and abandoned. But certain types of regulation serve a valuable purpose and should be preserved.

Utilities

Regulation in the utilities sector remains crucial, even in the wake of revolutionary technological changes. In telecommunications today, for example, signals traverse multiple network systems owned by different operators; power generators supply customers through common-carrier transmission lines. Real competition can occur only if regulatory rules mandate easy interconnection and specify how interconnection prices will be determined.

Regulation is also a vital tool in protecting private investors from the risk of expropriation. If a government has a change of heart, utilities are particularly vulnerable because their assets cannot be redeployed for other uses. Thus, in the absence of a clear regulatory framework, investors run the risk that governments may initially offer them attractive terms only to impose costly demands later. A well-designed mechanism that commits the regulator to a clearly defined course of action can offer the reassurance needed by potential investors.

A cross-country comparison of telecommunications reform illustrates the options available to countries with different levels of institutional capability with respect to how much flexibility they give their regulatory agencies. At one extreme are industrial countries such as New Zealand and the United Kingdom, where institutional checks and balances are strong enough to permit experimentation with highly flexible regulatory approaches without scaring off private investment. The United Kingdom, for example, imposes an overall ceiling on utility prices based on the annual rate of inflation minus an adjustment factor set by the regulator. Price-cap regulation gives the utility an incentive to be efficient and can encourage innovation, but it also gives the regulator substantial discretionary power. A better option for countries with weaker checks and balances might be to combine price-cap regulation in which the adjustment factor is fixed with an agreement to share unexpectedly high profits on the basis of a prespecified formula. Between these two extremes, we find Jamaica, which has given its regulatory agency limited flexibility.

The long-term goal for countries with weak background institutions must be to strengthen them. In the short term, one option is to substitute an international mechanism for the missing national foundation. The Philippines has attracted independent private generators of electric power by agreeing on very rigid "take-or-pay" contracts that are enforceable offshore. The World Bank Group offers guarantees for infrastructure projects to protect private investors and lenders against noncommercial risks, including the risk of administrative expropriation.

Banking

The case for regulation in the financial sector is also compelling. The goal should be not to channel credit in certain predetermined directions but to safeguard the health of the financial system through prudential mechanisms. In the absence of regulatory incentives to provide reliable information, banks can easily disguise the extent of nonperforming loans in their portfolio—and their own lack of solvency. Information asymmetries in the banking sector can be destabilizing. Without reliable information, depositors might rush to withdraw their funds when there are rumors about troubled banks. When banks go under, nervous depositors can start runs on other banks, with potentially severe macroeconomic consequences.

To reduce the risks and costs of bank failures, countries with strong administrative capabilities and well-functioning legal systems generally promulgate detailed regulations and assign a central role to bank supervisors. Key elements of such banking systems include capital adequacy and entry criteria; restraints on insider lending; rules for banks to classify the quality and risks of their loan portfolio; and regulations that banks must meet minimum auditing standards and disclosure requirements. But these types of measures will be difficult to implement unless reasonably reliable accounting and auditing information is available on the financial health of a bank's borrowers and unless there are a sufficient number of supervisors who are not only skilled enough to do the job but politically independent enough to do it impartially.

Especially if institutional capabilities are weak, more emphasis can be put on making the incentives and interests of bank owners, managers, and depositors compatible with prudent banking. Recently, for example, the World Bank and the European Bank for Reconstruction and Development (EBRD) collaborated in Russia to onlend funds through participating banks that agreed to submit to annual audits by international accounting firms and to adhere to prudential norms.

Industrial Policy

In cases where externalities, a lack of competition, and other market imperfections drive a wedge between private and social goals, there is general agreement that states can enhance welfare by regulating markets. There is much more controversy about whether states should try to accelerate market development through activist industrial policies. The rationale for industrial policy in developing and transition economies is that their information and coordination problems are especially acute and pervasive. This is because, in countries where the number of market participants is small, information is a source of power and therefore tightly guarded, and because the institutional arrangements that evolve as markets develop to facilitate economically beneficial coordination remain weak. With appropriate institutional capability, governments can support industrial development by acting as brokers of information and facilitators of mutual learning and collaboration.

A key distinction needs to be made between initiatives that require only a light touch from government and those that require more intense government involvement. The latter should be approached cautiously or avoided, except by countries that have unusually strong institutional capabilities.

Postwar Japan's development of the steel, coal, machinery, and shipbuilding industries offers a rare example of successful government activism. In contrast, the Philippines' experience with industrial policies in the 1970s and 1980s shows what can happen when large ambitions are not matched by institutional strengths and government is swayed by powerful private interests. In 1979, the Philippine government announced a new $5 billion program of "major industrial projects," all in heavy, capital-intensive industries. By late 1987—but only after intense pressure by critics and a change of government—5 of the 11 initial projects, accounting for almost $4 billion, had been shelved.

Industrial initiatives that require a light touch from government—inexpensive public-private partnerships intended to foster the provision of intra-industry public goods—offer more flexibility. In mature market systems, networks of private firms flourish. Domestic, regional, and international networks create sources of learning and open up opportunities for firms; specialized buyers open up new market niches and offer information on product standards; equipment providers transfer technological know-how; input suppliers help with product and process innovations; and competitors are a rich source of new ideas. Often, clusters of firms, buyers, equipment suppliers, input and service providers, industry associations, and other specialized organizations come together in the same region. But in countries with underdeveloped markets, a catalyst (public or private) may be needed to set this process in motion.

Catalytic initiatives can be directed either at individual firms or at groups of firms. Some successful initiatives have focused on events, such as joint participation in trade fairs. Others (in Chile and Denmark, for example) have aimed at achieving a broader shift in the business culture to favor cooperative efforts that can lead to increases in productivity. A promising approach involves giving matching grants to firms, typically on a 50:50 cost-sharing basis, to help them penetrate markets and upgrade technologies.

Focusing on the Possible

In fostering markets, there is no "one-size-fits-all" formula. If institutions are strong, far-reaching state actions can contribute to economic well-being. Without strong institutional foundations, such actions are likely to prove ineffective— or even an invitation to capture by powerful private interests or for predatory behavior by the state.

How, then, should countries with limited institutional capabilities proceed? In the short term, until institutions can be strengthened, the first challenge is to focus on the essentials—establishing a lawful state and setting sound economic policy, for example—while setting a lighter agenda for state action. The second challenge is to find tools for state action that are better aligned with country capabilities. Two approaches appear to be particularly promising:

- specifying the content of policy in precise rules, and then locking in the rules using mechanisms that make it costly to reverse course; and
- working in partnership with firms and citizens, sometimes shifting the burden of implementation entirely outside government.

The results may not be first-best in a textbook sense. But as state capability grows, it will become possible to switch to more flexible tools that are capable of increasing efficiency gains. Throughout, states must maintain the confidence of firms and citizens that flexibility will not be accompanied by arbitrariness or else the foundation for development will crumble.

Brian Levy, "How Can States Foster Markets?" *Finance and Development* 34, no. 3 (September 1997): 21–23.

5

Improving the State's Institutional Capability

SANJAY PRADHAN

The state's power to intervene in economic activity is a double-edged sword. While the state may use this power to promote the well-being of its citizens, it may also abuse it, to their detriment. Countries therefore need to adopt mechanisms that give state agencies the flexibility and the incentive to act in the public interest while restraining arbitrary action and corruption. Unfortunately, the governments of many developing countries have failed to achieve this balance. As a result, their actions have not been viewed as credible, and investment and growth have suffered.

Three interrelated sets of institutional mechanisms can improve the credibility, accountability, and responsiveness of the state: restraints and rules, voice and partnerships, and competitive pressures.

- *Restraints and rules.* Many countries need to strengthen formal instruments of restraint, such as judicial independence and the separation of powers. Within the executive branch of government, credible rules can create an enabling environment for effective public sector performance.
- *Voice and partnerships.* Mechanisms such as public-private deliberation councils and client surveys, which give businesses and civil society a voice in state activities and foster partnerships between the state and its constituencies, allow external stake-holders to provide input and oversight and exert pressure for change.
- *Competitive pressures.* Competitive pressures from markets and civil society and other state organs check the state's ability to exercise a monopoly in policymaking and service delivery. Competition in civil service recruitment and promotion can help build a motivated, professional bureaucracy.

Formal Checks and Balances

Sustainable development requires that the state and its officials be held accountable for their actions. The two most important formal instruments for achieving accountability are a strong judiciary and the separation of powers.

For judiciaries to be effective, they must be independent and have adequate resources and instruments for enforcement. Judicial independence and enforcement have repeatedly been compromised in too many countries, however.

Even where judiciaries are capable of enforcing rules, the state's credibility can be limited if the public has little reason to believe that rules will be stable over time. One classic constitutional mechanism for avoiding excessive legislative change is to divide power horizontally (among the judiciary, legislative, and executive branches of government) or vertically (among different levels of government).

The broader the separation of powers, the more difficult it is to change rule-based commitments. The separation of powers thus increases the public's confidence that rules will be sustained or that changes will be made only after considerable negotiation. However, the presence of multiple veto points also has drawbacks: it can make it hard to change harmful laws or lead to gridlock in government. Nonetheless, many developing countries, even those with a formal separation of powers, have few effective checks and balances. In some countries, legislative oversight is weak because of poor capacity and inadequate information. In others, the executive branch dominates a compliant legislature.

To some extent, external restraints can substitute for limitations in national institutions. One option is to use extraterritorial adjudication to underpin the domestic judicial system or compensate for its weaknesses. Confidence in the Jamaican judicial system is buttressed by the fact that the United Kingdom's Privy Council serves as Jamaica's appellate court of last resort. Cross-border agreements such as the European Union, the North American Free Trade Agreement, and the West African franc zone are another mechanism for strengthening commitments.

Strengthening Policymaking

Instruments of restraint need to be balanced by arrangements that provide the executive branch with sufficient flexibility to formulate and implement policies and respond to changing circumstances. Although the institutional arrangements vary from country to country, the public sectors of the industrial countries and many East Asian countries have generally been characterized by a strong central capacity for macroeconomic and strategic policy formulation; mechanisms to delegate and debate policies among government agencies; and transparent links to external stakeholders. By contrast, policymaking capacity in many developing and transition economies is weak and fragmented, with little institutionalized input or oversight from stakeholders.

Australia provides an example of reforms aimed at creating a more transparent, competitive, and results-oriented policymaking process. Of particular relevance is the emphasis on publishing the medium-term costs of competing policies, facilitating debate and consultation within the government on policy priorities, setting hard budget constraints, and evaluating outcomes.

The United States and some continental European countries have instituted other mechanisms for consultation and oversight in policymaking. US executive agencies, for instance, are governed by the Administrative Procedures Act (APA) of 1946, which imposes procedural requirements—such as public announcements of new policy—that are enforceable in the courts. This approach assures accountability by involving the judiciary and giving citizens the chance to voice their views.

The successful East Asian countries have adopted similar approaches. In Korea, Japan, Malaysia, Singapore, and Thailand, policymaking has been delegated to elite central agencies staffed by professional employees recruited on the basis of merit. Private firms provide input and oversight to the agencies through public-private deliberation councils.

In many developing countries in Africa, Central America, and the Caribbean, the central government's capacity for the formulation of strategic policies is weak. The problem is compounded by poor discipline and an absence of competition. Often, budgets are unrealistic, and decisions are made in an ad hoc manner. In Tanzania, actual recurrent expenditures have been 50 percent higher, on average, than budgeted expenditures in recent years, and, in Uganda, 30 percent higher. There are long lags in the production of financial accounts and audits, and often no system of costing or contesting competing policies.

In aid-dependent countries, donors inadvertently exacerbate the problem. Decision making often becomes more fragmented as ministries and donors enter into bilateral deals on several projects without determining whether the cumulative effects are collectively sustainable or mutually consistent. In many countries, public investment programs have become passive repositories of donor-driven projects, and the future recurrent costs of projects have become unsustainable, as in Guinea. Lack of coordination between the ministries of planning and finance further impedes the integration of capital and recurrent expenditures. The result in many developing countries is that newly built roads fall into disrepair; schools find themselves without textbooks; and health centers have no drugs.

Several initiatives have been launched to address these problems. The Africa Capacity Building Initiative seeks to strengthen Africa's policymaking capacity through enhanced external inputs from African universities and civil society. Governments and donors have also launched sectoral investment programs that coordinate donor assistance. Countries like Malawi and Uganda are moving beyond coordinating donor policies within a given sector to developing a systematic process for strategic prioritization across sectors within total spending constraints. A few countries, such as Colombia, are instituting an ex post evaluation system to assess whether policies are achieving intended outcomes.

In the transition countries of Central and Eastern Europe and the former Soviet republics, the problem is not the shortage of administrative expertise but the lack of mechanisms for channeling that competence into coherent policy. When the communist regimes in these countries collapsed, so did the centralized decision making apparatus that coordinated the activities of ministries and departments. As a result, these countries developed confused, overlapping responsibilities and multiple, rather than collective, accountability—a surefire formula for disastrous policy formulation. The situation is improving in some countries, however; Georgia has already removed overlapping and conflicting positions, and Hungary and Poland have introduced reforms to streamline multiple and conflicting responsibilities and speed decision making.

Improving Delivery

Even well-designed policies can experience major implementation problems. In many developing countries, services are simply not delivered or delivery is marred by poor quality, high cost, waste, fraud, and corruption. Politicians often intervene in the day-to-day operations of public agencies, and managers have limited flexibility. There is limited accountability for the use of inputs and virtually no accountability for outcomes. And, in many countries, the public sector has a monopoly on delivery of service. To improve delivery, governments are experimenting with a range of institutional mechanisms.

The so-called new public management reforms in the industrial countries have sought to improve delivery primarily using market mechanisms and formal contracting. In New Zealand, for example, commercial activities have been spun off, corporatized, and often privatized. All remaining conglomerate ministries have been broken up into focused business units headed by chief executive officers given fixed-term, output-based contracts and considerable managerial autonomy, including the right to hire and fire.

What is feasible in New Zealand may not be in many developing countries, however. It takes considerable capacity and commitment to write and enforce contracts, especially for outputs that are difficult to specify, as is the case with social services. Indeed, the most appropriate method for improving performance should be determined by the characteristics of the service in question and the ability of the state to enforce contracts.

For contestable services (that is, those with scope for actual or potential competition), such as commercial products, telecommunications, and power generation, market mechanisms can generate strong competitive pressures. Deregulation of telecommunications and power generation has led to significantly lower unit costs and a rapid expansion of service in many countries. But the use of market mechanisms requires a well-developed regulatory capacity.

For services whose outputs the state can specify and enforce at low cost, contracting out to private firms and NGOs is an attractive option. In industrial countries, the contracting out of services to the private sector is now common. In Australia's Victoria State, for example, each local council is required to contract out at least half of its annual budget through competitive tender. In developing countries, contracting out easily specified services competitively can lead to efficiency gains. For instance, Brazil reduced the costs of road maintenance 25 percent by contracting it out to private companies.

Some governments are contracting out the delivery of services that are difficult to specify, such as social services. Bolivia and Uganda have subcontracted such services to NGOs that are committed to high quality or that are better able to serve certain groups because of their religious or ideological orientation. In general, however, the costs of contracting out complex or nonroutinized activities are high.

For activities that remain in the public sector, industrial countries undertaking public management reforms are setting up performance-based agencies and drawing up formal contracts even for complex activities such as defense, education, and health care. But countries with scarce capacity and weak bureaucratic controls need to proceed with caution. Industrial countries that have been able to relax detailed control over inputs have been developing credible restraints over a long period of time. Developing countries have often not been successful in enforcing contracts with public enterprises producing easily specified outputs.

Many developing countries need first to strengthen rule-based compliance and financial accountability, provide clearer descriptions of desired outcomes, and introduce ways to evaluate performance. A number of countries—such as Argentina and Bolivia—are now undertaking reforms to improve the quality and credibility of their financial accounting and auditing systems. As input controls are strengthened, countries such as Colombia, Mexico, and Uganda are introducing performance measurement.

Also needed are mechanisms to enhance the loyalty, motivation, and competence of the civil service. This requires recruitment and promotion based on merit, long-term career rewards, adequate pay, and mechanisms to instill esprit de corps.

Where internal monitoring and enforcement capacity are weak, pressures from clients can improve performance. Feedback mechanisms such as client surveys have been shown to increase transparency and accountability in India, Nicaragua, and Tanzania. Malaysia and the United Kingdom have set minimum service standards through citizen charters, which are being made public. With clear and specific standards, clients and staff know what is expected.

Corruption as a Symptom

Even if bureaucracies are flexible and subject to oversight and competition, the risk remains that individual officials will engage in self-seeking behavior, which can degenerate into corruption. Corruption, the abuse of public power for private gain, is symptomatic of the more general problem of perverse underlying incentives. Corruption flourishes where distortions in the policy and regulatory regimes provide scope for it and where institutions for restraint are weak.

Countries with highly distorted policies, as measured by variables such as the black market premium, provide more control rights to politicians and bureaucrats, and are more corrupt. Another cause of general corruption is a corrupt judiciary—lawbreakers see little risk of getting caught and punished. Finally, the punishment for corruption may not be severe enough to outweigh the rewards. Corruption often occurs in countries with large public-private pay differentials, or what is sometimes called the "rate of temptation." But simply raising civil service salaries may not reduce corruption; mechanisms that curb political patronage and create a more impartial public service may also be needed.

The battle against corruption requires a multipronged strategy. First, countries need to build a professional, rule-based bureaucracy with pay structure that rewards honest effort, a merit-based system to shield the civil service from political patronage, and credible financial controls to prevent the arbitrary use of public resources. Second, the discretionary authority of individual officials needs to be reduced and competition increased. Third, accountability can be increased by improving transparency and strengthening the mechanisms for monitoring the civil service and punishing wrongdoers—relying not only on criminal law but also on oversight by formal institutions (such as statutory watchdogs in Hong Kong, China) and ordinary citizens.

Institutions and Reforms

In some developing countries, reform-minded leaders cannot translate their goals into reality because the machinery linking policy statements to action has ceased to function. As a result, a vast gap has opened up between what the state says and what it does. The first step toward building a more effective public sector must be to close these gaps—to reestablish the credibility of the government's policies and the rules it claims to live by. This requires setting hard budget limits, making the flow of resources predictable, ensuring accountability for the use of financial resources, and making the civil service a meritocracy.

Building a professional, rules-based bureaucracy takes time. However, in the interim, measures can be taken that will yield early payoffs. Well-functioning policymaking mechanisms can make the costs of competing policies transparent and encourage debate and consultation. Using the market to deliver contestable services can lower costs and improve quality. Contracting out easily specified activities can reduce the burden on the state and improve efficiency. While the state builds internal mechanisms for monitoring and enforcement, the public can be encouraged to voice its opinions on performance, generating external pressure for improvement. These measures will also help fight corruption.

Sanjay Pradhan, "Improving the State's Institutional Capability," *Finance and Development* 34, no. 3 (September 1997): 24–27.

Section II

Explanations of Government Policy

How can we explain the policies that governments in Latin America have actually adopted? The readings in Section I canvassed many views about the proper amount of government involvement in economic affairs. The authors argued that under certain circumstances, a government could help overcome market failures that inhibit economic performance. As any student of Latin American affairs knows, however, government policy is not always motivated by concerns about aggregate welfare. Sometimes policy serves the narrow interests of a few political leaders or lobby groups rather than society as a whole. Thus, it is important to understand how government policy emerges from the clash of interests and why policies vary across countries and over time. The readings in this section provide a coherent framework for explaining government policy.

The process of explanation involves several steps. First, the analyst identifies the key players that influence government policy. Karl Marx, one of the first political economists, assigned primary importance to classes and claimed that in his time, capitalists occupied the driver's seat. Today, political economists are more eclectic in acknowledging the influence of many actors, including voters, interest groups, firms, political parties, elected officials, and bureaucrats. Obviously, these actors do not carry equal weight in every decision. To simplify the analysis, it is useful to focus on the subset of actors that are most salient for a particular issue.

Next, the analyst describes the fundamental objectives and policy preferences of the key actors. Modern political economy rests on the assumption that individuals seek to promote their utility, or happiness. Given the difficulty of specifying exactly what makes people happy, it is acceptable to suppose that most workers and firms want to maximize their income and that most politicians would like to remain in office. Some government policies will serve these objectives more effectively than others. We presume that actors are instrumentally rational, which means they prefer the policy that will bring them the greatest utility.

Finally, the analyst considers what strategies the actors will adopt to bring their desired policies to fruition. For voters, a strategy might involve casting ballots for the politician who seems most likely to put the ideal policy in place. The strategies of interest groups and firms could be more complicated and involve lobbying, campaign contributions, and bribes. Naturally, elected officials and bureaucrats will fashion their own strategies, which represent the best responses to the maneuvers of others. In all cases, actors must remain cognizant of political and

TABLE 2.1

	Alesina	Rodrik	Haggard/Webb
Politicians	*		
Voters	*		
Groups/Classes	*	*	
Ideas		*	
Foreign Pressure		*	*
Institutions			*

social institutions, which could make it easier or harder to achieve the desired result. By considering who wants what—and how they pursue it—the analyst can begin to explain government policies and economic outcomes in Latin America.

Frieden (reading 6) describes this method of analysis, which many authors apply in practice. For instance, Alesina (reading 7) asks why governments follow unsustainable economic policies even when it becomes apparent to everyone that reform is necessary. He proposes several models, including the "war of attrition," to account for this perverse outcome. In the war of attrition, two social groups would like the government to adopt a stabilization policy, but neither group wants to bear the costs of adjustment. As rational actors, each group plays a wait-and-see strategy, hoping that the other side will capitulate. At some point, the costs of delay become unbearable for one group, which concedes and therefore breaks the stalemate. The model helps explain why distributional conflicts can delay the adoption of economically efficient policies. The pieces by Rodrik (reading 8) and Haggard and Webb (reading 9) contain many other examples of how modern political economy can illuminate the choices that governments make.

The authors focus on somewhat different actors and variables, which are summarized in the table.

Nevertheless, the authors share a basic commitment to modern political economy and its assumptions about the rationality of political and economic actors. They assume that decisionmakers seek the most efficient means to achieve their given ends. In economic affairs, these ends are often presumed to be material, a view reflected in most of the readings in this book. It is important to recognize, however, that rational actors could pursue nonmaterial goals such as ethnic advancement, national cohesion, or cultural survival. Of course, the assumption of instrumental rationality is controversial, as Geddes (reading 10) notes. Any complete analysis of political and economic behavior would also need to account for habit, cognitive biases, human error, and other factors that might prevent people from acting in ways that maximize their well-being. Although they acknowledge the validity of this critique, the proponents of modern political economy believe that the assumption of rationality is a useful starting point for analyzing the sources of government policy in Latin America. In Sections III–VII, we will have many opportunities to see the fruits of this approach.

6

The Method of Analysis: Modern Political Economy

JEFFRY A. FRIEDEN

The framework used here is what I call modern political economy. The book's principal analytical goal is to examine the usefulness and implications of modern political economy for the study of politics and economics in the developing world.

Modern political economy as used here has four component parts: defining the actors and their goals, specifying actors' policy preferences, determining how they group themselves, and following their interaction with other social institutions.

Definition of Actors and Their Objectives

Actors are assumed to maximize utility, and to make cost-benefit calculations of how best to achieve this end. In this study, I also assume that actors maximize income. The desire to maximize income says only that workers prefer higher to lower wages, and capitalists prefer higher to lower profits.

The objective of income maximization leads actors to a variety of subsidiary concerns, including preferences for certain government policies. While capitalists and workers are assumed to have the same *objective* of earning as much as possible, their *policy preferences* may be different: capitalists might prefer taxes to be paid entirely by workers, while workers might prefer all taxation to be on capital. Changed conditions can lead actors to change their policy preferences (but not their income-maximization objective!): free-trade steelworkers might, with the rise of imports, become protectionist. However, individuals and firms, in my analysis, rationally calculate their policy preferences as a function of their goal of maximizing their incomes given their positions in the economy.

The assumption that actors are utility maximizers is straightforward. Analysis based on rational self-interested individuals and firms is common to neoclassical economics, its public-choice/rational-choice off-spring, and classical Marxism. However, criticism of models of social behavior that assume self-interested rationality are common. It would be impossible to engage all but the most widespread such objections.

Perhaps the most frequent charge leveled at those who assume rationality is that people do lots of irrational things. This can be distilled into two points. It might mean that there is a systematic bias to individual decision making—caring more about losses than about gains, for example—in which case analysts simply need to control for this bias. Alternately, it might mean that people make decisions at random, with no predictable pattern, in which case there is no room for social scientific analysis. Neither point invalidates the rationality assumption for those interested in normal social science.

A second common protest is that the world is so complex that even the most rational of individuals does not have enough information to make rational decisions. This misunderstands the issue: the rationality assumption means that people do their best given their circumstances, not that they are omniscient. Indeed, much modern game theory investigates the effects of different informational environments on social interactions.

A third mistake is to assert that rationality is the same as economic interest. Many critics object to the assumption of rationality because they believe that it implies assuming that all people care about is their income. They are mistaken. Rationality means only that individuals attempt to achieve whatever goals they have by the best means at their disposal. Politicians, for example, might be assumed to maximize the probability of being elected. It so happens that in this study I assume that income maximization drives economic policy preferences, but this is not inherent in the rationality assumption. My restrictive income-maximization assumption should not be confused with the much less limiting assumption of utility maximization.

Finally, many argue that the focus on individual choice—methodological individualism—is not adequate for explaining social outcomes; that the social whole is greater than the sum of its parts and that looking at the parts will not allow us to understand the whole. This may well be the case, but it is not an argument *against* understanding the parts and how they interact, and its validity depends on a demonstration that it is impossible to build an explanation from the bottom up, on firm microfoundations. Indeed, most modern political economists believe that many social outcomes are in some sense greater than the sum of their parts, inasmuch as they are not the intentional result of individual actions but rather the aggregation of individual behavior into unintended consequences. We need a baseline from which to begin this analysis, and the assumption of rationality provides such a baseline. There can hardly be a strong case made *against* wanting to build coherent arguments from elemental units up to final consequences.

Ultimately this is the simplest reason for the core assumptions of modern political economy: they allow us to develop logically consistent analyses, starting with the basic entities that compose society. They give us the opportunity to derive testable propositions about the behavior of individuals, firms, and groups, and about how their interaction produces social effects. Many objections are misguided, irrelevant, or not motivated by concern with the pursuit of social science. The modern political economy assumption that individuals rationally attempt to maximize their utility allows for the incorporation into analysis of confused or inadequate information, goals other than wealth or income, and social complexity. It provides a fruitful starting point for subsequent analysis.

Specification of Actors' Policy Preferences

In this framework, all else equal, social actors prefer public policies that maximize their incomes. Purely economic characteristics of the actors, therefore, determine whether they will seek government policies and what sort of policies they will seek.

Given stable property rights, economic actors—individuals and firms—earn income from their assets, and what their assets earn is a function of relative prices. Leaving aside for now problems of collective action, the extent to which an asset-holder tries to influence policy depends on how policy will affect returns on the asset, and on the availability of other uses to which the asset might be put. Both of these are a function of asset specificity.

First, an actor's policy preferences are a function of the susceptibility of the actor's assets to policy. The less policy can change the return on the asset—change the relevant relative prices—the less incentive the asset's owner has to try to affect policy.

Second, an actor's policy preferences are a function of the degree to which his asset has an available alternate use in which it earns a similar rate of return. The harder it is to move an asset from use to use, the more closely its owner is wedded to its current activity and the greater the incentive to obtain policies to favor this activity. At one extreme, if an asset can be transferred without cost from one activity to another, its owner has no reason to lobby for sector-specific policy, since the asset can be redeployed to earn the highest available rate of return. At the other extreme, if an asset is fully specific to a sector and cannot be employed in *any* other activity, its owner is completely dependent upon the sector's fortunes. By the same token, the more diversified an actor's asset portfolio, the less susceptible the actor is to policy. At the extreme, someone with equal shares of all firms would be indifferent among policies that take from some firms and give to others. The point is that if the owner of an asset can easily shift the asset from one activity to another, or is fully diversified, the owner has no incentive to support sector-specific policies. Other things equal, this means that those in industries characterized by specialized skills, machinery, supply and distribution networks, or other barriers to easy exit will be more motivated to influence policy toward their industries.

This abstract discussion can be made more concrete by describing the range of asset specificity found in the real world. Assets that are not specific at all are those that can easily be redeployed—demand deposits, financial assets more generally. Holders of completely liquid assets are indifferent to policy, for they can move their funds to whatever activity is earning the highest rate of return. Of course, these asset-holders have an incentive to oppose policies that repress the return to financial investments—interest-rate ceilings, for example—but beyond this they are indifferent as to the relative price structure. Similarly, physical capital of a standardized nature is relatively unspecific; if the machinery in a firm can easily be converted to another equally profitable use, its owner will have less incentive to lobby for government support.

Asset specificity is generally associated with industries with high barriers to entry and unique technology, skills, and networks. A firm producing turbines for a Venezuelan hydroelectric power plant is likely to have a larger proportion of its assets tied up in things specific to this use than a firm producing men's clothing or bricks. Industries to which entry is difficult—those using specialized technologies or specialized networks of suppliers or customers—typically have the most specific assets, and therefore the greatest incentive to lobby for industry-specific policies.

Aggregation of Actors into Groups

It is not enough for actors to have an incentive to lobby; they must organize to exert effective political pressure. The above discussion concerns economic determinants of policy preferences, but we also need to discuss the political determinants of the translation of these policy preferences into pressure on policymakers. This involves the organization of individuals and firms into groups.

Two complementary tools can be used to predict how socioeconomic actors combine in the political arena. The first is purely economic and groups individuals and firms by shared economic characteristic, similarity of asset. Those with like assets are affected analogously by relative price changes.

A second tool to determine what kinds of groups are likely to cohere is the logic of collective action. The literature on collective action is based on such observations as, for example, that while all workers may gain from a strong union, union membership may be irrational for each individual worker. A worker benefits from union strength but incurs costs in joining the union, and union strength appears independent of one individual's actions. After all, one member less or more makes no difference. The rational action for the individual can be to "free ride," take the benefits without incurring the costs. Thus no worker may have a reason to join the union.

Some groups unite more easily than others. Organizations can come and stay together by overcoming the contradictions of collective action, especially the free-rider problem. The literature on collective action suggests that cohesion depends on such factors as the size of the group (the smaller the group, the easier to police its membership) and its ability to provide selective benefits to members (health plans only for union members). More generally, better information or enforcement mechanisms make it easier to sustain an organization. The point is that we cannot assume that individuals or firms with similar assets will automatically come together, and collective-action considerations illuminate who will organize more easily.

The success of collective action depends in many ways on characteristics of industries that parallel the previous discussions of asset specificity and similar assets. The more concentrated the industry, the easier we would expect it to be able to exert political pressure. The greater the entry barriers, the more easily the industry will be able to avoid free riding by new entrants. The more similar the assets, the greater the ease of communication—including monitoring agreements—among those in the industry. As with asset specificity, then, we expect more concentrated industries able to exclude (or selectively include) members to be more politically influential.

Groups and Their Relations with Other Social Institutions

Once the policy preferences of socioeconomic interests are determined and their pattern of internal political organization is understood, the next step is to discover how organized interests work within or against existing institutions to achieve their goals. Institutions include lobbies and political parties: members abide by formal and informal rules in return for assistance from fellow members. Governmental structures are institutions: they exist only as social actors consent to observe their constraints. Specific public agencies are institutions: their employees, constituents, and targets all concede authority over some realm to the agency.

In the first instance, we take prevailing institutions as given and explore how rational self-interested actors use these institutions to satisfy as many of their needs as possible. With a given party structure, an interest group must determine which party or faction is most likely to champion successfully its policy preferences. With a given bureaucratic design, a group must decide which agency is most amenable to its demands and best located to meet them. The members of organized interest groups can carry out cost-benefit calculations as they weave their way through existing institutions in pursuit of their goals.

In this "static" picture, with institutions held constant, interest groups can strategize to form coalitions. If several weak groups ally against a strong group, they may prevail and obtain policies to their liking. Protectionist lobbies, each of which cares only about its own product, can support each others' demands in return for votes; the result might be that a free-trade group larger than any other *single* group is defeated by an alliance of all other groups united only by the logic of log-rolling. Political influence depends on coalition-building.

In the second instance, we relax the assumption that institutions are static and evaluate the determinants of institutional change. Even those with strong preferences and extensive alliances can be stymied by institutions biased against them. Literacy requirements inflate the impact of some groups or regions and reduce that of others; many parliamentary structures overrepresent rural voters. Restrictive labor or voting laws curtail the influence of the working class, while such ethnic restrictions as apartheid and Jim Crow impede political action. Biased institutions lead victims of bias to weigh the possibility of changing the institutions, although this may involve a long, hard struggle, as in the American South and South Africa.

In this "dynamic" picture in which institutions can be changed, socioeconomic groups evaluate whether complying with the requirements of existing institutional structures is in their interest. The first impulse is to abide by strictures imposed by an existing party, bureaucratic, or other arrangement, because the cost of destroying old structures and building new ones is usually considerable. But if the costs of *obeying* existing strictures is high, it may be more attractive to consider changing the institutions. Calculation of the costs of institutional stasis and the benefits of institutional change may lead a group to try to eliminate and replace the institution. Parties split, interest-group pressure leads to the creation of new agencies, elite discontent takes the form of support for the military elimination of democratic political systems.

The responsibility of the analyst here is to explain how the constraints set by existing institutions affect the political activities of socioeconomic interests. This involves illuminating the process by which social actors work through markets, parties, bureaucracies, and political systems to obtain as many of their goals as possible. It also involves exploring the circumstances under which social actors attempt to change, eliminate, or replace prevailing institutions.

Policies and Politics

The above overview of the analytical framework used in this study can be brought to bear on two outcomes of interest. First, we are interested in *policy outcomes,* what government policies are adopted. Inasmuch as actors accept the institutional restrictions upon them, we want to know how their interaction leads to the dominance of the policy preferences of one group or coalition over another. This tries to explain what economic policies governments undertake. Second, we are interested in *political outcomes,* in whether, how, and when actors decide to reject, reform, or build political institutions.

Where seeking to explain government policy toward a particular group, we begin with the costs and benefits to the government of supplying the policy. These costs are a function of the resources the government must expend to supply the policy; they decline as more resources become available. Taxes may increase; more important for our purposes, the interest rate charged to the government may drop. If interest rates fall and borrowing becomes easier, other things equal, we expect government to supply more of the policies demanded by society.

The benefits to the government of undertaking policies vary with the political pressure exerted by groups that stand to gain. This pressure is, as discussed above in detail, a function of economic and political characteristics of members of the various groups. On the economic side, the more specific a group's members' assets are to particular activities amenable to policy intervention, the more incentive they have to lobby for favorable policies. On the political side, the better able the group's members are to overcome collective action problems, the better able they will be to lobby for favorable policies. These are related to the level of asset specificity and concentration.

Where the thing to be explained is social behavior toward political institutions, we look at the costs and benefits to socioeconomic groups of accepting or rejecting existing political organizations. The less existing institutions provide the benefits a group demands, the more incentive it has to alter the institutions. The easier it is to alter an institution, the likelier it is that a disgruntled group will try to do so.

The general method to be used in this study can be summarized in four steps. The first step is to identify the policy preferences of individuals and firms, based on their position in the economy. The second step is to determine how they are grouped into politically relevant social forces, on the basis of both common economic interest and ability to overcome problems of collective action. The third step is to trace the aggregation of organized interests in the context of existing institutions, as they seek to obtain their preferred policies. The fourth step is to determine and trace the pressures for institutional change. The result is a series of new government policies and political institutions that create a new environment within which socioeconomic interests continue to contend.

Jeffry A. Frieden, "The Method of Analysis: Modern Political Economy," excerpt from *Debt, Development and Democracy: Modern Political Economy and Latin America*, 1965–1985 (Princeton, NJ: Princeton University Press, 1991): 15–41.

7

Political Models of Macroeconomic Policy and Fiscal Reforms

ALBERTO ALESINA

Economists typically study policymaking using models in which a benevolent social planner optimally chooses economic policy instruments in order to maximize the welfare of a representative individual, given certain resource constraints. From a *normative* point of view, these models are an extremely important tool of analysis. From a *positive* point of view, they cannot explain the occurrence of frequent and large departures from first-best policies. In addition, models with a social planner cannot explain why different countries at different points in time exhibit extremely different economic performances even though they face similar economic problems and have comparable resources.

A political-economic approach takes into account the institutional constraints and rigidities in which policymaking occurs by emphasizing the role of distributive conflicts, ideological and opportunistic incentives of the politicians, and other factors. Once these political variables are appropriately brought into the analysis, economic policy decisions that, at first view, appear wildly incoherent and suboptimal, can be interpreted as the rational outcome of a political-economic equilibrium. Such an approach not only is valuable from a positive perspective but also is rich in normative implications. In fact, it provides insights into how to design institutions that facilitate the achievement of efficient economic outcomes.

This chapter highlights how recent developments in political economics contribute to the understanding of macroeconomic policy and, more specifically, of the timing, design, and likelihood of success of stabilizations achieved through monetary and fiscal reforms.

In addressing these important issues, two basic and very general forces will always be crucial factors: (1) the policymakers' incentive to retain power and (2) society's polarization and degree of social conflict. These two elements of the analysis play a crucial role in both democratic and dictatorial systems, although they may manifest themselves differently, in different institutional contexts.

This chapter is organized as follows. First, the role of rationality in political-economic models and related methodological issues are discussed. Second, the timing of macroeconomic policy in general, and of fiscal reforms in particular, is addressed in relation to the timing of elections. This section focuses on how ideological and opportunistic considerations influence the choice of when to implement certain policies. It also reviews the literature on opportunistic and partisan political cycles and emphasizes what this literature offers to countries engaging simultaneously in policy reforms and democratization. Third, the related issue is examined of why stabilizations are delayed. The emphasis here is on why suboptimal economic outcomes such as hyperinflation and out-of-control budget deficits are not corrected for extended periods of time, even when something will obviously have to be done sooner or later. This section also emphasizes which political-institutional features are most likely to produce the timely adoption of successful stabilization programs.

Why Use Rational Models?

Political-economic models are often invoked to explain observations that seem to conflict with standard economic rationality. Thus, one is immediately tempted to abandon altogether the notion of rational behavior—defined as the maximization of individual utility under constraints—which also implies that all the available information is used to form expectations. Much too often, political-economic models hold the view that societies can be characterized as a bunch of crooks (the politicians) who manipulate a bunch of naive children (the citizens). It is often too easy to explain apparent departures from efficient collective behavior as the result of naïvité behavior, lack of understanding of basic economic relationships, shortsightedness, forgetfulness, or incoherence. Interpretive schemes and models in which behavior and expectations that are not rational play a crucial role should be used only as a last resort, after first considering other explanations.

Two compelling arguments justify this view. The first is that economic rationality (the maximization of individual utility under constraints) underlies our basic economic models. Why should analysts be so ready to assume that economically rational investors, consumers, and workers suddenly become dumb voters and naive citizens?

The second argument is that one of the most important contributions that the political-economic approach can make is to explain the large differences observed in the economic performance of countries with similar economic problems, resources, and level of development. If the observed outcomes are explained as a lack of rationality, then one has to believe that what differentiates various countries in the world is the degree of rationality of their citizens, consumers, voters, and leaders. This view is far from appealing.

The most common objections to the assumption of rationality in political-economic models can be summarized as follows:

First, some argue that voters have no incentive to gather information, and empirical evidence shows that they know very little about politics. But rationality simply requires that an agent uses efficiently all the information he has; rationality has nothing to do with the amount of information available. Moreover in many political models, very little is required of voters; in several spatial models of elections, for instance, voters are only required to know which party is on the left of the other.

There is a second argument against the assumption of rationality: not only are individuals self-motivated, they also have ideologies and may care about their fellow citizens, or at least some of them. But this is not inconsistent with rationality. In fact, this chapter discusses models in which partisan politicians act as if they followed an ideology, in addition to being self-interested. A rational approach only requires political and economic behavior to be consistent with given preferences, constraints, and information. Furthermore, an ideology can be interpreted as a systematic statement of preferences concerning political outcomes that are related to the resources and constraints of different actors.

According to a third argument, individuals cannot be expected to make all the necessary and complicated calculations needed to act rationally. But consumers are not required to take partial derivatives in order to compute marginal rates of substitutions when they shop in supermarkets. Nevertheless, economists believe in basic consumer theory and in the idea that demand curves are downward sloping. The same arguments apply to politics.

Finally, some say that leaders are not capable of acting rationally, because they and their advisers do not have enough technical preparation to adopt the correct policy decisions. In most cases, however, the crucial ingredients of policy reforms are simple. The real difficulties are political: for instance, how to share the burden of adjustment, how to implement the program without creating social unrest, and so on. Political issues are much more difficult than the technical issues of how to design the perfect program, from the point of view of economic theory. This is not meant to deny that good technical advice to leaders is not important; nevertheless, political conflicts and constraints are often much more difficult to overcome than technical difficulties. Otherwise, one would be led to the conclusion that, for instance, the far below-average economic performance of Latin America is due to the below-average competence of its economic advisers, a distasteful hypothesis. This does not mean, however, that government competence is irrelevant. More-competent governments are more likely than less-competent governments to minimize the costs of adjustments.

Political Cycles and Economic Cycles

This section reviews the theory and empirical evidence of political cycles in economic policymaking. Most of this literature has been developed with reference to advanced democracies, but some provides insights for analyzing systems that are not democratic or are in transition to democracy.

Different models of political cycles emphasize either the opportunistic or the partisan incentives of policymakers. In opportunistic models, policymakers maximize only their probability of being reelected or, more generally, their probability of surviving in office. In partisan models, different political parties represent the interests of different constituencies and, when in office, follow policies that are favorable to their supporting groups. Traditionally, left-wing parties are more concerned with the problems of unemployment, while right-wing parties are relatively more willing to bear the costs of unemployment to reduce inflation.

This literature has developed in two clearly distinct phases. The first one, in the mid-1970s, is due to the work of Nordhaus on opportunistic cycles and by Hibbs on partisan cycles. These papers share a prerational expectations model of the economy and are based on the existence of an exploitable Phillips curve, relating inflation and unemployment.

The second phase took off in the mid-1980s as a branch of the game-theoretic approach to the positive theory of macroeconomic policy. These newer models depart from their predecessors in two important dimensions. First, the assumption of economic agents' rationality makes real economic activity less directly and predictably influenced by economic policy in general and by monetary policy in particular. Second, voters' rationality implies that they cannot be systematically fooled in equilibrium; that is, a repeated, openly opportunistic behavior would be punished by the voters.

The Political-Business Cycle

The assumptions underlying Nordhaus's political-business cycle can be characterized as follows:

(2–1) The economy is described by a stable Phillips curve in which growth (and unemployment) depends on unexpected inflation.

(2–2) Inflation expectations are adaptive; that is, current expected inflation depends only on past inflation.

Combining these assumptions leads to the result that an increase in inflation *always* leads to a reduction in unemployment (and an increase in growth). Since expectations are adaptive, they catch up with a lag to actual inflation.

(2–3) Policymakers control the level of aggregate demand by means of monetary and fiscal instruments.

(2–4) Politicians are opportunistic: they only care about holding office, and they do not have partisan objectives.

(2–5) Voters are mainly retrospective: they judge the incumbent's performance by economic performance during the term of office and heavily discount past observations. Also, voters cannot distinguish between good economic conditions caused by luck and those caused by skillful policies.

Under these assumptions, Nordhaus derives the following testable implications: (a) every government follows the same policy, (b) toward the end of his term in office, the incumbent stimulates the economy to take advantage of the short-run more favorable Phillips curve, (c) the rate of inflation increases around election time as a result of the pre-electoral economic expansion; after the election, inflation is reduced with contractionary policies. Thus one should observe high growth and low unemployment before each election and a recession after each election.

Models of Rational Political-Business Cycles

More recently, authors have developed the model of the political-business cycle in a rational direction. In a nutshell, this line of work removes the second assumption and substitutes it with the following:

> (2–2') Economic agents have rational expectations concerning all the relevant economic variables.
>
> (2–2") Voters cannot perfectly assess the level of competence of the incumbent; that is, they can only imperfectly distinguish the effects of unlucky shocks to the economy from the effect of the government's lack of competence in handling the economy.

Assumption 2–5, which implies naive retrospective voting behavior, is substituted by the following:

> (2–5') Each voter chooses the candidate who is expected to deliver the highest utility for himself, given his rational expectations of postelectoral economic outcomes. In particular, the voters try, as best as they can given their information, to disentangle the effects on the economy of exogenous shocks from the effects of economic policy.

The competence of policymakers is defined as their ability to reduce waste in the budget process, to promote growth without inflation, or to react quickly to unexpected shocks. An important component of competence is the degree to which government officials are corrupted.

The basic assumption of this model is that policymakers are more informed than citizens about their own competence. By taking advantage of this informational asymmetry, and by trying to appear as competent as possible, politicians behave in a way leading to a Nordhaus-type political-business cycle. However, given voters' rationality and awareness of politicians' incentives, politicians are limited in their opportunistic behavior. If politicians appear to be too openly opportunistic, they might be punished by voters. Thus, electoral cycles in these rational models are more short-lived, smaller in magnitude, and less regular than they are in Nordhaus's model.

The Partisan Theory

A strong version of the partisan theory (Hibbs), based on a nonrational expectation mechanism, adopts assumptions 2–1, 2–2, and 2–3. Assumptions 2–4 and 2–5 are substituted by:

> (2–4') Politicians are partisan, in the sense that different parties maximize different objective functions. Left-wing parties attribute a higher cost to unemployment, relative to inflation, than right-wing parties do.
>
> (2–5") Each voter is aware of partisan differences and votes for the party that offers the policy closest to the preferred outcome.

This model implies that different parties choos°e different points on the Phillips curve: output growth and inflation should be permanently higher and

unemployment permanently lower with left-wing than with right-wing governments. More generally, fiscal policy will have a partisan bias (for instance, capital
taxation will be used more extensively by the left).

Rational Partisan Theory

Alesina develops a rational partisan theory by adopting assumptions 2–1, 2–28,
2–3, 2–4', and 2–5". This model generates a political cycle if nominal wage contracts are signed at discrete intervals (which do not coincide with the political
terms of office) and if electoral outcomes are uncertain. Given the sluggishness
with which wages are adjusted, changes in the inflation rate associated with
changes in government temporarily deviate real economic activity from its natural level.

More specifically, the following testable implications can be derived from the
model: (a) at the beginning of a right-wing (left-wing) government, output
growth is below (above) its natural level and unemployment is above (below)
it; (b) after expectations, prices, and wages adjust, output and unemployment
return to their natural level, and after this period of adjustment, which should
last no more than a couple of years, the level of economic activity should be independent of the party in office; and (c) the rate of inflation should remain
higher throughout the term of a left-wing government; that is, the time-consis-
tent (but suboptimal) inflation rate remains higher for left-wing parties even
after the level of economic activity returns to its natural level because of a credibility problem. The public knows that the left has a strong incentive to follow
expansionary policies to reduce unemployment. Thus, expected inflation is
high when the left is in office. In particular, because of rational expectations,
after the initial adjustment to the new regime, expected inflation is high
enough so that the government does not have an incentive to inflate more. Actual inflation is equal to expected inflation, and unemployment is at its natural
level.

In summary, this rational model differs from the traditional partisan one because it emphasizes how differences in growth and unemployment associated
with changes in government are only temporary. For example, a left-wing or a
populist government, strongly committed to reducing unemployment by means
of expansionary aggregate demand policies, is bound to succeed only in the short
run. After a brief period in which unemployment may actually fall, such a government will find itself trapped in a high-inflation equilibrium with no benefit
on the unemployment side. According to Hibbs's model, a left-wing government
could permanently lower the rate of unemployment by permanently increasing
the rate of inflation.

Empirical Evidence

Recent papers have provided several tests of political cycle models on a sample of
all the democracies in the Organization for Economic Cooperation and Development (OECD) for the period 1960–87. Their conclusions can be summarized in
two general points: (1) the new rational approaches to modeling opportunistic
and partisan cycles are much more successful empirically than their predecessors;
and (2) partisan effects are rather strong on economic outcomes, such as growth,

unemployment, and inflation, while opportunistic effects are small in magnitude and appear only on policy instruments, particularly budget deficits.

Empirical research on political cycles in non-OECD democracies is much more limited, and, therefore, any new results in this area would be valuable. It is important to distinguish between dictatorships and periods of transition to democracy.

Dictatorships are a heterogeneous group, beginning with the distinction between strong and weak dictators. The survival of strong dictators is not seriously threatened, given a certain domestic and international political and military balance. Strong dictators are themselves heterogeneous. Some have promoted economic growth and macroeconomic stability in their countries. Others have wrecked their countries' economy. Given such differences, any attempt to show that dictatorships as a group exhibit a superior (or inferior) economic performance than democracies as a group would be inconclusive. More generally, the vast literature on democracy and growth has not reached conclusive evidence regarding their relationship.

Weak dictators are in danger of being overthrown. In fact, if social discontent increases, the dictator's probability of survival decreases. When a dictator is in such danger, his incentives may not differ too much from those of an incumbent president or prime minister in a democracy before an uncertain election. Thus, one may look for opportunistic policies and loose fiscal policies when weak dictators are in danger of being overthrown. Ames studies the opportunistic behavior of Latin American rulers, with particular reference to budget cycles and fiscal and military policies. This author shows that Latin American dictators have followed fiscal policies that, in some respects, are a magnified example of the kind of opportunistic policies described above. Ames documents how rulers in danger of being overthrown used public expenditure to please key constituencies and, in particular, the military.

In fact, immediately before dictators are overthrown, they employ the worst opportunistic and self-interested policies, for two reasons. First, collapsing dictators are struggling for survival and are willing to do anything, since they feel that they have no future. Any consideration of good economic management is secondary to the goal of remaining politically (and physically) alive. Second, if a dictator becomes convinced that his time horizon in office is very short, he may simply decide to steal from the country's wealth for his personal gain and that of his close supporters.

As a result, collapsing dictators are likely to bequeath to their successors economies with serious macroeconomic imbalances, and new democracies thus inherit difficult economic problems. In addition, new democratic governments may feel particularly strong partisan pressures to do something for social groups that have recently obtained a voice in the political arena. Furthermore, new democracies are particularly subject to the risk of being overthrown and even more so when the groups and constituencies supporting the old regime have a voice and a political or military presence. As a result, new democracies face a difficult problem of survival and may find it particularly difficult to follow tough policies implying short-run economic costs: new democracies may have to be opportunistic to survive. Unfortunately, as argued above, new democracies may come to office exactly at a time when tough policies are called for and cannot be postponed.

Finally, the partisan theory implies a positive relationship between the degree of political and social polarization and the variability of macroeconomic policies, which, in turn, affects the variability and level of economic outcomes. In fact, as emphasized above, the partisan theory is based on the view that because different parties have different distributional preferences, they also have different preferences for macroeconomic policies. The more different these distributional preferences are, the more volatile is macroeconomic policy. From this perspective, populist cycles in Latin America magnify partisan cycles in OECD democracies. Populist policies are, in fact, defined as the use of aggregate policies (monetary and fiscal) to redistribute income and wealth. Populist governments are often followed by right-wing regimes that attempt to reverse these redistributions.

These macroeconomic policy cycles often introduce a large variance and unpredictability to expectations of future policies. Such uncertainty is likely to be associated with poor economic performance by making long-run planning more difficult. Recent results by Alesina and others suggest that the degree of political uncertainty and instability is linked with the level of investments and growth in large samples of countries, including Latin America.

Delays in Policy Reforms

One of the most puzzling observations in political economics is that several countries follow policies, for extended periods of time, that are recognized as not being feasible in the long run: in particular, rapidly accumulating public debts with skyrocketing ratios of debt to gross national product and hyperinflation. These observations are particularly puzzling when, as is quite common, the longer a country waits, the more costly the stabilization program is when finally adopted. Similar arguments apply to the apparently inexplicable delays in reforming trade policies to eliminate socially inefficient forms of protection. In its most general terms, the puzzle is the following: why are certain reforms delayed that are efficient in the sense that they increase aggregate welfare?

Clearly, no single model can explain every delay in reforming policy. Different explanations may play a role in different cases, although certain arguments appear, in general, to be more convincing than others. The following paragraphs review the least compelling explanations.

The first one is that countries that delay reforms do not understand that such reforms are unavoidable. This is not convincing since in most cases the macroeconomic imbalances are so macroscopic that the need for a monetary and fiscal stabilization is undeniable. Reasonable persons can, in some cases, disagree about the speed, urgency, and design of a stabilization program for technical reasons. Most often, however, these technical discussions reflect underlying distributional conflicts.

A second explanation is that governments wait to stabilize until exogenous shocks make the stabilization program less costly. Thus, there is an option value in waiting. Such an approach does not explain why, as is often the case, countries do not stabilize as soon as favorable shocks occur and why many stabilizations take place without any prior realization of particularly favorable economic shocks.

A third argument is that since stabilizations are costly in the short run, they are postponed until things get really bad. This is irrational, since the longer a country waits, the more costly the stabilization becomes. According to this model, different countries' experiences would be explained by different degrees of rationality, an argument that is hardly convincing.

Explanations based on collective rationality or an understanding of basic economic relationships are more sound. The remainder of this section highlights a few, organized by four types of models:

1. War of attrition models based on an uncertain distribution of the costs of delaying the stabilizations
2. Models focusing on the conflicting interests of specific social groups, such as labor and capital
3. Models emphasizing the uncertain outcome of the stabilization
4. Models emphasizing the role of certain institutional arrangements, such as the degree of independence of the central bank.

Stabilization as a War of Attrition

Alesina and Drazen argue that, often, the process leading to a monetary and fiscal stabilization can be described as a war of attrition between socioeconomic groups with conflicting distributional interests. The basic idea follows. Consider an economy where, for whatever reason, a budget deficit appears. A stabilization is defined as an increase in regular income taxes that eliminates the deficit. For simplicity and without loss of generality, government spending is assumed to be constant.

Before a stabilization occurs, government spending and the interest on the external debt are paid by the government, in part by borrowing abroad and in part by means of a highly distortionary tax. For concreteness, the tax before stabilization is thought of as an inflation tax, and it is assumed to be more distortionary than regular income taxes. In such a situation, a social planner managing an economy populated by identical individuals would *not* delay the stabilization program. In fact, delays are socially costly for two reasons: first, until the stabilization occurs, distortionary means of taxation are used; second, the longer one waits, the more the debt accumulates, and the higher the interest the government pays.

Even though a social planner would stabilize immediately, the political conflict between heterogeneous groups over how the burden of the stabilization will be allocated leads to rational delays. Suppose that the burden of the stabilization is not divided equally among groups. In particular, assume that there are two competing groups and that the loser will pay more than half of the stabilization costs (that is, income taxes). Suppose, further, that the two groups are not identical: in particular, they differ in the utility loss suffered in the period before stabilization. For instance, the high-cost group is the one whose costs of living in an unstable economy are particularly high. An important element necessary to obtain delayed stabilization is that each group's costs of delaying the stabilization are privileged information. Each group knows only its own costs and has a probability distribution over the opponent's costs.

The stabilization occurs when one of the two groups concedes, that is, accepts being the loser and agrees to pay a high fraction of the taxes needed to eliminate the deficit. Stabilization does not occur immediately because each group has a rational incentive to wait, hoping that the opponent will concede first. In equilibrium, the group with the highest costs of waiting will concede, but it is the passage of time that will reveal which is the high-cost group. The concession time is determined by the condition that the marginal costs of not conceding—the costs of remaining in the unstable economy for another instant—are equal to the marginal gains from remaining, which are given by the probability that the opponent will concede in the next instant, multiplied by the gains of being the winner (paying less than half the costs of stabilization). The asymmetry of information is important in generating the delay. If it is known from the start which group has the highest costs of waiting, then the loser is known from the start. Thus, the loser concedes immediately in order to avoid the costs of delays.

Alesina and Drazen derive several results concerning the expected time of stabilization, which make this war of attrition model useful for empirical analysis.

(1) *Political cohesion:* The more unequal the distribution of the costs of stabilization, other things being equal, the longer the stabilization is delayed.

If these costs are shared equally, stabilization occurs immediately, since there is no gain from being the winner. The more unequal the distribution of costs is, the higher the gain from being the winner and the higher the incentive to wait the opponent out. This suggests that stabilization will be delayed more in countries with less cohesion and with more political polarization and instability, in which it is more difficult to reach an equitable social contract with a fair allocation of costs.

(2) *Costs of delaying:* an increase in the costs of postponing the stabilization reduces the delay.

This somewhat obvious result becomes rather interesting if one thinks of these costs not only as the economic costs of inflation but also as political costs. For instance, the costs of political action that each group must pay in order to avoid being imposed upon increase that group's share of the costs of the stabilization. These costs of political action may be loss of wages and leisure time incurred by striking urban workers, the risks incurred by armed insurrectionists, the monetary costs incurred by the capitalists financing their representatives in the legislature, and so forth. Political institutions that make it easier for even small interest groups to block the legislative process by veto power are conducive to delayed stabilization. For instance, strictly proportional electoral systems are more likely to generate coalition governments in which legislative action requires the consensus of a large number of parties, each of which can veto an action. Thus even a small interest group can veto a stabilization program and procrastinate the war of attrition.

(3) *Income distribution:* The degree of income inequality has ambiguous effects on the amount of delay.

If political and economic resources are very unequally distributed, so that it is immediately obvious which group is stronger and has more resources to wait longer, the war of attrition ends immediately, since the identity of the winner is certain. However, if resources are dispersed across groups, maintaining the asymmetric distribution of information about relative costs, then delays increase.

Alesina and Drazen argue that this war of attrition model is consistent with three elements that are often (but not always) observed in stabilization processes:

1. There is an agreement over the need of a fiscal change but a political stalemate over how the burden of higher taxes or expenditure cuts should be allocated. In the political debate over the stabilization, this distributional question is central.
2. When stabilization occurs it coincides with a *political* consolidation. Often, one side becomes politically dominant. The burden of stabilization is sometimes quite unequal, with the politically weaker group bearing a larger burden. Often this means the lower classes, with successful stabilizations being regressive.
3. Successful stabilizations are usually preceded by several failed attempts; often a previous program appears quite similar to the successful one.

Further progress in an empirical direction can be made by defining more clearly what exactly is meant by a concession. In theory, a concession means simply that one of the groups accepts the role of loser. In practice, a concession may take different forms. One is a clear electoral victory for one side. This may make the legislative action easier for the winning side and raise to an unsustainable level the political costs to the opponent of vetoing stabilization plans. A second is the acceptance by one side of granting extraordinary powers to the government to avoid legislative deadlocks. A third is the recall of strikes, riots, and other political actions taken by the workers' movement if they are perceived to be too costly and unsustainable. A fourth is the achievement of a compromise accepted by all parts governing how the burden of stabilization will be allocated.

Drazen and Grilli extend the war of attrition model by emphasizing the possible benefits of economic crises. They show that if an exogenous shock aggravates the economic conditions, the war of attrition may be resolved because the costs of not stabilizing are even higher. In some cases, such crises increase aggregate welfare: in fact, the costs of the adverse shock are more than compensated by the benefits of the anticipated stabilization.

Finally, the war of attrition idea is applicable not only to delays in fiscal stabilizations but also to many other delays in the adoption of efficient reforms, such as the removal of price controls or trade restrictions. For a war of attrition to occur, the proposed reform should have substantial distributional effects and some uncertainty must exist about the relative strength of the various groups.

Class Conflicts

Different classes may have different perspectives about the urgency of a stabilization, and some may actually gain from delaying the stabilization. In other words, an unstable economy benefits some groups. For instance, in one model stabilization may be delayed if the asset holders perceive that they can escape taxation by exporting their assets abroad. He considers an economy with three broadly defined classes: capital owners, middle-class or skilled workers, and unskilled workers. Suppose that, because of a fiscal imbalance, aggregate demand is high and inflation is increasing; a social planner, once again, would choose to stabilize immediately. However, a political equilibrium may lead to postponements for the following reason. Suppose that in the period of high aggregate demand and high inflation, profits are increasing and wages of unskilled workers are indexed and approximately constant in real terms. Profits are increasing with aggregate demand, as are returns to capital.

Capitalists would like to postpone the stabilization, if they think that they gain first, because of the increasing returns, and that they can then move their profits abroad to escape the tax increase needed to stabilize. Unskilled workers are too poor to be taxed after stabilization. Thus, the cost of stabilization falls mostly, or exclusively, on the middle class. While the middle class would prefer to stabilize immediately to minimize overall costs, capitalists and unskilled workers may prefer to postpone the stabilization. If capitalists and unskilled workers together have enough political influence, the stabilization is delayed.

This model captures two important insights, which are much more general than the specific example: first, not everybody loses during the period preceding stabilization; second, the very rich and the very poor may be on the same side against the middle class. In fact, in several well-known cases of hyperinflation, the middle class has suffered the most.

In summary, these types of models suggest that in some cases certain coalitions actually benefit from a macroeconomic imbalance and manage to postpone the adjustment for their own advantage.

Uncertain Outcomes of the Stabilization

Fernández and Rodrik consider the case of a policy reform that improves the welfare of the majority of the population. For concreteness, removal of a tariff is the reform under consideration. All producers in the export sectors are better off with the reform; a fraction of producers in the import-competing sector have to move to the export sector and are better off after the reform and their move. Suppose that these two groups are a majority of the population. However, because of uncertainty about which agents in the import-competing industry will benefit from the reform, a majority of the population may vote against it.

This model emphasizes that uncertainty concerning the identity of the losers from a proposed reform may create a bias toward maintaining an inefficient status quo. Even though Fernández and Rodrik consider a trade reform, clearly their approach is much more general and applicable to fiscal reforms as well.

Milesi-Ferretti suggests another reason, based on uncertain outcomes, why monetary and fiscal stabilizations may be postponed. He considers a model in which the costs of stopping inflation are uncertain and depend upon how competent the government is in managing the reform; that is, there are competent governments, which manage to stabilize with small economic costs, and incompetent ones, which are capable of stabilizing but do so at higher costs.

If a stabilization is started and the government is discovered to be incompetent, the public may choose to elect the opposition, which is expected to be more competent. If, instead, the government does not begin a program, nothing is learned about the government's competence. In this case, if the public favors the opposition, the latter would have to solve the same problem faced by today's government. Thus, if it is in the interest of the current government to do nothing for fear of failure because of incompetence, the public may have no incentive to vote for the opposition because the latter would do the same, when in office. What is crucial, here, is that the *government itself does not know its own level of competence*, otherwise the choice of doing something or doing nothing would reveal some of the government's private information concerning its own competence.

This model is particularly appropriate for cases in which a policy reform is relatively new and has never been attempted before, making it difficult to predict the costs and the government's competence on such grounds. The case of new democratic governments facing economic crises may be a good example for this model. A new democratic leadership may be reasonably unknown to the public, since the new leadership has never been in office before. At the same time, the new democratic opposition is also new to the political arena. Thus, there might be very little available information on both the new democratic government and the new opposition.

Institutions

Different institutional arrangements may be more or less conducive to macroeconomic management and to a swift reaction to economic crises needing stabilization. The discussion of wars of attrition suggested that multiparty systems with coalition governments may find it difficult to achieve quick agreement on how to stabilize. This is because each member of a coalition government may have the power to veto and block any program that is disliked by a certain (even small) constituency. Coalition governments are more often observed in parliamentary democracies with proportional representation. Therefore, the institution of proportionality may not be conducive to swift fiscal reforms when they are needed. Empirical results on OECD democracies are consistent with these observations. Studies show that prolonged periods of fiscal imbalance leading to the accumulation of relatively high ratios of debt to gross national product have been common in parliamentary democracies with large coalition governments. On the other hand, single-party governments have reacted more quickly to prevent persistent deficits.

These arguments are not directly applicable to dictatorships. However, they are somewhat related to the previous discussion of strong versus weak dictators. A weak dictator may be the analog of a weak coalition government in a democracy. A weak dictator may have to please several constituencies with conflicting interests in order to survive and would find it difficult to resolve a fiscal crisis promptly.

A second institutional feature that may affect fiscal management and the implementation of fiscal reforms is the possibility of conflicts within a state or a bureaucracy over the allocation of spending and taxation. Fiscal federalism (that is, geographic decentralization of fiscal decisions) may make it difficult to act quickly when quick action is needed. First, if local authorities can, up to a point, transfer locally generated deficits to the federal system, they may choose to do so in time of need; that is, one may observe a prisoner's dilemma situation, in which different states or regions fail to cooperate. Second, there might be, once again, a veto power with which various states or regions block stabilization plans decided at the federal level.

A similar argument may apply to conflicts within a bureaucracy. Obviously, the relevance of these conflicts would depend on the degree to which the bureaucracy is independent of elected officers.

Third, an institutional feature that could be very important in the context of a discussion of monetary and fiscal stability is the degree to which the central bank is politically independent. A central bank independent of the treasury and firmly committed to monetary control reduces the degree of monetization of budget deficits. This has two effects: it keeps inflation under control, and it forces the government to find other sources of financing, ultimately forcing the government to raise taxes or cut spending.

Several authors have noted how, within industrial economies, countries with low inflation have independent central banks. Furthermore, such low inflation has not been accompanied by high unemployment, high real interest rates, or other undesirable, real consequences. Thus, central bank independence seems to have helped monetary stability with very small "real" costs.

Although a central bank with an established reputation of independence may improve policymaking, the process of establishing such a reputation may lead to periods of policy instability. In fact, suppose that the treasury runs budget deficits and does not raise taxes in an attempt to induce the central bank to monetize. The bank refuses to do so, precisely to establish a reputation of independence and induce the treasury to raise taxes and cut spending. This situation may lead to a sort of war of attrition between the treasury and the central bank. Before one of the two players gives in, taxes are not raised and the deficit is not monetized; such a combination leads to a rapidly growing ratio of debt to gross national product. On the one hand, institutional arrangements guaranteeing the independence of the central bank should ensure that such an institutional war of attrition does not occur because the treasury knows that the central bank will not concede. On the other hand, a war of attrition will not occur when the central bank has no independence at all, and the treasury can obtain as much monetization as it desires.

There are three ways of testing political-economic models of inflation, deficits, stabilization, or lack thereof: case studies, a comparative method in which several cases are examined jointly, and econometric studies of several countries. The first two approaches have been adopted mostly (but not exclusively) by political scientists. The third has been used mostly (but not exclusively) by economists. A survey of the empirical literature is, obviously, well beyond the scope of this chapter.

Conclusions

This chapter has reviewed recent formal developments in political economics that study the relationship between the timing of macroeconomic policy and political institutions. Two important issues have been the focus of this review: political-business cycles and monetary and fiscal stabilization policies.

Rather than review the results described in the previous pages, this section highlights several issues open for further research.

- Although a reasonably sound and extensive body of theoretical and empirical research exists on political-business cycles in advanced industrial democracies, much less has been done for developing countries. This research should tackle difficult issues, such as how to test for such cycles in nondemocracies.
- The periods of transition from dictatorships to democracies are extremely interesting situations for studying political-economic interactions. Researchers should devote careful and specific attention to such periods.
- Authoritarian regimes appear to be a heterogeneous group. Some have promoted growth and economic stability and have done better than the average democracy. Others have destroyed their economies. A further understanding of what explains these large differences is likely to have very high intellectual returns.
- The normative aspects of political economy should also be very high on the research agenda. Should a new democracy be advised to adopt majoritarian systems, set up independent central banks, include balanced-budget clauses in the constitution, limit the number of times incumbents can run for office, delegate fiscal authority to local authorities to have a bicameral system, and elect the president directly? These are only a few of the many questions facing new democracies.

Alberto Alesina, "Political Models of Macroeconomic Policy and Fiscal Reforms," in *Voting for Reform: Democracy, Political Liberalization and Economic Adjustment*, eds. Stephan Haggard and Steven B. Webb (New York: Oxford University Press, 1994): 37–60.

8

Understanding
Economic Policy Reform

DANI RODRIK

Introduction

The events of the last decade have underscored the need to understand the
political-economy of policy making. One of the eventual consequences of the
global debt crisis that erupted in 1982 was a wave of market-oriented economic
reforms, the likes of which have never been seen. The reforms were strongest and
most sustained in Latin America, where countries like Bolivia, Mexico, Argentina,
Peru, Colombia, and Brazil joined Chile in orthodoxy. But this was very much a
global phenomenon. "Stabilization" and "structural adjustment" became the primary preoccupation of government leaders in Asia and Africa as well, even
though the commitment to economic orthodoxy varied across countries and
over time. These countries were in turn soon joined by the previously socialist
economies of Eastern Europe and the former Soviet Union. Economists who had
cut their teeth in Latin America's economic quagmires became the advisors and
analysts of these transitional economies. Even India, the giant archetype of a
closed, import-substituting economy among developing countries, embarked on
a process of economic liberalization in 1991.

These reforms were encouraging to economists and a vindication of sorts to
those among them who had long advocated market-oriented reforms. But they
in turn raise their own puzzles. Most fundamental of all, why are so many governments reforming now, after decades of adherence to policies of an opposite
kind? This question poses a particularly important challenge to political economists: an understanding of these countries' experiences now requires a theory
that explains not only why seemingly dysfunctional policies had been initially
undertaken and then maintained for so long, but also why these policies were
suddenly abandoned en masse during the 1980s, often by the same politicians
who had been among their most ardent supporters. Second, while the reforms
were inspired at least in part by the East Asian experience, they took place much
more quickly and, in many areas, are going considerably beyond those undertaken in East Asia. This raises the question of whether the new wave of reform-

ers have internalized the correct lessons from the East Asian experience. Finally, are there any helpful rules for reformers to follow in guiding their policies through complicated political terrain? Can one hope to develop a "how-to" manual for the reformist politician?

The New Orthodoxy in Development Thinking and Enduring Puzzles

Once upon a time, there was something called the Third World and we thought we understood how it worked (or did not work). Countries of the Third World followed import-substitution policies, so called because the overarching objective of economic policy was to develop domestic manufacturing capability for goods previously imported. Such policies included import controls, overvalued exchange rates, binding ceilings on interest rates, a heavy dose of public ownership, and pervasive price regulation. The political-economy counterpart of these policies was the predominance of urban over rural interests, and within the urban sector, an uneasy alliance of sorts between the protected industries and the bureaucrats administering the protection.

Perhaps no other economist has done as much as Anne Krueger in documenting and popularizing the shortcomings of import-substituting policies. As she points out, there was a multitude of reasons for the initial adoption of these policies. Newly independent governments had a strong desire for industrialization, and the apparently successful example of Soviet planning invited emulation. Moreover, the economic ideas of the 1950s and early 1960s tended to dismiss the benefits from trade and emphasized the need for physical capital accumulation and infant-industry promotion. As Krueger puts it,

> [t]he underlying premises regarding markets and governments implicit in these policy prescriptions are obvious: There was a strong emphasis on the primacy of market imperfections. Market failures were thought to be relatively strong, while it was assumed that governments could correctly identify and perform economic functions. Virtually no attention was given to the possibility that there might be government failure.

And there was plenty of government failure. Not only did many infant industries fail to mature, but many countries succumbed to stop-go cycles driven by excessive government spending. Krueger explains that in viewing the government as a "benevolent social guardian" most economists had ignored a number of important forces at work. Individuals in the public sector were apt to follow their own selfish interests. They would be lobbied by pressure groups aiming to impose their own agenda on a largely docile majority. Policy interventions would create rent-seeking incentives diverting entrepreneurs from productive activities. Finally, the informational disadvantage of government bureaucracies over market participants would doom even the best-laid plans to inefficiency.

Meanwhile, four East Asian economies were making a mockery of the export pessimism that had persuaded policy makers elsewhere to follow an inward-oriented strategy. South Korea and Taiwan, in particular, were able to engineer a remarkable increase in their growth rates, thanks to sharp jumps in their investment and export efforts during the mid–1960s. What was the key to these economies' success? Among professional economists, there soon developed the view that the East Asian miracles could be attributed to market-oriented policies and the reduced role of government intervention.

So the new orthodoxy was built on two mutually reinforcing pillars: one was the set of policies that had been tried by the import-substituting countries and had failed; the second was the set of successful policies implemented by the East Asian tigers. These two sets of policies bear close scrutiny, as they overlap to a much greater extent than the orthodox case likes to admit.

Macroeconomic Disequilibrium or Import-Substitution Policies?

In describing the experience of developing countries it has become common to lump together a wide range of policies, under the label of "import-substitution policies." For descriptive purposes, this makes perfect sense. Except for a handful of countries in East Asia, most developing countries did combine illiberal trade and price policies with (at least occasional) fiscal profligacy and overvalued exchange rates. So there was a common syndrome, which perhaps does deserve to go under a single name. However, the practice has also frequently led economic analysis astray and generated confusion. The trouble is that failures were often misattributed to microeconomic policies, when their sources lay either with unsustainable macroeconomic policies or bureaucratic and institutional shortcomings.

The watershed event of the 1980s for most developing countries, the generalized debt crisis that followed the Mexican moratorium of August 1982, was a dramatic confirmation of the importance of prudent macroeconomic policies. Looking below the surface, it was evident that the crisis affected only those countries that did not respect budget constraints. India, the import-substituting country par excellence, managed to escape the debt crisis during the 1980s, thanks to its tradition of conservative monetary and fiscal policies. At the other end of the spectrum, South Korea experienced a payments crisis in 1979–80, *before* the Latin American countries, as a consequence of an ambitious investment program running ahead of available domestic savings. But the quick adoption of expenditure-reducing and expenditure-switching policies enabled a swift recovery, after a five percent contraction in 1980. Before long, Korea's crisis was forgotten. More broadly, there was no correlation between the propensity to fall into crisis and the nature of microeconomic policies proper. The countries that experienced a debt crisis in 1982 were those that failed to adjust their monetary and fiscal policies, and not those that had large microeconomic distortions or were confronted with particularly large external shocks.

This distinction between microeconomic distortions and macroeconomic stability is one that economists have long recognized. Yet it is also one that has made
little impression on the development profession. It became commonplace to view
the debt crisis as the consequence of import-substitution ("inward-oriented")
policies. The intellectual ground was therefore cleared for the wholesale reform
of prevailing policies in Latin America, Africa, and Asia. Orthodox economists
who had the ear of policy makers now had their chance to wipe the slate clean
and mount a frontal attack on the entire range of policies in use. After some delay, this produced dramatic results, especially in Latin America.

What Did the East Asian Governments Do Right?

Ironically, many governments (notably in Latin America) ended up implementing policies that went far beyond what the East Asian governments themselves
had adopted since the 1960s. As intimated above, many of the discredited policies
had long been in use in South Korea, Taiwan, and Singapore, and apparently to
good effect. (Hong Kong's policies have come closest to the laissez-faire ideal,
even though there is plenty of intervention in the housing market.) To appreciate
this point, it is useful to spell out in somewhat greater detail the elements of the
new orthodoxy, so we can compare them to East Asian policies.

Fortunately, we have a useful list of policy desiderata compiled by Williamson,
who has dubbed it the "Washington consensus." In Williamson's words, "[t]he
'Washington consensus' offers a description of what is agreed about the set of
measures that are typically called for in the first stage of policy reform. . . ." The
list is shown in Table 1 along with my own summary comments on the degree of
compliance exhibited by Taiwan and South Korea in each area of reform.

How well did South Korea and Taiwan do according to this list? Judging by
the number of the prescriptions these countries did or did not follow, we would
have to award South Korea a score of about five (out of ten), and Taiwan about
six. Neither country significantly liberalized its import regime until the 1980s.
Both countries heavily interfered in the investment decisions of private enterprises. And far from privatizing public enterprises, both countries actually increased their reliance on such enterprises during the crucial decade of the 1960s.
In short, where South Korea and Taiwan followed the orthodox path most
closely was in maintaining conservative fiscal policies and competitive exchange
rates; this accounts for their ability to avoid protracted periods of macroeconomic instability, particularly in the crisis-ridden decade of the 1980s. In the
area of microeconomic interventions, however, their experience diverged from
the orthodox path.

By contrast, it is striking how many Latin American countries have come
within reaching distance of completing the items on the "Washington consensus"
in a period of no more than a few years during the 1980s. Mexico, Bolivia, and
Argentina, to cite some of the more distinguished examples, have undertaken
more trade and financial liberalization and privatization within five years than
the East Asian countries have managed in three decades.

I will discuss the reforms of the 1980s at greater length later. First we have to
confront two puzzles that arise from the contrasting experiences of the East Asian
tigers and other developing countries prior to the 1980s. How could the East

TABLE 1   The "Washington Consensus" and East Asia

Elements of the Washington Consensus	South Korea	Taiwan
1. Fiscal discipline	Yes, generally	Yes
2. Redirection of public expenditure priorities towards health, education and infrastructure	Yes	Yes
3. Tax reform, including the broadening of the tax base and cutting marginal tax rates	Yes, generally	Yes
4. Unified and competitive exchange rates	Yes (except for limited time periods)	Yes
5. Secure property rights	President Park starts his rule in 1961 by imprisoning leading businessmen and threatening confiscation of their assets	Yes
6. Deregulation	Limited	Limited
7. Trade liberalization	Limited until the 1980s	Limited until the 1980s
8. Privatization	No. Government established many public enterprises during the 1950s and 1960s	No. Government established many enterprises during 1950s and 1960s
9. Elimination of barriers to direct foreign investment (DFI)	DFI heavily restricted	DFI subject to government control
10. Financial liberalization	Limited until the 1980s	Limited until the 1980s

Source: Williamson (1994) for first column, and author's evaluation.

Asian countries avoid the disasters that accompanied interventionist policies elsewhere? And why did most developing countries succumb so easily, and often periodically, to unsustainable fiscal and exchange-rate policies?

How Did East Asian Countries Manage to Intervene without Inviting Rent Seeking?

One major puzzle noted above had to do with the apparently successful pursuit of interventionist microeconomic policies by South Korea and Taiwan. Why did trade protection, industrial policy, and subsidized credit work in these countries when it failed most everywhere else? We can ignore purely economic aspects and narrow down the question to the following: how were the East Asian governments able to avoid the rent-seeking activities that typically accompanied microeconomic interventions?

Authoritarianism may have had something to do with the East Asian governance style, but there are too many mismanaged dictatorships around the world to take the hypothesis seriously. One need only look at Sub-Saharan Africa.

At least part of the explanation has to do with some of the special initial conditions that the East Asian countries shared prior to their economic take-off. Two such conditions stand out. First, by the late 1950s the East Asian economies had for the most part a much better educated labor force than would have been expected on the basis of their income levels. This may have made it easier to establish a competent bureaucracy (as well as enhancing the productivity of interventions aimed at boosting private investment). Second, and perhaps more importantly, in all of them the distribution of income and wealth around 1960 was exceptionally equal by cross-country standards. Equality may have been conducive to better governance for at least three different reasons.

First, these governments did not generally have to contend with powerful industrial or landed interest groups: therefore, policy making and implementation could be insulated from pressure-group politics. Second, the absence of large-scale inequities meant that governments felt no immediate need to undertake redistributive policies; they could concentrate on expanding the pie instead. Note that this point is analytically distinct from the previous one, since even a government which is completely insulated from lobbying groups would wish to redistribute income. Third, and related to these, the fact that the top political leadership was free to focus on economic goals meant that it could supervise the bureaucracy closely and make sure that the bureaucrats assisted rather than hindered private entrepreneurship. For bureaucracies are prone to two problems that are fatal to economic performance: they can be captured by the interests they are supposed to regulate, and they can create excessive red tape discouraging economic activity. In Korea and Taiwan, these problems were avoided because the bureaucracies were very closely supervised by the top political leadership.

The Political Economy of Macroeconomic Cycles

The continued existence of some of the policies that make up the "import substitution" syndrome, despite mounting evidence of their inefficiencies, can be understood in distributional terms: such policies redistribute income or rents to favored groups in society. Their beneficiaries—business and labor groups protected from foreign and domestic competition—are naturally resistant to their reform. But what is distinctive about large-scale deficit spending and overvalued currencies is that these policies are by their very nature temporary, and the longer they are pursued the more drastic their eventual reversal must be. Groups that benefit during the upswing of the joyride have to suffer losses during the downswing. Labor, for example, normally gains from expansionary "populist" policies, but also ends up as the greatest loser when the eventual crisis takes its toll on real wages and employment. Businessmen benefit from cheap imported inputs while the currency overvaluation lasts, but they are condemned to take a hit when the inevitable devaluation takes place (or when a large black-market premium makes its appearance). Therefore, short of attributing myopia or irrationality to the main political actors, it is hard to understand why such policies find support in the first place.

A fascinating case in point is the experience of Peru under President García (1985–90). Facing a stagnant economy, the new García administration launched a "heterodox program" in August 1985. The main thrust of the program was to boost consumption demand by increasing real wages, subsidizing consumption, and creating public-works programs. The government also instituted a freeze on prices, interest rates, and the exchange rate. And consumption did boom for a couple of years, raising output alongside it. However, the process was clearly unsustainable: the public-sector and current-account deficits both rose substantially and foreign reserves were depleted. By late 1988, the economy had collapsed and prices were near hyperinflation levels. Real wages, which had increased until 1988, took a sharp nose dive and in 1989 stood at a third of their 1987 level.

Peru's case may be extreme, but it is by no means unique. Observers of the developing world have long been fascinated by the prevalence of such boom-and-bust cycles.

Myopic behavior can take us only so far in understanding these policy cycles. For one thing, the underlying economics is straightforward: it does not require a Ph.D. in economics to realize that spending money one does not have can result in unpleasant consequences. For another, people ought to learn from their mistakes. To take one—not altogether extreme—example, since the 1950s Turkey has gone through *four* full boom-and-bust cycles, one per decade.

Several recent papers have proposed formal models that generate political outcomes that are inefficient *from the standpoint of the politically powerful groups themselves,* even though these groups behave rationally and non-myopically. The trick is usually performed by positing some kind of coordination problem among the contending actors.

For example, Alesina and Drazen show how a stabilization can be delayed, at great cost to the parties involved, thanks to a "war of attrition" between two groups, each of which is uncertain about the costs being incurred by the other group. It is individually rational to wait in this model because the group that caves in first is assumed to bear a larger part of the post-stabilization tax burden. Each group has the incentive to wait and see if the other group will throw in the towel first. Stabilization takes place only when one of the groups figures that it stands to gain more from assuming the cost of stabilization than from waiting another instant to see if its rival will do so instead.

But these papers leave hanging a key question: if distributional struggles are at the heart of inefficient policy choices and macroeconomic policy cycles, why do policy makers not design *compensation* schemes to neutralize political opposition? In the Alesina-Drazen model, for example, the distribution of the costs of stabilization is taken as exogenous. This is unsatisfactory because the design of the stabilization package can surely influence the distributional impacts. I will return to the issue of compensation toward the end of the paper.

Crisis and Reform During the 1980s

The 1980s experienced two events of lasting significance. First, much of the developing world became engulfed in a protracted debt crisis. Second, many countries began to shed their import-substitution policies and endorsed market-oriented ones. The reforms did not come immediately after the crisis. In fact, the typical pattern was for governments to respond to crisis by *tightening* their restrictions. Even Chile, which had already opened up during the 1970s under General Pinochet, initially chose to increase its (uniform) import tariff when the crisis hit. But after some delay, which differed across countries, countries in Latin America, Africa, and Asia jumped on the bandwagon of reform. Governments endorsed reform with varying degrees of enthusisasm. The most enthusisastic reformers by far were in Latin America, where the Chilean example played a major role. The developing countries were followed after 1989 by the socialist countries of Eastern Europe and the former Soviet Union, which embarked on their own transition to market economies.

Does Crisis "Cause" Reform?

It is natural to suppose that crisis and reform were somehow related. Indeed, if there is one single theme that runs through the length of the political economy literature it is the idea that crisis is the instigator of reform.

The idea that governments have to be up against the wall before they act may be valid, but it is not entirely free of problems from an analytical standpoint. First, note that there is a strong element of tautology in the association of reform with crisis. Reform naturally becomes an issue only when current policies are perceived to be not working. A crisis is just an extreme instance of policy failure. That policy reform should follow crisis, then, is no more surprising than smoke following fire. Furthermore, the hypothesis is virtually nonfalsifiable: if an economy in crisis has not yet reformed, the frequently proffered explanation is that the crisis has not yet become "severe enough." What we surely need to understand is why South Korea's politicians are ready to change course at the slightest hint of a crisis, while Brazil's will bring their economy to the brink of hyperinflation several times before they tackle the problem.

Some helpful hints come from Alesina and Drazen who show in their "war of attrition" model that the lower the "degree of cohesion" in society, which they model as the expected asymmetry in the burden of stabilization, the greater the delay before a stabilization takes place. One can loosely interpret this in the following terms. In societies where resources are evenly distributed, and the government has a good distributional track record, groups are less inclined to believe that the burden of adjustment will be one-sided. This places the East Asian countries in an advantageous situation, once again, where crises are concerned.

In addition, the emphasis on crisis has in itself little predictive content as to what form the response will take. Latin American countries eventually adjusted not only by balancing their fiscal accounts, but also by overhauling their trade and industrial policies and undertaking privatization on a major scale. As I have discussed above, these trade and industrial policies had little to do with instigating the crisis, and consequently their reform was not a logical necessity once decisive action was taken. In fact, some of the reforms in the area of trade liberalization almost surely complicated the macroeconomic stabilization effort. Therefore, the comprehensiveness of the reforms that the Latin American countries undertook still requires explanation.

Part of the explanation has to do with the advice that these governments received. As mentioned previously, many professional economists themselves tended to lump together all "import substitution" policies and to hold them equally responsible for the crisis. That was certainly the approach taken by the World Bank, the most important conduit of economic ideas to developing-country policy makers.

But how could these wide ranging trade and industrial policy reforms be rendered palatable to the interest groups that had been their beneficiary for so long? How were they persuaded to go along? Here again it is plausible that the atmosphere of crisis played a role. Crisis enabled reformist governments to package fiscal reforms, which were absolutely crucial for the return of price stability, with trade and industrial policy reforms, which were viewed as desirable in the longer run but were incidental to the immediate crisis. In other words, policy makers acted as agenda setters: They presented domestic interests with a package of *both* macroeconomic and microeconomic reforms. Because high inflation and macroeconomic instability hurt pretty much everyone across the board, influential interest groups felt compelled to go along. They may have preferred to have only the macroeconomic component of the package, but that was not the choice that they confronted.

The point is that the opportunity to do something that will benefit most everyone by a large margin—an opportunity that arises only when the economy is mismanaged terribly and falls into deep crisis—allows reformist policy makers to sneak in, alongside the stabilization, microeconomic, and structural reforms which have significant distributional implications and which would be difficult to implement under normal circumstances.

Does Reform Have Short-Term Costs?

The proposition that some of the major structural reforms of the 1980s and 1990s were adopted despite interest groups, rather than because of them, naturally raises the question of the sustainability of the reforms. Here we face two other conventional wisdoms of the political-economy literature: First, reforms become sustainable when they generate "winners" with a stake in their continuation. Second, and this one is the downer, reforms tend to make things worse before they make them better.

For a proposition that is startlingly lacking in empirical support, the second piece of conventional wisdom is surprisingly strongly held. It permeates practically every discussion of the political economy of reform.

The facts do not support such pessimism about long-delayed response. Once one makes allowance for the likelihood that the counterfactual—no reform—produces even worse results in the short run, the consequences of reform actually look pretty good. This shows up in a number of different areas. With regard to disinflation, most of the recent cases of exchange-rate based stabilizations, such as those in Israel (1985), Mexico (1987), and Argentina (1991), have been accompanied by consumption booms, rather than recessions. With regard to broader structural adjustment policies, the best statistical evidence to date is that such policies tend to significantly increase, rather than decrease, growth of output within two or three years, even if not immediately. Even in Eastern Europe, where there is genuine reason to believe that the transition may have short-term costs, the evidence indicates that reform *reduces* rather then intensifies the short-term costs. Output has fallen the least in countries like Poland and the Czech Republic which have had the most extensive reforms, and the most in countries like the Ukraine which have had the least.

Of course, structural reforms (and possibly stabilization as well) may have sharp distributional consequences, as discussed previously. But this is not a matter of the short run versus the long run, as with the worries reflected in the quotes above. Saying that reform is difficult because some powerful groups will be inevitably made worse off—in the long run as well as the short run—is distinct from claiming that reform is difficult because the net benefits from the reform come too late for politicians to reap the gains. It is the latter that seems empirically problematic.

None of this is to dismiss the obvious fact that reforms do arouse opposition, and that the opposition often tends to be strongest early on. The point is that we cannot really attribute these phenomena to presumed (rather than demonstrated) short-term costs of reform. Once irrationality and myopia are dismissed, the political economy of reform turns out once again to contain more puzzles waiting to be worked out.

Does Foreign Aid Help Reform?

If reform has short-term costs, as so many believe, then foreign aid should help reforms get launched (and sustained) by alleviating these costs. This indeed is the standard justification for the World Bank's and the IMF's "structural adjustment" lending as well as for official bilateral credits. But the logic of this statement is not unassailable, even if the premise is accepted. The reason is that external resources reduce the costs both of reform and of doing nothing—that is, avoiding reform. In addition, the *prospect* of aid can actually exacerbate the delay in stabilization, by inducing groups to postpone making sacrifices until aid actually materializes. The effect on reform is consequently ambiguous.

Advocates of aid would respond that donors must ensure the recipient governments will undertake the reforms before doling out the cash. More generally, aid must come with a heavy dose of conditionality. This is well recognized, and both the IMF and the World Bank make access to their resources conditional on good behavior on the part of the borrowing governments. But conditionality is no panacea, as conditionality can last (at best) only as long as net transfers are positive. In the end, sovereign governments are just that: sovereign.

In Search of a Manual for
Reformist Politicians

All of which raise the question, "what's a poor reformist politician to do?"

A fundamental fault line that divides the contributors to this literature is the issue of how participatory reform politics ought to be. Most economists are on the side of speed, stealth, and consequently of reform from above. In Sachs' view, it is at best a waste of time to seek a broad coalition for reform because most people have no understanding of what is required: "While the history of market-based reforms has repeatedly shown that free markets, open trade, and an economy fueled by private ownership are enormously powerful in stimulating rapid economic growth, the general public rarely knows it or believes it at the start."

What some may find striking in these statements is the lack of faith in the common sense of ordinary people and in the efficacy of political institutions, especially in new democracies. That economists should hold to these views is not without irony. After all, homo economicus is supposed to be rational and forward-looking, and to process all the information that comes his way in the most efficient way. Sachs' homo politicus is none of these things, or else is being held hostage to some grand coordination failure whose nature is unclear.

This irony is seized upon by Przeworski, who provides a serious challenge to the economists' preference for reform from above. Focusing on the Polish case, he faults the storm tactics favored by Sachs and others for both weakening democratic political institutions *and* making errors in economic policy more likely. He and his two co-authors (Bresser Pereira and Maravall) summarize their argument in their concluding chapter thus:

> we find that subjecting the reform strategy to the competitive interplay of political forces is superior on three essential grounds: It improves policy, it builds support for the continuation of reforms, and it helps consolidate democratic institutions. We do not see a trade-off between public discussion and the soundness of economic plans.

It is difficult not to feel sympathy for Przeworski's yearning for a more democratic style of reform. Yet my suspicion is that most observers of the Polish reforms would agree with Balcerowicz and Sachs that speed (and stealth) was of the essence. While there have been some reversals in the reforms, even with these reversals the Polish economy is in far better shape today than it would have been under a more gradual path.

This fascinating debate takes us back to the most fundamental issue in the political economy of policy reform, the one with which this essay opened: If the objective of reform is to make people better off, why does reform have to be shielded from the people? Furthermore, if the problem with reform is that powerful groups are hurt by it, why can't policy makers come up with compensation schemes that remove the hurdle? Myopia, to which many observers ultimately resort, appears to me to be as unsatisfactory an explanation here as in any area of conventional economics.

As I pointed out above, the analytical literature has begun to address these puzzles. For example Fernandez and Rodrik ask whether a rational electorate would ever reject a reform which is known to benefit a majority of the voters. We show that the answer is "yes." We also show that political systems in general have a bias toward the status quo even when the status quo is inefficient and individuals are risk neutral. The key to the argument is uncertainty of a particular kind: the identity of many of the gainers (as well as losers) from reform cannot be determined ex ante.

To see how the argument works, consider a democracy where a majority vote is needed before reform can be adopted. Let the economy have 100 voters and suppose that the reform in question will increase the incomes of 51 individuals by five zlotys each and decrease the incomes of the rest by one zloty each, leaving a net gain of $(5 \times 51) - (1 \times 49) = 206$ zlotys. In the absence of uncertainty, the majority of the population would vote in favor and the reform would be adopted. Assume that all these consequences of reform are common knowledge. Now suppose that while 49 individuals know for sure that they will gain, the remaining 51 are in the dark as to which among them will gain and which will lose. However, because aggregate consequences are common knowledge, individuals in the latter group know that two of them will eventually benefit while 49 will lose out. (Such uncertainty may arise, say, from incomplete information at the individual level about the skills needed to succeed in the post-reform environment.) This renders individuals in the second group identical ex ante, with an expected benefit from reform of $[(5 \times 2) - (1 \times 49)]/51 = -0.76$ zloty each. Hence the individuals in the uncertain group will reject reform, blocking its adoption.

The bottom line is that uncertainty about the consequences of reform at the level of the individual can prevent reform, even when it is recognized that reform will make a politically effective majority better off. Moreover, the same kind of argument explains why compensation, or the promise thereof, is not always an effective device to remove the distributional obstacle to reform. In the above example, ex ante losers know that if reform is passed, there will be an ex post majority in support of its continuation—even in the absence of compensation. Therefore, a promise to compensate losers ex post is not going to be credible. This kind of reasoning may explain why many reforms that would have been popular ex post are passed up ex ante. It may also explain why reforms that are instituted by an authoritarian regime against prevailing political sentiment survive the return of democracy (e.g., Pinochet's reforms in Chile).

Concluding Comments

Most economists have now come to the realization that good economic advice requires an understanding of the political economy of the situation. The result has been a remarkable degree of collaboration between economists and political scientists, as well as more work on political economy by younger economists. Both of these are good news. The bad news is that the habit of attributing myopia or irrationality to political actors—whether explicitly or, more often, implicitly—persists.

———————
Dani Rodrik, "Understanding Economic Policy Reform," *Journal of Economic Literature* 34, no. 1 (March 1996): 9–41.

9

What Do We Know About the Political Economy of Economic Policy Reform?

STEPHAN HAGGARD

STEVEN B. WEBB

This survey explores the politics of economic reform. We examine the influence of political institutions on the adjustment process, the links between economic conditions and the politics of reform, and the way in which the design of the program influences the pattern of political support or opposition.

Political Interests and Institutions

Authoritarian and Democratic Regimes

Any political analysis of reform demands attention to the interests at stake, but institutional factors also influence the policy process. One of the most contentious debates in comparative political economy concerns the implications of the type of political regime for reform and, more generally, for economic performance. In the 1980s numerous studies probed the relative capacity of authoritarian and democratic governments to maintain stable macroeconomic policies or to initiate broader market-oriented reforms. Several lines of argument suggested that authoritarian regimes might be more successful in initiating reform than democratic ones.

First, rent-seeking groups may have greater influence in democracies. Authoritarian leaders, by contrast, can override interest-group demands by fiat. Partly because of their ability to dominate interest groups, authoritarian governments also have longer time horizons. Many economic reforms, such as fiscal adjustment or trade liberalization, entail short-term costs while the benefits take longer to unfold. If the democratic politician cannot count on being in power long enough to reap the political gains from reform, optimal policies will be abandoned as interest-group lobbying or electoral pressures intensify. Authoritarian leaders might find it easier to take a longer-term perspective because they encounter weaker interest-group and electoral constraints.

The hypothesis that authoritarian regimes do better is not without empirical support—countries in Latin America and East Asia are often cited as examples. In a stylized sequence: weak democratic governments are unable to resist pressures to boost wages and pursue other populist but unsustainable fiscal and monetary policies. Inflation mounts and stabilization efforts founder. As the crisis deepens, the military seizes power and imposes the costs of adjustment on labor and other groups. This pattern is visible in the so-called bureaucratic-authoritarian regimes in Latin America (Argentina in 1966 and 1976, Brazil in 1964, Chile in 1973, and Uruguay in 1973) and elsewhere (Indonesia in 1966 and Turkey in 1971). The developing economies of East Asia—the Republic of Korea, Taiwan, Singapore, and Hong Kong—also undertook crucial policy reforms under authoritarian or administrative auspices, and China's recent reforms were undertaken on the explicit premise that economic and political liberalization need not go hand in hand.

The model of the authoritarian regime as a boon to developmental reform has two theoretical shortcomings. First, it assumes an enlightened leadership. A rational dictator might seek to maximize the present value of consumption through policies to enhance growth or through tax increases that are inimical to growth. The possibility of these diametrically opposed strategies of enlightened despotism and predatory behavior helps explain why economic performance seems to vary more among authoritarian governments than among democratic ones. Military governments in Latin America made policy mistakes as egregious as their democratic predecessors, and in some authoritarian countries, including Albania, Iran, Myanmar, and Romania, policies contributed to economic blight so severe that only a dictator could have sustained them.

The second difficulty concerns the assumption that authoritarian governments are immune to interest-group pressures and therefore have longer time horizons. Authoritarian governments may not be accountable to electorates, but they may nonetheless remain vulnerable to interest-group pressures. The absence of regularized turnover and political competition can give rise to corruption more pervasive and intractable than would be possible under accountable forms of rule. The Philippines under Marcos, Haiti under the Duvaliers, and Zaire under Mobutu are cases in point.

The few systematic comparisons of performance and policymaking in authoritarian and democratic regimes have yielded ambiguous results. The ambiguity of these findings suggests that the debate should move beyond simple distinctions between authoritarian and democratic regimes to greater differentiation within each category. For example, stable two-party democracies have a better record on macroeconomic policy than do authoritarian governments but authoritarian regimes are more likely to stabilize when inflation and social conflict are high. These findings suggest, however, that optimism about the effect of democratization on economic performance may not be warranted either. Whether economic performance improves depends very much on the nature of democratic institutions.

Transitions to and from Democratic Rule

The global wave of political liberalization and democratization since the mid-1970s has increased interest in the economic consequences of changes in regime. An incumbent regime that believes its days are numbered will be strongly tempted to drum up support through expansionist policies and delays of reform, even if this policy is self-defeating over the longer run. There is some empirical evidence that the political crises and stalemates that attend transitions from authoritarian to democratic regimes, and vice versa, are associated with macroeconomic instability. Here we focus on the problems of transitions to democracy.

Political and economic conditions at the time of the transition have an important bearing on the ability of the new government to manage the economy. Authoritarian governments that improved economic performance through extensive and difficult reforms are better positioned to control the pace and substance of the political transition when they relinquish power; Chile in 1989 and Turkey in 1983 are examples. The outgoing authoritarian leadership is also more likely to have built tacit or explicit bases of support for the new policy regime and to maintain control of the macroeconomic situation.

Many authoritarian regimes do not exit by choice, however, but rather come under pressure from popular protest, the defection of key economic elites, and internal divisions. A faltering economy seems to precipitate this type of transition. In many of the democratization experiences in Latin America, including Brazil in 1985 and Argentina in 1983, and in Poland more recently, the outgoing authoritarian leaders engaged in a last, desperate round of expansionist economic policies to shore up short-term support. Many of the economic imbalances that greeted the new democratic governments can be traced to the politically motivated actions of their predecessors.

Expectations about the policy behavior of new democratic governments may thus be somewhat contradictory. New democracies may have trouble maintaining stable macroeconomic policies and undertaking structural reforms. Democratization is accompanied by an increased level of political activity, which provides the opportunity for previously repressed groups, such as labor, to press their demands. Frequently, governments respond with expansionary fiscal policies and higher wage settlements, and changed expectations then lead to higher inflation.

Transitions to democracy increase budget deficits and inflation, according to cross-section statistical evidence. The evidence does not show, however, that new autocratic regimes systematically reduce public sector deficits on coming to office, as posited by the authoritarian hypothesis outlined earlier, although inflation does typically decline. And new democracies experience more inflation for a given budget deficit than their authoritarian counterparts.

Incoming democratic governments typically enjoy a honeymoon period, when they can trade short-term economic losses against various political gains. The new government can more easily gain support for broad initiatives if the regime change occurred because of failures in economic policy. One study on the politics of adjustment in new democracies finds several examples. The most striking is the comprehensive Polish program, initiated by a government with strong ties to the union movement. The social pact forged during the transition to democracy in Spain after 1977 also provides strong evidence that new democratic governments are more likely to succeed in initiating wide-ranging programs if they move quickly. By contrast, new democratic leaders in Argentina, Bolivia, and Brazil pursued more expansionist policies in their early days and delayed needed reform. When events finally forced them to adjust, the economic situation had deteriorated further, support for the government had dwindled, and its programs lacked credibility. Presidents Alfonsin of Argentina, Siles Zuazo of Bolivia, and Sarney of Brazil all left office with their economies in hyperinflation.

The Party System

A finding that emerges strongly from the comparative study of new democracies is the importance of the party system in organizing support for or opposition to reform. Dominant parties capable of ruling by themselves (and in presidential systems, presidents and legislatures of the same party) have the easiest time securing legislative support for their programs. Coalition governments fare less well, and minority governments and presidential systems in which the president and legislature are of different parties have the greatest difficulty. In general, fragmented party systems encourage bidding wars among contending political forces, make legislative support difficult to mobilize and ruling coalitions hard to sustain, and contribute to political instability.

Mexico provides an interesting example of the strong party case. Despite some political liberalization since the mid-1970s, Mexico's political system remains dominated by a powerful single party, the Partido Revolucionario Institucional (PRI), which has long controlled, co-opted, and reconciled contending social interests. The PRI's long-standing corporatist links with labor and the private sector were crucial elements in the president's ability to secure agreement and compliance with the heterodox stabilization program contained in the Solidarity Pact of 1989.

That the party system is important to cohesive economic policy is not simply an academic observation. Outgoing authoritarian leaders have openly altered electoral rules and party registration laws to extend their control into the next administration. Experiences in Turkey and Chile show how this can happen. In Turkey the political and economic difficulties of the late 1970s were attributed to an increasingly polarized and fragmented political system. The military-controlled election of 1983 was limited to three parties approved by the military. As the party system subsequently opened up, the constitution was amended, with electoral rules and thresholds designed to eliminate smaller parties from participating. The rules served as intended, providing a center-right, pro-reform party with a legislative majority in 1987, although it had received far less than a majority of the popular vote. The election of 1991 once again brought a coalition government to power, however, which would suggest greater difficulty in economic management than had been the case in the early post-transition period. Democratization in Chile took a different route, but Chile's experience shows how outgoing military regimes can control the transition. Pinochet was defeated in the presidential election of 1989 by a coalition of opposition parties, the Concertación. Before the transition, however, Pinochet had already established what

Arriagada and Graham call "authoritarian enclaves" in the new democratic order. Pinochet directly appointed a number of senators and oversaw changes in the electoral rules designed to guarantee "adequate" legislative representation for the right.

Governance and the Bureaucracy

The wide variation in the quality of economic policy within both democratic and authoritarian governments suggests that the prospects for policy reform also depend on characteristics of the state itself, particularly the discipline and competence of the bureaucracy. Consequently, many structural adjustment programs require a selective strengthening of the government's role in the economy rather than a simple reduction in government intervention.

An array of administrative and organizational factors contribute to the capacity of a government to function well. Among them are the efficiency with which information is collected, decisionmaking is organized, and tasks are allocated among implementing agencies; the quality of personnel; and the integrity and transparency of the financial workings of government, including audit and review functions. Administrative reforms in these areas are clearly important for strengthening the capacity of the state over the long run.

Being able to function efficiently is not simply a matter of administrative competence, however; reform programs must also consider the milieu in which the bureaucracy operates. Pervasive corruption can make the bureaucracy itself a powerful and well-positioned interest group, aligned against reform and capable of obstructing the implementation of adjustment programs. Even in the absence of corruption, bureaucracies are subject to interference from politicians as well. A proper system of delegation is often the solution. Because the effectiveness of policies depends on the widespread belief that they will be sustained, politicians can fortify their commitment by delegating decisionmaking authority to autonomous institutions. This reduces the capacity to reverse their decisions in response to short-term considerations.

Developing a bureaucratic apparatus that is reasonably well insulated from corruption and political power typically requires more than short-term reform efforts. Socialization to professional norms and institutional reform are usually long-term processes. But the incentives for corruption can be reduced through attention to institutional design. For example, one justification for a policy based on rules rather than discretion is to eliminate altogether agencies with discretionary powers that can serve as the locus for rent-seeking relations between the private sector and the government.

Economic Conditions

Economic conditions influence not only the policy agenda, but also the political actions of organized social groups and thus politicians' calculations about what can and what cannot be done. Three factors are especially relevant: the intensity and length of the economic crisis, the outcomes of previous reforms (or perceptions about those outcomes), and the distribution of income. External economic and political constraints also affect the adoption and implementation of programs.

Intensity of the Crisis

It seems intuitively obvious that crises trigger reform efforts. Crises increase a government's willingness to attempt remedial measures and the public's tolerance for them. Under democratic regimes, crises are likely to bring to office new governments with new programs. Economic crises also influence the balance of power among groups and the configuration of political interests by weakening some groups and strengthening others.

But the concept of crisis is much more elusive than first appears. Governments respond differently even to balance of payments difficulties, the most strictly binding of constraints. Countries may ultimately adjust their current account by cutting back on imports, but they do not necessarily follow up with an appropriate policy response. Not all countries recognize the same crises, and no theory has yet identified a crisis threshold that all nations would recognize. At various points in the 1980s, the Thai, Colombian, and Indonesian governments responded preemptively to warning signals and undertook important economic adjustments before economic difficulties slipped into crisis. At the other end of the response continuum are several African countries—Ghana is perhaps the worst example—that experienced full-blown economic disasters year after year but failed to deal with them effectively. When the Rawlings administration finally seized power, it was certainly responding to a crisis; but this begs the question of why no action had been taken two or five or ten years earlier.

A crisis in no way guarantees that any remedial actions taken will be sustained or institutionalized. As the crisis winds down, the urgency of reform lessens and the political forces resistant to reform typically revive. The outcome can be a cycle of policy deterioration, economic crisis, temporary or partial policy reform, recovery, and relapse.

Collective Memory—Instructive and Selective

Years after any traces of a direct effect on the economy have faded, economic successes or failures of the past continue to mold politicians' views on policy reform. Economic experiences—whether "golden ages" or "nightmares"—provide elites with lessons and analogies that shape their current decisionmaking, however different the conditions.

An example concerns countries that have experienced episodes of hyperinflation. West German interpretations of interwar history typically attach great importance to fiscal deficits and hyperinflation as causes not only of severe economic distress but also of the rise of fascism. Thus, West Germans tend to view price stability as a more important policy objective than full employment, even though Germany also suffered from extraordinarily high unemployment rates between the two world wars. These perceptions of cause and effect had a profound influence on postwar economic policy and institutions, such as the independence of the Bundesbank.

The institutionalization of import-substituting policies in Latin American countries following World War II similarly owed much to interpretations of past events. The policies grew out of the memory of the international environment between the wars and the mistaken belief that short-term declines in commodity prices in the 1950s represented a secular trend. The policies had an enduring influence, in part because policymaking institutions, such as those concerned with trade and industrial policy, grew up around them and provided political access for groups that stood to gain from import-substituting activities. Reducing the influence of such muddled legacies often requires not only changes in polices, but also institutional changes that reduce the incentives and possibilities for the undesirable policy to reemerge.

Income Distribution

A third economic factor that affects the success of policy reforms is the distribution of income. Sharply unequal income distribution creates social and political divisions that undermine consensus for economic reform, increases uncertainty about the actions of future governments, and shortens time horizons, producing such undesirable economic outcomes as tax evasion, capital flight, investment strikes, and unreasonable wage demands. When income distribution is seriously imbalanced, agreement on any package of major reforms will be complicated by considerations of whether to broaden the reforms to include a redistribution of income or even of assets.

External Influences

The influence of external economic and political factors on domestic policymaking in developing countries has been a subject of contentious debate for decades. Building on the structuralist economic arguments of Prebisch and Singer and a Marxist sociology, a wide-ranging literature has emerged on the (generally pernicious) role of external influences on economic development.

There are at least three channels through which the external milieu might influence policy choice. First, cycles of prices and demand can influence the propensity for reform. Some argue that policy changes in developing countries can be traced to fluctuations in world prices of primary products and to business cycles in industrial countries. Shifts to more outward-oriented development strategies are more likely during the boom phase of the cycle, when external conditions favor export diversification. Returns to more inward-looking strategies recur during the down phase. Although there appears to be some evidence of this kind of cycle in the past in Latin America, the current wave of reform contradicts the argument: external shocks have pushed several countries toward liberalizing reform.

Second, policy choices are influenced by international networks and socialization that result in the transmission of policy-relevant knowledge. These networks include foreign advisers, training programs for technocrats at foreign universities, government-sponsored exchange programs, and work experience in multinational corporations.

Finally, external actors seek to influence policy more directly through loan conditionality. At the center of the debate about the politics of conditionality—to be distinguished from the economic issue of whether programs will have the desired effects—is the extent to which outside agencies actually influence the policy process. On the one hand, unity among creditors and their power over the flow of financial resources provide them with substantial influence. Extra external resources can increase the political sustainability of reforms by allowing the country more consumption while sustaining higher levels of investment. In that way, external support can lengthen the time horizons of politicians.

On the other hand, creditor governments, the potential enforcers of these agreements, have multiple and conflicting goals with respect to debtors. The concern to support a strategically important client can easily override the interest in enforcing conditionality. Where leaders are already committed to a reform program, as in Turkey in the mid and early 1980s, additional finance may help it succeed, although usually by supporting efforts that would have been undertaken anyway. But when nonconditional resources are made available to countries disposed against reform, such as the Philippines under Marcos or Zaire under Mobutu, the additional finance creates perverse incentives, allowing governments to postpone adjustment.

The empirical evidence appears to support these expectations, although all studies in this vein note methodological problems of determining compliance. A survey of IMF Extended Fund Facility programs finds a high level of noncompliance and program cancellation due to domestic political factors.

Design of the Program

Initiatives are more likely to succeed if governments, particularly the implementing agencies, are somewhat insulated from interest-group pressures. We have already explored some of the conditions conducive to such autonomy, including the type of regime, timing relative to the electoral cycle, and the nature of the bureaucracy. Over the longer run, however, consolidating reform requires building and institutionalizing a new base of political support among emerging winners. So the crucial transition is from an initial position of autonomy (usually temporary), when supporters of the status quo are politically weakened, to a new equilibrium that consolidates the new bases of support that have emerged. We consider here two elements of program design that might affect this transition path: how quickly the program is initiated, and whether and how losers are compensated.

Tortoise or Hare

Most, but not all, political considerations support the argument for moving quickly. The way speed affects the political balance between winners and losers argues for rapid reform. Often, the fate of a reform program depends on the emergence of new beneficiaries to support it. A necessary, although not sufficient, condition for that to happen is rapid implementation, a condition that holds even in democracies. Pushing reforms rapidly through the system can also weaken interest groups that are tied to the status quo and give antireform forces little time to mobilize.

Putting reforms in place quickly at the beginning of a new administration also means that the reforms have time to put down strong roots during the honeymoon period, when support is high and opposition muted. A new government that takes office in the middle of a severe crisis and acts immediately can blame the decline in living standards on actions of the previous government. The longer the government delays, the more likely that the costs of adjustment will be attributed to the current government, increasing the level of opposition. New democratic governments taking over from authoritarian regimes are in especially good position to trade political gains against short-term economic losses. Spain in the late 1970s and Eastern Europe in recent years demonstrate this pattern.

Yet another argument for speedy reform rests on credibility. A government that acts without delay strengthens the public's belief that the reform will be maintained steadfastly over time. A reform-minded government could signal the seriousness of its commitment by overshooting—by initiating reforms of a magnitude or at a pace that an uncommitted government would never attempt.

Concerns about credibility can also support a more gradual approach. Rapid adjustments tend to provoke resistance because they are more unsettling and have higher short-run costs. Riots in response to rapid price reforms are typically cited as a cost of moving too quickly. Because firms and households can shift into new activities only with a lag after a program is put in place, shock programs face the hurdle of getting through an extended period of extremely limited support, because the economy has not yet responded. Going slow limits the initial costs and allows some of the front-end benefits to unfold and attract supporters before the next round of reform measures hits. This go-easy strategy seems more applicable to certain types of structural realignments than it does to macroeconomic policy, though, and has worked best in countries where macroeconomic imbalances are not severe.

Compensation

The political argument for compensation has been cast in normative as well as positive terms. Governments may have clear moral reasons for assisting the poor. It has also been argued that compensation may be necessary to secure political support for reform—or at least acquiescence.

There are three possible counterarguments to compensation. First, a country simply may not have the funds to compensate losers; this has been a recurrent theme in the literature on poverty alleviation during adjustment and an important argument for adequate external assistance. Second, some types of compensatory measures may undermine the reform. Compensating workers for a nominal devaluation by increasing wages directly undermines the objective of increasing competitiveness. And third, the likely recipients of politically motivated compensation may not be the poor.

Studies generally found, however, that some sort of compensation was crucial for securing support for programs. In the more successful cases—Chile, Mexico,

Spain, and Thailand—compensation came in the form of complementary reforms. The Concertación in Chile and the socialists in Spain (1982) came to power expecting to protect the interests of labor and the poor. Realizing that wage increases and direct subsidies would derail needed fiscal adjustments, they instead took measures to improve the distribution of health and education services and to widen the social safety net for the poor. International agreements with the United States and Europe to increase export opportunities helped compensate firms in Chile, Mexico, Poland, Spain, and Turkey that were accustomed to selling in protected domestic markets. So did export incentives in Thailand and Turkey, which accelerated the growth of exports and the expansion of pro-adjustment export interests.

Is Political Economy Analysis
Relevant for Policymaking?

Prescriptive ʃ   ʌy analysis by economists aims to identify measures that are optimal according ʟo such criteria as efficiency, stability, or growth. Positive political analysis, however, is often concerned with why optimal policies are not adopted. The findings of political analysis involve parameters that cannot be manipulated in either the short or the long run. What practical use is it, for example, to point out that inflation or trade policy are the result of the underlying social structure or the fragmentation of the political system?

Political analysis of economic policy can be of practical use in at least three ways. One is by taking into account the likely political fallout of a program when the program is being designed. An example is the need to complement the speedy initiation of a program with the right compensatory mechanisms to build support and blunt opposition. A second area is the design of institutions and decisionmaking processes within government. Some of the difficult problems of collective action, such as reconciling spending and revenue decisions, have to do with organizational features of the government that are amenable to change. Surprisingly little systematic work has been undertaken on how the organization of decisionmaking is likely to affect the success of adjustment efforts.

The final insight of the new political economy concerns the timing and content of conditionality. A program that raises expectations, engenders domestic hostility to external agencies, but is doomed to failure for political reasons can be worse than no program at all. Ill-timed external assistance can allow governments to continue misguided policies. Political economy has not yet devised a clear set of guidelines for making judgments about the wisdom of lending by the international financial institutions, but it can help sensitize these agencies to the likely outcomes of their efforts.

Stephan Haggard and Steven B. Webb, "What Do We Know about the Political Economy of Economic Policy Reform? *World Bank Research Observer* 8, no. 2 (July 1993): 143–68.

10

Uses and Limitations of Rational Choice

BARBARA GEDDES

In contrast to most arguments in the dependency, new institutionalist, and comparative historical sociology traditions, rational choice arguments use the individual, or some analogue of the individual, as the unit of analysis. They assume that individuals, including politicians, are rational in the sense that, given goals and alternative strategies from which to choose, they will select the alternatives that maximize their chances of achieving their goals. Factors that shape first-order preferences, goals, are outside the deductive structure of rational choice models (in the sense that models do not attempt to explain their origins), but goals, nevertheless, play a crucial role in rational choice arguments. The most compelling use of this approach results from the creative synthesis of the rational actor assumptions with, one, a plausible attribution of goals and, two, a careful interpretation of the effects of institutions and other factors on the feasible strategies available to actors for achieving these goals.

In this chapter, I show first, why those using the rational choice approach have had so much success constructing theories of democratic politics; and second, which parts of this theoretical literature can be most easily and fruitfully adapted to the context of politics in developing and newly democratic countries.

Misperceptions About Rational Choice

Many who have worked outside the rational choice tradition hold misperceptions that interfere with using the insights and methods associated with it. So, before considering the applicability of some of these ideas outside the context in which they emerged, the most common misperceptions need to be examined. They include contentions that rational choice arguments:

- assume that all people are motivated by material interests (the economists' famous *homo economicus*);

- are based on unrealistic assumptions—since people are not really rational, and they lack the information and calculating ability assumed by rational choice theory;
- are deterministic.

In the following paragraphs, I discuss each of these misperceptions in turn, including the grain of truth upon which each pearl of misperception has been accreted. This section aims to clear away some misunderstandings and to delimit the domain in which rational choice arguments are likely to be useful. Although none of the statements listed above is generally true, some are true in some instances; and, when they are true, rational choice arguments are not likely to provide much leverage for understanding events.

Goals

One misperception is that rational choice arguments assume that human beings are motivated by material interests. This is simply false. The "rationality" assumed by rational choice arguments is of the narrowest means-ends kind. No assumptions are made about the goals held by individuals. The approach only assumes that people (1) choose the means they consider most likely to result in desired ends; (2) can weakly order their goals (that is, given any set of alternatives, they will prefer one or the other or be indifferent); and (3) hold consistent preferences (that is, if they prefer Bill Clinton to George Bush and Bush to Ross Perot, then they prefer Clinton to Perot). Although one can think of situations in which the second or third condition might not hold, they are not common. If one limits the domain of rational choice arguments to areas in which these conditions seem plausible, the domain remains extremely broad.

Because the rational choice approach makes no assumptions about goals, the analyst who seeks to apply it to a particular problem must identify the goals of the actors involved. This is an empirical question. The analyst cannot usually offer direct proof, such as survey data, to show that actors really do have the goals imputed to them, since actors may have good reasons to lie about their goals. Nevertheless, checks on the analytic imagination are built into the rational choice approach: If the analyst misperceives actors' goals, then their behavior will differ from that predicted.

For most arguments in economics, and for some in political science, it is entirely plausible to attribute goals of material self-interest to actors. If one wants to explain how firms set their prices or which industries lobby for tariffs, it is reasonable to assume that material interests shape these decisions. There is, of course, nothing unique to rational choice in the idea that much of human behavior is motivated by material interests. It is an idea shared by most Marxist, neo-Marxist, pluralist, corporatist, ad hoc, and journalistic accounts of political behavior.

Many of the most interesting rational choice arguments about democratic politics, however, do not conceptualize the salient actor as *homo economicus*. Instead, they attribute to democratic politicians the goals of reelection, political survival, and career advancement. In some countries, the advancement of a political career may be the surest road to amassing a fortune, but, more commonly, officeholders could make more money doing something else. A rational choice argument might not offer a satisfactory account of why certain individuals choose politics though others choose business or professional careers. Once the choice has been made, however, it seems reasonable to attribute the goal of survival in office to those who have previously demonstrated a preference for office-holding, and rational choice arguments have had substantial success using this assumption to explain the behavior of politicians.

The theoretical bite of rational choice arguments depends both on the plausibility of the goals attributed to actors and on the ability of analysts to identify the goals a priori, that is, without reference to the specific behavior to be explained. Most of the time, analysts are on firm ground when they assume that actors prefer more material goods to less or that politicians prefer continuing their careers to ending them. It is obviously not true that all politicians prefer continuing their careers since some retire before every election, but if the average politician has this goal, then the argument that assumes the goal will explain average behavior. Rational choice arguments tend to become less persuasive and less useful as goals become more idiosyncratic. Thus rational choice arguments do a good job of explaining why most members of the U.S. Congress cater to the interests of their constituents, but they would not, in my view, do a good job of explaining why a few Russian intellectuals joined Lenin in his apparently hopeless struggle to overthrow the czar. It is possible to construct a rational choice explanation for this behavior, but it would leave unexplored one of the most puzzling factors needed to explain Lenin's followers: the origin of their unusual goals.

Plausibility of the a priori attribution of goals to actors thus limits the domain within which rational choice arguments are useful. Because the approach sets no limits on what the goals may be, it is possible to construct rational choice explanations for apparently irrational (in the every-day sense of the word) behavior by claiming that actors were rationally pursuing their own (idiosyncratic) goals. The person who, for instance, gives all his or her possessions to a religious cult can be said to be rationally pursuing the goal of self-abnegation. But when goals are directly inferred from observed behavior, rational choice arguments slide into mere tautology. Consequently, the appropriate domain for rational choice arguments, in my judgment, includes only situations in which plausible goals can be attributed to actors a priori.

Information and Calculating Requirements

Another objection to the use of rational choice arguments is that they make unrealistic assumptions about human calculating ability and information acquisition; it is argued that although people may try to pursue their goals efficiently, they lack sufficient information and calculating ability to do it. There is a sizable grain of truth in these claims, but the information requirements are more implausible in some situations than in others.

Rational choice arguments work best in situations in which actors can identify other actors and know their goals, and in which the rules that govern interactions among actors are precise and known to all. Many situations in democratic politics exhibit these characteristics, and, consequently, rational choice arguments have successfully explained a number of democratic processes. Interactions in legislatures, between legislatures and the bureaucracy, within party leaderships, within ruling coalitions, and in other political bodies established in democratic settings tend to involve easily identifiable actors whose goals are easy to establish and whose interactions are governed by precise, well-known procedural rules.

Rational choice arguments can even be used successfully in democracies that differ substantially from the ideal, as do many of the democracies in Latin America. Limitations on effective participation, representation, or party competition do not reduce the usefulness of rational choice arguments, as long as there is some competition in the system and interactions among political actors remain reasonably predictable and transparent to all involved.

Rational choice arguments are also more likely to be useful when explaining outcomes of high salience to the individuals involved. Actors spend more time and effort acquiring information when the results of their decisions have important consequences. The average citizen is often "rationally ignorant" about politics; his or her vote will have almost no effect on political outcomes, and therefore it would not be rational to spend time learning all about the issues and candidates. In contrast, the average legislator, whose career depends on making electorally correct choices, has good reason to use time and energy to stay well informed. Because of the visible and well-structured nature of governing institutions in established democracies and the importance to the careers of elected officials of making the right decisions, rational choice arguments have proved especially useful in explaining behaviors in these institutions.

Whether rational choice arguments can be used successfully to explain decisionmaking within authoritarian regimes depends on their level of transparency, stability, and predictability. Rational actor assumptions are likely to be plausible in regimes in which the rules governing survival and advancement are clear to both participants and observers and relatively unchanging, but not in regimes in which many decisions are made in secret by a small group of individuals and in which rules and rulers change frequently, radically, and unpredictably.

Rational choice arguments can be useful in some circumstances even when actors lack crucial information. Actors can sometimes learn through trial and error to choose the same strategies that they would have chosen if they had had full information and the unrestricted ability to calculate. Thus, if situations are repeated over and over again, people can be expected to learn over time to understand the situation and to make more effective decisions. The more important the outcome to the person, the more effort will be expended on learning.

Actors may also behave as if they were rational without conscious learning if some selection mechanism exists to weed out behaviors that lead to outcomes different from those a rational actor would have chosen. Just as differential survival rates eliminate less-efficient mutations in evolutionary theories, they can eliminate actors in other arenas who follow strategies that fail to converge with the outcomes that would have been produced by rational (that is, efficient) choices. It has been argued, for example, that firm managers do not actually think about profits when they make most decisions. Nevertheless, existing firms behave as though they were profit-maximizers because competition drives out of business those that deviate too far from profit-maximizing behavior. The same kind of argument can be made for politicians. Politicians may sincerely believe that they are ignoring constituency and interest-group pressures and are voting according to conscience, but if they deviate too far from behavior that maximizes their chances for reelection, they are likely to be defeated in the next election. As with learning, natural selection requires repetitions. Neither learning nor evolution can be used to support a claim that actors behave as if they were rational in unrepeated situations.

To summarize, the information and calculation requirements of the rational choice model are stiff. Rational choice arguments are more likely to succeed in explaining behavior when actors closely approximate these requirements. The appropriate domain of rational choice arguments thus includes situations in which outcomes are very important to actors, since that impels gathering knowledge; situations in which the rules governing interactions are clear and precise; and situations that occur repeatedly so that actors can learn, or efficient strategies can evolve even in the absence of conscious learning.

Determinism

The rational choice model, that is, the deductive logic that connects the choice of means to preexisting goals, is deterministic. This does not, however, imply that rational choice arguments make deterministic predictions of behavior. The most useful way to think of rational choice arguments is as if-then statements of the form: *if* actors have the goals the observer claims, *if* the information and calculation requirements are plausible (for any of the reasons noted above), and *if* the actors actually face the rules and payoffs the observer claims they do, *then* certain behavior will occur. Some slippage can occur at each *if* without necessarily eviscerating the whole argument. A few actors may have goals that differ from the majority's. For example, a few members of Congress may not care about reelection. If most do, however, the argument will still explain the behavior of most of them and therefore the outputs of the legislature. Some actors may lack information or the ability to calculate. For example, freshman legislators may not yet have "learned the ropes," but if most legislators are not freshmen, the argument will still hold. Or the observer may misunderstand the situation that faces some actors even though the situation facing most of them has been correctly interpreted. For example, the observer may incorrectly assume that payoffs to members of small parties are the same as payoffs to members of large parties. If so, the argument will still explain the behavior of members of large parties. In all of these examples, an empirical test of the argument (if one is possible) should show that the argument explains a substantial part of the outcome, though not every individual case. In other words, the argument results in probabilistic predictions and explanations, just as other social science arguments do.

This section has dealt with a series of misconceptions about rational choice arguments. It has shown that several of them are simply that: misunderstandings that should not be permitted to muddy the waters any longer. Other misperceptions bring to light serious impediments to using rational choice arguments to explain all conceivable human behaviors. I have argued that these objections should be taken seriously and used to delimit the domain within which rational choice arguments can be expected to be useful. I now turn to a different question: What really distinguishes the rational choice approach from others?

The Rational Choice
Approach

The defining features of the rational choice approach are (1) methodological individualism, usually applied to individual people but sometimes also to organizations that can plausibly be expected to behave as unitary rational actors; (2) explicit identification of actors and their goals or preferences; (3) explicit identification of the institutions and other contextual features that determine the options available to actors and the costs and benefits associated with different options; and (4) deductive logic. The rational choice approach has no monopoly on any of these features. Furthermore, most arguments originally posed within other frameworks can be translated into rational choice idiom. Advocates of structuralist arguments, for example, believe that structural conditions cause outcomes. They consider it unnecessary to spell out explicitly how structures determine the incentives facing particular individuals and thus determine their choices and, through their choices, social outcomes. Nevertheless, the analyst who wants to incorporate these intervening steps into a structuralist argument usually has no trouble doing so.

In short, there is nothing very unusual about the assumptions or structure of rational choice arguments. Nevertheless, the focus on the incentives facing individuals, the ruthless pruning of extraneous complexity, and the use of deductive logic have together resulted in a cluster of theoretical results both novel and fruitful.

I focus on the developments within rational choice theory that seem most potentially fruitful for the study of democratic (and quasi-democratic) politics in developing countries. I deal with three categories of arguments: those that depend on the unintended and nonobvious results of aggregating individually rational choices; those that unpack the black box of the state by looking explicitly at the individuals who actually make state decisions, the goals that shape their behavior, and the incentives they face; and those that treat political decisions as strategic interactions among actors rather than as decisions under external constraint.

The Consequences
of Aggregation

The theoretical development within the rational choice framework that has had the most radical and far-reaching effect on our understanding of the political world is the series of proofs that group decisions will not necessarily, or even usually, reflect the interests of the majority in the group, even if members of the group are entirely equal and decisions are arrived at democratically. Among a number of nonobvious and sometimes perverse aggregation effects, two stand out in terms of their political and theoretical consequences: the proof that majority rule does not necessarily result in policies that reflect majority preferences; and the demonstration that individuals who would benefit from public goods will not, if they are rational, usually help achieve them.

Cycles Under Majority Rule and the
Effects of Intralegislative Institutions

Kenneth Arrow developed the original proof that the aggregation of preferences through majority rule (given a set of plausible conditions) may lead to policy cycles. A series of votes in a representative institution, such as a legislature, can result in any possible policy outcome, depending on the *sequencing* of votes on different options—usually called agenda control. Thus one need not posit powerful interest groups that buy votes through campaign contributions or hegemonic classes to explain the failure of legislatures to represent the interests of the majority of voters. Powerful groups *may* greatly influence policy—whether they do is an empirical question—but the mere existence of unrepresentative policies does not show that they do. The consequence of this result is to focus attention on the leadership and institutions within representative institutions in order to figure out who controls the agenda and how, and to figure out what causes policy stability when Arrow's proof leads to the expectation of cycling.

An enormous rational choice literature has arisen, most of it focused on the U.S. Congress, that seeks to explain how congressional institutions and procedures lead to relatively stable policy outcomes. Implicitly or explicitly, these arguments also address the question of how representative legislatures are likely to be under different institutional arrangements (especially rules governing the role of committees, assignment to committees, and amendments from the floor).

Research in this area could help to explain differences in representativeness across countries, tendencies toward immobilism versus legislative effectiveness, and biases in policy outcomes. It would also, by broadening the range of institutions across which comparisons could be made, make an important contribution toward the development of theories about the effects of intralegislative institutions. In order to apply these models to legislatures in developing countries, assumptions about the functioning of the institutions themselves would obviously have to be revised. Since Latin American political systems resemble the U.S. system in terms of the fundamental division of power between the president and the legislature, however, there is reason to believe that models developed to explain outcomes in the United States would provide a useful starting point for the study of intralegislative institutions in Latin America.

Collective Action Problems

Nearly thirty years ago, Mancur Olson demonstrated the political consequences of combining standard assumptions about individual rationality with the notion of public goods developed by economists. Public goods have the following properties: Once supplied to a target group, no member of the group can be excluded from enjoying them, whether the person helped to create them or not; and use of the good by one individual does not reduce its availability or usefulness to others. The standard example is clean air. Once laws limiting pollution have been passed, clean air (the public good) can be enjoyed by all. Whether or not a person did anything to bring it about—work to pass a clean-air law, pay for an antipollution device for his or her car, or do whatever might be necessary to create clean air—

no one can be denied its use, and, in most circumstances, the fact that many other people are breathing it does not crowd anyone out or reduce the air's healthful effects.

Consequently, it is not rational for any individual to contribute toward attaining the good. If, on one hand, enough people are already willing to do the work or pay the cost to bring about the public good, there is no reason to do anything oneself, since one will enjoy its benefits when it arrives regardless of whether one worked for it. But if, on the other hand, there are not presently enough individuals at work to produce the public good, there is still no reason to contribute, since any one person's efforts are extremely unlikely to make the difference in whether the public good is produced. There are, as it turns out, certain conditions under which it is rational for individuals to band together in collective action, but the conditions are somewhat stringent and often go unmet. Hence effective collective action toward a commonly held goal often fails to develop, even when it seems to a casual observer that it would be in everyone's interest to cooperate.

The logic of collective action leads to devastating revisions of some standard ideas about politics. It breaks the link between individual interests and group political action that underlies virtually all interest-based understandings of politics, from Marxist to pluralist. The failure of lower-class groups to organize to defend their interests, for example, is transformed from an anomaly to be explained by false consciousness or Gramscian hegemony into the behavior expected of rational actors from the lower-classes.

The effects for democratic theory are equally serious. The logic of collective action leads to the expectation that the interests of average citizens are unlikely to influence policymaking, since ordinary people are unlikely to organize to express their interests effectively. In general, government policies that supply benefits to groups are public goods for the group, even if the goods themselves are privately consumed. Organizing to press for benefits is costly to the individuals who could benefit from the goods if they were supplied, and, because the goods are public, it is not rational for individuals to bear these costs if they can "free ride" instead.

The logic of collective action has a number of frequently observed but—prior to Olson—misunderstood substantive consequences. Groups in which resources are distributed unequally, for example, are more likely to be able to organize than are groups in which members are more equal; inequality increases the likelihood that one member of the group will receive enough benefits from a public good to be willing to shoulder the costs of lobbying, regardless of the free riding of others. This argument has been used to explain why industries that contain one or a few very large firms are more likely to be protected by tariffs.

Small groups are more likely to be able to organize to press for the policies they prefer than are larger groups. In small groups, members can recognize whether others are contributing and punish those who free ride. As a result, they can solve the collective action problem by changing the incentives facing individual members. This explains why special interest groups are often effective in the policy arena even when most citizens disagree with them or could benefit from different policies. The relationship between group size and the ability to organize also helps explain the prevalence of agricultural pricing policies in Africa that benefit the relatively small number of urban consumers (and their employers, since low food prices reduce the demand for wages) at the expense of large numbers of rural producers.

Previously organized groups are more likely to achieve the policies they want than are the unorganized. Because organization is costly, groups that have already paid start-up costs have an advantage over groups that have not. It is easier to change the purpose of an existing group than to form a new group. This argument has been used to explain why political leaders in new states often mobilize followers along ethnic lines. It is more difficult to form new groups than to turn to new purposes ethnically based organizations that already exist.

Most of these substantive arguments have been made in the context of either the United States or Africa. Nevertheless, their implications for other countries are obvious. Tariffs elsewhere have also tended to protect large industries. Pricing and other policies affecting the relative welfare of urban and rural dwellers have, on average, disadvantaged the less-organized rural inhabitants. The barriers to the entry of new parties representing recently enfranchised groups have, on average, been high. The logic of collective action implies that policies, *even in fair and competitive democracies,* will tend to benefit the rich and well organized at the expense of the more numerous poor and unorganized, simply because the former are more likely to be able to exercise their rights effectively; it thus offers a possible explanation for one of the central characteristics of policy choice in most of the world.

Inside the Black Box of the State

A second stream of rational choice theorizing has moved further from its roots in economics to focus on the actors inside the black box of the state. Despite the emphasis placed on the state recently by new institutionalists and others, rational choice arguments are the only ones that make systematic links between particular institutional characteristics of states and the behavior of elected and appointed officials. Practitioners of rational choice were not the first to notice the autonomy of the political (or the state), but they have been the most successful at producing theories that use state or political characteristics to explain policy outcomes.

Rational choice arguments about state or government actors begin with explicit attention to their goals and then consider the ways that various behaviors and choices can affect the achievement of goals in given institutional settings. The keystone of the approach is a simple model of politicians as rational individuals who attempt to maximize career success. In the U.S. context, this is often simplified to maximizing the probability of reelection, but somewhat broader conceptions of what it is that politicians maximize have been suggested and successfully used by comparativists. Using this one simple assumption about goals and a small number of characteristics of the U.S. political system, rational choice arguments have explained many of the behaviors that characterize members of Congress: the devotion of large amounts of resources to constituency service; the preference for pork; position taking and credit claiming; the avoidance of votes on controversial issues; and the assiduous pursuit of media coverage.

Other rational choice arguments link election-seeking or survival-maximizing to particular kinds of policy outcomes. Still other rational choice arguments examine coalition formation, the relationship between politicians and bureaucrats, and the creation of new political institutions. In short, a set of extremely simple arguments that begin with the assumption that politicians are self-interested maximizers of the probability of political survival or reelection, along with a context supplied by the institutions of a given political system, provide explanations of many of the political outcomes scholars would most like to understand.

Strategic Interactions Among Political Actors

The final subset of rational choice arguments to be discussed here is game theory. To the standard apparatus of rational choice arguments in which individuals respond to a particular set of institutional incentives, game theory adds the idea that individuals strategically interact with each other to produce social outcomes. That is, game theory "seeks to explore how people make decisions if their actions and fates depend on the actions of others." In nongame theoretic arguments individuals are assumed to pursue their goals within constraints imposed by the environment. In game theory, actors decide how best to pursue their goals after taking into account both environmental constraints and the equally rational and strategic behavior of other actors. Since strategic behavior and interdependence are fundamental characteristics of politics, game theory offers a particularly useful approach to understanding political actors and processes.

One of the most revolutionary contributions of game theory to thinking about politics is the prisoner's dilemma. The prisoner's dilemma game describes the logic of situations in which two or more individuals would all end up better off if they could agree among themselves to cooperate, but, if binding agreements are impossible, each will be better off if he or she chooses not to cooperate. Since it is rational for each individual to refuse to cooperate, none do; the goal is not achieved and all are worse off than they might have been had they cooperated. This may have a familiar ring to it, and it should. The prisoner's dilemma game is a generalization of the collective action problem discussed above. Much of the work on prisoner's dilemma games has focused on the difference between single interactions and interactions that are repeated (or "iterated") over time. Although it is always rational for all players to defect in single games, under some circumstances cooperation is rational when games are repeated.

Prisoner's dilemma games have been used to explain many situations in international relations. They can also offer leverage for explaining domestic political outcomes, for example: interactions among coalition partners; pacts such as the Colombian National Front, in which traditional enemies agree to cooperate to limit competition in order to secure the democratic system that benefits both and to exclude other potential competitors; and the pervasiveness of patron-client relationships. Other simple games illuminate the logical structure of other situations.

Game theory is the most exciting and potentially fruitful strand of the rational choice approach. Its strategic and interactive image of politics is realistic, and it can be used to illuminate political situations without recourse to advanced mathematics. Although theoretical developments in game theory will continue to be made by the mathematically gifted and trained, substantive progress can be made using the simple logic that game theory provides.

Rational Choice and the
Latin American Research Frontier

To some extent, the choice of which intellectual perspective to embrace is simply a matter of taste. The appeal of the rational choice approach, in my view, lies in its substantive plausibility in numerous political situations, its theoretical coherence, the fruitful simplification of "buzzing blooming" reality it offers, which facilitates comparative work, and its capacity to explain puzzling outcomes and generate nonobvious conclusions.

Rational choice arguments deal only with systematic patterns of incentives that lead to systematic patterns in outcomes. In contrast, more contingent political arguments focus on the specific conjunctural circumstances that make particular decisions understandable. The strength of such contingent political explanations is that they offer a very complete treatment of events; their weakness is that they do not easily lend themselves to the construction of general theories. Rational choice arguments have the opposite strengths and weaknesses. They invariably omit from the analysis colorful and arresting details that some observers consider important. But, by abstracting from the specifics of particular cases, they make theory-building possible and facilitate comparisons across cases that may at first appear too different to compare.

Many criticize rational choice models on the grounds that they simplify reality to such a degree that the model seems to bear no resemblance at all to the real world. And some work unquestionably deserves this stricture. Rational choice arguments can easily cross the line from simple to simplistic. Persuasive and useful applications of the rational choice approach, however, take into account the most important features of the social and institutional setting. They also draw insights from important abstract arguments. The bite of good rational choice arguments comes from the synthesis of empirical evidence from the cases under examination and abstract deductive logic.

Using rational choice models requires the analyst to identify relevant actors, to determine their preferences, and to present a plausible justification for the attribution of preferences. Observers can, of course, make mistakes in their attribution of preferences, but rational choice models do "have the advantage of being naked so that, unlike those of some less explicit theories, [their] limitations are likely to be noticeable." The rational choice approach does not prescribe any particular methodology for testing hypotheses, but persuasive work combines deductive rational choice arguments with examinations of evidence to see if it conforms to the expectations generated by the deductive model.

This summary of rational actor explanations has dealt only with some of the best-known arguments that directly address questions fundamental to understanding democratic politics. Even this brief survey shows that there is a well-developed rational choice literature replete with theories that have only begun to be extended and modified for use in Latin American countries. Analysts so far have made use only of the simplest of the theories about parties and legislatures that have emerged in the context of U.S. politics. With increasing democratization, this literature should begin to seem more relevant to scholars interested in understanding politics in Latin America.

Two areas seem to me especially overdue for systematic attention from rational choice practitioners. The first is the emergence and consolidation of democracy. Scholars working on developing countries have in the past focused so heavily on economic, cultural, and social structural causes of political outcomes that many have found themselves at a loss to come up with systematic explanations of democratization—since underlying economic and cultural conditions have changed little—and thus they have fallen back on ad hoc inductive generalizations. Rational choice arguments that focus on the incentives facing political actors during democratization have the potential for producing much more satisfying explanations. A start has been made on the task of illuminating democratization through the use of rational choice arguments and game theory, but much remains to be done. Little analysis of legislatures and party systems in new democracies has been carried out, and most of what exists is theoretically primitive. Some interesting and insightful studies of particular parties exist, but these studies do little to explain the interactions among political actors that determine how political systems work.

The second and, to my mind, most exciting area for new research involves the creation of new institutions. Rational choice arguments about the creation of institutions are in their infancy. Most explanations of institutional change by economists assume that efficiency gains explain changes, without considering who reaps the benefits of efficiency gains and who loses as a result of changes. The challenge for rational choice theorists is to revise such economic arguments by incorporating the effects of different actors pursuing their own, often inconsistent goals, and the nonobvious effects of the aggregation of individual choices.

Current events in Latin America and Eastern Europe provide a great opportunity for building theories to explain institutional creation precisely because so many institutions are being created, changed, and destroyed. Struggles over the design of new political institutions have recently taken place in several countries, and many more can be expected during the next few years. Compelling explanations of such important institutional changes would have a tremendous impact not only in our own field but in political science as a whole, reflecting back on how Western Europe and the United States arrived at the institutions that now rigidly structure their politics. We have a large and sophisticated theoretical literature on which to build. Progress should be rapid, once work begins.

Barbara Geddes, "Uses and Limitations of Rational Choice," in *Latin America in Comparative Perspective: New Approaches to Methods and Analysis*, ed. Peter H. Smith (Boulder, CO: Westview Press, 1995): 81–108.

PART TWO
Applications

Section III

The Political Economy of Growth since Independence

Latin America's contemporary circumstances are the product of a complex history spanning many centuries. Each country in the region has a unique trajectory, but some commonalities can be identified that help us understand how Latin America came to be what it is today.

The modern history of Latin America began with the colonial rule of Spain and Portugal (and for some small nations in and around the Caribbean, France, and the United Kingdom). Iberian policies were based on the precepts of *classical mercantilism*, which subordinated the developmental needs of the colonies to those of the metropolitan countries. Crown governments controlled the valuable precious metals of the region and parceled out land and other riches to their supporters. The colonies were typically forced to trade primarily with the mother country, so that they received less than world prices for their exports and paid more than world prices for their imports. This relationship—as in North America—served to channel resources from the New World to Europe. At the same time, Spanish and Portuguese socioeconomic and political institutions were transplanted (often after much transformation) to the colonies. These institutions tended to be autocratic, based as they were on centralized monarchies. They also tended to be hostile or indifferent to local economic needs, such as the development of efficient transportation and communications and of a system of general education. Colonialism was not all negative, of course, and much of Latin America was relatively prosperous during colonial times. Indeed, by some measures, the gap between Latin America and North America was smallest during the colonial period (Coatsworth, reading 11). Nonetheless, some of the negative aspects of Iberian rule would have enduring effects on the region (Engerman and Sokoloff, reading 13).

Independence, achieved by most of the continent between 1810 and 1830, was typically followed by sociopolitical conflict and often civil war. After the postcolonial dust cleared, most Latin American countries oriented their economies toward the production of primary commodities—raw materials and agricultural products—for export to Europe. This orientation was only natural, given the region's extraordinary natural resource base and the booming European demand for such products as coffee, sugar, cotton, wheat, copper, and nitrates. At the same time, Latin America borrowed heavily from British and other investors in order to build railroads, power plants, ports, and other industrial facilities. Again, heavy borrowing made sense given Europe's search for profitable investments and Latin America's chronic shortage of capital.

From the 1860s to 1914, this *primary exporting* model brought the region very rapid rates of economic growth. Some of the developmental successes were stunning indeed: On the eve of World War I, Argentina was one of the world's wealthiest countries, with a per capita gross domestic product (GDP) roughly equal to that of Canada and higher than that of almost every country in Europe.[1] However, success was not universal, and even in relatively successful countries there were serious weaknesses. Generally speaking, and especially in comparison with North America, the economic infrastructure was poorly developed: Transportation, communications, education, and the financial system all lagged (Coatsworth, reading 11; Leff, reading 12). Among the many reasons for the poor infrastructure, the great inequality of the region's social systems played an important part (Engerman and Sokoloff, reading 13).

The years between 1914 and 1945 were a watershed in Latin American economic history. Over these decades, the region shifted from export-oriented primary production to domestically oriented industrialization. Both external and internal factors contributed to this shift. Internationally, World War I, the Great Depression, and World War II all tended to force Latin America away from its prior integration into the world economy—whether due to wartime conditions or to the collapse of international markets. Continued specialization in the export of primary products and reliance on imported manufactures would have been exceedingly difficult in these troubled times. Foreign conditions forced the region back in on its own resources, and especially required it to satisfy much of its own demand for industrial products with domestic production. This situation led to a process of natural *import substitution*, a market-driven replacement of manufactured imports with domestic production.

Domestically, between 1914 and 1945 previously dominant primary producers and exporters tended to weaken and new socioeconomic groups tended to become stronger. Wheat farmers, copper miners, cattle ranchers, and coffee growers all declined in economic and political importance as their crops became less profitable and less important to the national economy. At the same time, natural import substitution led to very rapid industrial growth and urbanization. The urban middle and working classes, industrialists, and public employees of the growing state sector came to dominate national political economies.

The economic and sociopolitical predominance of the new urban groups was associated with the rise of Import Substituting Industrialization (ISI) as a conscious development strategy. Indeed, ISI itself tended to be part of a turn toward economic nationalism, populism, and developmentalism. Economic nationalism privileged domestic businesses over foreign. Populism aimed to redistribute income toward the urban middle and working classes. Developmentalism evinced a reliance on government involvement in the economy to speed industrialization, whether by subsidies and incentives or direct state ownership of steel mills, power plants, and other facilities.

By the 1940s, modern Latin America had emerged. It had substantial farming and mining sectors, but they had taken second place to the drive for industrial growth. Government policy and politics were increasingly oriented toward the development of modern manufacturing and urban centers, with all they implied.

---

[1] Angus Maddison, *Monitoring the World Economy 1820–1992* (Paris: OECD, 1995), pp. 194–202.

11

Obstacles to Economic Growth in Nineteenth-Century Mexico

JOHN H. COATSWORTH

I

National income per capita in Mexico was closer to that of Great Britain and the United States in 1800 than at any point thereafter. In that year Mexico produced more than a third of British income per head and nearly half that of the United States. The gap in productivity between the Mexican economy and that of the advanced countries of the North Atlantic has never been so small. By 1877, Mexico's per capita income had fallen to a little over one-tenth that of the industrial nations. It has fluctuated between 10 and 15 percent of U.S. per capita income ever since.

Two aspects of the comparison stand out. The first is the substantial difference between the economies of Mexico and the United States at the beginning of the century. In 1800 the United States was still a predominantly agrarian country, decades away from its industrial revolution. Mexico in the same year counted as Spain's richest colony in the New World, with an advanced mining industry exporting vast quantities of processed metals. Indeed, the values of U.S. and Mexican exports at the end of the eighteenth century were quite similar. Why did the Mexican economy begin the nineteenth century less than half as productive as that of the United States? The second striking aspect of the data is the extent to which the gap between Mexico and the industrializing countries widened between 1800 and the last quarter of the century. Had Mexico's economy kept pace with the growth of the United States for the entire century, Mexico would have reached its 1950 level of per capita income before the Revolution of 1910. Had the gap between Mexico and the United States remained the same from 1800 to the present, Mexico would now rank among the world's industrial powers. From the standpoint of the twentieth century, the question might be reversed: Why did the Mexican economy fall so far behind the industrializing giants of the North Atlantic during the nineteenth century?

II

Three main obstacles to economic growth have been postulated to explain Mexico's relative backwardness at the end of the colonial period: Spanish colonial rule, the system of land tenure, and the Roman Catholic Church. On the basis of evidence of direct economic effects, regardless of more general problems, all must be rejected.

First, since Spain managed, or mismanaged, its New World colonies for three full centuries, it cannot be denied that Spain was responsible for whatever the colonies achieved or failed to achieve—a truism that has been repeated by scholars and historians ever since Baron Alexander von Humboldt made it popular in his monumental studies of the Spanish colonies in the first decade of the nineteenth century. But emancipation from Spain promised few benefits. For purposes of measurement, the costs of Spanish colonialism are defined as those economic constraints that independence actually eliminated: (1) mercantilist restrictions on direct trade with foreign countries and (2) the uncompensated export of gold and silver extracted by the colonial government as net fiscal revenues.

The total cost of Spanish sovereignty came to a little more than seventeen million pesos per year. By contrast, the cost of British colonialism was only half a million pesos. The Spanish burden was, therefore, thirty-five times greater than that of the British. However, the Spanish burden amounted to less than three pesos per capita at the beginning of the nineteenth century. It is arguable, of course, whether the psychic splendors of Spanish citizenship were worth that much. In economic terms, fully 7.2 percent of the colony's 1800 income was lost, an amount by no means negligible. But even if this estimate were five or ten times too low, independence would not have eliminated the gap in productivity between the Mexican and U.S. economies in 1800. Adding three pesos to Mexico's per capita income would still have left it at less than half that of the United States.

Many Mexicans in the nineteenth century, and not a few historians thereafter, have wondered why independence failed to stimulate the Mexican economy. Many have sought the answer to this question in the turmoil of the struggle for independence and the political instability that followed. Certainly these phenomena helped to depress the economy after 1810, but Mexico's income did not increase dramatically because independence had direct adverse economic results, which more than offset the benefits. Indeed, the continued depression in the crucial mining industry that persisted well into the nineteenth century was largely the result of an unanticipated cost of independence: the loss of assured supplies of mercury—indispensable for processing low-grade ores—that Spain had provided at low, fixed prices from the huge state-owned mercury mine at Almaden.

Second, a major obstacle to economic advance cited in the conventional accounts is the system of land tenure or, more precisely, the organization of Mexican agricultural production into large estates called *haciendas*. This general explanation can be divided into a number of distinct assertions, of which at least two can now be rejected: (1) that the large estates of both the colonial period and the nineteenth century were inefficiently organized and badly managed and (2) that concentration of land ownership *per se* caused waste and misallocation of resources. Full discussion of the system of land tenure is impossible in so short a space. Fortunately, it is now possible to rely on a large body of *hacienda* studies.

Collectively, the *hacienda* and regional studies have transformed the traditional view of Mexican agriculture and estate management. Not one estate owner has been found who might qualify as the sort of aristocratic, prestige-oriented, economic nincompoop once thought by many to be typical of Spanish American *hacendados*. Each was greedy in the ordinary way—even the managers of Church estates, for the income went for good works after all. Every one of them demonstrated a primordial desire to maximize income and to minimize production costs. During periods of prosperity, estate owners invested in their operations, experimented with new crops and new methods, and sought new markets. In periods of economic decline, they shifted from crops to livestock, reorganized their estates into tenancies, sold out to cut losses, or abandoned their holdings altogether. Given the relative costs of labor, capital, and especially management and supervision, their economic rationality was comparable to that of modern entrepreneurs. No evidence has yet been found to sustain the hypothesis that the estate sector of Mexico's agricultural economy wasted resources that might have been put to more productive use under different land-tenure conditions.

The picture of colonial and nineteenth-century agriculture in Mexico that emerges from the evidence now available suggests two main conclusions. Estate agriculture enjoyed advantages not available to Indian villagers, small landowners, or tenant farmers: economies of scale, access to outside credit, information about new technologies and distant markets, a measure of protection from predatory officials, and greater security of tenure. But these advantages, important as they were, did not eliminate small-scale production because they were not sufficient to offset the high cost of recruiting and supervising labor. The large estates held a competitive advantage in the production of cattle, sheep, wool, food grains, pulque, sugar, and sisal. In other products that required very close supervision (or highly motivated workers) either to produce or to transport without great losses, the villages and small-scale producers held the advantage: fruits, garden products like tomatoes and chiles, silk, cochineal, small animals including pigs, poultry, eggs, and the like. Even cotton, tobacco, and wine were commonly produced by villagers and small landholders. Product specialization among units of varying size, location, and organization made Mexican agriculture more efficient than it would otherwise have been. The discipline of local and regional markets, moreover, acted to push the size of production units toward what a modern economist would describe as an "optimal mix." Far from distorting resource allocation in agrarian Mexico, concentration of landholding functioned to allow more efficient production of crops suitable for large units and did so without sacrificing the advantages of small-unit output for other produce.

In the late nineteenth century the increasing availability of new transport and production technologies made the historic division of labor between estate-and nonestate agriculture inefficient. The economic balance tipped dramatically in favor of the large *haciendas*. Agricultural productivity, stagnant during the half century after independence, increased rapidly as the estates expanded at the expense of the free villages and small landowners. Additional evidence may be adduced from comparative data. In 1800, between 70 and 80 percent of the Mexican labor force worked in agriculture to produce approximately 40 percent of the colony's gross product. Almost identical are the best estimates for the United States in the same year: slightly more than 80 percent of the labor force in agriculture produced approximately 40 percent of the nation's income. The gap in agricultural productivity between the two regions was exactly equal to the gap in nonagricultural productivity between the two economies. Mexico was only half as productive as the United States in both agricultural and nonagricultural production. In comparative terms, the agricultural sector of the Mexican economy did not, therefore, act as a drag on the nation's growth. Although this evidence is not decisive, it does at least suggest that historians should, in searching for obstacles that hindered Mexico's economy in the colonial era and the nineteenth century, look less at a single sector, important as it was, and more at conditions affecting the economy as a whole.

Third, the Roman Catholic Church purportedly retarded Mexico's economic growth during the colonial period and for at least three decades after independence, until the liberal revolution succeeded in expropriating the Church's wealth and reducing its role in the nation's political life. The anticlerical argument runs through volumes of highly charged prose and involves not only the Church's strictly economic activities but its political, social, and cultural influence as well. The portion of the argument that can now be rejected is that which assigns significance to the Church's strictly economic activities: (1) the tithe, (2) mortgage lending, and (3) ownership of real property.

The tithe was a 10 percent tax on gross output charged mainly on the agricultural and livestock production of the private estates. Like any direct tax today, the tithe reduced the profitability of agricultural enterprise. But by how much did this tax reduce Mexico's gross national product? It has often been implicitly assumed that agricultural production (and thus GNP) was reduced by the amount of the tax—that is, by 10 percent—as though the tithe collectors made off with a tenth of every harvest and burned it as a sacrifice. Even if this entirely inappropriate measure were adopted, the per capita drain of the tithe in 1800 would have amounted to less than half a peso—a little more than 1 percent of national income. By the time of independence (until 1833 when the tithe was abolished as a legal obligation of the citizenry), Church revenues from this source had already dropped to negligible sums.

An appropriate measure of the impact of the tithe would have to take into account its effect on the profitability of private agricultural enterprise. By reducing profits in private agriculture, the tithe reduced employment and investment in that sector of the economy and pushed labor and capital into other, less productive activities. The negative effect on GNP is thus the difference between what the labor and capital pushed out of private agriculture actually produced elsewhere and what they would have produced (in the absence of the tithe) had they remained on the farms and estates. The amount of labor and capital pushed out of private agriculture was negligible; thus, the amount of this difference was close to zero, even when tithe collections reached a maximum at the end of the eighteenth century. Not only did the Church itself and the Indian villages produce a major portion of the colony's farm products and livestock (thus removing a sizable portion of agriculture from the full effect of the tithe), but differences in productivity between private agriculture and the rest of the economy indicate that nonagricultural pursuits were already more productive than agriculture. Therefore, the most important effect of the tithe was distributional: a larger portion of land remained in the hands of the Church and the Indian villages than would have been the case if the tithe had not been levied.

Even when historians have realized that tithe collection did not directly reduce the gross national product, they have often suggested that the Church used this income unproductively: instead of investing its revenues in new industries and enterprise, the Church dissipated a tenth of the economy's output on new religious construction or on the wages of priests. There are two problems with this contention. First, the multiplier effect of "unproductive" expenditure in modern times has proved reasonably effective in stimulating, rather than depressing, economic activity; and there is no reason to assume, *a priori,* that this effect was absent in colonial Mexico. Second, the Church did invest a sizable portion of its revenues in mortgage loans to private entrepreneurs. Indeed, the Church probably raised the rate of investment in the economy above what it would have been had the tithe revenues remained in private hands.

The Church's role as the country's chief banking institution has also been misunderstood. The Church earned a net income from the tithe, private donations, and its various properties. In addition, it acted as fiduciary agent for trust funds left in its care. The Church invested a large portion of its net income and all of the trust capital it managed, usually at 6 percent interest on the security of real property. Because it charged a low, nonmarket interest rate, the Church dominated the mortgage-lending market. What effect did this have on economic activity? Practically none at all. Once again, the main effect was distributional. The Church lost money when it lent funds below the market rate of interest, while the recipients of Church credit gained. It performed like a modern development bank, charging taxpayers to subsidize the accumulation of private capital. The Church imposed no legal or practical obstacles to prevent recipients from investing in factories rather than *haciendas* or high living. If factories were not built, reasons other than interference by the Church were involved.

Finally, the Church was a property owner. Studies of Church-owned estates suggest they were at least as well managed as those in private hands. The larger Church estates enjoyed considerable advantages, including a long-distance communication network which made it possible to plan both sales and purchases to take advantage of prevailing market conditions in widely scattered areas. Most Church estates after independence were rented to individuals, so the efficiency of these properties did not depend on Church management at all. The major difference between the eccesiastical and the private sectors lay in the Church's exemption from most of the taxes levied on private enterprise by colonial and, later, national governments. There is no evidence, however, that public authority would have put revenues gained from taxing the Church to better use; and much evidence, in fact, suggests the contrary. After expropriation, for example, a large number of Church-supported charitable activities disappeared, so the short-run effect of moving Church properties into the taxable private sector seems to have been a drop in the welfare of poor people.

III

There were two main obstacles to economic growth in colonial Mexico which together explain most of the difference in productivity between the Mexican and U.S. economies in 1800: inadequate transport and inefficient economic organization—geography and "feudalism."

Mexico's population and economic activity have always been concentrated in highland valleys and plateaus far from the sea. Inland waterways did not exist, nor could they have been constructed. The entire economy, therefore, depended on costly overland transportation to move goods and people. One example will suffice to show how geography affected transport costs and thus both the development of markets and the growth of productivity. In the late eighteenth century the Mining Deputation of Guanajuato estimated that this city received its supply of maize from estates located within a radius of ten leagues (fifty-five kilometers). At prevailing rates in this area, producers had to pay between one and one and one-third *reales* (0.125 to 0.166 pesos) per ton kilometer to ship goods commercially. The price of maize fluctuated widely, but for purposes of illustration it may be put at thirty pesos per ton. Estates at the margin of this radius had to pay more than eight pesos (40 percent of the sale price of maize) just to carry it to Guanajuato. If maize producers had been able to ship by water to Guanajuato, at the same rates paid for shipments by canoe on the lakes surrounding Mexico City, Guanajuato's supply radius would have increased to between 485 and 725 kilometers. The effects of such cheap transport can only be imagined, but the impact on national income would have been very large: increased regional specialization and division of labor, new centers of production previously undeveloped because of distance from centers of population and markets, greater reliance on markets to exchange products, greater mobility for both capital and labor, external economies due to better communication, and the like. The United States, of course, already possessed these advantages. Had Mexico shared them, the difference in productivity between the Mexican and U.S. economies would have been reduced, all other things being equal, by at least one-third.

This conclusion is based on what actually happened when railroads were constructed during the Porfiriato. Freight-transport costs fell to less than one-tenth of their prerailroad levels. Social savings by 1910 amounted to at least 10.8 percent of gross domestic product, equivalent to-one-third of the productivity gains of the Mexican economy between 1895 and 1910. If Mexico had been endowed with a system of rivers, like those along the eastern seaboard of the United States, a major portion of the U.S. advantage at the beginning of the nineteenth century would have been eliminated.

All other things were not, of course, equal. The viceregal government might well have decided to raise internal customs duties (*alcabalas*) to match reductions in transport costs. Or Madrid could have ordered the colonial government to deny licenses to entrepreneurs clamoring to take advantage of lowered transport costs and ready to invest in new productive enterprise. Or the crown could have decided to make transportation a royal monopoly (*estanco*, from which *estancar*, to stagnate) and control the supply of shipping and charge inflated rates. Or the Council of the Indies might have urged the king to protect the indigenous population by forbidding its employment in the production of goods sold in faraway places. Or, after multiple lawsuits lasting several decades, the Audiencia might have decided in favor of the petitions of muleteers, wagonmasters, and hotel keepers and ordered that all boats, rafts, and canoes in the colony had to be owned exclusively by former muleteers, wagonmasters, and hotel keepers who registered with the authorities and agreed to lend the king ten thousand pesos.

The very plausibility of measures such as these suggests a seriously deficient institutional environment for entrepreneurial activity. Indeed, the second of the two main obstacles to Mexican economic growth was inefficient economic organization. This term does not mean, for example, that private estates or mining companies wasted resources, given the environment they faced. It refers instead to an ensemble of policies, laws, and institutions that magnified, instead of reduced, the gap between the private and the social benefits of economic activity. During the colonial period and most of the nineteenth century, activities which could have contributed to economic growth were never undertaken because they promised too small a return to potential owners and producers. Either existing law and practice discouraged more productive enterprise or new laws and practices needed to protect and stimulate more productive activity never developed.

In the colonial period, legal constraints on the mobility of capital and labor inhibited the development of factor markets. Minute public regulation of economic activity for fiscal and other purposes raised start-up costs and discouraged enterprise. The judicial system increased the risks of entrepreneurial activity by failing to enforce a well-defined set of property rights. Fiscal policy made transactions more costly, discouraged use of markets as a means for exchanging products, and contributed to the geographical isolation of those regional and local markets which did develop. Royal monopolies on the production and distribution of many commodities distorted prices and reduced production. Investment by public authority or voluntary agencies in infrastructure or human capital was negligible. No general legislation existed to promote the realization of economies of scale through joint stock companies or corporations. Innovation was discouraged by a system of privileges that did not guarantee a return to inventors or investors in the application of new processes. Corporate exemptions from a portion of the risks and constraints imposed on the rest of society were distributed by the crown to favored groups and individuals, with the net effect of increasing the burden on others. The special courts established to hear cases involving members of each corporate group compounded the ordinary chaos of the judicial system with interminable litigation over which court was appropriate to hear each case and thus increased the uncertainty that plagued the legal environment. The property of Indian villages, town councils, certain public bodies, entailed estates, and the trusts administered by the Church were defined by law as inalienable. The land thus held could not be used as collateral for mortgage loans, rented for extended periods of time to a single tenant, or sold to anyone. However much evaded or even violated in practice, these constraints helped immobilize resources or divert them to less productive uses.

At the apex of this system of government sat the crown, whose power was constitutionally absolute. No rights of citizens and no law, regulation, or settled custom bound the king's freedom of action in the colonies. All legislative and judicial acts derived their authority from the crown. The king could, and often did, grant individual exemptions from the application of his own laws or issue judicial decisions on appeal that controverted his own decrees in order to take into account the personal merits of the litigants. Not infrequently, the king's ministers, viceroys, and appellate courts acted in the same way.

The interventionist and pervasively arbitrary nature of the institutional environment forced every enterprise, urban or rural, to operate in a highly politicized manner, using kinship networks, political influence, and family prestige to gain privileged access to subsidized credit, to aid various stratagems for recruiting labor, to collect debts or enforce contracts, to evade taxes or circumvent the courts, and to defend or assert titles to land. Success or failure in the economic arena always depended on the relations of the producer with political authorities—local officials for arranging matters close at hand, the central government of the colony for sympathetic interpretations of the law and intervention at the local level when conditions required it. Small enterprise, excluded from the system of corporate privilege and political favors, was forced to operate in a permanent state of semiclandestinity, always at the margin of the law, at the mercy of petty officials, never secure from arbitrary acts and never protected against the rights of those more powerful.

This system of government made "free" enterprise impossible. It was not merely a matter of specific policies, laws, and institutions or their collective impact at a particular point in time that discouraged enterprise. The chief obstacle was the nature of the state itself, its operating principles, the basis for all of its acts. Mexico's economic organization could not have been made more efficient without a revolution in the relationship between the state and economic activity.

Unfortunately, the cost-benefit approach so helpful in identifying the impact of economic organization in theoretical terms cannot be applied quantitatively. It is possible to know the direction (positive or negative) of the effects of specific laws, policies, or institutions but not the magnitude of their impact. Direct measurement is impossible in practice, even to distinguish the relative importance of the various components of the system. Some advances may come from the aggregation of individual case studies at the enterprise level, but these may not be of much help in estimating the loss from economic activities that never got started in the first place. Treating the impact of economic organization as a residual is scarcely satisfactory, especially when the size of the residual is suggested by an international comparison rather than an estimate of Mexico's own potential for growth. Nonetheless, a starting point for future work might well be the hypothesis that most of the gap between the Mexican and U.S. economies in 1800 was due to differences in economic organization.

IV

The two main obstacles to economic growth in colonial Mexico—inadequate transport and inefficient economic organization—could have been eliminated early in the nineteenth century. Independence in 1821 emancipated the country from the source of the policies, laws, and institutions that inhibited enterprise. And railroad technology developed in the 1830s and could easily have been imported by 1840. By the time of independence, the liberal Spanish Cortes, established to resist the Napoleonic invasion and later revived under popular pressure, had already eliminated many important constraints on economic activity. Ethnic distinctions between citizens in employment, taxation, and justice were abolished; corporate property rights were restricted to the Church and the Indian villages and town councils; the number of royal monopolies was reduced and their activities were curtailed; the corporate privileges of certain groups, including most of the guilds, were eliminated; efforts were made to streamline the judicial system; and revision of the antiquated law codes was begun. But then Mexico plunged into a half century of political, social, and international warfare. The collapse of stable government mullified the potentially positive effects of the changes that accompanied independence and deprived both the new government and the private sector of the resources needed to improve transportation.

Mexican independence came through a virtual coup d'état by the colony's Creole elite, carried out largely to separate Mexico from the liberalizing process under way in the mother country. For the next half century, repeated efforts were made to recreate the arbitrary centralism of the colonial state. The principal proponent of these conservative efforts was a limited social group of major landowners and industrialists in the center of the country (often residents of Mexico City), who had been the principal beneficiaries in the colony of the crown's interventionism or who, like the large merchant houses of the capital, sought to regain privileges the crown itself had abolished in the reforms of the late Bourbon era. Allied with this group were the Church, seeking to preserve its privileged status and to reverse the anticlericalism of the later Bourbon kings, and the new professional army, endowed with privileges in the early constitutions, whose chief *raison d'étre* was to be found as enforcer of the new centralism against regional demands for greater autonomy and liberal clamorings for reform.

Traditional accounts of Mexico after independence have attributed the conservative orientation of the new country's early governments to the influence of a "feudal" or "semifeudal" landowning class. Early national governments were weak. The nation disintegrated into a multiplicity of regional satrapies controlled by local *caudillos*. The parallel to Europe's Middle Ages seemed very apt. The chief problem with this interpretation has been and remains a lack of systematic data on the social composition of the political forces that fought for control over the new nation's destiny. Aside from the small group of magnates in the capital, there is little evidence to suggest widespread support for conservative centralism among Mexico's landowners. Many—including important regional chieftains—supported the liberal cause, because it promised less interference by the national government in local affairs. This support, in turn, aided the Church in its efforts to convince the Indian population to support the capital against the local liberals.

Feudalism, in the broad conception of Marxist historians, is usually linked to serfdom. Serfs were peasants permanently attached to the persons or properties of aristocrats. They labored with their own implements and were obligated to yield up a portion of their product or to contribute a portion of their labor to the lord. In Mexico, however, legal serfdom did not exist and recent research has demonstrated that debt peonage (often assumed to be its New World equivalent) was effectively practiced only in parts of the sparsely populated geographical extremities of the country. Indeed, Mexico's landowners enjoyed none of the privileges of the old European nobility, either before independence or after. Spanish *raison d'itat*—principally the fear of an American nobility rising to claim sovereignty over New World populations—prevented any such development. Indian access to land came from the crown in the form of corporate, and thus inalienable, land grants to villages. The crown never countenanced legal obligations between Indian villagers and landowners, save those regulated by royal decree and administered by royal officials. The royal courts and the tenacious resistance of the villagers themselves prevented the incorporation of villagers and their lands into the *haciendas*. Preservation of nonexistent servile obligations or other privileges played no role in determining the social composition of the warring parties in independent Mexico.

If Mexico's landowners were not privileged, neither were they powerless. By designating the villages as corporate entities, the crown had virtually tied the bulk of the Indian population to specific pieces of real estate. Geography, culture, and lack of communication restricted Indian mobility still further. Most Indian villagers worked as seasonal labor on the great estates in the vicinity of their homes. Often, they did so out of need—village land grants in the sixteenth and seventeenth centuries were inadequate for the rising population in later periods. In the eighteenth century the royal courts became less protective of village land titles as the large estates expanded to profit from the colony's prosperity. In many areas seasonal labor on the estates acquired the force of habit over many years or continued as a form of rent charged for access to estate water, salt, or woodlands.

Coercion, however, was widespread and pervasive. Usually it involved various kinds of pressures applied by landowners in cooperation with local civil and ecclesiastical authorities. The stratagems employed varied from place to place, as did the success of the landowners who employed them. The colonial authorities resisted these informal attempts to obligate local villagers but their efforts were never entirely effective, for the landowner's capacity to manipulate the local environment was always decisive. Far from desiring a restoration of Bourbon centralism, most landowners wanted to be allowed a free hand to control their immediate surroundings.

The social composition of what became the liberal movement has not received adequate attention from researchers. The only significant study of this question—a survey of the delegates to the Constitutional Convention of 1856–57—has revealed that most of the participants were either lawyers or generals in the liberal forces. In the port cities on the Gulf of Mexico, support for liberal governments was apparently quite strong, which suggests ties to merchants and tradesmen in addition to local landowners and *caudillos*. The liberals also appealed to the "professional classes, lawyers, doctors, small property owners, merchants, the middle ranks of the clergy and military. . . ." While the thrust of liberal demands for change—at least those emanating from liberal political leaders who assumed command of the movement at the national level—was for institutional change modeled on the example of the United States and Western Europe, Mexico's bourgeoisie—under any definition of the term—constituted a small, weak, and highly fragmented social grouping. Neither landowners nor capitalists can be said to have formed a national governing class in independent Mexico. With more than fifty changes of government in a half century, no group effectively dominated national government.

Because it fought to prevent institutional change, the Church did constitute an important obstacle to economic growth, even though its strictly economic activities did not directly impede progress. The lack of evidence demonstrating systematic support for the conservative cause by Mexico's landowners, however, makes it impossible—even in this general sense—to describe the system of land tenure as a significant obstacle to economic advancement. The social base of

Mexico's conservative movement was not determined by the nature of rural so-cial relations but by the pattern of relations between a narrow stratum of the eco-nomic elite—however their fortunes were made—and the central government. In both colonial and independent Mexico, Enrique Semo's observation was bril-liantly precise. "Feudalism in Mexico," he wrote, "was strongest at the level of su-perstructure."

V

For a multitude of reasons that need not detain us here, liberalism emerged tri-umphant from Mexico's postindependence turmoil. The last hope for restoration of the colonial pattern of government ended when the short-lived regime of Em-peror Maximilian (1862–67) embraced an essentially liberal program and moved rapidly to remove the same obstacles to capitalist development that his liberal en-emies hoped to abolish. Not only did Maximilian promulgate the nation's first modern commercial code to replace the Ordenanzas of Bilbao, but his govern-ment used French aid to push construction of the nation's first railroad as well.

When the apparatus of national government fell to the liberal regime of Benito Juárez in 1867, the first and most important step in the transformation of prop-erty rights proclaimed in the Constitution of 1857 was already an accomplished fact. Most of the wealth of the Church was now in private hands. Little more was accomplished during the decade of the Restored Republic. The liberals did man-age to produce a new civil code (1870) to recognize the new status of Church-state relations, but the commercial code was revoked and nothing was enacted to replace it. Tariff reform, which affected the largest source of federal government revenues, was enacted by Congress in 1872, but modernization of the tax system and reform of the antiquated and inefficient treasury were postponed. The judi-ciary was reorganized and purged, but the main qualification for appointment was loyalty to the new regime and the judicial system remained as chaotic as ever. The Juárez and Lerdo regimes lacked the resources to repair roads, subsidize rail-road construction, build schools, or lower taxes. The Veracruz-Mexico City rail line was finally completed in 1873, but the debt-ridden company that owned it charged rates only slightly below the cost of shipments by wagon or mule.

When Porfirio Díaz seized power in 1877, nothing had been done to reform the colonial mining code since the 1820s, when Congress abolished the mining guild and relaxed the prohibition on foreign investment. No legislation existed to encourage the formation of corporations with limited liability. No banking laws were passed, except for concessions to particular banks. No mortgage-credit law existed to protect long-term-investment and replace the spiritual sanctions on which the Church had relied. A modern patent law did not exist. Despite consti-tutional provisions that specifically outlawed them, colonial fiscal measures like the internal customs still provided most of the revenue for state and municipal governments. Economic activity of all kinds still required special permits and li-censes for which special taxes and fees were charged. Though Church wealth had been expropriated, the corporate holdings of the Indian villages remained unaf-fected throughout most of the country. The liberal movement had destroyed the political power of the Church, seized the apparatus of government, and changed the constitution. But a new superstructure of laws and institutions for a capitalist society had yet to emerge.

The Porfirian military coup occurred at a fortuitous moment. In a short time, the Díaz regime issued major railway concessions for lines running across the Central Plateau and northward to the U.S. border. Railroad concessions raised land values along projected routes and precipitated wide-spread usurpations of Indian village lands by estate owners and land companies. Needless to say, the railroad companies reported no difficulties in recruiting thousands of property-less wage laborers for the massive construction projects that got under way in late 1880. In the next three years, nearly five thousand kilometers of track were built by tens of thousands of Indian workers, many of whom had only recently been driven from their lands. As cheap transport and the nation's new prosperity re-vived the profitability of the estates, expropriation of village lands progressed apace. The dispossessed villagers swelled the ranks of the nation's landless rural and urban proletariat. Capitalist modernization had begun.

As railroad lines spread throughout the countryside and the first signs of mas-sive foreign interest in Mexican resources appeared, a series of major legislative reforms was enacted. In 1884, Congress passed a new commercial code, the single most important piece of economic legislation since independence. (The new code had to be reformed—ironically, the revisions were modeled after Spain's 1885 code—in 1889, largely because it did not make adequate provision for lim-ited-liability corporations.) In 1887, a new mining code followed. Banking, first included in the commercial codes, became the object of special legislation in 1897 and 1908. Reform of the fiscal system, begun in 1881 with reorganization of the treasury, continued in stages for the rest of the decade until new tax laws, tar-iff schedules, and public-debt reorganization had been achieved. After more than a decade of virtual isolation, the Mexican government signed commercial treaties, first with the United States and, later, after successful renegotiation of the foreign debt, with all of the European powers.

VI

The simultaneous development of transportation and a more efficient economic organization made possible the economic growth of the Porfirian era. That growth had characteristics that made Mexico's advances in this period markedly different from the economic and institutional development of the industrial economies of the North Atlantic. While Mexico was resolving its internal con-flicts, exacerbated as they were by foreign wars and invasions, the Industrial Rev-olution brought Europe and the United States to new heights of productivity. The main significance of Mexico's greater relative backwardness lay in the vast comparative advantages of foreign technology and resources for the development of Mexico's own economy. No Mexican government, whatever the social compo-sition of its leaders and supporter, could have long resisted the benefits offered by foreign participation in Mexico's economy. What Mexico might have done on its own when it first won independence could no longer be done without a far greater sacrifice of palpable immediate gains by the 1870s.

The participation of foreign capital in Mexico's first period of sustained capitalist growth had five main consequences. First, the construction of railroads and subsequent development of major export industries interrupted the gradual disintegration of the large estates into smaller units, which had begun in 1810 with the outbreak of the independence movement. The new prosperity also ensured that the properties expropriated from the Church passed into the hands of large-scale operators. Second, the new industries developed by foreign capital and by Mexican entrepreneurs with foreign financing also operated on a large scale. In both agriculture and industry, large-scale units ensured more rapid growth. They also defined the nature of the institutional changes Mexico adopted to facilitate capitalist development.

Third, Mexico's numerous class of petty tradesmen and small-scale producers were therefore assigned a position in Mexico's new society similar to that which it had occupied in the colonial era. Since it was clearly marginal to the country's economic progress, it suffered from the same arbitrary treatment and operated in the same netherworld of semiclandestinity as before. Nor did that numerous class of independent farmers envisioned by some liberal leaders ever emerge. Without either force, Mexican governments reverted to authoritarian models from the colonial past, despite the new institutions of the liberal era, and spent their increasing resources on more important projects than the development of the nation's human resources.

Fourth, the Revolution of 1910 was produced by the discontent of precisely those elements in Mexican society whose importance in the nation's political and social life would have increased, rather than diminished, in the absence of foreign resources: the dispossessed villagers who never became family farmers and the "middle sectors" that continued to suffer exclusion from both political and economic opportunity. Fifth, foreign resources established a pattern of economic activity that fixed Mexico's position in the world economy at the most unfavorable moment in the nation's economic history. Foreign resources attracted their Mexican counterparts to produce, labor, and invest in activities made profitable by Mexico's short-term comparative advantage in the production of raw materials and agricultural products for export. It may be doubted, of course, that Mexico's present condition would be more favorable had the nation followed a different course. But it is clear enough, in any case, that the path Mexico did follow promised no more than a long-term dependence on foreign technology, resources, and markets.

John H. Coatsworth, "Obstacles to Economic Growth in Nineteenth-Century Mexico," *American Historical Review* 83, no. 1 (February 1978): 80–100.

12

Economic Retardation in Nineteenth-Century Brazil

NATHANIEL H. LEFF

Unlike the United States and the other regions of recent settlement, nineteenth-century Brazil did not develop as an economy characterized by relatively high wages. At first appearance this may seem surprising, for Brazil also had an abundance of land and high land–labour ratios, and might have been expected to follow a similar course with respect to productivity and to the distribution of income.

The Brazilian case also does not fit some other standard explanations of the economic retardation of the less developed countries. During most of the century the country was free both from far-reaching colonial domination and from the substantial political instability which affected some other Latin American countries following independence. Brazil's overall economic retardation can also not be attributed to some of the conditions characteristic of an enclave "export economy" in which expanding exports have only limited effects on aggregate development. As noted below, conditions in the export activities made for a high foreign-trade multiplier; and after the 1840's the country implemented a protective tariff policy which stimulated domestic manufacturing and led to the formation of strong linkages between export growth and industrialization. Thus, the nineteenth-century Brazilian experience offers an opportunity to focus on the causes of overall retardation in conditions which appear to have been relatively favourable for development.

I

In 1800, Brazil's population numbered approximately 3.6 million people. During the nineteenth century the population grew rapidly, at an annual geometric rate of 1.4 per cent from 1800 to 1849, and one of 1.8 per cent from 1850 to 1900. This was mainly the result of natural increase and the importation of slaves; for reasons discussed below, Brazil did not attract much free immigration until the 1870's. In 1920, the country's population was 27.4 million.

Estimates of Brazilian national product are not available for the years before 1920. However . . . the statistics on the currency supply can be used to form an idea of broad trends in Brazilian national income during the nineteenth century. These estimates suggest that for the country as a whole, *per capita* income was probably increasing at only a moderate rate between 1822 and 1900. This aggregate picture is, of course, highly important, and much of this article is directed towards explaining it. However, the aggregate view does obscure one of the major features of nineteenth-century Brazilian development, a marked disparity in regional rates of development. The south-east region (Rio de Janeiro and São Paulo provinces), which enjoyed favourable expansion of coffee exports, experienced considerable economic progress. By contrast, the large north-east region, which had a poor experience in its overseas exports of sugar and cotton, did not do well during the nineteenth century.

II

Despite an abundant supply of land *in natura*, and high land-labour ratios, nineteenth-century Brazil did not develop as a relatively high-wage economy. First, even in the more advanced agricultural export activities, production techniques seem to have been extremely primitive. In addition, although rivers and coastal shipping were used for transportation, Brazil's large hinterland did not have an extensive network of internal navigable waterways in the habitable areas comparable to the Mississippi and Great Lakes systems in the United States. Man-made transportation facilities were also noticeably lacking. Consequently, transportation costs from the agricultural areas to the markets were very high. In these conditions of low physical productivity and high-cost transportation, abundant land was not associated with a high value of output per worker in agriculture.

The highest productivity sectors in agriculture were in the export activities. This is indicated by the ability of the plantation-owners concerned in the major export products, coffee and sugar, to bid away scarce factors from other activities in their respective regional economies. Access to these activities was limited, however, by relatively large minimum scale, high capital intensity, and imperfections in the capital and land markets. The principal export commodities required substantial capital, both for production and for processing (which was usually done by the same enterprise). Because of capital-market imperfections, large and medium-size plantations dominated the major export activities, and there was little supply from peasants or family farms. Furthermore, in contrast with the United States, where following the Revolution a more equal distribution of power and a more egalitarian political ethos dictated a liberal land policy, the Brazilian government did not make available public lands in relatively small lots and on favourable credit terms for family farmers. On the contrary, one of the main effects of the country's first land legislation, in 1850 and 1854, was to facilitate appropriation of land by the large plantation-owners, to the detriment of squatter families. As oligopsonists in local labour markets, the large landowners also used their economic and political power to deny freeholders secure tenure of land in plantation areas, in order to lower the cost of such free labour as they employed. These general conditions affecting the value of output per worker were especially important, for they helped prevent Brazil from beginning the twentieth century with a relatively high level of labour productivity. In a comparative perspective, the Brazilian experience suggests how relatively unimportant abundant land was *per se* in the economic development of the United States.

III

Wages and the demand for labour within Brazil were also very much influenced by the institution which dominated the country's labour market—slavery. The effects of slavery on wages were especially important in nineteenth-century Brazil, for slaves were used in plantation agriculture throughout the settled regions of the country. This situation contrasted with that in the United States, where slavery was concentrated in one region, the South, and did not directly influence labour-market conditions in the rest of the economy.

Slave labour was a close substitute for unskilled (as well as for skilled) free labour in production. The user cost of slave-labour services was determined by (*a*) the costs of capturing and transporting slaves from Africa, (*b*) the interest rate on the capital employed in the stock of slaves, and (*c*) the maintenance costs of slaves. Interest costs appear to have been relatively high in Brazil, but the standard of living provided for slaves was very low. Until 1850, moreover, when the British government stopped the importation of slaves from Africa, the supply price of slaves was apparently very low in relation to the income stream produced with their labour.

The supply price of free labour was determined primarily by the opportunity cost of the income forgone in its alternative occupations. This labour was mainly confined to the domestic agricultural sector where, for the reasons cited, its productivity was not high. Nevertheless, people in this sector had an income (which included leisure as well as the returns to their capital and entrepreneurship) which was appreciably above the user costs of slave labour. This is attested by the fact that slaves were used in preference to free workers in Brazil's major export activities during most of the century. In addition, whenever proposals were discussed for replacing slave labour in Brazil, it was usually in terms of importing indentured workers from Europe or the Orient (or occasionally, in terms of forced impressment of workers from within Brazil): the wages necessary to attract free workers from the domestic agricultural sector were considered relatively high.

The availability of slave labour during the first half of the century, then, imposed a ceiling on the wages which employers were willing to offer free workers in Brazil. As a consequence, free workers were not widely used in the activities with a high marginal value-product of labour during the first half of the century. Apart from its implications for the distribution of income, the elastic supply of labour which was made possible by the importation of slaves limited the extent to which the expansion of output in Brazil's higher productivity export activities led to absorption of domestic workers, eventually with rising real wages, from the domestic subsistence sector. Thus, this was a case of "unlimited supply" of *imported* labour to the expanding, more productive sector. In this respect, the Brazilian case seems closer to the model discussed by Myint in connexion with the "opening" of Africa and Asia than to closed-economy models of unlimited labour supply. The lower labour costs made possible because of slavery also reduced the pressures for capital deepening or technical progress.

With the suspension of overseas importation of slaves, the internal price of slaves rose sharply. The country's dwindling slave population was then reallocated to the activities (mainly coffee production on new lands in São Paulo) where, because their marginal value-product was greatest, the highest prices could be paid for slaves. At the same time, free workers were increasingly employed in the export sector, albeit not in the products in which labour productivity was highest, where, for the reason just mentioned, slaves continued to be used. The planters also began adopting rationalization practices and labour-saving techniques on a wider scale. The way in which Brazil dealt with the long-term labour problem posed by the abolition of slavery, however, reversed this movement and resulted in a reversion to the earlier pattern. As pressures for the end of slavery increased and the percentage of slaves in the Brazilian labour force declined, large-scale European immigration to Brazil began. This immigration was attracted, however, not by rising wages in Brazil but by the Brazilian government's payment of the immigrants' transportation costs, thus increasing the net private returns to immigration. The inflow of unskilled workers from abroad was so great that real wages of the immigrants in São Paulo province may actually have fallen between the 1880's and 1914, a period of rapid economic growth in that region.

IV

The transition to a free labour force in Brazil meant that an increasing percentage of the labour force was placed in a situation of more competitive rather than predatory wage determination. The market position of free workers in Brazil may have been strengthened because of the alternative opportunities afforded by the availability of land in the Brazilian hinterland, where they had an income higher than the implicit wages to slaves. Because of the higher opportunity income available to free workers in Brazil, the decline in slavery and the transition to free labour may have led to an improved distribution of income in favour of the lower classes. Consequently, at least until the 1870's and the onset of large-scale immigration, their welfare may have improved at a rate greater than indicated by the growth in *per capita* income alone.

The fall in the number of slaves also helped smooth Brazil's course through the political crisis engendered by the campaign for abolition. Although the use of slavery remained privately profitable until the end, it did not loom large enough in the economy for abolition to cause a major upheaval, as it did in the United States. Finally, the decline of slavery also stimulated Brazil's efforts to attract European immigration. It was only after the cessation of overseas slave importation that Brazil began to attract substantial European immigration. These immigrants, however, came largely from southern Europe rather than from the technologically more advanced European countries. Moreover, most of the immigrants were unskilled and uneducated. Consequently European immigration probably did not make as large an absolute contribution to the Brazilian human-capital stock as did European immigration to the United States. Without denying the contribution which immigrants sometimes made with entrepreneurship and specific skills, it would be misleading to overlook the fact that the greatest effect of large-scale immigration was to increase the supply of labour and exert a downward pressure on wages.

V

For the country as a whole, *per capita* income in nineteenth-century Brazil seems to have increased at only a moderate rate, but grew at an accelerated pace after 1900. The conditions affecting economic development in this economy will now be considered.

Rates of capital formation do not appear to have been high in Brazil during most of the nineteenth century. Investment data for these years are not available, but statistics on the composition of Brazilian imports from the United Kingdom in 1835 do not give the impression of a high rate of fixed investment. Only £153,000, or less than 6 per cent of imports from the United Kingdom, consisted of hardware or iron. Much of Brazilian capital formation during these years was in the form of newly cleared and planted land, and imported iron and hardware would have been required because Brazil did not have a domestic iron industry. The low percentage of iron or hardware in Brazil's imports from the United Kingdom is especially noteworthy since the share of imports in Brazilian national income was low in the nineteenth century, while the United Kingdom dominated in the overseas supply of investment goods to Brazil.

Later in the century, the share of capital goods (defined more broadly than iron and hardware) in Brazilian imports from the United Kingdom rose—to 16 per cent in the 1850's and 1860's, 25 per cent in the 1870's, 28 per cent in the 1880's, and 38 per cent in the 1890's. This change in the composition of imports may in part reflect a substitution of imports for domestically made investment goods—e.g. railway cars for traditional means of conveyance. Aggregate investment rates may therefore not have risen as much as did the share of capital goods in imports from the United Kingdom. Moreover, the shift in the composition of imports occurred during a period when the value of *per capita* foreign trade in Brazil was rising at only a modest rate, 1.6 per cent per annum. Consequently, if total investment was proportionate to imports of capital goods, these data would still not indicate a very high rate of capital formation. In the last quinquennium of the century, capital-good imports from the United Kingdom amounted to an annual average of only £12.1 million.

If we attempt to take account of the capital formation which occurred in the form of newly cleared and planted land, a similar picture emerges. The most prosperous sector was coffee, where the quantum exported grew at an annual trend rate of 5.3 per cent between 1822 and 1873, and at 3.8 per cent between 1874 and 1913. Assuming no significant technical progress or changes in factor proportions, the capital stock in coffee would have grown at a rate approximately similar to the growth in the export quantum. By all accounts, however, coffee was the most rapidly expanding part of the agricultural sector. At the same time coffee, and indeed total exports, did not account for an overwhelmingly large share of total agricultural output in Brazil. Consequently, the rate of capital formation in the agricultural sector as a whole may have been well below the rate in coffee.

Why aggregate rates of capital formation may have been low in nineteenth-century Brazil is another question. Indeed, it might have been expected that in an economy with chronic inflation, wealth-holders would hold a relatively large portion of their assets in real capital rather than in money. One possible explanation is that a low rate of real capital formation may have been due to the possibilities for accumulating wealth in land—to which access was limited by institutional conditions—rather than in fixed capital. In any case, a relatively low rate of measured saving and investment in Brazil as compared with, say, the United States, cannot simply be attributed to attitudes biased towards present consumption; for rates of return on investment may not have been similar in the two countries. The material, cited below, on the relatively small magnitude of British investment in Brazil during most of the century suggests that (private) rates of return may indeed have been relatively low, perhaps due to an absence of external economies.

Finally, we should note that the impact of the capital formation which did occur on capital-labour ratios—which is the relevant consideration from the viewpoint of economic progress—was mitigated by the high rates of growth of the country's population and labour supply. This was particularly the case in the advanced sector of the economy, where the labour force grew at an especially rapid pace, both because of such internal labour reallocation as took place and because the imported slave and immigrant labour were directed to the advanced sector.

VI

Exports seem to have been the principal avenue to economic development in nineteenth-century Brazil. It was mainly access to the world market and the demand conditions that it offered to a producer with Brazil's factor endowment that permitted growth in income despite a rate of fixed investment and of technical progress which, as discussed below, seem to have been very low. Growth in income based on exports and a high foreign-trade multiplier, in turn, provided a domestic market which permitted rapid industrial development. After 1850, a textile industry emerged in Brazil, whose output grew at an annual rate of 10 per cent in the fifty years before 1914. There is also evidence for similar development in other industries during this period. As a result of the growth of exports, therefore, the region which enjoyed a rapid expansion in trade—Rio de Janeiro and São Paulo—experienced considerable development during the nineteenth century. The main difficulty for a broad process of export-led development in nineteenth-century Brazil was simply that a large part of the country did not experience a rapid increase, on a sufficiently large scale, in the value of *per capita* exports.

A standard two-sector growth process, in which the rate of growth is augmented by a significant rate of technical progress in the "advanced" sector, may also have been hampered in Brazil because the rate of productivity increase in the "modern" sector of export agriculture and manufacturing seems in fact to have been low. New activities such as coffee, railroads, and manufacturing emerged and permitted a rise in total factor productivity. The productivity increase, how-ever, seems to have been limited mainly to a once-for-all shift, due to intersec-toral factor reallocation. Within the new activities, large, continuing productivity increases, which might have been a major source of autonomous development, do not seem to have occurred. Although there are reports of individual producers improving their efficiency in the use of capital and labour inputs, the general rule appears to have been traditionalism and relatively static technology. Some evi-dence for this suggestion is available from the data on productivity increase in the cotton textile industry.

Substantial increased efficiency did not occur over a fifty-year span in this in-fant industry. If anything, the facilities for technical progress were probably greater in manufacturing than in agriculture; both because of the larger scope for learning-curve gains, and because more productive technology developed in the advanced countries could be readily imported in the form of equipment. In agri-culture, by contrast, improved techniques suitable for tropical commodities had to be developed domestically or, at the least, adapted to local ecological condi-tions.

A low rate of technical progress and a low level of technology in nineteenth-century Brazil may clearly have been related to the country's meagre human-capital stock. Only 7 per cent of the cohort aged 7–11 is estimated to have been enrolled in primary schools in 1857. Educational enrolments were much lower than in countries which were experiencing substantial economic development during the nineteenth century. Although Brazil's enrolments grew rapidly during the second half of the century, as late as 1907 only 20 per cent of the cohort aged 7–11 was enrolled. The percentage enrolments in secondary and university edu-cation were even lower.

The reasons for the low level of the Brazilian human-capital stock are not en-tirely clear. It cannot be attributed simply to the special conditions created by slavery. Indeed, as late as 1877 only some 22 per cent of the *free* population (in-cluding immigrants) was literate. With slave labour a non-competing factor, an abundance of slave workers would, of course, *raise* the rates of return to educa-tion for the free population. In any case, at least after 1869 (see Table 3), the an-nual rates of growth of primary-school enrolments were not low. Hence a policy on the part of the *élite* to limit the availability of education does not seem plausi-ble for that period. The low percentage of enrolments at the end of the century therefore seems to be the result mainly of the poor initial condition of the schooling system, and the effects of rapid population growth in diluting the ab-solute increase in enrolments.

VII

Like most other studies of the nineteenth-century Brazilian economy, the discus-sion thus far has focused on the relatively small, higher-productivity sector of the economy. The greater availability of data for this sector, however, should not lead us to exaggerate its importance. The main reason for the slow growth of *per capita* output in Brazil before 1900 undoubtedly lay in the conditions of the do-mestic agricultural sector, which employed a large portion of the country's labour force. Detailed data on this sector are scanty, but the main lines of the picture appear clear.

This sector seems to have consisted of two parts. First, there were free men living in or near the areas of export production. The access of these people to secure tenure of land was, however, limited by the country's land policies. Their productivity in the occupations in which they engaged was probably also affected adversely by low educational levels. In addition, part of the labour force in the domestic agricultural sector was engaged in farming on the abundant lands in the interior of Brazil, relatively far from the areas of export production. Output consisted largely of cattle-ranching and especially of semi-subsistence agricultural cultivation. In the latter case, in the absence of marked economies of scale in the technology used and in the commodities produced, production was mainly in the form of small-scale, family farming under the overlordship of a local large landowner. With labour scarce relative to land, cultivation was extensive. And, since population in this sector was growing exogenously while abundant lands existed farther in the interior, the frontier shifted ever farther from the centres of consumption. During the first three-quarters of the century, there is no reason to believe that the rate of growth of output *per capita* in this sector was, at best, more than extremely modest. The poor growth conditions in the domestic agricultural sector slowed the pace of aggregate economic development both by employing such a large share of the country's labour force in this sector and, indirectly, by depriving the industrial sector of a large internal market.

Railways might have helped this situation by lowering transportation costs. This would have provided a necessary condition for linking part of the domestic agricultural sector with the rest of the economy, and permitting it to shift from subsistence to market-oriented production (for the domestic market or for exports), whether in family farms or in large-scale agriculture. Lower transportation costs would have provided producers with the stimulus of market demand and with the incentive of new, market-produced, consumption goods. On the demand side, this might have affected the marginal rate of substitution between consumption and leisure and led to higher output levels. On the supply side, producers would have been able to reap the gains from specialization and comparative advantage. However . . . large-scale railroad construction began very late in Brazil. To give some comparative perspective we should note that in 1900 railway mileage in the United States was almost 20 times as great as in Brazil. In 1914, after the large post–1900 increase in railway construction, Brazil had only 16,400 miles of track, a figure which the United States had surpassed by the 1850's.

Moreover, most of the early railway construction was limited to the areas of export agriculture, and did not serve the more distant areas of the domestic agricultural sector. The great increase in railway construction reaching beyond the export agriculture areas began only in the 1890's, and the largest absolute rise in railway track occurred as late as the twenty years before 1914.

Once the railways were extended beyond the areas of export production, however, development does in some cases seem to have proceeded along the lines outlined above. Producers appear to have responded with increasing output, raising income and further integrating the economy by import-substitution in foodstuffs. Thus, the extension of the railway network, with its associated linkage effects, may have been a key factor responsible for the onset of sustained Brazilian growth after 1900. This experience is also consistent with interpreting the country's earlier stagnation as at least in part due to the absence of low-cost transportation, which was of special importance to a land-surplus economy like Brazil.

VIII

Why were the railways built so late in nineteenth-century Brazil? Some of the first railroads in the coffee region were built with local capital participation. In general, however, construction of Brazil's railways depended heavily on foreign investment, which in the nineteenth century was largely British. British investment was not directed to Brazil by non-market considerations such as imperial policy. And the private rate of return on Brazilian railway investments was apparently not high enough to attract substantial British capital from its alternative opportunities during most of this period. Just as Brazil was unable to compete with the United States to attract much of the international flow of human capital during the nineteenth century, so too the country did not receive much of the limited flow of financial investment before the turn of the century.

It is not surprising that private investors were not eager to build railways through the Brazilian hinterland. Such railways, through sparsely populated and undeveloped land, could have been justified only in terms of external economies and social returns. This development task could have been undertaken only by government—central, provincial, or local—as were some of the "public improvements" in the nineteenth-century United States.

Brazilian government in the nineteenth century had notable achievements to its credit. The imperial regime was able to avoid the frequent armed strife that characterized some other Latin American countries during the century. It was also able to hold the country together, coping successfully with the threat of territorial fragmentation. With its gradualist policies, it also spared Brazil a cataclysmic crisis in dealing with abolition. Although Brazilian governments in the nineteenth century were able to ensure relative political stability, until the turn of the century they did not fill a major entrepreneurial role, and did not provide on a sufficient scale the external economies needed for the country's economic development.

IX

This discussion raises an important identification problem. Was the government's failure to play a larger entrepreneurial role until the turn of the century due primarily to conditions on the "demand" side—the pressures which made themselves felt in terms of the current ideology, political conditions, and regime? Or was it due largely to conditions on the "supply" side—a lack of the financial, administrative, intellectual, and political resources required to implement a large infrastructure programme?

The material necessary to answer this question definitively is not available, but a number of relevant points should be noted. First, "demand" conditions do not seem to have been the major problem. This is suggested by the fact that nineteenth-century Brazilian governments did implement measures—for example, subsidized immigration, protective tariffs, and loose monetary policies—which were believed to be developmental but which did not require a large resource input on their part. This presence of favourable demand conditions for developmental policies in a country dominated by large landowners should not, of course, be surprising. On the contrary, following Schumpeter's insight concerning the convergence of monopoly and socialism, large landowners should be especially energetic in pressing for public investment, because with their extensive holdings and market power they can internalize and appropriate much of the benefits of infrastructure facilities. Furthermore, given elastic supply conditions for public goods, in a system with a small number of very large landowners the availability of public goods should be closer to the social optimum than in a more egalitarian society, for the returns to individual participation in public affairs are greater.

It has been suggested, however, that landowners may have opposed the building of railroads, especially to the hinterland, because such construction would have raised their labour costs: first, by creating new demand for workers in construction, and second, by lowering the costs to their workers of outward migration to the abundant unoccupied lands of the interior. These considerations do not appear relevant in the Brazilian case, however, because of the elastic supply of manpower from overseas. In addition, lower transportation costs from the interior might even have reduced wage costs, by shifting downward the supply curve for (wage-good) foodstuffs and by increasing its elasticity.

Turning to the supply side of inputs to a large-scale programme of government infrastructure activity, during the nineteenth century the expenditures of the central government did grow rapidly. With the exception of the period 1878–97, the central government was able to increase its expenditure, in real terms, steadily and at a relatively high rate. This was particularly the case, however, in the period following 1897, when expenditure in constant sterling grew at an annual trend rate of 10 per cent.

Detailed data are not available on the allocation of these growing expenditures, or the efficiency with which they were used. However, central government expenditure was not allocated as single-mindedly to the military as has sometimes been supposed.

Despite the rapid growth of central government finance, however, the absolute magnitude of the financial resources available to the government until the turn of the century may not have been sufficient to mount a large-scale public investment programme. Government taxation revenues were heavily dependent on duties on foreign trade, which were administratively relatively easy to collect. As in other large countries, however, the size of the external sector was not great in relation to the rest of the economy. In these conditions of limited resources, the government understandably concentrated on providing infrastructure facilities for the export activities, where immediate returns—not least, to itself—were highest. In this process the development of the large Brazilian hinterland was delayed. It is also noteworthy that the emergence of more energetic efforts to develop the interior followed the establishment in 1889 of a federal constitution. This new governmental structure decentralized power and functions, and gave individual states greater capacity to promote their own development.

X

The foregoing explanation of Brazil's economic stagnation during the nineteenth century in terms of externalities and the inadequate entrepreneurial performance of government may appear supremely conventional. However, the discussion does omit some other factors which have sometimes been suggested as serious obstacles to economic development.

It appears, for example, that the importance of Brazil's cultural tradition as a barrier to economic development has previously been overstressed, for much of the country's economic retardation can be explained in terms of structural economic and political conditions. Indeed, there is even some evidence that despite the alleged limitations of the Iberian cultural heritage, the Brazilian export sector was characterized by a relatively rapid supply adjustment process. There is, of course, more to economic development than rapid supply adjustment, and socio-cultural conditions may clearly have been at the root of the country's technical backwardness and low educational level. Even here, however, "values" *per se* should not be invoked as a blanket explanation or a substitute for analysis of relevant political and economic structural conditions.

Brazil's social structure also seems to have been less rigidly cast in a two-class, master-slave mould than has sometimes been suggested. Even in the heart of the coffee region, in 1872, fully 49 per cent of the population was free, and only a small percentage of these were plantation owners. In addition, the decline of the percentage of slaves in the population was accompanied by a sharp rise in the number of free mulattoes, who came to constitute a lower-middle stratum in the country's social and economic structure.

Furthermore, Brazilian policy-makers were not, as has sometimes been suggested, culturally alienated and constrained by an undue deference to orthodox economic ideology and policies "developed elsewhere but inappropriate for a country like Brazil". In fact, Brazil displayed considerable flexibility and heterodoxy in its economic policies, for example, following a protectionist trade policy, and a paper money rather than a gold standard foreign-exchange regime. In addition, the Brazilians early perceived the possible advantages of loose monetary and fiscal policies. The result, however, was chronic inflation. Despite generally favourable movements in the terms of trade, monetary expansion was such that the exchange rate depreciated at an annual trend rate of 1.2 per cent between 1822 and the world depression year of 1873; and at 1.7 per cent between 1874 and 1914. Although rapid monetary expansion may at times have facilitated industrial growth, it did not lead to generalized development of the Brazilian economy.

Colonialism has also been proposed as an explanation of economic stagnation in the less developed countries during the nineteenth century. Although Brazil was not formally a colony, it has been suggested that the country was part of the "informal" British Empire, and that the political and economic relations which this entailed slowed economic development. Great Britain did have considerable diplomatic influence in Brazil, and an 1810 treaty which, until 1844, limited Brazil's freedom to impose protective tariffs probably did retard Brazilian industrialization. Brazil might have been better off as an exporter, indeed, had it been part of the *formal* empire, for Brazilian exports of sugar, coffee, and tobacco were excluded from the British market during the first half of the century. Neither of these conditions, however, had much impact on the central feature of nineteenth-century Brazil's economic stagnation—the failure to develop the domestic agricultural sector. Responsibility for this task necessarily lay with the Brazilian government, and it is hard to see how colonialism prevented the government from proceeding with this task. In fact, when the Brazilian government did begin moving more energetically to develop the country with infrastructure programmes, it found that access to the London financial market provided it with significant capital resources. In 1913, the value of British investments in Brazilian government loans and railway securities amounted to a sum which, in terms of contemporary prices, income levels, and population, can only be considered impressive, £179 million.

The Brazilian experience thus suggests that absence of some of the often cited barriers to development may be a necessary, but not a sufficient, condition for economic development. Political independence and an absence of imperialist domination, the existence of an elastic money supply, supply responsiveness, and relative political stability seem to fit into this category.

XI

This article has attempted to reconstruct and analyse the main features of the Brazilian economy and its development in the nineteenth century. It has also analysed the conditions underlying the slow growth of *per capita* income for the country as a whole before 1900. The institutional mechanisms employed to permit low labour costs and to control access to land combined to prevent "real" factor endowments from inducing a high labour-productivity form of agricultural exploitation. The concentration of Brazil's landowners on increasing the supply of labour in order to maintain their returns—rather than, or in conjunction with, a similar emphasis on capital formation and technical progress—had important consequences both for productivity and for the distribution of income. Finally, the government failed to provide early in the century and on a sufficient scale the external economies in transportation and education which were necessary for the development of this sector.

The Brazilian experience suggests that even in a country with abundant resources of land, rapid population increase which permits a continuing situation of "unlimited" labour supply may not be consistent with generalized economic development. In the nineteenth century, the elastic supply of low-cost (unskilled) labour came from abroad, in the form first of slaves from Africa and subsequently of immigrants from southern Europe. In the twentieth century, populist and national policies led to the restriction of this immigration. By that time, however, internal rates of population increase had so risen that the pattern of economic growth with abundant labour supply, with its attendant effects on the growth of labour incomes, continued.

Nathaniel H. Leff, "Economic Retardation in Ninetheenth-Century Brazil," *Economic History Review* 25, no. 3 (August 1972): 489–507.

13

Factor Endowments, Institutions, and Differential Paths of Growth Among New World Economies:

A View from Economic Historians of the United States

STANLEY L. ENGERMAN

KENNETH L. SOKOLOFF

Economic historians of the United States, with their traditional reliance on Europe as the reference point, normally focus on factor endowments in accounting for the record of economic growth. They routinely attribute the country's long history of high and relatively equally distributed incomes, as well as impressive rates of advance, to an extraordinarily favorable resource endowment.

Puzzles arise, however, when scholars of the United States turn to the experiences of Latin American economies. These other New World societies also began with—by European standards of the time—vast supplies of land and natural resources per person and were among the most prosperous and coveted of the colonies in the seventeenth and eighteenth centuries. Indeed, so promising were these other regions that Europeans of the time generally regarded the thirteen British colonies on the North American mainland and Canada as of relatively marginal economic interest—an opinion evidently shared by Native Americans who had concentrated disproportionately in the areas the Spanish eventually developed. Yet, despite their similar, if not less favorable, factor endowments, the United States and Canada ultimately proved to be far more successful than the other colonies in realizing sustained economic growth over time. This stark contrast in performance suggests that factor endowments alone cannot explain the diversity of outcomes. In so doing, however, it raises the question of what can.

Those seeking to account for the divergent paths of the United States and Latin America have usually made reference to differences in institutions, where the concept is interpreted broadly to encompass not only formal political and legal structures but culture as well. Many specific contrasts in institutions have been proposed as being potentially significant, including the degree of democracy, the extent of rent seeking, security in property rights, the inclination to work hard or be entrepreneurial, as well as culture and religion. Where there is explicit discussion of sources of institutional differences, the norm has been to relate them to presumed exogenous differences between British, Spanish, Portuguese, and various Native American heritages. Although the possible influences of factor endowments on the path of economic and institutional development have been neither ignored nor excluded, few scholars have attempted to identify or explore systematic patterns. It is as if the deviance of the Latin American economies from the United States model has in itself been viewed as evidence of the predominance of exogenous, idiosyncratic factors. In reality, of course, it is the United States that proved to be the atypical case.

In this chapter, we explore the possibility that the role of factor endowments has been underestimated and the independence of institutional development from the factor endowments exaggerated.

A Brief Sketch of the Growth of the New World Economies

Systematic estimates of the records of relative per capita income over time have not yet been constructed for many of the New World economies, but the existing figures suggest that the advantage in per capita income enjoyed by the United States (and Canada) over Latin American economies materialized during the late eighteenth and nineteenth centuries, when the United States (as well as Canada) began to realize sustained economic growth well ahead of its neighbors in the hemisphere. Indeed, as John Coatsworth has suggested, there may have been virtual parity (given the roughness of the estimates) in terms of per capita income in 1700 between Mexico and the British colonies on the mainland that were to become the United States. Moreover, product per capita appears to have been far greater in the sugar islands of the Caribbean, where David Eltis finds that in Barbados the level was more than 50 percent higher. If the current estimates are correct, then those of European descent in Mexico and Barbados were much better off than their counterparts on the North American mainland, because they accounted for a much smaller share of the population and their incomes were far higher than those of the Native Americans or slaves. Estimates of per capita income for other Latin American economies do not extend as far back, but it does seem apparent that they must have been closer to U.S. levels during this era than they have been since. Moreover, by the same logic as proposed for Mexico, incomes for populations of European descent must have been comparable or higher in South America and the Caribbean than in the northern parts of North America.

Although all of the major New World colonies may have provided high living standards for Europeans, it is clear that they evolved dissimilar economic structures and institutions early in their histories. This divergence has long been noted and explanations have often made reference to differences in the origins or backgrounds of the settlers. With the recent accumulation of evidence of wide disparities among colonies of the same European country, however, alternative sources of diversity deserve a re-examination. We argue that the United States and Canada were relatively unusual among New World colonies, because their factor endowments (including climates, soils, and the density of native populations) predisposed them toward paths with relatively equal distributions of wealth and income and corresponding institutions that favored the participation of a broad range of the population in commercial activity. This is significant, in our view, because the patterns of early industrialization in the United States suggest that such widespread involvement in commercial activity was quite important in realizing the onset of economic growth. In contrast, the factor endowments of the other New World colonies led to highly unequal distributions of wealth, income, human capital, and political power early in their histories, along with institutions that protected the elites. Together, these conditions inhibited the spread of commercial activity among the general population, lessening, in our view, the prospects for growth.

It is convenient for both our exposition and analysis to define three types of New World colonies. The usefulness of these abstractions, drawn from the uniqueness of each society, must be judged ultimately by how meaningful and coherent our stylized types are and by the explanatory power they help provide. Our first category encompasses those colonies that possessed climates and soils that were extremely well suited for the production of sugar and other highly valued crops characterized by extensive scale economies associated with the use of slaves. Most of these sugar colonies, including Barbados, Brazil, Cuba, and Jamaica, were in the West Indies, but there were also a number in South America. They specialized in the production of such crops early in their histories, and through the persistent working of technological advantage their economies came to be dominated by large slave plantations and their populations by slaves of African descent. The greater efficiency of the very large plantations, and the overwhelming fraction of their populations that was black and slaves, made their distributions of wealth and human capital typically extremely unequal. Even among the free population, there was greater inequality in such economies than in those on the North American mainland.

Although the basis for the predominance of an elite class in such colonies may have been the enormous advantages in sugar production available to those able to assemble a large company of slaves, as well as the extreme disparities in human capital between blacks and whites, the long-term success and stability of the members of this elite was also undoubtedly aided by their disproportionate political influence. Together with the legally codified inequality intrinsic to slavery, the greater inequality in wealth contributed to the evolution of institutions that commonly protected the privileges of the elites and restricted opportunities for the broad mass of the population to participate fully in the commercial economy even after the abolition of slavery. Progress in these postemancipation economies was further slowed by the difficulties of adjusting to the loss of the productive technology on which they had long been based.

A second category of New World colonies includes exclusively Spanish colonies like Mexico and Peru, which were characterized by relatively substantial numbers of natives surviving contact with the European colonizers and by the distribution among a privileged few (*encomenderos*) of claims to often enormous blocs of native labor, land, and mineral resources. The resulting large-scale estates, established by grant early in the histories of these colonies, were to some degree based on preconquest social organizations, whereby Indian elites extracted tribute from the general population, and endured even where the principal production activities were lacking in economies of scale. Although small-scale production was typical of grain agriculture during this era, their essentially nontradeable property rights to tribute (in the form of labor and other resources) from rather sedentary groups of natives gave large landholders the means (a major competitive advantage) and the motive to continue to operate at a large scale. For different reasons, therefore, this category of colony was rather like the first in generating an economic structure in which large-scale enterprises were predominant, as was a very unequal distribution of wealth. This second type of colony relied on the labor of natives with low levels of human capital instead of slaves; in both cases, however, the elites were racially distinct from the bulk of the population. Instead of the existence of scale economies in slavery supporting the competitive success or persistence of the largest units of production, large-scale enterprises in this second class of colonial economies were sustained by the disinclination or difficulty of the natives in evading their obligations to the estate-owning families and in obtaining positions that allowed them to participate fully in the commercial economy. These estates were not unlike feudal manors, where lords held claims on the local population that could not be easily transferred and where labor mobility was limited.

To almost the same degree as in the colonial sugar economies, the economic structures that evolved in this second class of colonies were greatly influenced by the factor endowments, viewed in broad terms. Although the Spanish need not have treated the native population as a resource like land, to be allocated to a narrow elite, the abundance of low-human-capital labor was certainly a major contributor to the extremely unequal distributions of wealth and income that generally came to prevail in these economies. Moreover, without the rich supply of native labor, it is highly unlikely that Spain could have maintained its policies of restriction of European migration to its colonies and of generous awards of property and tribute to the earliest settlers. The early settlers in Spanish America endorsed having formidable requirements for obtaining permission to go to the New World—a policy that undoubtedly limited the flow of migrants and helped to preserve the political and economic advantages enjoyed by those who had earlier made the move. A larger number of Europeans vying for favors would have raised the cost of maintaining the same level of benefits to all comers, as well as increased the competition, political and otherwise, for the special privileges enjoyed by the early arrivals. Because of the differences in settlement patterns, the fights for control between creoles and *peninsulares* took a quite different form in Spanish America than did the colonial-metropolitan conflicts of British America.

Paths of development similar to that observed in Mexico are repeated in virtually all of the Spanish colonies that retained substantial native populations. During the initial phase of conquest and settlement, the Spanish authorities allocated *encomiendas,* often involving vast areas along with claims on labor and tribute from natives, to relatively small numbers of individuals. The value of these grants was somewhat eroded over time by reassignment or expiration, new awards, and the precipitous decline of the native population over the sixteenth century that necessarily decreased the amount of tribute to be extracted. These *encomiendas* had powerful lingering effects, however, and ultimately gave way to large-scale *estancias* or haciendas, which obtained their labor services partially through obligations from natives but increasingly through local labor markets. Although the processes of transition from *encomienda* to hacienda are not well understood, it is evident that large-scale agriculture remained dominant, especially in districts with linkages to extensive markets. It is also clear that the distribution of wealth remained highly unequal, not only at given points in time but also over time, because elite families were able to maintain their status over generations. These same families, of course, generally acted as *corregidors* and other local representatives of the Spanish government in the countryside, wielding considerable local political authority.

The final category of New World colonies is best typified by the colonies on the North American mainland—chiefly those that became the United States, but inclusive of Canada as well. With the exception of the southern states of the United States, these economies were not endowed with substantial indigenous populations able to provide labor nor with climates and soils that gave them a comparative advantage in the production of crops characterized by major economies of scale or of slave labor. For these reasons, their growth and development, especially north of the Chesapeake, were based on labor of European descent who had similar and relatively high levels of human capital. Correspondingly equal distributions of wealth were also encouraged by the limited advantages to large producers in the production of grains and hays predominant in regions like the Middle Atlantic and New England. With abundant land and low capital requirements, the great majority of adult men were able to operate as independent proprietors. Conditions were somewhat different in the southern colonies, where crops like tobacco and rice did exhibit some limited scale economies, but even here, the size of the slave plantations, as well as the degree of inequality in these colonies, was quite modest by the standards of Brazil or the sugar islands.

Spain had several colonies on the South American mainland that might also be placed in this category. Most notable among them is Argentina, although the Indian share of the population there remained high into the 1800's. Despite not being suited for growing sugar as a major crop, and ultimately flourishing as a producer of grains, the economy came to be characterized by substantial inequality in the distribution of land. Rooted in large grants to military leaders and favored families, this inequality may have persisted because of scale economies in raising cattle on the pampas. Argentina failed to attract many immigrants until well into the nineteenth century and remained a relative backwater, partially because of Spanish restrictions on European immigration and on trade, as well as the relative absence of lures like valuable mineral resources or stocks of readily available native labor (these were concentrated in the southern part of the country). Despite such ambiguous cases, however, there appears to be no serious question that the structure of the economies in the northern colonies of the North American mainland was quite different from those of their counterparts elsewhere in the New World.

In our discussion of the first two categories of New World colonies, we raised the possibility that the relatively small fractions of their populations composed of whites, as well as their highly unequal distributions of wealth, may have contributed to the evolution of political, legal, and economic institutions that were less favorable toward full participation in the commercial economy by a broad spectrum of the population. The deviant case represented by the United States and Canada highlights this point. It seems unlikely to have been coincidental that those colonies with more homogenous populations, in terms of both human capital and other forms of wealth, evolved a set of institutions that were more oriented towards the economic aspirations of the bulk of the adult male population.

The Role of Institutions in Shaping Factor Endowment

We have suggested that various features of the factor endowments of three categories of New World economies, including soils, climates, and the size or density of the native population, may have predisposed those colonies toward paths of development associated with different degrees of inequality in wealth, human capital, and political power, as well as with different potentials for economic growth. Although these conditions might reasonably be treated as exogenous at the beginning of European colonization, it is clear that such an assumption becomes increasingly tenuous as one moves later in time after settlement. Factor endowment may influence the directions in which institutions evolve, but these institutions in turn ultimately affect the evolution of the factor endowment. It is our contention, however, that the initial conditions had long, lingering effects, both because government policies and other institutions tended generally to reproduce the sorts of factor endowments that gave rise to them and because certain fundamental characteristics of the New World economies and their factor endowments were difficult to change.

Crucial legislation influencing the evolution of the factor endowment, as well as the pace and pattern of economic development in the New World colonies, were those relevant to land policy, policy regarding immigration, and the regulation of trading arrangements between colonies, the metropolis, and the outside world.

During the colonial period, there were significant differences throughout the New World in immigration patterns and policies.

The British, fearing overpopulation at home and responding to the perception in the colonies of an acute scarcity of labor, actively encouraged immigration to their colonies, first those in the Caribbean and then those on the mainland. Indeed, the right to migrate to British colonies remained open for people from other European countries, generating a more diverse white population and a broader base of participation in the commercial economy than was to be found elsewhere. In stark contrast, Spanish immigration was tightly controlled and even declined somewhat over time. Not only was Spain believed to be suffering from underpopulation rather than overpopulation, but the advantages that served as implicit subsidies provided to those who migrated led to a concern for limiting the flow as well. The authorities in Spain were motivated by a desire to keep costs down, while those who had already migrated sought to maintain their levels of support and privileged positions. A restrictive stance toward further immigration could not have been retained, however, if there had not already been a substantial supply of Indians to work the land and otherwise service the assets owned by the elites and the Spanish Crown; in this sense, at least, the policy must have been due to the factor endowment.

After the wave of independence movements early in the nineteenth century, most nations introduced or followed a relatively free immigration policy to attract new workers, mainly from Europe, with only a few restrictions on the racial or ethnic composition of the immigrants. Indeed, several countries advertised for migrants and attempted to induce, by subsidy (including land grants) or other measures, more permanent arrivals. Despite the marked easing of restrictions on immigration by Latin American countries, however, by far the dominant stream of European transatlantic migratory flows over the nineteenth century was directed to the United States, reflecting both the larger size of its economy as well as the hoped-for greater opportunities possible with the higher per capita income, the more equal distributions of wealth and political power, and the greater availability of small landholdings. It was not until late in the century that the Latin American economies received substantial new inflows of labor from Europe.

There was, even here, another important difference in the nature of the immigrants to the United States, Canada, and to Latin America. The former two received migrants primarily from northwestern Europe, where economic growth was already under way and literacy was expanding. The major recipients in Latin America drew mainly from areas that had lagged, such as Argentina from Italy and Spain and Brazil principally from Italy and Portugal. Thus, even after restrictions on European migration were lifted, it is probable that those going to the United States and Canada had generally higher levels of human capital than those moving to Latin America.

Because the governments of each colony or nation were regarded as the owners of the land, they were able to set those policies that would influence the pace of settlement for effective production, as well as the distribution of wealth, by controlling its availability, setting prices, establishing minimum or maximum acreages, granting tax credits, and designing tax systems. Land policy could also be used to affect the labor force, either by encouraging immigration through making it readily available or by increasing the pool of wage labor through limiting availability. In most cases, although there were initial attempts at a slow, orderly process of settlement, this became more difficult to control over time. In the United States, where there were never major obstacles, the terms of land acquisition became easier over the course of the nineteenth century. Similar changes were sought around the middle of the nineteenth century in both Argentina and Brazil as a means to encourage immigration, but these seem to have been less successful than in the United States and Canada in getting land to smallholders. That the major crops produced in the expansion of the United States and Canada were grains, permitting relatively small farms given the technology of the times, may help explain why such a policy of smallholding was implemented and was effective. But as the example of Argentina indicates, small-scale production of wheat was possible even with ownership of land in large units, maintaining a greater degree of overall inequality in wealth and political power. Argentina, in the second half of the nineteenth century, was somewhat unusual in not having a national land policy, that being left to individual state governments. Unlike in the United States, however, where rivalry among the sub-federal governments seemed to spur investment in transportation infrastructure and banks, accelerating the pace of economic growth, no such beneficial effects were manifest in Argentina. Thus, the nature of factor endowments (inclusive of soils, climates, the composition and relative sizes of populations, and existing distributions of land and political power), as well as the particular crops grown, did influence land policies, and the particular land policies pursued in different areas had significant impacts on future levels and distributions of income.

The basic tripartite classification of New World colonies indicates that the United States (particularly the northern states) and Canada, with their reliance on grain agriculture and relatively small landholdings, were unique both in their rates of long-term growth and degrees of equality. The basic influence of their factor endowments was reinforced by their policies of offering small units of land for disposal and maintaining open immigration, particularly by Europeans. Elsewhere there were large landholdings, greater inequality, and ultimately, a later achievement, if any, of modern economic growth. In much of the Caribbean, this reflected the importance of sugar plantations producing for world markets and the large number of slaves in their populations. In areas such as Mexico (where corn was the principal crop), Peru, and Argentina, land and labor policies led to large landholdings and great inequality, whether on the basis of large numbers of Native Americans (as in Mexico and Peru) or with immigrant renters (as in Argentina). The latter nations had relatively few Africans and only a small plantation sector, but their patterns of land distribution during the earlier stages of settlement meant that more substantial inequalities were generated than in the United States and Canada.

The Extent of Inequality and the Timing of Industrialization

We have argued above that, despite the high living standards all New World colonies offered Europeans, fundamental differences in their factor endowments, which were perpetuated by government policies, may have predisposed them toward different long-term growth paths. Most of these economies developed extremely unequal distributions of wealth, human capital, and political power early in their histories as colonies and maintained them after independence. The United States and Canada stand out as rather exceptional in being characterized from the beginning by high material living standards among both elites and common people, as well as by relative equality in other dimensions. It may, we suggest, not be coincidental that the economies in this latter group began to industrialize much earlier and thus realized more growth over the long run.

The idea that the degree of equality or of democracy in a society might be associated with its potential for realizing economic growth is hardly new. On the contrary, controversy over the existence and nature of the relationship can be traced back a long way. Those who favor the notion that relatively unequal distributions of wealth and income have proved conducive to the onset of growth traditionally credit higher savings or investment rates by the prosperous. Their focus on the capability for mobilizing large amounts of capital stems from a belief that either major capital deepening or the introduction of a radically new generation of technologies and capital equipment was necessary for sustained growth, and skepticism that labor-intensive sectors or enterprises of small scale could have generated much in terms of technological progress. Proponents of the opposite view have held that greater equality in circumstances has historically stimulated growth among early industrializers through encouraging the evolution of more extensive networks of markets, including that for labor, and commercialization in general. This provided impetus to self-sustaining processes whereby expanding markets induce, and in turn are induced by, more effective or intensified use of resources, the realization of scale economies, higher rates of inventive activity, and other forms of human capital accumulation, as well as increased specialization by factors of production. This perspective views the acceleration of economic growth as the cumulative impact of incremental advances made by individuals throughout the economy, rather than being driven by progress in a single industry or the actions of a narrow elite. By highlighting how the extension of markets elicits responses from broad segments of the population, this school of thought suggests a greater potential for economic growth where there are both high per capita incomes and relative equality in circumstances.

Despite the complexity of the relationship between equality and the onset of growth, and the likelihood that it varies with context, we believe that recent studies on the processes of early industrialization in the United States provide support to the hypothesis that those New World economies with more equality were better positioned to realize economic growth during the eighteenth and early nineteenth centuries. The new evidence comes primarily from investigations of the sources and nature of productivity growth during that era when the United States pulled ahead. Studies of both agriculture and manufacturing have found that productivity increased substantially during the first stages of industrialization and that the advances were based largely on changes in organizations, methods, and designs that did not require much in the way of capital deepening or dramatically new capital equipment. Estimates of manufacturing productivity growth between 1820 and 1860 indicate that a wide range of manufacturing industries were able to raise productivity at nearly modern rates, despite the small firm sizes and limited diffusion of mechanization and inanimate sources of power characteristic of most industries until the 1850's.

This pattern of relatively balanced productivity growth across a broad spectrum of industries is difficult to attribute to a fundamental break-through in technology or a general increase in the capital intensity of production. On the contrary, it appears instead to be more consistent with the hypothesis that firms and individuals throughout the economy were responding to a common environmental stimulus for improvements in technology—like the dramatic expansion of markets that characterized the period. Indeed, this view, that broad advances in productivity were induced by the growth in volume and geographic extent of commerce, originating in the extension of networks of low-cost transportation and increases in income, has received strong support from recent scholarship. Studies of agriculture have found that farms with easy access to major markets became more specialized, used their labor more intensively, and were more apt to adopt new crops and products. Studies of manufacturing have found that firms in proximity to broad markets maintained higher average levels of productivity and were generally distinguished by operating at a larger scale, with a more extensive division (and perhaps intensification) of labor, and with a more standardized product—but without markedly different ratios of capital to labor.

Recent work with U.S. patent records has perhaps more directly demonstrated that the growth of inventive activity was strongly and positively associated with the extension of markets as economic growth began to accelerate during the first half of the nineteenth century. Not only was patenting higher in districts with such access to broad markets, but the construction of canals or other additions to the transportation infrastructure yielded immediate and large jumps in patenting activity. Also indicative of the importance of contact with the market, and economic opportunity more generally, was the widening range of social classes represented among patentees in those geographic areas where patenting per capita rose. The proportion of urban patentees who were from elite occupations fell sharply as rates of patenting first began to rise rapidly from 1805 on.

A broad spectrum of the population appears to have become engaged in looking for better ways of carrying out production, spurring the rate at which improved methods diffused as well as boosting rates of invention and innovation. Moreover, the association between patenting and access to broad markets held for ordinary patents as well as for the presumably more important patents (on average) awarded to the "great inventors." Evidence that manufacturing firms in districts with higher patenting rates, holding other factors constant, had higher total factor productivity provides further support to the interpretation that invention and technical change were genuinely induced by the expansion of markets.

There are several reasons for believing that the association of markets with economic growth during the first half of the nineteenth century is relevant to the question of whether the condition of greater overall equality was an important contributor to the earlier onset of industrialization in the United States than elsewhere in the New World. First, the coincidence of high per capita incomes with equality would be expected to attract relatively more resources to the production and elaboration of standardized manufactures, because free whites of the middling sort would ultimately expend higher shares of their income on manufactures than would the poor (or than slaveholders would expend on their slaves). Moreover, although the wealthy might also devote large shares of income to manufactures, they generally consumed manufactures that were nonstandard or customized. This is significant, both because markets were more likely to develop around goods or assets with uniform characteristics and because many of the most fundamental advances in technology during the nineteenth century were concerned with the production of standardized manufacturing products.

Second, greater equality in wealth, human capital, and political power likely promoted the evolution of broad, deep markets through the supply side as well. In some cases, the stimulus was associated with the existence of scale economies in activities, such as transportation or financial intermediation, with high fixed costs or capital intensity. Greater densities of potential users and beneficiaries raised the projected returns on investment in such projects and facilitated the mobilization of necessary political and financial backing. In the northeast region of the United States, for example, the great majority of banks and much of the transportation infrastructure (roads and canals) in place during the initial phase of growth were organized locally and relied on broad public participation and use. Without the substantial numbers of small businesses (including farms) and households seeking better access to product and capital markets, there would have been less potential for realizing the substantial scale economies characteristic of transportation and financial intermediation—and much less investment in these crucial areas.

Greater equality in economic circumstances among the U.S. population not only encouraged investment in financial intermediaries and transportation directly through the structure of demand but also through a legal framework that was conducive to private enterprise in both law and administration. The right to charter corporations was reserved to state governments, and this authority was generously wielded in order to promote investments first in transportation and financial institutions but ultimately in manufacturing as well. Responding to widespread sentiment that there should be few obstacles to private initiatives, as well as to opposition to privilege, many state governments had in effect routinized the process of forming a corporation with general laws of incorporation by the middle of the nineteenth century. Another example of a legal system that encouraged private enterprise is provided by the relationship between equality and rates of invention. Not only is it likely that the greater equality in human capital accounted partially for the high rates of invention in the United States overall, but the more general concern with the opportunities for extracting the returns from invention contributed to a patent system that was probably the most favorable in the world to common people at the time. This pattern stands in stark contrast to that in Mexico and Brazil, where patents were restricted by costs and procedures to the wealthy or influential and where the rights to organize corporations and financial institutions were granted sparingly, largely to protect the value of rights already held by powerful interests. Differences in the degree of equality in circumstances between these economies and the United States seem likely to play an important role in explaining the divergence in experience. For a variety of reasons, therefore, a large degree of inequality might be expected to hamper the evolution of markets and hence delay the realization of sustained economic growth.

One might ask whether one can legitimately draw inferences about what the experiences of the New World economies in Latin America could have been like from the experience of the United States. Our implicit assumption is that there was a fundamental nature to the process of early economic growth during the eighteenth and nineteenth centuries, prior to the widespread introduction of mechanization and other heavily capital-intensive technologies, that was essentially the same across all economies.

Many scholars have long been concerned with why the United States and Canada have been so much more successful over time than other New World economies since the era of European colonization. As we and others have noted, all of the New World societies enjoyed high levels of product per capita early in their histories. The divergence in paths can be traced back to the achievement of sustained economic growth by the United States and Canada during the eighteenth and early nineteenth centuries, while the others did not manage to attain this goal until late in the nineteenth or in the twentieth century, if ever. Although many explanations have been offered, in this chapter we have highlighted the relevance of substantial differences in the degree of inequality in wealth, human capital, and political power in accounting for the divergence in the records of growth. Moreover, we have suggested that the roots of these disparities in the extent of inequality lay in differences in the initial factor endowments of the respective colonies. Of particular significance for generating extreme inequality were the suitability of some regions for the cultivation of sugar and other highly valued commodities, in which economies of production could be achieved through the use of slaves, as well as the presence in some colonies of large concentrations of Native Americans. Both of these conditions encouraged the evolution of societies where relatively small elites of European descent could hold highly disproportionate shares of the wealth, human capital, and political power—and establish economic and political dominance over the mass of the population. Conspicuously absent from the nearly all-inclusive list of New World colonies with these conditions were the British settlements in the northern part of the North American continent.

We have also called attention to the tendencies of governmental policies toward maintaining the basic thrust of the initial factor endowment or the same general degree of inequality along their respective economy's path of development. The atypical immigration policies of Spanish America have been given special emphasis in this regard; while other European nations promoted and experienced mushrooming immigration to their New World colonies, Spain restricted the flows of Europeans, leading to a stagnant or declining number of migrants to its settlements during the late seventeenth and eighteenth centuries. It was not until late in the nineteenth century that former Spanish colonies like Argentina began to recruit and attract Europeans in sufficiently large quantities to shift the composition of their populations and erode the rather elite status and positions of the small communities of old families of European descent. The New World economies that had long histories of importing slaves to exploit the advantages of their soils and climates for the production of crops like sugar also continued to be characterized by much inequality and to be dominated by small, white segments of their populations. Why extreme inequality persisted for centuries in these classes of New World economies is unclear. Certainly large deficits in wealth, human capital, and political power, such as plagued Native Americans and slaves (and free blacks, after emancipation), are difficult to overcome, especially in preindustrial societies. Elites would be expected to (and did) use their political control to restrict competition they faced over resources, and large gaps in literacy, familiarity with technology or markets, and in other forms of human capital could take generations to close in even a free and seemingly evenhanded society. Indeed, these factors undoubtedly go far in explaining the persistence of inequality over the long run in the New World cases of concern here. The close correspondences between economic standing and race, however, may also have contributed to the maintenance of substantial inequality, either through natural, unconscious processes or by increasing the efficacy of direct action by elites to retain their privileged positions and holdings.

Stanley L. Engerman and Kenneth L. Sokoloff, "Factor Endowments, Institutions, and Differential Paths of Growth Among New World Economies," in Stephen Haber, ed., *How Latin America Fell Behind: Essays on the Economic Histories of Brazil and Mexico* (Stanford: Stanford University Press, 1997): 260–304.

14

Latin American Manufacturing and the First World War

RORY MILLER

Introduction

In the last decade there has appeared a considerable amount of research on the early history of manufacturing industry in Latin America, which has thrown into some doubt the analysis of earlier economists, writing in the 1950s and 1960s. Many, especially perhaps those connected with the United Nations' Economic Commission for Latin America, and the earlier writers of the "dependency" school, once saw the most important periods of industrial growth in Latin America as coinciding exactly with weakened links between the international economy and the region. In the words of Frank:

> It is clearly established and generally recognized that the most important recent in-
> dustrial development—especially that of Argentina, Brazil, Mexico, but also of other
> countries such as Chile, has taken place precisely during the periods of the two world
> wars . . . Thanks to the consequent weakening of trade and investment ties the satel-
> lites initiated marked autonomous industrialisation and growth.

This paper raises substantial doubts about the idea that the First World War was a period of major industrial advance in Latin America.

The paper concentrates on the experience of five countries—Argentina, Brazil, Chile, Colombia and Peru—and draws heavily on discussions of textile industries. This, however, was a major area for import substitution, a sector where the market was established, technology was readily available, raw fibres often obtainable locally, yet still, in 1919, a vital part of Britain's export trade to Latin America.

Industry Before 1914

Although some historians, in the 1940s and 1950s, commented on the pre-war roots of industrial growth in Latin America, only in the last decade has it become possible to obtain a more reliable and detailed picture of industry in the period before 1914, especially in the medium-sized economies. Estimates for Argentina suggest that manufacturing already contributed around 14% of GDP in 1900–1904, a proportion maintained, despite rapidly rising exports of primary products, until the war. Indeed exports and factory expansion were intricately linked, the most important plants being in areas like meat-packing and flour-milling. The converse of this concentration of Argentina's industrial effort in export-processing was a relatively slow rate of import substitution. This contrasted with Brazil where import substitution, especially in the field of cotton textiles, had made impressive advances by 1914.

Industrial growth, whether linked to export processing or to import substitution, was not confined, before 1914, to the two or three largest economies. Textiles, matches, soap, hardware, beer, cigarettes and similar products were all being produced in local factories in Chile, Peru and Colombia before 1914. In Chile, after the Pacific War (1879–1883), local foundries had even turned out locomotives for the state railways as well as machinery for the nitrate industry, expanding into export markets in neighbouring countries. In Peru favourable movements in tariffs and exchange rates, late in the 1890s, had provided some protection for local factories, the most impressive growth taking place in textiles where local supplies of cotton and wool were abundant. Though not on the scale of Brazil or Mexico, Peruvian mills were producing 23 million yd of cloth even in 1905—over 40% of the domestic market, from which they had almost eliminated imports of unbleached cloth. In both these countries there are perhaps some signs of a loss of the initial dynamism immediately before the war, but in Colombia industrial expansion was still proceeding rapidly, especially in Antioquia, under the impetus of a succession of protective measures. Indeed a sign of the industrial growth was the occurrence, in each of these countries sometime in the 20 years before the First World War, of a vigorous debate between industrialists favouring protection and an opposition coalition, which included both exporters and workers and drew attention to the harmful effects of "artificial" industries (like flour-milling and matches in Peru and Colombia or sugar refining in Chile) on government revenues from import tariffs and on prices.

The War and Industry

Initially the war seems to have further exacerbated the existing lack of business confidence in Latin American markets. Reports from throughout the continent remarked on the high level of stocks of imported and local products which could only slowly be released onto the market. One of the two cotton mills in Cartagena was consequently closed for the first half of 1915. As import shortages grew, however, the opportunity arose for traders to dispose of their stocks at high prices, which also gave some impetus to branches of local manufacturing industry. Reports later in the war noted several instances where the war had stimulated local production: dairy products and quebracho extract in Argentina, textiles, footwear and meat-packing in Brazil, textiles in Colombia. Selected cases of growth in output do not, however, incontrovertibly prove the importance of the war to industry. Some countries may have benefited more than others, some sectors stagnated because of wartime, in others prices and profits rose but without a corresponding increase in output and investment.

The only substantial industrial growth in Argentina during the war occurred in textiles, where the value of production doubled between 1914 and 1919. Textiles, however, accounted for only 5% of industrial production. Diaz Alejandro accepts a decline in Argentine manufacturing in real terms of 17% between 1913 and 1917. This recession, he argues, remained the severest on record in the 20th century until the 1960s. Using the same figures Gallo notes a revival in manufacturing only in 1918. Even this represented only a recovery to the 1913 level.

Brazilian manufacturers did benefit from the war, producing more and selling it at higher prices. However, there is little evidence of any major new investment. The clearest example of a new activity occurred not in a business affected by import shortages but in meat-packing for export. Moreover, the south and centre may have gained more than the north.

As in the Brazilian case, interpretations of Chile's industrial performance have been substantially revised, particularly with the development of more trustworthy estimates of industrial production before and during the war. After a full analysis of the statistical data Kirsch concludes: 'A closer examination of the available data and other ancillary material cause far more moderate enthusiasm with respect to the significance of the war to domestic manufacturing . . . There was, however, an upturn from 1917.' Peruvian manufacturers, according to American reports, profited greatly from the high prices obtainable during the war. This, however, must be put into the perspective of de Lavalle's post-war lament that 'unfortunately the war has created no new industry in our country'. The experience of Colombia also provokes scepticism. The cotton mills earned large profits and imported much new machinery, particularly for spinning and dyeing processes, after the armistice. However, Colombia did not until then reduce its dependence on imported yarn, changing instead from British to American supplies. The profits and post-war expansion of cotton textiles must again be placed in context. The trend towards spinning yarn in Colombia had begun before the war, and the war may have delayed it by hindering imports of capital goods. High profits later in the war had to make up for the business depression and mill closures of 1914–1915. Moreover the experience of cotton textiles may not have been typical of industry as a whole. One American consul reported from Cartagena in 1917 that the European conflict 'has disorganized business in general and discouraged any attempt to extend the existing industries or to undertake new ones until peace is restored'. His Barranquilla counterpart noted at the same time: 'Cotton growing, spinning, and weaving were the only industries which did not suffer as a result of the general world conditions.'

Overall, therefore, the performance of Latin American industry during the war does not agree with the expectations of proponents of the 'adverse-shocks' theory of Latin American development. It seems unlikely that the war stimulated any upward trend in the rate of growth of the manufacturing sector. High prices and profits arising from the utilization of excess capacity after 1915 must be balanced against the extremely difficult year of adjustment after the outbreak of war, the continuing problems of many branches of industry, and the shortage of new investment until after the peace. Rising output seems to have been confined either to existing industries with spare capacity (and even there, as the cases of brewing and flour-milling in Argentina show, it was not automatic), or to activities linked to exports like meat-packing, or to those organized in fairly small plants using local inputs like the dairies and wool-washing plants in Argentina, and leather products in Brazil. It is the poor performance of Latin American industry during the war, in particular the lack of new investment and diversification, that needs analysing.

Some Explanations

One starting point is to consider the level of economic activity and the pattern of demand for industrial products. Aggregate demand depended heavily on export earnings, foreign investment, and government expenditure. Latin American exports suffered almost immediately on the outbreak of war as a result of the rapid stockpiling of essential supplies by the belligerents coupled with shipping shortages and rising freight rates. Thereafter some export prices increased, but there were marked variations from one product to another. Consequently some countries benefited quickly but others took longer to recover. At the one extreme Peru made exceptional profits from the high prices attained by the country's major exports, cotton and sugar. There is little evidence, however, that this brought any significant expansion of the local market, since real wages were falling, or that the profits accumulated were used later for investment in manufacturing. At the other extreme both Brazil and Colombia suffered from low coffee prices until frosts and state intervention in Brazil pushed prices up again in 1919.

Argentina was especially affected by the halting of further inflows of foreign capital. Construction activity, a key indicator of the health of the economy, fell, for example, by over 80% between 1913 and 1917. Overall it is doubtful that new investment from the United States could come near to counteracting the withdrawal of access to British, French and German capital markets, though there might be exceptions. Government revenues and expenditure must also have suffered in a period of business depression and low imports, which, in normal times, provided an important source of income. Even in Peru, whose trade began to recover earlier than most, government expenditure did not exceed the 1913 level until 1918.

Poor export prices for certain products, the withdrawal of access to foreign capital markets, and the curtailment of government expenditure all depressed demand in Latin America until the second half of the war, and, in some cases, until after the armistice. It emphasized, at least in the short term, the dependence of Latin American industry on domestic markets fuelled by rising exports and foreign investment. For the most part, moreover, Latin American industrialists in 1914 relied on the sale of articles of high mass consumption: foodstuffs, beverages, tobacco, textiles, clothing and foot-wear. In Brazil in 1919, 80% of value added came from consumer goods, one-third from food-processing alone. The Chilean figures for 1917 show that the products mentioned accounted for over 75% of industrial output.

Changes in real wages would thus be vital to the prospects of manufacturing. Wage/price data for Latin America in this period, even for the capital cities, are extremely unreliable. Qualitative and quantitative evidence would, however, suggest a decline in real wages, which contributed to the wave of strikes through Latin America in the second half of the war and following the peace. In Argentina real wages fell by one-third between 1914 and 1918. Wages both in Peruvian export agriculture and in Lima appear to have remained static until 1918, despite the doubling of prices of foodstuffs, like sugar, rice, lard, meat, and of rents. The American consul in São Paulo noted there the enormous rise in the price of staple foodstuffs. In fact some of the market distortions caused by the war hindered the growth of manufacturing. High export prices for Peruvian products diverted land away from foodstuffs, leaving less income available to the consumer of manufactured products. High prices and profits for one group of industrialists reduced the opportunities for others.

The overall picture, therefore, is one of high prices and profits for existing manufacturers who could use excess capacity to take advantage of the distortion in international trade caused by the war. The problems of the export sector, however, and the decline in real wages limited the possibilities of expansion, despite growing shortages of some imports once the overstocking of 1914 had disappeared and the United States entered the war. Several new plants were founded during the war, especially in Brazil, but on the whole the level of new investment appears to have been very much less than in the 20 years before 1914. To explain this in more detail it is necessary to consider businessmen's perceptions of the future, their dependence on imports of machinery and other inputs, and changes in tariffs and exchange rates which helped to reduce the competitiveness of Latin American industry.

In August 1914, after a year of recession in Latin American markets, importers and wholesalers were holding large stocks, and most, in Latin America as in Europe, expected the war to last only a few months. Business confidence did not totally revive after 1915–1916. Throughout the war Colombian textile mills feared an imminent drop in prices, their current profits being seen very much as a windfall. News of the armistice in November 1918 provoked an immediate fall in prices to clear stocks in the expectation that European manufacturers would immediately begin exporting. Only in mid–1919, with stocks low and demand buoyant as a result of record coffee exports, did it become clear that Colombian industry could still expect good profits. Colombia was not unique. Many Latin American businessmen, quite justifiably, viewed the wartime conditions as exceptional and remained unprepared to make significant new investment in areas where they feared renewed competition from imports after the war.

Latin American industry relied both on imports of equipment and machinery and of other inputs. In Chile and Colombia textile mills depended on imported yams. Flour mills and breweries needed foreign technology and materials. Argentina could not survive without imported fuel. Argentine imports of coal from Britain fell from an average of 3.4 million tons in 1911–1913 to less than 300,000 tons in 1918. Imports from the United States, which did not exceed a million tons until 1920, failed to fill the gap. Cotton textiles needed British machinery, the lack of which prevented one mill in Peru from opening until after the war. The inability to secure machinery limited the extension of factories in Brazil after 1915, even before the market became demoralized in 1918. More expensive cottons needed imported bleaches and dyes. Local supplies of cotton and wool fibres rose in price for local industrialists because of export demand later in the war. There was little incentive to switch to American sources of machinery. The American commercial statistics show that the value of exports of shoe machinery to Latin America, despite the rise in its price, did not exceed the 1913 level until 1919. Imports of textile machinery from the United States showed some growth late in the war in Argentina, Chile and Peru, but the real expansion did not occur until 1919–1920.

Tariff and exchange rate movements also discouraged import substitution. Both Argentina and Peru suffered from high exchange rates. The common use of specific duties, which did not keep pace with inflation, rather than *ad valorem* tariffs, led to a decline in the level of effective protection. In Peru duties had been 22% of the value of imports in 1913, but fell to 10% in 1918. For Colombia the corresponding figures were 44 and 22%. In Argentina effective protection declined in 1917 to 69% of the 1914 level, and in 1918 to 48%.

Conclusions

The 'adverse-shocks' theory overestimated the importance of the First World War to Latin American industry through the failure to appreciate the extent of growth in the 1895–1913 period and by overlooking the serious hindrances to expansion created by the war. The wartime years fell into two phases: an initial period of depression followed by a recovery which allowed manufacturers to utilize excess capacity to take advantage of high prices. In some countries, however, such as Argentina and Colombia (with the exception there of textiles), the recovery from the 1913–1914 recession did not develop real momentum until after the war. New investment remained low, reviving in 1919–1920 only under the stimulus of an export boom. The manufacture of new products was severely hindered by the shortage of capital goods and other inputs, although there were several examples of some import substitution where new plants could take advantage of local raw material supplies. Some growth also occurred in some export-processing activities. In retrospect one must conclude that in none of these five countries can the wartime period be distinguished as one of significant and lasting initiatives in manufacturing industry, but rather as one of windfall profits and limited expansion on the basis established before 1914.

Rory Miller, "Latin American Manufacturing and the First World War: An Exploratory Essay," *World Development* 9, no. 8 (August 1981): 707–16.

15

Latin America in the 1930s

CARLOS F. DIAZ ALEJANDRO

Introduction

Latin American development experienced a turning-point during the 1930s. The contrast between 'before and after 1929' may often be exaggerated, but there is little doubt that the decade witnessed a closing toward international trade and finance, and a relative upsurge of import-substituting activities, primarily but not exclusively in manufacturing. Other trends visible before 1929, such as urbanisation and a growing interest by the State in promoting economic development, continued into the 1930s and accelerated in some countries. Memories of the 1930s have profoundly influenced the region's attitude toward international trade and finance; per capita foreign trade indicators reached by the late 1920s were not surpassed in many nations until the 1960s.

At least some Latin American economies performed surprisingly well during the 1930s, relative to North America, and relative to what average opinion would have expected to happen in quite open, primary-product exporting nations. This essay will view the economic performance of each country as the result of the magnitude of the exogenous external shock received, of the policy measures undertaken by domestic authorities to speed adjustment to those shocks, and of the resilience of local private agents in responding to the new constellation of profit opportunities, including those opened up by new technologies and products. Shocks, policies and capacities to transform differed substantially from country to country.

Ability and willingness to manipulate policy instruments such as nominal exchange rates, tariffs and domestic credit were greatest in countries which were either relatively large, such as Brazil, or had relatively autonomous public sectors, such as Costa Rica and Uruguay. Smaller countries, e.g. Honduras, or those with highly dependent governments, e.g. Cuba, had less room for policy manoeuvre. The generalisation that largeness and policy autonomy were favourable to performance covers only republics with nominal sovereignty. Paradoxically, some clear-cut colonies in the Caribbean appear to have performed better than Cuba or the Dominican Republic.

The rest of the chapter will chronicle how various Latin American countries coped with the crisis and the extent to which they were able to mobilise mechanisms of adjustment beyond deflation. The nature and magnitudes of the external shocks will first be narrated. Second, the various policy reactions to those shocks will be discussed, covering measures seeking to regain external and internal balance, as well as policies targeted toward longer-term goals. Then the global, sectoral and welfare performances will be explored, and the sense in which economies did or did not do reasonably well will be analysed. In evaluating performance, emphasis will be placed on quantitative indicators. An overall interpretation of events during the 1930s will close the paper.

External Shocks and Trends

The breakdown during 1929–33 of the international economic order was transmitted to Latin America first of all by sharp changes in relative prices: dollar export prices collapsed more steeply than dollar import prices. Within four years the terms of trade fell by 21 to 45% in countries for which comparable data are available. Latin American terms of trade had, of course, experienced steep declines before, as during 1920–1, but the magnitude of the collapse combined, for many countries, with the continuation of unfavourable terms of trade throughout the rest of the decade, in spite of some post–1933 recovery, was unprecedented at least during the era of export-led growth. The terms of trade deterioration may be regarded as primarily exogenous to Latin America; countries which could influence the international prices of their exports, such as Brazil, had been doing so since earlier in the century. During the early 1930s other Latin American countries began regulating their traditional exports so as not to worsen further their dollar prices.

For a country with a ratio of exports to Gross National Product (GNP) of one-third a deterioration of the terms of trade by 30% would represent a loss in real income of about one-tenth, assuming no change in physical output.

During the late 1920s Latin American payments balances were bolstered by large capital inflows, with New York replacing London as the leading source of long-term portfolio funds. Already during 1929, well before Latin American countries showed signs of skipping scheduled servicing of the external debt or blocking profit remittances, gross capital inflows fell sharply. After mid-1930 little fresh capital came in. With the dollar price level falling unexpectedly by no less than one-quarter between 1920–9 and 1932–3, debt servicing rose dramatically in real terms, compressing the capacity to import beyond what data on the purchasing power of exports suggest. During the early stages of the crisis the import quantum fell even more than the purchasing power of exports in most countries, as they struggled to meet debt obligations in spite of the cessation of capital inflows. Defaults started in 1931 and by 1934 only Argentina, Haiti and the Dominican Republic maintained normal servicing of their external national debt. From then to the end of the decade import volumes as a rule recovered faster than the purchasing power of exports.

Direct foreign investment, in magnitudes more significant for specific branches of production than for the balance of payments, did not disappear during the 1930s, but shifted its marginal orientation away from traditional exports, export-oriented services and social overhead capital, and toward import substituting activities, with the important Venezuelan exception. This trend had been visible already during the 1920s, particularly in the more developed countries of the region. Exchange controls and multiple exchange rates discouraging profit remittances may have induced in the short run some reinvestment of profits in new local activities, especially after the early 1930s. The late 1930s also witnessed the inflow of refugee capital from Europe, and there were even proposals to make Buenos Aires an international money centre, replacing those threatened by European tensions.

The emergence of a protectionist and nationalistic Centre was the greatest shock to Latin American economies during the 1930s, going beyond its direct negative impact on the region's terms of trade. As late as 1931 it was still unclear whether the decline in economic activity in industrialised countries was another passing recession or something more serious. But by that date it seemed very likely that one was witnessing the end of *laissez-faire* and of the commitment of leading countries to relatively free trade. Already during the 1920s imperial preferences were advocated in Britain by influential groups, and the 1928 presidential election in the USA was accompanied by a protectionist wave. That ferment was followed by passage of the Smoot-Hawley tariff in 1930 and the British Abnormal Importations Act of 1931. Even if prosperity returned to the Centre, the outlook for Latin American exports competitive with production in industrial countries or in their colonies or commonwealths, ranging from sugar and copper to meat, corn and wool, looked grim. As the Depression deepened, protectionism gained ground: British Commonwealth preferences were adopted in Ottawa in 1932, while France, Germany and Japan also reinforced their protectionism and discriminatory trade arrangements for areas under their political hegemony.

It is true that in 1934 Cordell Hull, US Secretary of State, started a policy of reducing US tariffs, but such policy made slow progress, and had to whittle down a tariff wall raised not only by the Smoot-Hawley Act, but also by the deflation-induced increase in the incidence of specific duties. The brightest and best-informed observers of the international economy as it stood by 1934 probably had difficulty in forecasting the shape of the new international economic order for the next ten years, but it is unlikely that they would have urged Latin American countries to wait for export-led expansion. As it turned out, by that date circumstances had pushed many Latin American policy-makers into considerable experimentation, without the need of sage foreign advice, which had sharply depreciated during the crisis.

Policies

As early as 1930 some Latin American policy-makers began to reconsider the wisdom of remaining faithful to the orthodox rules of the game. The reconsideration was not due to new theoretical insights, but to the pressure of circumstances. Maintaining gold parities when foreign-exchange reserves were disappearing and foreign capital markets were practically shut to new Latin American bond issues became foolhardy. Balancing the budget when customs revenues were collapsing and civil servants were rebelling became nearly impossible. Timidly at first and loudly promising a quick return to late 1920s parities and practices, policy-makers in countries where instruments were at hand or where sufficient autonomy allowed their creation began to replace gold-exchange standard rules with 'emergency' discretionary tinkering. Peripheral shame and self-doubts gradually gave way to self-confidence, especially after Britain abandoned the gold standard in 1931 and Germany and the USA embarked on their own experiments.

The thrust of policies adopted by the more autonomous and reactive republics may be viewed as attempts to avoid the costs of the deflation called for by the classical mechanism of adjustment, and to speed up the achievement of a new constellation of relative prices and resource allocation consistent with the post-1929 realities of the international economy.

Exchange-rate Policies

Reactive countries by 1933 had nominal exchange rates relative to the dollar significantly above the late 1920s parities. Lip service was paid to an eventual restoration of the gold standard, but policy-makers in reactive countries went no further than checking 'excessive' depreciations.

Small or very dependent countries, such as Honduras, Haiti, Dominican Republic, Panama and Cuba, maintained their peg to the US dollar throughout the 1930s. The last two countries did not even have a central bank or a corresponding monetary authority, such as those of Brazil or pre-1935 Argentina. Exchange-control measures in the small or passive countries were on the whole less forceful than in reactive countries.

Data on price levels and money wages are scarce for the 1930s, especially for the smaller countries. Nevertheless, available information indicates that nominal devaluations in the reactive countries had weak inflationary consequences, contrary to the experience in later years. By 1930–4, therefore, *real* import-exchange rates with respect to the dollar, which take into account price-level changes domestically and abroad, had risen (depreciated) between 30 and 90% in Argentina, Brazil, Chile, Colombia, Mexico, Peru and Uruguay, relative to 1925–9 levels. Such real prices of dollars in terms of local currency remained at those depreciated levels also during 1935–9.

For the smaller or passive countries one may conjecture that there was no such rapid and large real depreciation of exchange rates. In the Caribbean and Central America the sharpest Depression-induced devaluation occurred in Costa Rica, with a smaller one occurring in El Salvador; other small countries maintained their pegs to the dollar or underwent monetary changes due to domestic turmoil. Some countries having a steady peg to the dollar attempted to raise the ratio of the exchange rate to nominal wages by extraordinarily repressive labour policies; such was the case of Guatemala under General Ubico, at least until 1934.

Regardless of the exchange-rate policy followed, a country subjected to an exogenous and permanent worsening of its international terms of trade should witness over the long run a decline in the price of its non-traded goods and services (or money wages) relative to the domestic price of importable goods, encouraging a movement of resources, including fresh investments, toward the import-competing sector, additional to that generated by the decline in exportable-goods prices. A permanent decline in net long-term capital inflows would also induce a decline in the prices of non-traded goods relative to all traded goods. Countries willing and able to devalue their exchange rate moved toward the new constellation of domestic relative prices more speedily and less painfully than those with fixed rates, limiting both price and monetary deflation, containing their negative impact on real output, or reducing pressures to depress money wages by extraordinary measures.

Trade Policies

The domestic price of importable goods relative to non-traded goods prices, or to money wages, also received an upward push in many Latin American countries as tariffs rose and quantitative restrictions, via import or exchange controls, were introduced. Contrary to what would happen in the late 1940s and 1950s, exchange-rate and *de facto* protectionist policies reinforced each other as import-repressing mechanisms, especially in Brazil and the Southern Cone.

The small or passive countries appear to have been, with some exceptions, as impotent regarding protection as with nominal exchange-rate management. Cuba actually lowered tariffs in 1934, undoing much of the protectionist effect of her anomalous Tariff Act of 1927. Even larger countries were pressured into reversing some of their early-1930s tariff increases; wielding the threat of Commonwealth preferences and meat import quotas, the UK obtained tariff concessions from Argentina under the controversial Roca—Runciman treaty of 1933. Argentina and Cuba shared awkward memberships in 'informal empires', although the autonomy of the former country was, of course, much larger than the latter.

Tariff rates appear to have undergone few changes in levels or structure in Mexico and Peru. These countries also behaved in a manner more like the smaller countries in regard to import and exchange controls; in contrast with Brazil and the Southern Cone they employed those instruments only sparingly. Colombia, as usual, had an intermediate set of policies: most of the change between 1927 and 1936 in the prices of her imported non-traditional manufactures has been attributed to devaluation rather than tariff increases, although increments in effective protection stimulated some industries, including cement, soap and rayon textiles. Colombia also exercised import and exchange controls with greater vigour than did Mexico and Peru.

Debt Policies

Toward the end of the 1920s the stock of British and US investments of all kinds in Latin America amounted, in per capita terms, to about one-sixth those in Canada. The heaviest concentration occurred, in descending order and still in per capita terms, in Cuba, Argentina, Chile, Mexico, Uruguay and Costa Rica. Both in Canada and Latin America the two major foreign investors had accumulated claims of all kinds of around four times the annual value of merchandise exports. Assuming a 5% rate of return, profits and interests of foreign capital must have accounted for about 20% of annual export earnings, and were punctually transferred abroad. With the exception of Mexico the 'investment climate' appeared reasonably good; the nineteenth-century defaults on bonds issued in London had been settled, and while numerous frictions were generated by direct investments they seemed negotiable.

The unexpected post-1929 fall in dollar and sterling prices sharply increased the real cost of external obligations denominated in those currencies. Servicing the Argentine public debt, for example, which had absorbed about 6% of merchandise exports during the late 1920s, by 1933 reached nearly 16% of exports. Chile in 1932 faced interest and amortisation charges, including those on short-term maturities, far exceeding export earnings. The ratio of the stock of long-term external public debt to yearly merchandise exports for all Latin America rose from 1.5 in 1929 to 2.3 in 1935. The drying up of foreign capital markets made roll-over operations for both long- and short-term debt very difficult. The collapse of import-duty revenues cut a traditional budgetary source for payments on the external debt.

Starting in 1931, authorities delayed granting exchange to importers for settling their short-term debt and to foreign companies for profit remittances. Also in 1931, many Latin American countries began to skip scheduled servicing of the external long-term public debt. Defaulting countries did not dramatically repudiate their obligations, but asked foreign creditors for conversations aimed at rescheduling and restructuring the debt. Different countries carried out those conversations with various degrees of enthusiasm: Cuba, for example, while servicing her debt irregularly during the 1930s maintained better relations with her creditors than Brazil, whose dealings with creditors during the late 1930s, especially with British ones, were acrimonious. For many countries those negotiations were to stretch out well into the 1940s, and into the 1950s in some cases. The contrast between Argentine and Brazilian policies toward debt service in the 1930s casts light on the nature of international economic relations during those years. The relative abundance of exchange reserves in Argentina, whose gold holdings remained one of the highest in the world, gaining an important windfall by the increase in the international gold price during the 1930s, plus the fact that a substantial amount of the Argentine sterling- and dollar-denominated debt was held by Argentines (just as a share of 'domestic', peso-denominated debt was held by foreigners) also contributed to punctual servicing of even dollar-denominated bonds, presumably mostly held in the USA, in spite of British hints about the convenience for Anglo-Argentine trade of defaulting on that part of the debt. Furthermore, tampering with the normal servicing of the Argentine debt would have involved not only a bruising commercial clash with the UK, but probably also a major restructuring of the Argentine domestic political scene at the expense of groups linked with Anglo-Argentine trade.

There is little reason to doubt the consensus among those who have examined the Latin American defaults of the 1930s: if the Depression had been mild, and if the steady expansion of world trade and capital flows had been continued, defaults would have been infrequent and could have been settled without much difficulty. Once the Depression came and productive resources were allowed to go to waste in idleness, while countries everywhere restricted imports to protect jobs, it made no economic sense to insist on the transfer of real resources as debt servicing. No doubt the capital markets of the 1920s contained significant imperfections: during the 1930s many underwriters were accused not just of negligence in seeking information about borrowers and their projects, but also of deliberately misleading bond-buyers, motivating New Deal regulatory legislation. Latin American countries were encouraged to borrow excessively, and a good share of the funds went into projects of doubtful social productivity. But one may question whether these microeconomic factors were decisive. One may also note that the industrialised countries themselves led in the undermining of belief in the sanctity of contracts; examples include the British default on the war debt, Germany's failure to make payments on the greater part of her international obligations, the derogation of the gold clause in the USA, and domestic moratoria legislated in several countries.

By the late 1930s foreign-exchange availability had improved and indeed some debt servicing was paid by defaulting Latin American countries throughout the 1930s. Some countries purchased their own partially or wholly unserviced bonds selling at a discount in foreign markets; those bonds by the late 1930s were probably held mostly by speculators. Such 'repatriations' of the debt avoided a rigid settlement schedule at a time when the international economic outlook was very uncertain, and were carried out by central banks, whose financial positions were generally better than those of the Treasuries, which still suffered from the fall and change in composition of imports and the induced decline in duties.

In spite of exchange controls regulating profit remittances abroad by foreign enterprises, direct foreign investments occurred throughout the 1930s, although in amounts more significant for the expansion of specific branches of production than for balance-of-payments equilibrium. It has been argued that the local reinvestment of foreign-enterprise profits may have been encouraged by limitations on remittances abroad, an argument more plausible in the short run than in the long. In some countries exchange controls were also employed to ward off unwanted short-term capital inflows, as in Argentina during the late 1930s; such 'hot money' movements were perceived as destabilising macroeconmic balance. Capital accompanying European refugees was considered a more permanent and welcomed addition to local resources and these combinations of entrepreneurship and finance were important in the expansion of several economic (and cultural) activities in many Latin American countries.

Monetary and Fiscal Policies

The decline in exports and capital inflows signalling the beginning of the crisis was accompanied at once by balance-of-payments deficits which drained reserves and money supplies, according to gold-standard, fixed-exchange rates rules. The export fall had important multiplier effects. This section will examine responses to those deflationary pressures on aggregate demand.

Money-supply data indicate that reactive Latin American countries show briefer or shallower post-1929 declines in nominal money supplies than the USA. By 1932 the Brazilian nominal money supply exceeded that of 1929; the corresponding Colombian date is 1933. The end of convertibility into gold was helpful in stemming the loss of liquidity among reactive countries. In contrast the Cuban inability to break out of the then orthodox rules led to a monetary deflation even greater than that of the USA.

The increase in real money supplies of reactive countries was not just the result of automatic mechanisms of adjustment triggered by the fall in the international price level, but also the result of domestic policies.

Maintenance of liquidity was not simply a matter of ending convertibility into gold or foreign exchange at the old parities. Even after the abandonment of the gold standard some countries, such as Argentina, shipped gold to service the external debt and sold some foreign exchange to stem currency depreciation. Both measures cut the monetary base if orthodox practices were followed. But as early as 1931 South American monetary authorities adopted measures which would have been regarded as unsound during the 1920s. Thus, the Argentine Caja de Conversión whose only classical duty was to exchange gold and foreign exchange for domestic currency at a fixed price, and vice versa, starting in 1931 began to issue domestic currency in exchange for private commercial paper, relying on obscure and nearly forgotten laws, and later on even issued domestic currency against Treasury paper, which was also accepted as payment for gold sent abroad for public debt servicing. Young technocrats in charge of Argentine monetary policy successfully resisted pressures from the orthodox to 'redeem' the Treasury paper, recall the new currency issues, and return to the old parity. The Colombian Central Bank in 1930 for the first time engaged in direct operations with the public, discounting notes and lending on the security of warehouse receipts; during 1931 ingenious subterfuges were found by the Bank to grant credit directly to the central government, involving as 'collateral' future public revenues from a salt mine. Government bonds were purchased from private banks in large quantities by the Colombian Central Bank since 1932. In Colombia, as in other reactive countries, since the introduction of exchange controls in 1931 international reserves ceased to govern monetary issue, which from then on was predominantly influenced by internal considerations of economic policy or budgetary expediency.

The South American and Mexican monetary policies, started around 1932, were in some ways a relapse into past inflationary propensities, a past which was supposed to have been exorcised by the adoption during the 1920s of gold-standard rules and up-to-date budgetary and monetary mechanisms.

The financial impotency of passive countries may be illustrated by the experiences of Cuba. In Cuba modest issues of silver coins were made during 1932–3, and in 1934 a revolutionary government appeared to herald a bold new monetary system independent of the dollar by planning new issues and by making silver pesos full legal tender for the discharge of old as well as new obligations contracted in dollars or in old Cuban gold pesos. Shortly thereafter a mild form of exchange control was decreed. Foreign banks on the island apparently threatened to export all dollars from Cuba; capital flight followed. The government caved in, lifting rather than expanding controls. Only the legal tender status of silver for all contracts in such currency remained of the 1934 reform. Even a Central Bank was to wait until 1948.

Fiscal policy in reactive countries appears to have contributed to the maintenance of aggregate demand, at least in the sense of *not* balancing the budget in the midst of the crisis, in spite of the protestations of policy-makers that they intended to do so. Although data are particularly shaky in this field, real government expenditures were not significantly cut during the early 1930s, while real tax revenues fell as imports collapsed, inducing an increase in fiscal deficits in spite of new taxes and higher tariffs. The financing of budget deficits even in re-active countries during the early 1930s was not all particularly expansionary; payment delays to civil servants and government suppliers increased the 'floating debt', a debt whose holders usually could only turn into cash at huge discounts, thus coming close to forced loans.

Whatever the hesitations and improvisations of the early 1930s, by the second half of the decade the reactive Latin American countries had developed a re-spectable array of both monetary and fiscal tools, as well as the will to use them to avoid deflation.

In passive countries an activist fiscal policy continued to be checked by exigu-ous foreign and domestic demand for public debt, and by convertibility into dol-lars at fixed rates that limited monetary expansion not backed by international reserves.

Performance

Reactive countries on average performed better than passive ones, and in both types of nations some regions did much better than others. National accounts for the four largest Latin American countries (Argentina, Brazil, Colombia and Mex-ico) register growth rates for Gross Domestic Product (GDP) steadier and higher than those of Canada and the USA for 1929–39.

In reactive countries GDP recovery apparently started in 1932, earlier than in the USA. Neither the 1929–32 decline nor the 1932–7 recovery were as dramatic as those in the USA.

Economic performance during the 1930s for the reactive Latin American countries looks even more impressive when attention is focused on manufactur-ing. While growth in this sector during the 1940s and early 1950s was to exceed that for the 1930s in most countries, manufacturing growth rates for 1929–39, ranging from more than 3% per annum in Argentina to more than 8% per an-num in Colombia, far outstripped those of the USA and Canada, which hovered around zero. The relatively modest Argentine manufacturing expansion was higher than that of Australia, even though both countries experienced roughly similar GDP growth rates between 1928 and 1938. In the important Brazilian case, manufacturing growth during the 1930s, of more than 6% per annum, was significantly higher than during the 1920s; the pace of Colombian industrialisa-tion during the 1930s could not have been much behind that of the 1920s, if at all. Another interesting comparison involves Chile and Uruguay, on one side, and Cuba, on the other; the former reactive countries experienced manufacturing ex-pansion of 3 to 5% per annum, while the latter country saw its total industrial production shrink even more than in the USA.

Growth of manufacturing during the recovery phase of the 1930s relied heavily on import substitution. Leading sectors typically included textiles, petroleum re-fining, tyres, pharmaceuticals, toiletries, food-processing for the home market (e.g. vegetable oils), chemicals, cement and other building materials. Cotton and wool textiles were the most important leading sectors, often providing more than 20% of the net expansion of value added in manufacturing, and growing at annual rates above 10%. Between the late 1920s and late 1930s cement production multiplied by more than 14 times in Colombia, by more than 6 times in Brazil and by almost 4 times in Argentina. Even in passive countries one finds some import-substituting industries growing very fast, such as milk-processing and cotton cloth in Cuba, but in the midst of depressed export-related manufacturing.

The industrialisation of the 1930s, at least in South America, was quite labour-intensive, and involved many small- and medium-sized firms. Between 1930 and 1937 industrial employment in São Paulo grew at nearly 11% per year.

Import-substitution also relied heavily on new national and foreign-born entrepreneurs, including fresh immigrants from the troubled Europe of the 1930s. The rise of Hitler and Franco led to significant gains of human and financial capital for Latin America. There was also direct foreign investment in import-substitution by tariff-jumping enterprises, whose home markets showed weak prospects. For sectors like tyres and cement these investments and the technology they supplied provided significant impetus.

New import-substituting activities clustered, not surprisingly, mainly around major consuming centres, such as Buenos Aires, Mexico City and São Paulo. While industrialisation thus contributed to support ongoing urbanisation trends, the latter appear to have had a dynamism of their own, making one sceptical of any close short-term links between the two phenomena.

Import-substitution was the engine of growth during the 1930s, but not just in manufacturing. The rural sector also witnessed gains in the production of goods sold in the domestic market relative to those primarily sold abroad. Food-importing countries, such as those in the Caribbean and Central America, engaged in either modest import-replacement, as in Cuba, or more ambitious efforts as in Guatemala. Countries which during the 1920s imported beverages and cooking oils, like Argentina, turned to domestic substitutes during the 1930s. Cotton textiles imported during the 1920s were replaced partly by value added in expanding local production of cotton, which later led to exports. In contrast with import-replacement in industry, much of agricultural import-substitution was at the expense of intra-Latin American trade, e.g. Argentine production of *yerba maté* was at the expense of imports from Paraguay.

Import-substitution extended to services; those of foreign labour and capital were to a large extent replaced with local inputs or dispensed with, while it is likely that many Argentines substituted visits to Bariloche and Mar del Plata for vacations in Paris. Among expanding sectors one can also find, especially in reactive countries, some producing non-traded goods and services using relatively few imported inputs, such as construction, housing and government.

On the whole income and wealth distribution during the 1930s were buffeted by contradictory influences. Groups linked to traditional exports must have seen their relative and even absolute position decline, in spite of government actions aimed at ameliorating the external blows. Entrepreneurs in import-substituting agriculture and industry must have accumulated handsome profits, with their output fetching high domestic prices while labour and raw-material costs were unusually low. Entrepreneurs who had inherited excess capacity from the 1920s were especially fortunate, receiving unexpected capital gains. High- and middle-class families, with budgets having low shares for foodstuffs and high shares for imported consumer goods, faced unfavourable relative price trends. Beloved durable goods, such as automobiles, or European vacations, became very expensive, and their consumption often was to be postponed for many years. For lower-income groups, whether urban or rural, it is unlikely that real income gains in terms of foodstuffs could have been very substantial; the best guess is that even in reactive countries performing reasonably well by the late 1930s real wages for unskilled and semi-skilled labour, taking into account all components of their consumption basket, were no higher than a decade earlier. Gains in employment security arising from new labour legislation were limited to pockets in the labour force and of moot significance even for them. The tax reforms carried out in several countries were more important for public revenue raising and diversification than for significant changes in income distribution. Perhaps with the exception of Mexico, the 1930s did not witness a discontinuity in the inherited trends for public services in education and health. Secular improvements in literacy and health indicators appear to have continued without obvious leaps or retardations, seemingly following more the sluggish urbanisation trends than the vagaries of import substitution.

A Concluding Interpretation

Much of the evolution of Latin American economies during the 1930s, particularly the coexistence in reactive countries of vigorously growing branches of agriculture and manufacturing with declining or stagnant foreign trade, can be explained as a response to incentives created by policies aimed primarily at coping with balance-of-payments disequilibria generated by the unexpected worsening of the terms of trade and the abrupt cessation of capital inflows. As it became clear that the new constellation of external and domestic relative prices were not fleeting phenomena, and that the international economy was not to return to the pre-1929 rules of the game, both private and public agents reoriented their production and investment plans.

Countries willing and able to devalue their exchange rate forcefully early in the decade moved toward the new pattern of accumulation more speedily than those nations which kept their exchange rate fixed or devalued slightly.

The abandonment of the old parities and of unlimited convertibility into foreign exchange allowed in several countries the maintenance and expansion of domestic liquidity, which combined with other policies led to the reasonably good economic performance in reactive countries. The balance-of-payments crisis and the threat of financial collapse were of greater significance in the adoption of those policies than whether the new governments which came to power during the 1930s represented a shift to the right, as in Argentina, or toward more reformist positions as in Colombia and Mexico. Purely domestic political factors may have accounted for whether or not a country engaged in land reform during the 1930s, but those factors had much less to do in reactive countries with the adoption of policies which induced import substitution. The latter depended on the magnitude of the foreign-exchange and financial crisis, and on country-specific characteristics of the external sector. Thus, revolutionary Mexico was more timid regarding exchange control than conservative Argentina, largely because of its open border with the USA. Policymakers who abandoned gold convertibility, allowed the exchange rate to depreciate, supported banks at the edge of bankruptcy, permitted budget deficits induced by economic and foreign trade decline, and financed them by monetary expansion, on the whole did so moved by survival instincts rather than inspired by the writings of economists, either defunct or live. But in reactive countries, including Chile and Uruguay, the institutional structure was compatible with actions involving a degree of policy autonomy, while in smaller or passive countries, such as Cuba, it was less so.

While the economic performance of reactive countries was reasonably good, per capita real incomes grew less during the 1930s than during the 1920s or 1940s. Had the industrialised countries maintained full employment, open markets for foreign goods and bonds, and a peaceful international environment, it is likely that the aggregate output performance in reactive countries (and of course in passive ones) would have been better. Sectoral patterns of growth would have been different, and it is likely that under such counterfactual circumstances some activities, like cement and textiles, would have grown less than they actually did during the 1930s. The diversification which took place in agriculture, manufacturing, exports and government revenues, as well as in the geographical sources and destination of exports, could very well have been less under the hypothesised counterfactual conditions. It is also conceivable that institutional reforms in banking, taxation and even land tenure would have been weaker. Under the counterfactual circumstances there might have been less structural change but more growth not just in aggregate output, but also in physical and technical capacity. Output growth during the 1930s wore out much of the capital stock accumulated during the 1920s and earlier and was accompanied by relatively little fresh investment and technical change. At the outbreak of the Second World War, a good share of the Latin American social overhead capital and industrial capacity was already stretched thin and at the verge of obsolescence; war shortages were to aggravate these conditions.

The crisis at the Centre did induce policy experimentation in the Periphery. The disastrous news from the rest of the world reaching Latin America during the 1930s made policy-makers and informed opinion feel not only that local conditions were not so bad, after all, but also that no one knew, in Centre or Periphery, exactly what were the roots of the crisis nor how it could be overcome. After a terrible fright, this stimulated an almost exhilarated creativity. The old authorities and rules on economic policy were shattered. It was a time calling for reliance on one's discretion.

Carlos F. Diaz Alejandro, "Latin America in the 1930s," in *Latin America in the 1930s: The Role of the Periphery in World Crisis*, ed. Rosemary Thorp (London: MacMillan, 1984): 17–49.

Section IV

Foreign Trade and
Industrial Policy

One of the most celebrated doctrines in classical economics concerns the superiority of free trade. When goods and services move freely across borders, each country can specialize in items that it produces relatively cheaply and import whatever else it needs. For instance, Venezuela might export oil in exchange for machinery and grain, thereby exploiting its comparative advantage in petroleum. By keeping costs low, this kind of specialization advances the welfare of consumers at home and abroad (Dornbusch, reading 18). Although economists disagree about many subjects, their faith in the benefits of free trade is nearly universal.

Notwithstanding the apparent intellectual consensus, we almost never observe free trade in practice. All countries use import taxes, quotas, or licenses to restrict the flow of international commerce. Why do governments fail to embrace laissez-faire, and why are some administrations more protectionist than others? These questions are central to modern political economy and are particularly salient for Latin America, a region with a checkered history of liberalism and protectionism. The readings in this section help explain the evolution of trade policy in Latin America during the twentieth century.

At the dawn of the twentieth century, many Latin American countries were open to trade. The pattern reversed itself during the Great Depression, when governments throughout the region raised tariffs and began a phase of Import Substituting Industrialization (ISI). Under ISI, each country began producing domestic versions of the machinery and other finished products that it had previously bought from the industrialized North. Policies of ISI persisted until the 1970s, when military dictatorships in the Southern Cone began edging toward freer trade. The real rush toward liberalization began in the 1980s and 1990s, however. During the final two decades of the century, governments throughout Latin America have lowered barriers to imports and signed international trade agreements committing them to keeping their economies open.

Why did Latin American governments adopt ISI in the first place? The economic shocks of the Depression and World War II forced many states to turn inward, but the intellectual influence of Raul Prebisch and his colleagues at the Economic Commission for Latin America (ECLA) also contributed to protectionism. Challenging the conventional wisdom about the advantages of free trade, ECLA economists argued that ISI could help Latin America develop. They reasoned that ISI would reduce the region's vulnerability to volatile commodity prices, arrest the downward trend in the terms of trade, and shelter "infant" industries until they were mature enough to compete in world markets. Cardoso and Helwege (reading 16) rehearse the intellectual case for ISI, note the genuine problems that ISI created, and indicate why countries were primed for a return to free trade.

Of course, Latin America was not the only developing region to experiment with ISI, but protectionist policies lasted longer in Latin America than elsewhere. Why did East Asian countries, such as Korea and Taiwan, turn from ISI to export-oriented growth at an earlier stage? Mahon (reading 17) considers several explanations, which reflect the main analytical approaches in Section II. He examines the alignment of interest groups, the power of state institutions, and the severity of the external crises, but attaches greater importance to the abundance of natural resources in Latin America. This cornucopia became a curse by creating an overvalued exchange rate and making it more difficult for Latin American manufacturers to compete in world markets. Students of international economics will recognize the parallels to the "Dutch Disease," which afflicted the Netherlands in the 1970s. Correcting the problem in Latin America would have required a massive and politically unpopular devaluation.

One of the first Latin American countries to abandon ISI was Mexico. During the 1980s, Presidents Miguel de la Madrid and Carlos Salinas lowered barriers to imports, joined the General Agreement on Tariffs and Trade, and entered a free trade agreement with the United States and Canada. What were the origins of this free trade policy? In searching for an answer, Pastor and Wise (reading 19) scrutinize several key variables, including the rise of intra-industry trade, the weakening of antitrade lobbies, the configuration of political institutions, and the beliefs of Mexican leaders. To these, the authors add another explanatory factor: the link between trade and inflation. By 1987, Mexican inflation was running at 160 percent per year, and the government desperately needed a program to stabilize prices. By subjecting the economy to foreign competition, free trade helped arrest inflation, which in turn broadened the antiprotectionist coalition.

Trade liberalization has occurred not only in Mexico but also in Central and South America. An important example is Mercosur, a customs union involving Argentina, Brazil, Paraguay, and Uruguay. Unlike a simple free-trade agreement, Mercosur requires its members to establish a *common trade policy* toward the rest of the world. Manzetti (reading 20) explores the political economy of Mercosur. He claims that the union was formed to foster peace between Argentina and Brazil and to consolidate democracy in the region. If correct, his argument suggests how political concerns can drive what might otherwise be seen as purely economic policy. Like any trade policy, the Mercosur agreement creates winners and losers at the national and subnational levels. Manzetti identifies the affected parties and indicates why distributional conflicts remain a thorn in the side of the organization. This emphasis on distribution is a hallmark of modern political economy and will reappear in the remaining sections of the book.

16

Import Substitution Industrialization

ELIANA CARDOSO

ANN HELWEGE

From the 1930s to the early 1960s, a growth strategy known as import substitution industrialization (ISI) dominated economic planning in Latin America. Although the region has long since undergone a reversal of the ideology associated with ISI, the economic structure in place today contains vestiges of this attempt to achieve industrial self-sufficiency. Factories constructed under ISI continue to operate today, and policies from this era remained intact well into the 1980s despite disillusionment with them. As antecedents to current economic problems in the region, ISI policies have had a profound effect.

The Great Depression backed many Latin American countries into an ISI strategy by default. The drop in international commodity prices left Latin Americans with little foreign exchange to spend on imports, forcing them to produce substitutes for imported essentials. This is not to imply that the crash stimulated growth in the region; real incomes plummeted with lower export earnings. However, political agitation in urban areas prompted governments to finance new industrial projects to create employment. Protectionist barriers were also erected to cope with balance of payments problems and protect local jobs.

World War II accelerated industrialization. Capacity shortages existed throughout the industrialized countries. Latin Americans enjoyed a recovery in the demand for their raw materials and were even able to compete in some markets for manufactured goods. At the same time, they were unable to import goods with their new export earnings. Unsatiated domestic demand stimulated expansion in the region's industrial capacity.

These secular influences on policy were complemented by the support of intellectuals who viewed ISI as a means of escaping dependence on unstable world markets. Although ISI was well underway as a strategy of development by then, R. Prebisch's work in 1949 for ECLA, arguing for changes in the structure of production in the periphery, became the classic doctrine of this growth model.

Arguments in Favor of ISI

Economists joined politicians in their support for ISI, calling attention to the lack of foreign exchange as an important constraint on growth. In a world where the terms of trade moved against traditional primary export products, domestic production would have to substitute for nonessential imports, freeing foreign exchange for needed inputs. Moreover, while technical progress in agriculture would leave labor unemployed, industry could absorb the growing population with increasing productivity and incomes. In the microeconomic sphere, markets in developing countries were thought to operate imperfectly, failing to make full use of an economy's resources. Expansion of domestic production required protection against imports and active government support in reducing barriers to industrial growth. The most common rationales in favor of ISI follow.

Volatility of Primary Commodities Prices

Primary commodity markets are unstable, and the concentration of exports in primary goods is risky. Good harvests worldwide can lead to a collapse of agricultural prices, especially in markets for tropical commodities, which do not benefit from price stabilization programs.

Mineral prices are also unstable; demand is highly sensitive to recessions in industrialized markets because metals like copper are heavily used in construction and new equipment. This instability is exacerbated by speculative stockpiling.

Latin American countries have seen their markets in guano, cochineal, cotton, rubber, hemp, tin, and copper erode as a result of innovation. Technological change also destroys markets for manufactured goods, but critics of primary export dependence argued that retooling factories for new products is generally easier than shifting the use of natural resources.

Declining Terms of Trade

The Prebisch-Singer hypothesis argued that there is a structural tendency for the terms of trade of developing countries to deteriorate because of the concentration of their exports in primary commodities. The terms of trade of Latin America are defined as:

$$\frac{\text{Latin American}}{\text{Terms of Trade}} = \frac{\text{Dollar Price of Latin America's Exports}}{\text{Dollar Price of Latin America's Imports}}$$

Trends in Latin America's terms of trade between 1930 and 1985 tend to support the Prebisch-Singer hypothesis, but studies using different end points often reject it.

Underlying the deteriorating terms of trade observed by Singer and Prebisch are several factors:

- Demand for primary goods expands less rapidly than demand for industrial goods due to a lower income elasticity (Engel's Law). A 10 percent increase in world income does not raise demand for coffee by 10 percent. In the long term, there is a shift in consumption to goods that involve more skill and less raw material.

- The technological superiority of the industrial countries means that their exports embody a more sophisticated technology and their prices embody profits from innovation, including the development of synthetic substitutes for primary commodities.
- The structure of labor markets is different in industrial and developing countries. In industrial countries, technical progress leads to higher factor incomes rather than lower prices of exports. In developing countries, productivity gains are not translated into higher wages because of widespread unemployment; instead, prices decline. An increase in productivity thus benefits overseas consumers rather than developing country producers.

Dynamic Nature of Resource Endowments

The theory of comparative advantage, which underlies arguments for free trade, implies that countries gain by exporting goods that intensively use their relatively abundant factors. In Latin America, these are natural resources and labor. The theory fails to take into account, however, the dynamic nature of resource endowments. Developing countries are capital poor, but capital is not a natural endowment; it is accumulated in response to market conditions. Supporters of protectionism argued that concentration in labor-intensive exports would simply trap workers in low wage industries. Governments must provide incentives— protection and financing—to attract investment in factories and equipment, shifting the resource balance from capital poor to capital rich.

Infant Industry

A related argument is that efficiency improves with experience. Whereas developed countries have moved well along the learning curve, Latin American industrialists are just starting out. The point of protection is to enable the firm to acquire the experience necessary to be competitive and perhaps eventually to export its product.

Caveats against infant industry protection were no different in Latin America than elsewhere: how can governments identify potentially competitive firms that merit protection? How long should consumers pay triple the international price of a washing machine for the sake of establishing a washing machine industry in Colombia? And if this industry is so promising, why won't private investors absorb the initial costs needed to establish the firm? For the most part, Latin American policies of protection have done little to ensure long-run competitiveness. This stands in contrast to Asian NICs, which made success in export markets a condition for continued government support. An exception is Brazil, which set an eight-year limit on protection given to its computer industry.

Linkages

Promoters of ISI argued that key industries have positive spillover effects. An automobile assembly plant generates demand for parts and steel, stimulating domestic production. As more supplier industries grow, bottlenecks that stymie other industries are eased. But the private sector may not be in the position to set this kind of growth in motion. Without a supply of steel, potential owners of a tool factory do not enter business, yet entrepreneurs considering construction of a steel plant reject the idea for lack of apparent demand. Government intervention is necessary to break this knot of inaction.

Elasticity Pessimism

ISI offered a solution to balance of payments deficits, at least in the short run. The assumption is that it is easier to cut imports by blocking their entry than it is to entice producers to increase exports. Policymakers who believe a real devaluation will have little positive impact on the trade balance are called elasticity pessimists. They are bound to be right in the very short run. A real devaluation takes time to work because resources must be transferred from nontraded goods to traded goods. But it is now widely believed that a real devaluation helps the external account in the medium run.

Export promotion might also face restrictions abroad. In 1982, for instance, almost half of Brazilian exports to the European Community and to the United States were affected by trade restrictions in these regions.

Implementation of ISI

In practice, ISI differed from protectionism in industrialized countries. Whereas protectionism in developed countries has typically been aimed at helping specific industries, ISI was adopted as an economy-wide strategy. Moreover, the goal of ISI was to establish new industries, not simply to protect existing firms. Governments were expected to play an active role in the economy, with benefits extending beyond the small number of workers already employed in industry.

The main tools used to implement an ISI strategy were import licensing, tariffs, overvalued exchange rates, and direct government investment in key industries. Import licensing enabled the government to control the composition of imports in order to promote specific activities. Essential goods—mainly food, capital goods, and intermediate inputs—were given preference, while imports of final consumer goods were discouraged with administrative red tape. Essential goods entered under lower tariffs and at preferential exchange rates. Multiple exchange rate systems served as an important mechanism for subsidizing favored goods.

Governments themselves constructed plants in heavy industries—steel, cement, utilities, and airplanes—where the amount of start-up capital involved was thought to discourage private investment. New plants in automobiles, pharmaceuticals, and grain processing were set up as joint ventures with foreign firms. Foreign firms provided access to technology, while government ownership limited the repatriation of profits abroad.

Latin American governments also stimulated industry through low interest rates and easy access to credit under soft monetary regimes. Publicly owned enterprises subsidized intermediate goods like electricity and steel by running in the red. Price ceilings on wage goods, especially food, helped to keep down labor costs for urban employers.

Consequences of ISI

The ISI model made sense, but it downplayed market forces and confronted three major limitations:

1. Protection led to overvalued exchange rates and hence to slow export growth.
2. In sectoral terms, import substitution policies exaggerated industrial growth at the expense of agriculture. Relatively capital-intensive manufactures absorbed only a fraction of the labor force, which grew with urban migration, placing pressure on government to serve as an employer of last resort.
3. As revenues from primary export taxes failed to increase, subsidies to industrial investment and growing government responsibilities put pressure on the budget. Monetization of the deficit led to persistent inflation.

ISI policies also had positive effects. They did indeed stimulate industrialization in Latin America, reducing the share of the labor force employed in agriculture. The counterpart of this phenomenon was the increasing relative importance of manufacturing. Some industrialization would have occurred anyway, but the marked shift of resources into industry contrasts sharply with the slow development of manufacturing before World War I. At the height of ISI's influence in the mid-1950s, industrial growth rates were high not only relative to agriculture but to industrial performance in developed countries as well. Furthermore, to the extent that reduction of dependence on world markets was a goal of ISI, import coefficients in the region did drop, although this change was misleading because the region remained dependent on inputs of essential goods.

Although difficult to measure, the ISI phase probably had a positive effect on the development of attitudes of social responsibility toward the poor. The idea that an increased supply of skilled labor was necessary for industrialization justified more spending on education. The stronger voices of union activists helped to establish at least some minimal social security programs. And greater expectations were placed on governments to provide infrastructure to support industrialization.

One can ask whether these gains would have occurred anyway, given the prosperous world economic climate of the late 1940s and 1950s, but at least the ideology associated with ISI ran in their favor. Critics of ISI argue that the poor lost out on growth that would have occurred had Latin American countries followed a policy of laissez-faire. It is hard to conjecture about growth under this hypothetical alternative, but even had overall growth rates been higher, one wonders how output would have been distributed, given the history of Latin American class relations prior to the ISI period.

A close look at the industrialization process shows a checkered pattern of success and failure, sometimes even within the same sectors. The Brazilians and Mexicans managed to establish successful automobile industries, but the Chileans and Peruvians wound up with a host of inefficient assembly operations. Efficient steel production was established in Argentina and Brazil, but attempts failed elsewhere. As a generalization, assembly of consumer durables went well, while few countries succeeded in getting capital goods and intermediate input industries off the ground. Perhaps because of their larger domestic markets, Brazil and Mexico managed better than other countries in the region.

Criticisms of ISI

Problems with import substitution strategies became increasingly apparent by the late 1950s. Criticisms came from both the left and the right. Leftists argued that ISI increased Latin America's dependency on imports, put power in the hands of industrialists and MNCs, and perpetuated the exploitation of peasants. Conservatives argued that the strategy misallocated resources; instead of enjoying rapid growth rates through export promotion, Latin American governments were creating hopelessly inefficient industries that depended on huge bureaucracies, which in themselves were a drain on the economy.

Uneven Protection

The overall level of protection is measured by the effective rate of protection (ERP). ERPs measure the degree of protection accorded to value-added in domestic industries, taking into account the level of protection afforded to both inputs and output. Value-added is the value of a firm's sales minus the cost of materials it buys to produce its goods:

$$\text{ERP of industry i} = \frac{(\text{Value-added in domestic prices})}{(\text{Value-added in international prices})} - 1$$

For a given level of nominal protection, the lower the protection of inputs is to an industry, the higher is the degree of effective rate of protection. Conversely, if the inputs to an industry are heavily protected, the effective rate of protection of the industry could be low although the nominal protection may be high. Brazilian agriculture in the 1970s, for example, suffered from tariff protection given to fertilizer and farm machinery. The more heavily an industry uses untaxed imported inputs and enjoys protection on its final output, the greater the protection is likely to be. Under ISI, effective rates of protection tended to favor investment in assembly industries rather than in basic goods. Parts for refrigerators and cars entered with low duties, while high tariffs kept out imported final goods. Thus, it is not surprising that the backward linkages that planners had hoped for failed to materialize. In some periods, the presence of multiple exchange rates compounded the distortions due to uneven effective protection.

Estimates of effective rates of protection in different industrial sectors should be interpreted with care because of the lack continuity in data and the differences in methodology. With these caveats in mind, before 1975 Chile had not only large effective rates of protection but also a huge dispersion of ERPs across industrial sectors. Generally a larger dispersion of ERPs will lead to greater distortion across sectors.

High levels of effective protection and overvalued exchange rates contributed to a situation in which domestically produced goods were often priced well above world prices. In 1969, the Chilean domestic price of electric sewing machines, bicycles, home refrigerators, and air conditioners was, respectively, three, five, six, and seven times higher than international prices. At these relative prices, any consumer with access to foreign exchange and import licenses would buy foreign goods. At the same time, producers enjoyed profitable domestic markets but did not stand a chance of exporting.

Overcapacity

ISI was also marked by overcapacity in many industries. The typical plant size exceeded domestic demand and operated at high average cost. This was especially evident in the automobile industry. In the late 1960s, Latin America had ninety firms producing 600,000 cars, or an average annual output of just 6,700 cars.

Agriculture

Agriculture was seriously hurt by ISI. Credit was diverted to industry, making it difficult for farmers to finance seasonal costs or investment in irrigation and equipment. Public expenditures on roads, water, and electricity services were biased toward urban areas. Little effort was made to integrate the peasantry into the modern sector through technical assistance and land reform. Overvalued exchange rates reduced the profitability of agricultural exports and at the same time made it difficult to compete with cheap imports of food. Price controls were used to keep wages down for urban employers, at the expense of farmers. Not only did Latin America become increasingly dependent on imported food, but its traditional source of foreign exchange, the agricultural sector, could not keep up with the need for foreign exchange.

Budget Deficits

The heavy involvement of governments in setting up new industries and providing credit to private firms contributed to public deficits. Subsidies and bureaucratic growth added to expenditures, while the failure to promote export growth cut into revenues from a sector that traditionally has paid a large percentage of taxes. In the absence of easy borrowing from abroad, monetary expansion financed deficits and spurred inflation.

Interest Rates

The use of low interest rates to encourage investment had two negative side effects: industry was excessively capital-intensive and savings rates were low. Large savers with connections abroad shifted their wealth to foreign banks. Allocation of scarce credit at negative real interest rates became subject to arbitrary bureaucratic decisions that often reflected inefficient, even corrupt, choices.

Labor

Progressive governments of the period supported labor through minimum wage legislation, but promotion of capital-intensive industries resulted in a two-tiered labor structure: those who had jobs enjoyed relatively good pay, but many workers were either unemployed or forced into the traditional sectors neglected by governmental emphasis on modernization. Labor is a relatively abundant factor in Latin America, but ISI programs failed to take advantage of this resource. At the same time, very high population growth rates contributed to underemployment. Industrial employment could not keep up with the growth in the labor force.

Foreign Direct Investment

Joint ventures with foreign firms brought in the same technology used in industrialized countries. Capital-intensive plants employed few unskilled workers. Expatriates filled highly skilled jobs, causing disappointment in the progress at which local workers gained technologically advanced skills. These joint ventures often involved a ban on exports; foreign firms had no interest in trying to coordinate international marketing decisions with Latin American governments. Yet despite these criticisms of foreign involvement, foreign firms provided capital necessary to finance some major investments. The ISI experience perpetuated a love-hate relationship between Latin Americans and multinational firms. On the one hand, Latin Americans objected to the extraction of profits and the enclave nature of foreign operations, but on the other, they saw MNCs as sources of technology and capital vital to the realization of economic independence.

The End of the Golden Years

Ironically, these complaints about import substitution emerged in the 1960s, a period of relatively strong growth in Latin America. The average real rate of growth in the region exceeded 4.5 percent between 1940 and 1968. By comparison to the 1.2 percent rate of the 1980s, the ISI years seem golden. Average inflation rates were also relatively low; whereas 100 percent inflation was shocking in the 1950s, triple-digit inflation was common in the region during the 1980s. The ISI era was also marked by important improvements in literacy rates, mortality rates, and access to electricity and water. Yet disappointment was understandable, particularly by the early 1960s; on a per capita basis, Latin American income rose only 2.1 percent per year between 1960 and 1967, significantly less than the 3.7 percent growth of per capita income in developed countries and the 6.4 percent growth rate characteristic of Asian developing countries. Inflation rates were high relative to the rest of the world. Perhaps most indicting was the fact that the

Southern Cone countries, which had applied ISI most thoroughly, had postwar growth rates below the regional average.

As theorists argued the demerits of ISI, some practical factors intervened to draw this phase of Latin American economic planning to a close. On a political level, labor unions had gained enormous strength under ISI. Demands for higher wages and improved benefits threatened the share of income going to the upper tiers of the class structure. Government efforts to placate worker demands through fiscal expansion fueled inflation, further eroding the support of the wealthy. Growing balance of payments problems made it impossible to squeeze more real output from the economy to keep everyone happy. Class tension was erupting into full-fledged political crises.

The first failed attempts at reversing ISI policies occurred in the late 1950s as conservative regimes briefly took control in Chile (1956–1958) and Argentina (1959–1962). In the 1960s, other countries, notably Brazil and Colombia, recognized the limits of ISI and introduced modifications to commercial policy. Crawling-peg exchange rate systems accommodated high domestic rates of inflation and averted the overvaluation earlier so predominant. Explicit concern for inducing nontraditional exports produced special export-subsidy programs in many countries after 1965. In the context of a more buoyant international market, such reinforcements produced positive results, and export growth and diversification in the region increased.

At the same time, borrowing became an option for several countries. From the end of the 1960s but notably after 1973, governments could finance both more imports and larger public sector deficits. The commitment to industrialization remained, and that meant an intrusive role for the public sector even under the "orthodox" policies pursued by military governments. In Brazil's "miracle" between 1968 and 1974, the large domestic market still dominated production decisions.

This period of adaptation and relatively successful adjustment of the earlier model came to an end with the international disequilibrium brought by the oil price rise in 1973. Mounting indebtedness and deterioration of domestic policy in a more difficult external environment marked the postoil shock.

Trade Reform

Changes in the international economic environment in the 1970s led to important splits in the region's economic history. While we can generalize about import substitution throughout the region in the mid-twentieth century and comment on the uniformly dismal experience of the debt crisis in the 1980s (admitting a few exceptions among the smaller countries), the experiences of Latin American countries in the 1970s are less consistent. Although import substitution was deemed inefficient, the policies that were adopted in the wake of its demise depended to a large extent on how successful a country was in its export markets.

The oil-importing countries did not fare well. Military regimes in Chile (1973), Argentina (1976), and Uruguay (1974) ushered in the end of inward-looking ISI strategies. Austerity measures took hold. Although the military regimes favored the elite, the tension that preceded the coups gave these regimes support that reached into the very classes bound to bear the brunt of stabilization programs. Unemployment, price hikes, and political repression were silently accepted by many as a bitter but potentially viable alternative to failed populist agendas.

Stabilization called for lower real wages, cuts in government spending, incentives for private investment, devaluation, and reduced protectionism. The market liberalization programs in Argentina and Chile in the 1970s were intended to improve industrial efficiency and hasten the transition from ISI to industrial exporting. Trade was opened up: in Chile, tariffs were reduced from an average rate of 94 percent in 1973 to an average rate of 33 percent in 1976. By mid–1979, all tariff rates had been reduced to 10 percent. However, the exchange rate was allowed to appreciate in real terms in both countries. The outcomes were surging consumer imports (table 4.10), partial deindustrialization, and financial bubbles that collapsed with disastrous consequences.

Mexico represents a more recent example of trade reform. After 1985, Mexico not only joined the General Agreement on Tariffs and Trade (GATT) but also engaged in a substantial trade liberalization. Trade reform complemented privatization and deregulation as measures to increase domestic competitiveness.

In the 1950s, development economists overemphasized the need for state intervention to promote investment and growth. In the 1980s, the fashion turned 180 degrees to favor nonintervention, privatization, and liberalization. It is now widely recognized that in small countries, import substitution policies (based on quantitative restrictions, differentiated tariffs, and a lack of commitment to competitive exchange rates) lead to disaster.

Eliana Cardoso and Ann Helwege, "Import Substitution Industrialization," in *Latin America's Economy: Diversity, Trends, and Conflicts* (Cambridge, MA: MIT Press, 1992): 84–103.

17

Was Latin America Too Rich to Prosper? Structural and Political Obstacles to Export-Led Industrial Growth

JAMES E. MAHON, JR.

Introduction

Much of recent discussion about the political economy of development has turned upon a contrast between Latin America and East Asia. East Asian growth, seen largely as the result of dynamic export-oriented industrialisation (henceforth EOI), has been juxtaposed with a relatively more sluggish Latin American performance. This has raised the question: why did Latin America persist for so long with a more protectionist model emphasising import-substituting industrialisation (henceforth ISI), despite foreign exchange crises and IMF prodding? One common answer implicates political weaknesses that bloated the state, protected urban industrialists, and coddled labour unions. Alternatively, the divergence is explained with reference to the wishes of foreign actors, especially the US government. This essay emphasises another dimension of the contrast: the size of the structural and hence political obstacles faced by middle-income developing countries in the turn to exporting low-wage manufactured goods.

Why Did Latin America Not Follow the East Asian Path?

Apparently, the East Asian countries followed a development strategy more appropriate to the international environment than that pursued by most of Latin America. Hence the puzzle which preoccupies many recent observers: why the contrast between the relatively smooth, unproblematic, and generally sustained transition from ISI to EOI in Taiwan and South Korea, and the more partial and difficult policy reorientation in much of Latin America before the debt crisis?

Answering this question involves accounting for the differing capabilities of governments to respond to foreign exchange crises by effectively turning policy from ISI to EOI. I would like to suggest that there are four dimensions to the explanation: first, the differing alignments of interests in civil society (the relative power of rural vs. urban groups, the role of multinational corporations, etc.); second, the power of the state over these societal interests (institutional insulation, repressive capability, foreign support); third, the severity and duration of the crises; and finally, the objective difficulty of an effective policy reorientation. That is, 'successful' countries may have had more societal allies and fewer enemies of policy change than did other countries; they also may have had stronger states, may have experienced more severe crises that provided stronger motivations for change, or may have faced a much more manageable task than did others.

In this section I will review and assess the literature on this problem and then present evidence supporting the fourth dimension.

Civil Society

Let us begin with arguments based upon the character and relative weight of interests in civil society. According to Sachs, a crucial variable is the breadth of property distribution in the rural export sector. Where industrial activities are heavily protected they have a vested interest in a relatively appreciated exchange rate, above all on their imported inputs (capital and intermediate goods). What keeps them from getting their way for very long, in East Asia for example, is broad land distribution in tradeable-good agriculture that creates a large bloc in opposition to an appreciated currency. In Latin America, exchange rate depreciation is unpopular because it transfers income from workers and capitalists to a small, politically regressive class of landholders or export proprietors. Hence, by this argument, ISI and overvalued exchange rates were gone from South Korea and Taiwan by the mid-1960s, in favour of outward-oriented industrialisation, while overvalued rates hung on in Latin America.

The Sachs argument does catch an important aspect of the South Korean case. The 1960 student revolution fought expressly against the corrupt government–business ties that characterised ISI under Syngman Rhee. The new urban industrial economy became the focus of dissent not only for students but also for the peasantry. The participants in the 1961 coup and subsequent governments, who considered themselves heirs to the 1960 movement, were overwhelmingly of rural origin. They were 'populist' in one sense—they sought to redistribute wealth to farmers. In 1963, when Park Chung Hee sought an electoral mandate, one of his key slogans was 'Agriculture First'.

Latin American policy experiences from the late 1950s to the debt crisis also provide some confirmation of the Sachs thesis. In Colombia, with a relatively broadly-held rural export sector, a powerful coffee interest organisation (FEDE-CAFE), and two major parties having strong rural organisations, policy has shown more attention to rural exporters. Lleras Restrepo's comprehensive 1967 foreign exchange reform did not have the same retrograde political significance as a similarly pro-export policy would have had elsewhere. There were many rural producers that stood to benefit to be sure, in a sector characterised by grossly inequitable land distribution because they were export producers also. In contrast, despite the spur of chronic exchange problems, in Brazil and Chile pro-export exchange reforms (1959 and 1961; 1965) failed to persist under elected governments. In neither case was the export sector as broadly owned as in Colombia. In Brazil, low commodity prices and protests at the inflationary results of devaluation led to back sliding under Goulart. In Chile, the Christian Democrats returned to fixed exchange rates under electoral pressure in 1970. Seemingly, when the immediate beneficiaries were a small oligarchy or big foreign firms, pro-export exchange policies were hard to sustain under elected leaders.

State Autonomy

In his multifaceted comparison of economic development in East Asia and Latin America, Evans argues the importance of state power to successful policy reorientation. This was due to the fact that the state in East Asia was powerful and had consolidated its dominance over the (former) landed elites prior to the shift to EOI and the opening to direct foreign investment by multinational corporations (MNCs). State power was enhanced by the strong administration and industrial assets left behind by Japanese colonial rule: by close external threats to political survival; and in Taiwan, by the cohesive nature of the Kuomintang ruling elite that arrived fully formed from the mainland. This power was most important in dealings with MNCs and especially with ex-landlords. It showed itself in land reform and rural development policies, which tended to give urban labour greater market power and led to a trend of rising real wages, which reduced overall inequality in Taiwan.

Others have also pointed to an inter-regional contrast in the relative power of states over civil society. These authors point to states insulated from domestic societal interests (though not from the US), in which technocrats had a relatively broad power to impose the kind of policy reforms that were often desired but proved difficult in Latin America: land reform, restrictions on MNC investments, or large real depreciations that cut real wages in the short run.

Severity of Balance-of-Payments Crises

One may argue that foreign exchange crises give policy reform a degree of urgency proportional to their magnitude, much as Diaz Alejandro observed about Latin American policy innovation in the 1930s. Some note that the transition from ISI to EOI was 'forced by development crises' in South Korea and Taiwan. Traditional export markets had been lost and foreign investment was scarce, which led to a dependence on US aid that was greater than any external dependence felt by Latin America. In the late 1950s the US sought to cut its long-term aid commitments to the region. Given this, 'both countries faced the task of earning foreign exchange'. Policy changes brought on by cyclical deterioration in the terms of trade are 'vulnerable to backsliding' when the situation improves. According to this argument, recurrent but shorter Latin American exchange crises would have been less effective in provoking large and sustained reorientation of policy.

Cost of the Shift to EOI

The fourth explanatory dimension relates to the objective size of the task implied by a reorientation of policy from ISI to EOI. Arguments of this type point to the factor cost differentials between regions. Most Latin American countries have an 'unbalanced productive structure,' one with a substantial productivity differential between the primary-product export sector and the manufacturing sector. Because of abundant primary exports, the equilibrium exchange rate is a relatively appreciated one. At this exchange rate the country's manufactures are relatively uncompetitive internationally and import-competing activities have to be protected in other ways. Pro-EOI reforms thus bear a large short- to medium-term cost in domestic income and wages, from the huge real devaluation that is required in order to make manufactured exports competitive and protection unnecessary. It also means that the political difficulty in reorienting policy toward low-wage manufactured exports will be greater as a country's primary exports are relatively more productive.

The 'unbalanced productive structure' argument helps us understand a criticism that could be levelled at the Sachs hypothesis: whatever the relative power of rural and urban sectors, moving from ISI to EOI will be politically easier where its objective costs are lower. Where the productivity of the export sector is low, the country's manufactures might be competitive internationally even at an exchange rate typical of ISI. In this case, the extent of real currency depreciation and the sacrifices involved in embracing an entry-level EOI model (in terms of real wage losses and import cost increases) would be much smaller.

Of course, that East Asian economies are resource-poor has been widely noted. One expert concluded that 'as compared with the other LDCs, the common denominator of the East Asian NICs has been their relative shortage of natural resources'. But few have argued that there is an advantage in resource poverty.

Evidence on the Wage Cost of the Shift to EOI

For the sake of a more detailed comparison, let us assume equal productivities across countries in Latin America and East Asia in the late 1950s and early 1960s. Thus export competitiveness may be approximated by real wage levels.

This assumption permits the comparison which appears in the following table (Figure 1) of current-dollar wage rates for ten countries, including the USA and Japan. For those countries with multiple exchange rates or official rates that were significantly supported by controls, wages are converted to dollars at a midyear parallel market rate. A focus on the parallel market lets us look past artificially appreciated official rates and see the effect of the productive structure on 'equilibrium' currency values.

Venezuela is clearly our most egregious example of what Diamand called an 'unbalanced productive structure'. Venezuela's postwar model for rapid growth depended on expanding oil revenues. The sacrifices involved in making Venezuelan manufactured exports competitive in world markets, through a unified ex-

FIGURE 1   Hourly Wage Rates in Manufacturing, All Industries, 1955–70 (current US dollars)

Country	1955	1958	1959	1960	1961	1962	1963	1964	1965	1970
Argentina	.20	.32	.25	.36	.32	.27	.30	.33	.25	.41
Brazil	.19	.20	.20	-	-	.19	.21	.24	.26	.36
Chile	-	-	-	.26	.30	.21	.16	.16	.20	.23
Colombia	.17	.14	.12	.23	.22	.223	.29	.33	.19	.27
Mexico	.22	.28	.30	.34	.36	.38	.45	.50	.54	.70
Venezuela	-	-	-	-	-	-	-	.82	.87	1.07
S. Korea	.08	.09	.10	.08	.09	.10	.07	.06	.07	.19
Taiwan	.06	.07	.06	.08	.10	.10	.11	.11	.11	.19
Japan	.21	.24	.25	.28	.31	.34	.38	.44	.49	1.06
U.S.A.	1.86	-	-	2.26	-	-	-	-	2.61	3.36

change rate alone, would have been dramatic. In 1965 Venezuelan dollar wages would have had to fall to about one-eighth their existing level in order to compete with Taiwan's, or to about one-twelfth to match Korea's. In 1970, Venezuelan wages were still higher than Japan's in dollar terms.

The situation was less dramatic but similar elsewhere in Latin America. Even measured by parallel market rates—those which often served as the target when the IMF recommended 'realistic' currency values—Latin America appeared a high-wage part of the world compared to Taiwan and South Korea. Latin American wages were closely comparable with those of Japan for much of this period. Where Latin American parallel-dollar wages dipped most steeply, this often had much to do with a black market made jittery by political events or economic news (Colombia 1958–59, Chile 1964 or 1970).

We can create a simple illustrative model of the choice that might have faced Latin American policy-makers. If they sought to export manufactures in competition with Taiwan and South Korea—and not with Japan—they would have had to devalue the currency mercilessly, far in excess of what the IMF typically recommended. They might have asked: how quickly can I expect real wages (in current parallel dollars) to recover fully from this devaluation? Taking 1962 wage figures—the competitive wage would be $0.10/hour—and generously assuming an annual dollar wage regain of 15 per cent, the results would be as follows (1962 wages in parentheses):

Argentina (0.271), 63 per cent devaluation, recovered in 7 years;
Brazil (0.186), 46 per cent devaluation, recovered in 4.5 years;
Chile (0.211), 53 per cent devaluation, recovered in 5.3 years;
Colombia (0.234), 57 per cent devaluation, recovered in 6 years;
Mexico (0.384), 74 per cent devaluation, recovered in 9.5 years.

Notice that for Argentina and Brazil, 1962 shows parallel-dollar wages well below their average trend, and that the competitive wage is based partly upon Korea before its 95 per cent devaluation of 1964.

To complete the scenario, one would have to add the doubt in the decision-maker's mind about the near-term viability of exporting manufactures (probably to the USA and Europe), relative to the prospects for an upturn in primary exports. One would also have to note that a return to previous dollar wage rates would come much sooner than would a recovery of the total dollar buying power lost in the interval, sooner still than the recovery of buying power measured at official dollar rates in countries where these were supported by controls. Then, we would have to assess the likelihood that the politician or someone with whom he identified would still be around to reap the eventual political benefits of success, however defined. Considering all these factors, it would seem that this distant, uncertain future attainment of economic 'success' would be very heavily discounted indeed. Moreover, we have not even considered whether the IMF would have allowed this kind of competitive devaluation.

This discussion may also shed light on the behaviour of multinational corporations. Did the vastly different profile of MNC investment in the two regions, much more prominent in Latin America than in Taiwan and South Korea, affect the likelihood of successful policy reform? As Evans notes, MNC investment in East Asia was practically non-existent until after economic policy had been reoriented toward exports; but it was present from an early date in Latin America. Would an established MNC have sought to block host country initiatives to raise manufactured exports because these conflicted with global corporate strategy?

One could argue that this strategy would have been shaped by relative costs and by timing. Once MNCs had made a commitment to exporting worldwide from one low-wage area, their enthusiasm for exporting from other, higher-wage countries would have lessened. Better, in this case, to continue selling in the protected market of countries whose domestic buying power would surely suffer from drastic policy reform. This analysis offers one reason why MNCs in manufacturing industry might have been, at best, indifferent to radical pro-export policy reforms in higher-wage developing countries.

Dependency and the 'Unbalanced Productive Structure'

Central to most accounts of twentieth-century Latin American political and economic development is an appreciation of the difficulty involved in breaking with an economic model of primary-product export that favoured a traditional, chiefly land-based oligarchy and its foreign allies. Industrialisation was delayed and difficult to achieve politically because the groups that commanded the majority of the productive base, the consumption share, and the political apparatus were positively against it. The Depression served as a catalyst for change because to varying degrees it weakened these established forces, often forcing them to rely on the state to support their income, while creating the conditions for industrial growth. But even after some amount of import substitution had been spurred on by the currency depreciations of the 1930s or by the trade disruption of the Second World War, the traditional oligarchy was still strong, especially if allied with the military in an anti-democratic conspiracy.

In short, it appeared that the crucial barrier to continued industrial development presented by the primary export sector (whether foreign or domestically controlled) was its political resistance. From this perspective, many of the roots of dependency could be traced to the persistence of an export sector which reflected the nineteenth-century conditions of its origin and often fought to reestablish them.

If the hypothesis of the 'unbalanced productive structure' has merit, it shows another side of Latin American dependency under ISI. A thoroughgoing insertion of a country into the world market on the basis of its primary exports (Argentina is the archetype) would have discouraged industrial exports for other reasons. The most fundamental would have been the effect of high primary-export productivity on the exchange rate.

This conclusion puts the postwar history of Latin American development in an interesting light. The catastrophe of the 1930s pushed the major countries of Latin America to undertake an import substitution process that was driven mainly by real depreciations that made all imports expensive. Postwar ISI differed. It would hew more closely to an easier but less sustainable path of making selected imports cheap to selected buyers, while exploiting the favourable trends in Latin American terms of trade in the decade after 1945.

The new postwar policies responded more to an economically stronger and ideologically more assertive industrial bourgeoisie, and less to the interests of the traditional export sector. While the social base of the top industrialists was often not very distinct from that of the traditional rural elites (especially in the smaller countries), the economic base had changed, with commerce and primary commodities weakened and industry strengthened by a decade and a half of reduced or interrupted trade. Still, factory owners were not the only supporters of the new set of policies. The pro-ISI enthusiasm was shared by most sectors of the military, labour, and many technocrats.

Reasons for avoiding devaluation could be traced to both new and old elements of this political economy. The most important foes of devaluation were urban industrial capitalists, who tended to be favoured by the exchange control systems erected in lieu of devaluation, and urban workers, who would lose from any acceleration of inflation not compensated immediately by equivalent nominal wage gains. Organised labour was especially prominent in postponing devaluation. Policy-makers also found good 'technical' reasons for resisting devaluation—the crucial one being an 'elasticity pessimism' about the probable response in supply and (if the country was a dominant world producer) international price of the country's key commodity to the move. Meanwhile, clamouring for devaluation and trade liberalisation were the traditional export sectors and international financial interests. All in all, many found it easy to see which side of the issue was the popular, 'national', and reasonable one.

These trends led to the familiar policy deadlock. A period of recurrent exchange crises accompanied industrial growth. By the time the crises put policy reform on the agenda, the interests holding fast to ISI were even stronger than they had been in 1945.

Many policy-makers understood that the problem lay in the export sector. Accepting that the country could not expect permanently rising export revenue from primary products, it was clear that other (perhaps more income-elastic) exports had to be substituted. But the high productivity of the primary sector made this difficult. Beginning in the 1960s, one had to compete in the new sectors with exporters of similar productivity, whose exchange rates were not buoyed up by the material legacy of a 'successful' primary-export stage.

More: in Taiwan and Korea the material legacy of primary-export development was practically insignificant. Even within East Asia, Taiwan and South Korea are distinguished by the disastrous declines of their primary export sectors after 1945. The difference between Latin America and these two countries was especially striking in the first postwar decade. In 1954 Latin America was just coming off a fairly sustained rise in its terms of trade. The coffee boom was still on; the metals bonanzas had ended with the Korean War a year earlier. Still, relative prices were ahead of 1945 (and 1939). In contrast, South Korea's export sector was in shambles. Exports in 1956 had fallen to less than half of their real value of 1950. In Taiwan, the loss of the Japanese market for tropical foodstuff exports compounded the countrywide problems of hyperinflation and rapid real depreciation, attendant upon civil war in 1945–49. One result of these disasters was the abject dependence of both East Asian countries on US aid to finance imports. Another was a depreciated level of parallel exchange rates, despite the aid inflow.

The poverty of primary exports in the two Asian countries had other social consequences, too. Because this resource poverty permitted an ISI process only at a low level of income, the pie was too small for it to be used, Argentina-style, as a basis for a strong political alliance of newly-mobilised labour and domestically-oriented business. It was less tempting to continue with it, and its limitations meant that the interests defending it would be relatively weak.

For Latin American politicians to have duplicated the disaster that befell the primary export sectors of Taiwan and South Korea, they would have had to re-create the Depression experience through state policy. This, of course, was inconceivable to them.

I am not trying to argue that only one feature distinguishes Taiwan and South Korea from Latin America. I have simply tried to provide one more reason why urban consumption interests were more powerful in Latin America. It was not just a matter of relative state power, societal interests, exchange crises, or international forces. Relative to Latin America, in East Asia the transition to EOI bore a much smaller income cost. This is a contrast that is often hidden when the successes of Taiwan and South Korea are compared to the less adept or permanent policy changes in Latin America.

James E. Mahon, Jr. "Was Latin America Too Rich to Prosper? Structural and Political Obstacles to Export-Led Industrial Growth," *Journal of Development Studies* 28, no. 2 (January 1992): 241–63.

18

The Case for
Trade Liberalization in
Developing Countries

RUDIGER DORNBUSCH

In a broad swing of the pendulum, developing countries have been shifting from severe and destructive protection to free trade fever. Many of the notable examples are in Latin America.

This new enthusiasm for freer trade stems from four overlapping sources:

Anti-statism. The world has seen a broad intellectual swing away from emphasizing the beneficial role of the state in the 1980s, and protection is seen as one of the manifestations of an overly intrusive state.

Poor economic performance. Many developing countries have suffered dismal economic performance and declining productive potential. Much of the reason can be traced to populist macroeconomic policies that engendered debt crises and hyperinflation. Of course, part of the reason was also a very adverse external environment. But since the days of plentiful external credit are gone, attention must shift to productivity gains as the source of growth. Trade may offer part of the solution.

Information. Citizens worldwide are exposed to more information about the opportunities available in other countries. It is no longer possible to conceal that goods in a country cost three or four times the world price or that they are not available. The elite want their BMWs, almost as a civil right; and the poor want cheap food and low cost consumer durables that are available in world markets; firms know what technologies and inputs their competitors abroad can use and insist on the same access. It is no longer possible to assert that liberal trade policy must immiserize a country; on the contrary, many economic actors now see access to imports as a way of stretching their buying power.

World Bank pressure and evidence of success. Major research projects under the auspices of the NBER and the World Bank have documented the problems of inward-looking trade strategies and discerned the lessons from successful trade strategies. The research helped diffuse the black-and-white debate—free trade versus protection—to reach a more differentiated judgment involving the importance of neutral trade regimes as opposed to regimes that are biased against exports. The favorable performance of countries which adopted outward-oriented policies served to make trade liberalization, broadly understood, a central condition for World Bank lending.

This paper next reviews the actual situation of protection in developing countries, to set the stage for a discussion of the prospective gains from liberalization. Three experiences with liberalization are then briefly sketched and the question is raised as to what can go wrong. The paper concludes by taking up two directions in which liberalization is now moving, regional free trade zones and liberalization of trade in services.

Protection in Developing Countries

Protection became the mode for most developing countries during the 1930s. During the Depression, industrial countries adopted restrictive trade policies and commodity prices—a major source of earnings for developing countries—collapsed. The pursuit of a policy of industrialization behind protective walls of tariffs and import quotas took hold first as a means of saving foreign exchange for debt payments, and then became viewed as a development strategy. The strategy was predicated on the assumption that primary producing countries would face inevitably a deterioration of the terms of trade; growth in demand for primary commodities was believed to be small because of low income elasticities for commodities and ongoing substitution toward alternative materials. At the same time, high rates of technical progress on the supply side would create a situation of excess supply and declining relative prices.

Trade policy changed little in the period immediately after World War II. Industrial countries continued for some time with highly restrictive trade policies, while many developing countries did not face foreign exchange problems due to their accumulation of foreign exchange reserves during wartime and a subsequent boom in commodity prices during the Korean War. But then commodity prices collapsed again, and developing countries faced stark questions of the appropriate trade and exchange policies. As industrial countries moved gradually in the direction of trade liberalization and currency convertibility, should the developing world follow?

The prevailing view, especially in Latin America, was the doctrine from the United Nations Economic Commission for Latin America, more commonly known as ECLA. In this view, developing countries should pursue an import substitution industrialization strategy to avoid the problem of secularly deteriorating terms of trade. Import substitution meant the development of domestic industry behind a high protective barrier of tariffs, quotas and licences. That policy was pursued vigorously. Direct foreign investment helped industrialization proceed, in some cases with extraordinary success, as in Brazil.

There was an intellectual counter-current supporting the classical case for free trade, notably in Jacob Viner's (1952) Rio de Janeiro Lectures. The debate carried into the 1960s when the protection doctrine became the main fare in the newly formed UN Conference on Trade and Development (UNCTAD), the intellectual forum in which developing countries shaped their views on trade and development strategy. Interestingly, while major progress was made in trade liberalization among industrial countries under the GATT, that same GATT allows developing countries substantial leeway in maintaining trade protection. This seems peculiar today, since poor countries especially ought to focus on making the best of their resources, but it fit the prevailing ECLA doctrine that protection was a pathway to development.

In the late 1960s and 1970s, protection in developing countries softened in at least one direction. Many countries recognized that protection by tariffs and quotas did keep imports out, but that the resulting decline in demand for foreign exchange also led to an appreciation of the currency and hence a severe tax on exports of both traditional commodities and emerging industrial goods. Unstable real exchange rates added to the hazards of export activities. Moreover, duties on imported intermediate goods first implied a tax on export activities using these goods, and then helped cause a currency overvaluation which hurt export competitiveness of these products.

From an industrialization standpoint it made sense to avoid the anti-export implications of protectionist policies by reducing duties and pursing policies for stable exchange rates. Countries which adopted outward-oriented policies, at least to the extent of neutralizing anti-export bias, performed better than countries who failed to recognize the adverse effects of restrictions on their export potential.

Recently, many developing countries have gone beyond compensation for anti-export bias to more radical reform. Quotas are being turned into tariffs, tariffs are being more tightly focused, and tariff rates are being reduced. Invariably, trade policy reform has also been part of a much broader program of policy reform including domestic stabilization and deregulation.

Gains from Liberalization

The channels through which trade liberalization could bring benefits are broadly these: improved resource allocation in line with social marginal costs and benefits; access to better technologies, inputs and intermediate goods; an economy better able to take advantage of economies of scale and scope; greater domestic competition; availability of favorable growth externalities, like the transfer of know-how; and a shakeup of industry that may create a Schumpeterian environment especially conducive to growth. This section will comment on each of these factors.

The static gains from improved resource allocation are the classical source of a gain from freer trade. Under perfect competition a small, price-taking country will gain by eliminating tariffs. Consumers are better off because their incomes stretch further, and resources are used more efficiently because they are no longer used to produce goods that could be imported at a lower price. As one early example of measuring these potential gains, Harberger (1959) estimated the welfare cost of protection in Chile to amount to 2.5 percent of GNP, as opposed to 10 percent for domestic distortions.

While the traditional discussion often focuses on final, homogeneous goods, the case for freer trade is enriched by including the facts that trade liberalization increases the variety of goods, and raises productivity by providing less expensive or higher quality intermediate goods. If appropriate intermediate goods can be imported, a country may easily become an exporter of labor intensive tasks such as assembly services; without such imports, that value-added opportunity is lost, along with the opportunity to graduate over time from assembly to tasks with higher value-added.

Free trade leads to a more economically rational market structure. Gains from liberalization also result from scale economies and economies of scope that arise in wider markets. Moreover, markets in protected economies are narrow and lack of competitors from the rest of the world fosters oligopoly and inefficiency. Protectionism can create market power for domestic firms, where under free trade there would be none. The casual evidence of these effects is striking. For example, when Mexico liberalized, firms put under pressure by import competition rationalized their activities to the point that they became export competitive. In fact, they looked to export markets to achieve a scale that would allow them to be competitive.

Beyond the general benefit of exposure to an advanced, competitive world market, the act of trade liberalization also carries the potential of dynamic benefits. An aggressive trade opening may well qualify as a Schumpeterian change that triggers growth. In Schumpeter's analysis, the discontinuity of events and opportunities is the critical ingredient in promoting a new growth environment, it is *change* that is the source of increased productivity. Such a discontinuity involves, specifically, the introduction of a new good: the introduction of a new method of production; the opening of a new market; the conquest of a new source of supply of raw materials or half-manufactured goods; and the carrying out of the new organization of any industry. Together, deregulation and trade reform can shake an economy out of a slow-growth trap, toward an acceleration of growth which then develops its own dynamics and financing. Of course, there is no basis here for a *sustained* increase in growth. Rather, the model suggests a temporary acceleration of growth that need not be sustained indefinitely but will have shifted the economy to a higher growth path.

The Schumpeterian model has substantial theoretical support. For example, firms may well have available better techniques and good ideas, but they are unwilling to implement them except in the favorable setting of economy-wide, major and irreversible change. Once a program of liberalization is put in place, adaptation must take place and that is the occasion to implement major productivity improvements that had been on the shelves. The coordinated response to the change both acts to trigger externalities and it assures thereby that a reversal becomes far less likely. High rates of investment and the associated increase in productivity are a natural by-product of a successful break away from a trapped slow growth economy. Trade liberalization is also a time when opportunities open up, because access to cheap inputs creates export opportunities, which carry rents and profits that can be invested in capital goods, which in turn yield further productivity gains.

What Can Go Wrong?

One problem for trade reform is political. Too long a phase-in period with too many safeguards for those who might be adversely affected is an invitation to disruption and reversal. The other risk comes from the exchange rate. The elimination of obstacles to trade invariably creates an immediate increase in imports. But although inputs become more readily available and technology improves, the beneficial rise in exports does not happen immediately, even if a real depreciation is undertaken. For example, when Chile first liberalized imports almost fully in the late 1970s (but overvalued its managed exchange rate) import levels exploded and the exchange rate collapsed. Another stabilization had to be undertaken. Without a real depreciation, exports will scarcely help pay for the higher imports.

Because of balance of payments problems, comprehensive trade reform requires one of two conditions: either the country must be politically in a position to have a major real depreciation of the exchange rate (to help boost exports) or else it must have access to foreign exchange for a substantial period of time. Real depreciation is a problem because it means a fall in real wages unless offset by the improvement in the standard of living that stems from reduced protection. If reserves are not available and depreciation is impractical, the only realistic option for trade policy is to approach liberalization more gradually.

Rudiger Dornbusch, "The Case for Trade Liberalization in Developing Countries," *Journal of Economic Perspectives* 6, no. 1 (Winter 1992): 69–85.

19

The Origins of
Mexico's Free Trade Policy

MANUEL PASTOR AND CAROL WISE

In this article, we combine political and economic analysis in an attempt to account more fully for both the origins and sustainability of Mexico's commercial opening during the 1980s.

We begin the article with a brief review of the major turning points in Mexico's trade liberalization. We then apply some of the most prominent international political economy explanations for trade policy to the Mexican case and find them lacking. We subsequently attempt to systematize an alternative explanation of Mexican trade liberalization and provide evidence for our view.

Mexico's Trade Liberalization:
Critical Turning Points

While Mexican trade liberalization began in earnest after 1983, significant efforts in that direction were underway in the previous decade. For example, the balance-of-payments disequilibrium caused by import substitution industrialization (ISI) led President José Lopéz Portillo (1976–82) to try to rationalize trade through moderate liberalization and export diversification. Licenses were replaced with tariffs, which were then reduced; official prices for imports and exports were gradually removed; and exports were promoted through new fiscal incentives and trade credits to foreign countries. The country even came close to joining the General Agreement on Tariffs and Trade (GATT), an idea scrapped in 1980 as surging prices for Mexico's oil exports and an increasingly acrimonious domestic debate over GATT entry led government policymakers to postpone the decision. In 1981–82 surging imports, falling prices for all of the country's commodity exports, and burgeoning external debt service payments led the government to abandon the nascent trade liberalization program; by 1982, 100 percent of all imports were again covered by licenses.

Phase one (1983 to mid-1985) of the 1980s liberalization effort came as President Miguel de la Madrid's (1982–88) administration loosened the restrictive import regime adopted to address the country's debt crisis and continuing balance-of-payments shortfall. In 1984 the government reduced the percentage of imports subject to license coverage first to 83 percent and later to 27 percent, and adjusted tariffs downward on intermediate and capital goods. This first phase also saw the relaxation of export controls on 44 percent of non-oil exports as well as the signing of a U.S.-Mexican bilateral trade agreement geared toward further liberalization and the elimination of export subsidies.

Phase two (mid-1985 to late 1988) of the program upped the ante considerably. In 1986, the government announced a new four-step tariff reduction schedule that would end by 1988 with tariffs ranging between 0 and 30 percent. The original schedule was soon accelerated for two reasons. First, Mexico's accession to the GATT in mid-1986 meant a commitment to eliminate all official prices for imports and exports by the following year. Second, in December 1987 the government launched an inflation-combatting Economic Solidarity Pact, which included new wage and price guidelines and a lower 0–20 percent tariff target range designed to promote external competition as a way to restrain domestic prices. This period also brought the signing of a broader Framework Agreement with the United States in 1987 and a shift in export promotion tools from subsidies to temporary exemptions of tariffs and licenses on crucial imported industrial inputs.

By the time President Salinas (1988–94) had taken office, Mexico's commercial liberalization basically had been completed. Thus, phase three (1988–90) consisted mainly of fine tuning: tariffs were further reduced for those goods that were still registering unusually high price hikes (and hence contributing to inflationary pressures) and increased for those consumer goods sectors experiencing an import surge, the sum of which produced a slight increase in both the mean and weighted tariff rates in 1990. In mid-1990, the Salinas administration went well beyond previous efforts and initiated NAFTA negotiations with Canada and the United States. The implementation of NAFTA will represent phase four of Mexico's trade opening. Given the country's burgeoning trade deficit, however, this phase will likely also include some temporary backtracking on liberalization, along the lines of the mid-1993 tariff hikes on more than a dozen categories of imported goods.

The Mexican Case and Standard Theoretical Explanations for Trade Policy

The trade liberalization history detailed above is quite dramatic: ten years ago, the country's current degree of exposure to international trade (which approaches that of the European Community and the United States), not to mention a NAFTA-style arrangement, essentially was unthinkable. Moreover, while Mexico is certainly in the forefront of such liberalization, much of Latin America has now joined step in abandoning the protectionist trade regimes that characterized the region's postwar development strategies. Unfortunately, much of the literature on Latin America, having internalized the region's previous free trade pessimism, offers an abundance of criticisms of liberalization but a shortage of explanations—aside from the power of international financial institutions—for why it has occurred.

As such, explaining the Mexican liberalization requires an examination of the wider body of international political economy literature on trade policy. This literature focuses on four broad explanatory categories: global political-economic structures; factor endowments, sectoral concerns, and related interest group politics; national political institutions; and leaders' values and beliefs. Below, we conclude that these theoretical explanations are incomplete and must be supplemented with an alternative approach that draws on the tools of modern political economy.

Global Political-Economic Structures

As preferable as free trade may be for growth, efficiency, and income gains, international trade theorists usually assume that a country facing Mexico's situation in 1983—massive debt, declining terms of trade, industrial bloc protectionism, and domestic macroeconomic crisis—is not likely to reduce tariffs and nontariff barriers. Yet Mexico has steered hard in the direction of economic orthodoxy since the early 1980s. This is, of course, partly due to the dicta of international creditors and financial institutions whose leverage over Mexican policy was enhanced by their control of scarce foreign exchange, and hence it is tempting to side with those who have concluded that the rush toward free trade is evidence of imperialist imposition. Nonetheless, the fact that Mexican liberalization took place in the face of such adverse circumstances defies traditional logic; many of the most dramatic moves toward reform, including the acceleration of tariff reductions in late 1987, seem to have been more connected to domestic than to foreign pressures and politics.

One way to fill this explanatory gap at the international level would be to draw on the recent literature that attributes a nation's preference for open trade to the local presence of globalized industries dependent on exports, capital goods imports, and intrafirm or intraindustry trade. There is in fact strong evidence of the growing importance of such intraindustry trade in Mexico.

Intraindustry and intrafirm traders tend to favor liberalization on the grounds that such a policy reduces the costs of their imported inputs, whereas trade protection puts them at a competitive disadvantage both at home and abroad. Thus, when Mexico's entry into GATT was considered in the late 1970s, internationally oriented capitalists, represented by such business lobbies as the Confederation of Chambers of Industry (CONCAMIN), which consists of larger manufacturing firms, the Employers' Confederation of the Mexican Republic (COPARMEX), which was strongly tied to northern entrepreneurs with exporting interests, and the Confederation of National Chambers of Commerce (CONCANACO) supported Mexico's participation in GATT but lacked sufficient strength and perhaps motive to force through GATT entry. By 1986 those businesses most likely to benefit from freer trade had grown in both numbers and influence and were thus better positioned to finesse GATT entry. In short, the forging of stronger intraindustry trade links is one very plausible reason why Mexico responded to the worsening international economy by opening rather than closing its borders.

Factors, Sectors, and Interest Group Politics

The discussion of intraindustry trade raises the broader question of the policy preferences and lobbying actions of economic agents. The political economy literature suggests three approaches to these issues, all of which hypothesize with limited success the conditions under which a country like Mexico is likely to embrace trade liberalization. The first is the "factors of endowment" framework. Mexico may be classified as a "backward" country—abundant in land and labor but poor in capital. Given this, "expanding trade . . . benefits farmers and workers but harms capitalists; . . . contracting trade, in such an economy, benefits only the owners of capital and injures both workers and farmers." Thus, the theory predicts that domestic capital generally will fight increased exposure to trade, while farmers and workers will support a more liberal commercial policy.

As has long been recognized in the analysis of Organization for Economic Cooperation and Development trade policy, however, a straightforward factor endowments analysis is less relevant when trade becomes increasingly dictated by scale economies and international firms, i.e., intraindustry trade. Thus, it is no surprise that the complex domestic politics of Mexican trade policy, particularly before 1983, do not fit a simple factors model. Despite conditions of capital scarcity, for example, Mexican capitalists were increasingly divided over trade opening, with old-fashioned ISI-style local capital opposed to the free trade preferences of intraindustry internationalists. Meanwhile, Mexican workers frequently were protectionist, an outcome again at odds with the simple factors model.

A second approach relies on analyzing "the policy preferences of relatively united economic sectors" rather than factors or classes. In the Mexican trade debate, for example, landed agribusiness interests persuaded their rural labor allies to push for a more competitive exchange rate and an end to import restrictions on manufactured goods, while organized urban workers banded together with small and medium-sized industrialists in an attempt to preserve high tariffs, manufacturing rents, and jobs. In understanding the politics of Mexico's 1980s liberalization, some early winners (auto engine, microcomputer, and pharmaceutical sectors) and losers (textile, shoe, basic metals, and wood furniture sectors) have begun to stand out, and a sectoral analysis does square with these differing levels of support. What is most striking, however, is that many sectoral losers now at least nominally support free trade.

A third basic approach to explaining trade policy focuses on how concentrated interest groups may be better able to overcome the usual collective action problems associated with realizing common objectives. For example, as desirable as free trade may be for the majority of consumers, the bulk of the population has less incentive to organize in favor of free trade than does the minority bloc of losers; for the losers (industrial producers and labor), the costs from foreign competition are tangible and immediate, whereas for the winners, such gains as price reduction, quality control, and bureaucratic cleanup, are diffuse. Such interest group dynamics were evident when the largest business organization, the National Chamber of Manufacturing Industry (CANACINTRA), representing some sixty thousand small and medium-sized Mexico City industrial firms, joined together with nationalist intellectuals and a majority of government ministries (including the ministry of industry) and successfully deterred President López Portillo from signing the earlier GATT protocols. But why then was the country able to overcome this collective action problem and proceed with unilateral liberalization and GATT entry just six years later? What, in short, happened to the approximately one hundred thousand small and medium-sized producers which comprise over 90 percent of the Mexican business community and which had successfully stymied liberalization in the past?

Part of the answer is that in the wake of the debt crisis and first wave of unilateral commercial opening, some of the protectionist opposition had already washed up on Schumpeter's shores of "creative destruction." While it is difficult to separate the deleterious effects of import penetration from those of an adjustment-related contraction in industrial demand, the point here is simply that the hardest-hit sectors (textiles, shoes, consumer electronics, basic metals) during the mid-1980s also constituted some of the core membership of the adamantly protectionist CANACINTRA. The weakening of this lobby due to the economic ill fate of many of its members sheds some light on their inability to head off the subsequent GATT victory in 1986.

What is surprising and uncaptured by interest group analysis, however, is the breadth of support for free trade now expressed by even those smaller businesses least likely to succeed in the face of increasing import competition. While there are some direct beneficiaries from open trade, such as northern exporters with strong ties to U.S. markets, most small and medium-sized producers largely have failed to cash in on Mexico's recent export boom. Yet our research interviews with small and medium-sized Mexican producers reveal that most support the opening for two related reasons: (1) liberalization is perceived as part of an overall package to stabilize and reform the Mexican economy; and (2) these macroeconomic concerns, especially the desire to maintain low inflation, are eclipsing any serious debate over the microeconomic consequences. We develop this argument more fully below.

National Political Institutions

Another strand of explanation for trade policy relies on institutional analysis; "trade policy formation under different organizational and legal arrangements will yield corresponding differences in policy content." One standard argument here, illustrative of the impact of institutions, is that since the volatile Smoot-Hawley era the U.S. temptation to raise tariffs has been mitigated by the increasing delegation of commercial policymaking authority to the office of the U.S. executive, with the Congress playing less of a direct role in deciding on trade matters.

There is rich evidence to suggest that an organizational overhaul, particularly at the level of the state, played a strong role in facilitating the successful implementation of Mexico's trade reform. The neutralization of protectionist demands, for example, was helped by the extraction of trade policy from its traditional location in the trade ministry and its placement within other, more insulated state agencies such as the Secretariat of Finance and Public Credit and the Secretariat of Programming and Budget. On its own, however, a state- or institution-centered explanation is at best an intervening variable: it tells us how a new trade regime was implemented but not where it came from.

Leaders' Values and Beliefs

While most analysts agree that cognitive factors (or ideas) can affect policy, there is disagreement about the extent of this effect. In the Mexican case, there has indeed been a massive shift in the ideological orientation of key political and economic actors. For the first time during the postwar era, Mexico's most powerful leaders share a consensus concerning past excesses of statism and protection and seem unequivocal in their commitment to free trade. Moreover, this set of beliefs now appears to be broadly held throughout the public and the private sectors; our interviews, both with bureaucrats working directly on trade policy and with leaders of the small and medium-sized business sector, revealed a new and general openness to neoliberal thinking.

We concur with those who stress the importance of cognitive factors but worry that ideologically based explanations are too often focused on belief change per se. As Judith Goldstein has observed, "ideas influence policy only when they are carried by individuals or groups with political clout." Thus, any analysis of the training, beliefs, and values of President Salinas and his inner circle of technocrats must be connected to institutional factors, underlying political coalitions, and actors' access to economic and political resources. An obvious institutional factor, for example, is Mexico's highly presidential, low-accountability political system, a feature that has made it easier for the President and his U.S.-trained advisers to instill their own free trade preferences. Equally important is that the antiprotectionist leanings of Presidents de la Madrid and Salinas merged well with the preexisting mindset of the internationalist faction of the Mexican business community. Finally, the power of the neoliberal faction was enhanced through contact with its counterparts in international financial institutions and was bolstered by the fact that the latter held the keys to foreign exchange during the capital-scarce years of the debt crisis.

A second problem is that ideological explanations for policy change sometimes fail to systematize the exact way in which ideas influence policy. As rational actors, after all, politicians are unwilling to bear infinite costs even in the pursuit of their most cherished ideological precepts. In our view, ideology has import in that if decisions correspond with decision makers' values, they may be willing to accept higher political costs than would be the case if their focus was on, say, reelection or other so-called opportunistic goals.

Summary

This brief review of prominent explanations for trade liberalization yields both insights and shortcomings. Global economic structures certainly contributed to the Mexican opening in that an externally induced crisis helped prompt policy change, and increasing intraindustry trade helped catalyze a new constituency in favor of liberalization. The trade policy shift also was pushed along by (1) the greater insulation of trade policymakers by relocating them to certain key state institutions and (2) by the unprecedented ideological free trade consensus shared by today's generation of politicians and economic managers.

We are still left, however, with the perplexing resistance of the Mexican case to the more classic factorial or sectoral explanations. Our approach, detailed below, tries to address this as well as to fill other gaps in the standard explanations for trade liberalization. We are better able to explain why the Mexican free trade consensus includes likely "losers," as well as to identify the risks in the present reform effort.

An Alternative Approach

While the debt and foreign exchange crisis of the early 1980s played a critical and indisputable role in triggering Mexican liberalization, we find the most striking feature of Mexico's trade reform to be its profoundly domestic character. The most dramatic phase of the liberalization, the acceleration of tariff rate reduction in late 1987, was linked to an overall domestic strategy to contain inflation and went well beyond the GATT timetable. The subsequent NAFTA negotiations were initiated not by the United States but by President Salinas; indeed, the U.S. administration was at first taken off guard when a number of Latin American nations followed in Mexico's footsteps by enthusiastically taking up the invitation for hemispheric free trade issued within the context of President Bush's June 1990 "Enterprise for the Americas Initiative." It is therefore inside the Mexican political economy that we should look for the origins of trade liberalization.

A critical factor influencing policy choice is the linkage of one policy with another. In such a case, the set of potential supporters can widen as various interest groups accept the costs from one government action in order to obtain the benefits from another part of the policy package. For example, in numerous Latin American countries, including Mexico, trade liberalization has been associated with inflation reduction. Thus, even those likely to experience sectoral or distributional difficulties because of trade liberalization expect to gain from the creation of a more level macroeconomic playing field. To the extent that macroeconomic stabilization also promises subsequent growth, those that may have expected to find their resources unemployed by import penetration are now more confident that the adjustment period will be shorter. Losers, in short, lose less and winners gain more.

As well-told a story as Mexico's adjustment experience in the 1980s may be, the linkage between macroeconomic stabilization and trade liberalization has been stressed by just a few authors. Again, the key episode in this regard was the December 1987 launching of the Economic Solidarity Pact. Under the pact, business and labor agreed to wage-and-price controls and the government firmly committed to slow dramatically the rate of currency devaluation and to liberalize trade further, mostly through tariff reductions. In other words, trade opening was an evident and seemingly irreversible policy from the pact's beginning; in particular, import competition, coupled with a nearly fixed exchange rate, was expected to provide a second level of control over domestic inflation.

This new approach to inflation control did manage to bring inflation down from nearly 160 percent in 1987 to just 20 percent in 1989. Growth was low but positive; the negative features of the program showed up in a doubling of the import bill, a 33 percent real appreciation of the peso, and an over $6 billion loss in reserves. To alleviate foreign exchange pressures, Mexico sought to reduce its external debt through the U.S.-sponsored Brady Plan and finally reached an accord in July 1989. While the agreement with international creditors was not implemented until early 1990, the expectation of debt reduction made more credible the promise to maintain the nominal exchange rate and therefore helped the government keep domestic price and wage inflation in line. Although imports stayed high, Mexican policymakers believed that the trade imbalance could be financed, primarily because they also believed that the combination of reduced debt and low inflation would attract foreign investors. To test the waters, President Salinas set out in January 1990 to Europe. Marketing Mexico proved unexpectedly difficult: Western European investors were more interested in the emerging opportunities in the former socialist countries to their east. Capital flows, so necessary to sustain the anti-inflation program, were going to have to be generated elsewhere.

Salinas returned to Mexico and initiated two dramatic strategies. In May 1990 he proposed the denationalization of the banking system, a measure that was passed in just two weeks by the Mexican Congress. While denationalization had many purposes, one was to attract new capital flows, both through foreign investment and the repatriation of flight capital by Mexican citizens. Then in June—after months of denials by lower-level officials hoping to stave off organized opposition—Mexico and the United States announced that they would begin talks on a bilateral free trade pact. Again, one of the purposes in at least the timing of NAFTA was to attract the capital flows that were needed to maintain the exchange rate and combat inflation.

This linkage of macroeconomic stabilization with trade liberalization and the embodiment of both in the NAFTA initiative help to explain why the coalition of free trade supporters includes small and medium-sized businesses. In the words of one top analyst of the Mexican economy, "Firms think that NAFTA is good for Mexico as a whole even if it's not great for them," mostly because it will raise overall economic efficiency and "stabilize the policy environment," a point confirmed in interview after interview with Mexican business people and decision makers. In short, macroeconomic objectives have led many economic and political actors to set aside microeconomic concerns.

Manuel Pastor and Carol Wise, "The Origins and Sustainability of Mexico's Free Trade Policy," *International Organization* 48, no. 3 (Summer 1994): 459–89.

20

The Political Economy of MERCOSUR

LUIGI MANZETTI

Four countries of South America—Argentina, Brazil, Paraguay, and Uruguay—joined together to create the Common Market of South America (*Mercado Común del Sur,* or MERCOSUR) in March 1991, the most ambitious attempt yet toward regional integration in Latin America.

Drawing upon recent concepts in political economy and international relations, this article focuses upon the political motivations and processes behind MERCOSUR.

MERCOSUR and Its Antecedents

This is not the first time that Latin America has attempted to organize a regional integration arrangement. As early as 1960, the region launched the Latin American Free Trade Association (LAFTA) under an ambitious program. However, despite good intentions, its member states failed to agree on the breadth and scope that the nascent integration process should encompass, which led to the demise of LAFTA before the end of the decade. During the 1970s, the focus of attention shifted toward more modest efforts at the subregional level, such as the Central American Common Market (CACM) and the Andean Pact. However, following a period of early success, both had fallen into obscurity by the early 1980s, when the initial goals of liberalizing trade and coordinating macroeconomic policies became first delayed, then implemented only half-heatedly, and eventually postponed indefinitely.

However, the mid-1980s were not without hope in this area. In 1986, Brazil and Argentina put aside longstanding rivalry to enter into a cooperative relationship termed the Argentine-Brazilian Economic Integration Program (ABEIP), a formal program for economic and political cooperation. From a political standpoint, the ABEIP aimed to strengthen the infant democratic regimes which had emerged in each country, following prolonged periods of military rule, during the mid-1980s. In the economic realm, the goal of the ABEIP was to expand, and diversify, bilateral trade between their two countries *via* protocols that emphasized, on a sector-by-sector basis, such domestic products as capital goods, agribusiness, and the automotive sector.

However, the favorable economic situation which had prompted Argentina and Brazil to embark upon the ABEIP in 1986 soon turned sour in the years that followed due to (1) failure of domestic macroeconomic policies and (2) external constraints imposed by their respective foreign debts. By the end of the decade, both Argentina and Brazil found themselves in deep economic crisis which slowed, even further, any progress toward economic integration.

Any misgivings about the future of the projected integration were quickly dispelled after two new presidents came to office in each country: Carlos Menem of Argentina, in mid-1989, and Fernando Collor de Mello of Brazil, in early 1990. Both Menem and Collor de Mello adopted free-market economic policies that differed appreciably from those of their predecessors; both re-affirmed their commitment to, and desire to push forward with even greater zeal, the integration effort. Indeed, economic integration was a key component of both their foreign policies. In July 1990, Menem and Collor de Mello signed the Buenos Aires Act, which called for establishing a common market by the end of 1994. A month later (August 1990), both Paraguay and Uruguay joined the proposed integration scheme. Though Chile was invited to join also, it declined the offer. On 26 March 1991, the Foreign Ministers of Argentina, Brazil, Paraguay and Uruguay signed the Treaty of Asunción, which called for the creation of the *Mercado Común del Sur* (MERCOSUR) or South America Common Market. The main provisions of the Treaty of Asunción were the following:

1. An **across-the-board tariff reduction** would replace the sector-by-sector approach used by the ABEIP.
2. The **coordination of macroeconomic policies** in accordance with the tariffs reduction schedule and the elimination of non-quantitative restrictions.
3. The **establishment of a common external tariff** for trade partners outside MERCOSUR, with the objective of increasing the competitiveness of the member countries.
4. The **development of accords for specific sectors of the economy** in order to optimize the use and mobility of production factors and achieve efficient economies of scale.
5. The implementation of an **institutional framework to solve trade litigation.**

Motivations

Over the last 15 years, scholars involved with international relations theory and political economy have increasingly turned their attention to the role of institutional cooperation in the area of international trade. According to one study on the subject, intraregional cooperation is a function of three broad considerations: (1) political/security concerns; (2) expectation of gains from liberalizing international trade; and (3) expectation of gains from regionalizing production and the international transfer of capital and technology. Let us see to what extent these motives apply in the case of MERCOSUR.

Political/Security Concerns

The most successful integration experiences have political purposes that are central to the overall mission. In fact, some feel that one of the reasons why regional integration schemes have had such a poor track record in Latin America has been their lack of a clearly defined political agenda that would, as in the European Community, direct the economic objectives. Nevertheless, a political agenda seems to have been the guiding principle behind the Argentine-Brazilian scheme (ABEIP) and, later, that of the MERCOSUR as well. MERCOSUR, like the European Community itself, has placed consolidating democracy and preserving peace in the Southern Cone among its paramount objectives. Indeed, a fundamental prerequisite for new members is that their governments be democratically elected.

How can we interpret this important shift? Taking a broad view, one author hypothesizes that the "lessened need for cross-regional security alliances increases the likelihood of regional integration". However, and as noted earlier, Argentina and Brazil have long been divided by ambitions to become regional powers, a goal which dates back to the early days of their independence, from Spain and Portugal respectively. During the 1970s, both countries had military governments that engaged in arms races of their own, which encompassed the production and import of a wide variety of sophisticated weaponry, as well as development of a nuclear power capability.

Argentina's defeat in its war with Britain over the Falklands/Malvinas Islands (1982), and the subsequent withdrawal of the armed forces from power in both Argentina and Brazil, made security concerns based on military considerations a very low priority. For the civilian administrations that ensued, security took on a new meaning: the preservation of regional peace and democracy.

Not surprisingly, some of the most important achievements of MERCOSUR to date have been in the political realm. MERCOSUR has provided its member states with a forum for discussion of sensitive policy issues, such as those in relation to transport and communications, nuclear proliferation (Argentina and Brazil signed a nonproliferation treaty in 1991), environmental protection, military cooperation, illegal immigration, and the drug traffic.

Moreover, the deep economic crisis in which the Southern Cone countries found themselves, plus their increasingly marginal role in world trade, took on the character of a security issue. As large trading blocs emerged, and spread, in other parts of the world (North America, East Asia, and Europe), Latin America's decision-makers lived in fear of being inexorably cut off from the reconfiguration of the world economy—with predictable consequences. This perception served to strengthen the incentive of many Latin American countries to seek out, and pursue, closer economic links, a view which gained added impetus from the Enterprise for the Americas Initiative (EAI) announced by President Bush in June 1990. Thus security took on a broader connotation: that of enhancing domestic competitiveness in the world economy, penetrating new markets, and improving one's bargaining position in trade negotiations. Renewing the emphasis on regional integration could provide the means by which to satisfy these security concerns, newly defined. As President Menem declared, MERCOSUR allows, "the possibility of uniting [its member countries' efforts] to compete in a new global market in which the strength of the trade blocs has become more important than that of individual countries." Seen in this light, MERCOSUR is meant to increase the bargaining power of its member countries in their dealings with the trade blocs of the industrialized world to a much greater extent than would be possible *via* the old go-it-alone approach. Through MERCOSUR, South American leaders are trying to develop a common agenda of policy priorities, which can then be negotiated in the General Agreement on Tariffs and Trade (GATT), as well as with the members of the NAFTA and the EC.

Gains from Liberalization of International Trade

Latin America's early attempts at integration were conceived as an integral part of import-substituting industrialization (ISI), a strategy strongly advocated and supported by the Economic Commission for Latin America (ECLA), an organ of the United Nations [known more widely in Latin America by its Spanish nomenclature: *Comisión Económica para América Latina* or CEPAL]. For ECLA/CEPAL, regional integration offered a way to provide markets large enough to satisfy economies of scale which would, in turn, strengthen the import-substitution process. Non-reciprocity and preferential treatment were to be granted in accordance with, or dependent upon, the level of economic development of individual countries. Tariff barriers against countries outside the region would serve to protect Latin American products and enable them to compete more effectively against foreign imports. In brief, the ECLA recipe for regional integration was an inward-looking strategy, conceived and understood as a "collective defense" for sheltering Latin America from adverse fluctuations in the world economy.

In the 1980s, however, the collapse of many Latin American economies called the ISI strategy into question. As a result, by the early 1990s most countries in the region had adopted neo-conservative economic policies to address the problems posed by large foreign debts, high inflation, and huge fiscal deficits. The ultimate goal of the neo-conservative economic prescription was to push through deregulation and trade liberalization so that the market, rather than the state, would be the ultimate referee on how resources would be allocated. Thus country leaders came to believe that trade liberalization maximizes the gains from inherited comparative advantage and encourages efficiencies from specialization and economies of scale. For one thing, many Latin American countries constitute markets too small to achieve effective economies of scale. Free trade-*cum*-integration offers the possibility of overcoming that problem, as this combination is capable of providing larger markets, a greater volume of trade, and better opportunities to develop specialization. At the same time, liberalizing first with neighbors, if they are major trading partners, provides many benefits while still ensuring regionalized protection against more efficient global producers.

Consequently, regional integration has assumed a new meaning. It has turned from being a defensive, into an offensive, strategy. Whereas, during the 1950s and 1960s, the prescription for regional integration tended to promote an inward-looking economic model, the emphasis today is on export-led growth—and regional integration is understood as an element of the overall outward-oriented strategy.

Gains from Regionalized Production and International Transfer of Capital

Regional integration can also serve as a powerful magnet to attract new external investment and technology into a country. Such arrangements provide the opportunity for capital, both foreign and domestic, to expand into larger markets *via* common external tariffs, rules of origin, and regulations regarding local content which, if exploited, hold out the prospect for winning, or increasing, market share. Integrated markets may promise other advantages as well, such as access to a low-wage labor force or the availability of highly skilled workers. A foreign multinational may decide to set up factories in more than one country within a given regional bloc, thus availing itself of lower costs (in transportation, communication and, possibly, of salaries) derived from having plants in neighboring or adjacent countries. The multinational can thus enjoy the best of both worlds: on the one hand, it can exploit the regional market under advantageous conditions while, on the other, it can also ship its products abroad, outside the region, where it may find itself at a competitive advantage due to its lower costs of production. Undertakings may extend from simple assembly lines for low-tech goods up to, and encompassing, more sophisticated consumer and durable goods. In this way, developing economies are enabled to reap the benefits of global interdependence through the net transfer of new capital and advanced technology to the recipient country.

Some of these trends have indeed been present in the case of MERCOSUR. Unlike previous Latin American attempts at integration, where the private sector deferred to government leadership, some entrepreneurial sectors have taken the lead in this integration effort.

Multinational corporations have been active as well. The prospect of serving a much greater market has induced many multinational corporations to reorganize their production and marketing operations in the four MERCOSUR countries. This is particularly true in the automotive sector, where both Ford and Volkswagen have merged their South American operations.

Who Gains?

Earlier, the discussion focused on the strategic motives that lead nations to join regional organizations today, and on how these considerations apply to MERCOSUR. How are integration-related benefits distributed among, and across, the member countries? In other words, who gains (and who loses) from integration? Do the payoffs justify the effort? Do some partners reap benefits at the expense of others? In the end, these are the crucial considerations that determine the ultimate success or failure of regional cooperation/integration over the long run.

Scholars of the so-called "realist" school of international relations, which holds that states operate at the international level in a state of anarchy, contend that this situation makes for a sufficient level of insecurity as to mitigate against the kind of institutional cooperation required for genuine integration. Consequently, prospects for institutional cooperation are limited. Not only do states worry about how they will fare *within* cooperative agreements (absolute gains), but they are equally, if not more, concerned with how well they will fare compared to other states (relative gains), fearing that their partners may cheat and/or obtain an advantage over them. If the perception arises that the gains from cooperation are being distributed unequally, a problem of "relative gains" occurs. If this perception then leads a state to try to advance itself relative to its neighbor or fellow member, the concept of cooperation immediately falls into decline (or falls apart); once such a decline sets in, the process tends to accelerate.

However, there are other theorists who recognize the problem incumbent upon relative gains on the one hand, but who believe that it is neither so pervasive, nor so threatening to the prospects of cooperation, as "realists" would have us believe on the other hand. The problem of relative gains may work to limit the range of viable cooperative agreements because states will not accept deals that provide disproportionately greater benefits to another. However, if distribution is the primary relative-gains problem, states can alter the terms of the cooperative behavior or offer side payments until the distribution is sufficiently proportionate. Nonetheless, such arrangements are not always made nor, even when offered, can they always satisfy the needs of the disaffected partner; thus the relative gains problem lingers on as a factor capable of hampering, if not crippling, cooperative arrangements.

This discussion over relative gains is relevant to an understanding of (1) some of the difficulties MERCOSUR has been experiencing in trying to meet its Asunción Treaty targets, and (2) the extent to which these difficulties may be successfully resolved in the future.

First, there are asymmetries in market size, which have been a major source of controversy. Brazil's economy far surpasses that of its partners: its GDP is 3.7 times larger than that of Argentina, 50.7 times larger than that of Paraguay, and 37.4 times larger than that of Uruguay. By itself, Brazil accounts for 75% of the total MERCOSUR gross domestic product (GDP) and for 80% of its industrial manufactures. As a result, analysts from the countries with smaller economies— Argentina, Paraguay, and Uruguay—have argued that Brazil is bound to garner most of the benefits from MERCOSUR, since it enjoys an economy of scale whose potential is far beyond the capacity of its partners to match. Thus, there is widespread fear in these countries that they will become relegated to the position of serving as suppliers of raw materials and intermediate products to Brazil's industrial sector unless appropriate industrial policies are adopted to forestall it.

Those who argue that Brazil will end up reaping most of the MERCOSUR benefits point to the fact that Brazilian companies have been the most active in every area: not just in selling to the markets of their partners, but also setting up intermediate processing plants in Argentina and participating in joint ventures with third-country firms to establish processing plants in Argentina, Paraguay, and Uruguay. While it could be argued that specialization responds to the criterion of comparative advantage, it is also true that it could undermine the industrial conversion now underway in Argentina, Paraguay, and Uruguay.

Problems of relative gain also arise from asymmetries in domestic macroeconomic policies. Coordinating economic policy among members, which should be another cornerstone of a common market, has also lagged. The three smaller partners—Argentina, Paraguay, and Uruguay—have made painful progress in

lowering inflation and slashing their respective fiscal deficits. They have combined policies of structural adjustment with a unilateral approach to liberalizing
trade that has served to open up their economies to foreign competition and investment. Brazil, however, is another matter. That country has been unable to implement a coherent stabilization program due, at least in part, to strong opposition from the domestic lobbies affected. Brazil has also been much more cautious
in moving toward liberalizing trade. Even though it has made a start on leaving
the protectionism of previous administrations behind, its approach has been so
gradual that whole economic sectors remain highly sheltered from international
competition. At the root of the problem is the fact that Argentina, Paraguay, and
Uruguay have given up the idea of retaining manufacturing and service sectors
that are not truly competitive and have retreated to a development model based
upon traditional exports. In contrast, Brazil is still trying to hang on to most of
its domestic manufacturing and service industry in the hope that, if the transition to free trade is slow enough, those sectors will be able to adjust to a more
competitive business environment. However, this has meant that Brazil's macroeconomic policies have been at odds with those of its partners as well as with the
provisos of the Asunción Treaty.

Within this scenario, exchange rate policy has also proved a troublesome issue.
While the smaller partners have recently been able to maintain fairly steady rates
of exchange, the Brazilian government again is the exception: it has been following a policy of mini-devaluations. This has elicited strong protests from its partners. The latter governments, pressed by their own domestic business sectors,
complain that Brazil's unilateral decision to devalue gives an unfair advantage to
Brazilian exporters, enabling them to undersell their competition in the other
MERCOSUR countries. Discrepancies in exchange-rate policies have resulted in
trade imbalances between Brazil and Argentina, at the expense of the latter.

Conclusion

This discussion has tried to place the experience of MERCOSUR within the
framework of current theories of political economy and international relations.
Both the changed (and changing) nature of the world economy, as well as domestic crises within the Southern Cone, have combined to create the incentive to organize a new type of integration scheme. In its first years of existence, MERCO-
SUR has achieved remarkable results, politically and economically. However, as
integration increasingly binds the four countries more closely together, problems
of relative gains have begun to arise. Thus far, the four countries have been able
to address most of the disputes that have arisen more or less successfully, either
through new internal arrangements or the offer of side payments. Nonetheless,
many problems, many derived from asymmetries among the partners, still persist
and offer no easy solution.

Luigi Manzetti, "The Political Economy of MERCOSUR," *Journal of Interamerican Studies and World Affairs* 35, no. 4 (Winter 1993): 101–41.

Section V

Foreign Capital and the Macroeconomy

For hundreds of years, businesses and individuals from rich countries have found it profitable to invest in poor countries, and poor countries have found it attractive to use foreign capital to help them develop. But the economic and political effects of foreign investment remain controversial, and national policies toward international capital have varied a great deal.

Foreign investment in Latin America has typically taken two forms: foreign direct investment (FDI) and loans (see Baer and Hargis, reading 21). FDI is the establishment by a multinational corporation (MNC) of a branch plant or subsidiary in another country. Managerial control remains with the home company, which also bears all the risks of the investment. FDI is sometimes criticized because it can leave important portions of the national economy in foreign hands—multinationals have indeed dominated some major Latin American industries, such as automobiles. On the other hand, the host country bears no direct responsibility to ensure the profitability of the investment, so that FDI does not expose national governments to substantial risk. And MNCs can bring with them technological, managerial, and marketing expertise that is not otherwise available.

International loans are extended either by commercial banks or the purchasers of bonds. In both instances, and in contrast to FDI, an international loan carries a legal commitment to pay but confers on the investor no managerial control over the use of the funds. A debtor country can, of course, refuse to pay its debts, but it would then be in violation of an international contract, and this violation can be costly to the country's reputation and can also expose it to retaliation. In normal times, governments and firms prefer to service their debts. Critics charge that international borrowing can mortgage too much of the nation's patrimony to wealthy foreign creditors, that borrowed funds are often misused, and that the requirement to pay debts even in difficult times exacerbates social suffering and unrest. Supporters believe that foreign loans can be fruitfully employed and that the obligation to repay is worth the gain in control over the borrowed funds.

In the 1960s and 1970s, FDI was especially controversial in Latin America as many local residents watched the increasing dominance of North American, European, and Japanese firms over portions of their economies. Many governments imposed stringent controls on FDI, even prohibiting it from certain industries. Since the early 1980s, most Latin American countries have become more eager to attract FDI, which is generally seen as less volatile than foreign finance (see Bergsman and Shen, reading 24). Nonetheless, national policies toward FDI continue to diverge, and MNCs remain restricted in many activities (Haggard, reading 25).

Foreign debt has been a Latin American constant since independence. It has fueled some episodes of rapid growth, such as in Argentina between 1870 and 1914. It has also been the source of great adjustment difficulties, as in the 1930s and 1980s. Indeed, the debt crisis that began in 1982 launched one of Latin America's most difficult decades. The foreign debt became an object of intense political debate, and in most cases, it ended up being a tremendous drain on the national economy. Some blamed foreign bankers for this situation; others looked at features of national policy and the national political economy (Sachs, reading 22).

After the troubled years of the debt crisis and recovery, since the early 1990s capital has flowed back toward Latin America in large quantities. The process has not been without difficulties, such as several rounds of currency and financial crises. But most of the region now seems both willing and able to attract FDI and foreign lending in large quantities (Calvo, Leiderman, and Reinhart, reading 23).

21

Forms of External Capital and Economic Development in Latin America: 1820–1997

WERNER BAER

KENT HARGIS

Introduction

Policy makers in emerging economies choose the forms by which foreign investors can participate in the domestic economy. Implicit in this choice are the benefits and costs of each form of external capital inflow. Among the benefits are the enhanced ability to finance domestic investment in excess of domestic saving to achieve faster rates of economic growth, smooth fluctuations in income and diversify the risks of the domestic economy. Costs include the drain on the balance of payments resulting from profit remittances and debt servicing, and the risk that actual capital inflows will fall short of expected inflows, increasing costs of economic adjustment. Another cost, and one of the most sensitive aspects of reliance on external capital, is the constraint placed on domestic policy makers in pursuing certain economic and political goals. To the extent that explicit or implicit conditions for obtaining and maintaining access to foreign resources and honoring these obligations prevail over the aims of domestic groups, the result is a decline in national sovereignty.

When attracting external capital, domestic agents must first decide the risks and constraints under which they will accept each form of financial contract and then determine at each point in time whether it remains optimal to honor these contracts. Creditors' recourse in the event of default is limited by the inability of international courts to enforce contracts across national borders and of external assets to be seized to cover the default. Consequently, with the exception of infrequent military intervention by creditor countries, the constraint is whether a domestic agent is willing to honor foreign financial contracts, rather than their ability to do so. The contract will only be honored if the direct or indirect cost of default is greater than the benefit, as the country always has the option of autarky in trade and capital flows.

Three distinctions are important in determining the risks and constraints of each form of capital inflow. First, the maturity structure determines whether the creditor has the option to refuse renewing credits. Short-term credits are riskier because the debtor may be forced to amortize the debt rather than simply keep up interest payments. The possibility that a costly liquidation of assets may be required when short-term debt is not rolled over was a key feature of the Mexican crisis.

Second, the risk sharing nature of debt and equity contracts are different. While payments are required under good and bad states of nature for debt contracts, equity holders only receive the residual claim on the earnings of the company. The degree of risk sharing with debt contracts also depends on the currency of denomination, whether the inflow is at fixed or floating interest rates and implicit government guarantees.

Finally, official, multilateral and private sector lenders may have different motivations and allow for different uses of credits. While official lenders have political motivations and multilateral creditors have economic development goals, private lenders may only be interested in the profitability and repayment of the loan.

After entering into the contract, the debtor must determine if the costs of servicing the contract exceed the expected benefits. The sovereign lending literature provides several motivations for why debtors will repay their debt. Costs may take the form of direct sanctions such as foreign invasion, seizure of foreign assets or exclusion from world capital and goods markets. The willingness, however, of creditor governments to intervene militarily on behalf on creditors has been limited since the early 20th century and the magnitude of external assets to be seized are unlikely to be sufficient to deter defaults.

Therefore, the more important cost is exclusion from future access to international capital markets. The severity of this exclusion depends on the existing prospects for trade and capital flows and the linkages among different forms of debt inflows or between debt and equity inflows. Government defaults and violation of implicit government guarantees on the banking system may have more widespread linkages than defaults of individual private sectors creditors. The ability to enforce this exclusion depends on whether creditors can form effective coalitions, between private sector creditors or among the private sector, multilateral institutions and national governments, to punish debtors.

Independence Loans

From the early years of independence (1820s) until WWI there were three principal periods of foreign capital inflows to Latin America: a brief boom during the 1820s, a more sustained movement in the 1860s and a large inflow in the decade prior to 1914. During the period after independence, bonds issued to private investors were the dominant form of capital inflow while the costs of not honoring these obligations were limited by the absence of government intervention or organized bondholder committees to coordinate creditors when debt servicing difficulties arose.

In the 1820s bonds were issued in London by several newly independent Latin countries and the funds obtained ". . . were mainly intended to meet obligations resulting from the wars of liberation and also current governmental expenditures and only to a limited extent for public works directly or indirectly stimulating production." Latin government bonds were the largest single category of new investment in London during 1822–25. This early dependence on foreign finance and the political support of Great Britain in guaranteeing independence had its counterpart in the openness of these economies, especially to British manufactured goods, which had privileged access to most of the newly independent countries, and which stifled the early development of domestic manufactures. By the end of the 1820s, however, most of the bonds had fallen into default and were not settled until the 1860s in many cases. With declining customs revenues and export earnings, Latin governments simply did not have the financial resources to pay off the contracted debts.

The ability of private bondholders to impose sanctions during this period was hindered by the lack of government involvement in international financial relationships and their own inability to coordinate penalties. Intervention by the British government on behalf of bondholders was limited during the defaults of the newly independent Latin American governments and throughout the 19th century, with trade relations often taking precedence. The assessment of one historical account that "It simply had not been conceived as a national interest to help bondholders" stands in stark contrast to the extensive involvement of multilateral institutions during the 1980s. The ability of private creditors to collect debt payments was also hindered by the lack of permanent bondholder committees to negotiate settlements or penalize debtors. The difficulty in obtaining repayment is reflected in the fact that defaults for all British foreign bonds during this period lasted an average of 14 years.

Primary Export Period 1860–1914

After 1860, foreign inflows evolved from long-term bonds to different forms of direct and portfolio equity investment, helping to achieve greater risk sharing. Creditors were able to impose harsher sanctions than earlier in the 19th century because of the greater perceived costs to domestic policy makers of exclusion from future international capital and trade flows, the formation of permanent bondholder committees and occasional government intervention.

Investments flowed into the development of mines and plantations, railways and port facilities, and by the end of the century and early 20th century into banks and such public utilities as electricity generation and distribution, gas companies and telephones. Initially, foreign capital was in the form of government bonds, accounting for 76% of total British investments in 1865 and 64% in 1885. Maturities were long-term and at fixed rates of interest, helping to reduce interest rate risk and the need to roll over loans frequently.

After 1885, British and US investments increasingly focused on direct and portfolio investment in private companies. Between 1885 and 1913, 50% of additional British investment was in the form of direct investment with another 19% in corporate securities. Interestingly, an increasing proportion of portfolio investment was in the form of portfolio equity, similar to the expansion of these flows after 1990, while most portfolio investment in corporate securities was in US and Canadian controlled companies.

Both foreign investors and the host governments at the time had interests in expanding international trade and capital flows. The latter were dominated by the land-owning elites and exporters who benefited enormously from the emphasis on the primary export model and foreign investment in infrastructure. One author found that the favorable treatment of foreign creditors was not surprising since ". . . the small Latin American states had no alternative but to make concessions if they wanted to return to the fold of creditworthy nations and to spur a new current of direct investments from abroad." Latin American governments guaranteed property rights, placed few restrictions on foreign trade and for certain sectors offered extra-market incentives. For instance, almost all Latin American governments offered large subsidies of cash or land or both, and guaranteed rates of return to foreign companies investing in railroads.

The period also accounted for the few instances of British military intervention in the region, with its involvement in the blockade of the Venezuelan port in 1902 and the 1862 invasion of Mexico. Of greater importance was that private creditors were now able to coordinate and impose stricter conditionality than after the defaults of the 1820s. The Council of the Corporation of Foreign Bondholders was formed in 1868, giving a permanent organization to negotiate settlements and coordinate creditors. The Council's linkage to the London Stock Exchange and ability to refuse future access to governments in default enhanced the power of private creditors.

The growing influence of private foreign creditors on domestic economic policy is demonstrated by the resolution of the Peruvian default of 1876 with the Grace contract in late 1889. This settlement led to the exchange of debt for the creation of the Peruvian Corporation, which was given the entire national railway for 66 years, guano deposits and customs revenues. The period also witnessed the largest number of British default settlements resulting in some economic control over Latin America. Although this occurred in only 8% of all British foreign settlements from 1821 to 1975, 77% occurred in Latin America between 1871 and 1925. These included Colombia (land in 1873), the Dominican Republic (railways in 1893). Ecuador (railways in 1897), El Salvador (railways in 1899) and Paraguay (land in 1885). The expanding influence of foreign private creditors and governments helped to reduce the average duration of default for all British loans during the period to 6.3 years from 14 years in the earlier period.

In other cases, such as the 1898 Funding Loan in Brazil, private bondholder committees were able to demand conditionality terms "as harsh as those imposed by an IMF agreement" or arrange for a relatively quick settlement. In the case of Argentina in 1890, however, when the government borrowed excessively in the international capital market and was unable to meet its payments to the House of Baring, a rescue operation was organized through the Bank of England. The Argentine government was eventually able to obtain some debt reduction, with a 30% reduction in interest payments for five years, and suspend amortization for eight years.

The Interwar Period

During the Interwar period, the United States surpassed the United Kingdom as the leading creditor to the region with debt financing being most important. But, the collapse of world trade and capital flows during World Depression of the 1930s limited the costs of exclusion from world markets and was demonstrated by the higher degree of autonomy displayed by Latin. American policy makers. In addition, the lack of existing bondholder committees to coordinate US creditors and limited US government intervention on behalf of creditors enhanced this autonomy.

During the 1920s many Latin American governments were anxious to contract loans in the US capital market and they absorbed 32% of all US foreign loans over 1925–29. During 1914–30, the share of portfolio capital in the balance of US foreign investment in South America increased from 11% to 46% while government debt accounted for 97% of the balance of portfolio investments in 1930. Their motive was in part to raise funds to cover government budget deficits. Government expenditures for debt service were covered by "refinancing loans." Another motive for government borrowing was ". . . the widespread conviction among Latin American elites that they could carry out public works and urban modernization projects with cheap money from New York. This urge led them to contract a number of 'development' loans during the years 1925–28."

In order to make New York banks more amenable to the granting of loans, financial experts from the United States were contracted by various Latin American governments. The most famous external financial expert was Edwin Kemmerer, a Princeton professor of economics, who headed six missions to Latin America. Prior to the era of multilateral institutions and missions by the International Monetary Fund (IMF), the Kemmerer missions performed a similar role by intermediating between US creditors and debtors in Latin America. Kemmerer, like the IMF, was not officially tied to the US government and could therefore claim some degree of neutrality in negotiations, although the IMF and Kemmerer usually recommended policies similar to the wishes of the US government. The missions usually recommended changes in public accounting systems, balanced budgets, adherence to the gold standard, and the creation of central banks along the lines of the Federal Reserve system of the United States. Similar to the Argentine government's acceptance of IMF monitoring of its fiscal accounts after the Mexican crisis in 1995, advisors appointed by Kemmerer were at times allowed to supervise the government budget and customs revenues to help attract US investments.

The seal of approval of these advisors often helped to attract new loans and foreign investment. US experts would help to legitimize proposals of local elites and justify austerity measures to domestic interest groups. Kemmerer's approval helped to reassure foreign investors, expand government spending and stabilize exchange rates while retaining a larger degree of national sovereignty than countries in the Caribbean. Although these missions were privately contracted by Latin American governments, the US government and bankers were looked upon as extremely useful, and the leaders of most Latin American governments involved ". . . were not opposed to this foreign intrusion in the management of the finances of their states because they believed that the presence of the advisers might help attract new loans and investments from abroad." The missions were relatively more successful than the IMF in attracting new external capital to the region because of its greater abundance in the 1920s than the 1980s.

At the beginning of the crisis of the 1930s Latin American countries continued to service their debts even though capital inflows and export earnings declined. It was only in 1931 with a spreading world recession and further declines in export revenues that nearly all of the region's countries, with the exception of Argentina and some smaller debtors in Central America and the Caribbean, declared complete or partial moratoria on their foreign debts.

In contrast to the 19th century, policy makers realized that external trade and capital were unlikely to resume quickly. The availability of foreign capital practically disappeared and default was not viewed in quite as negative a light as in previous epochs. Due the fact that the whole world was in crisis, there was no pressure to structure policies in such a manner to please foreign investors and lending institutions as in the defaults of the late 19th century. Consequently, an inward oriented development strategy was pursued.

Most countries of the region adopted a series of measures which were quite unorthodox, but which it was felt were important to minimize the negative impact of the World Depression. Brazil under president Getulio Vargas promoted import-substituting sectors, used exchange controls, followed unorthodox policies to sustain its coffee sector, and founded state firms. In Mexico, Cardenas undertook the most extensive land reform since the 1910 revolution and at the end of the decade nationalized foreign (mainly US) petroleum firms. These measures reflected a greater independence of the region's policy makers from the wishes of foreign creditors and investors than in prior defaults.

The fact that outright defaults were more common in the 1930s also resulted from the lack of a coordinating mechanism among US bondholders versus the experience of UK bondholders in the late 19th century and bank lending in the 1980s along with limited US government involvement. Prior to formation of the Foreign Bondholders Protective Council for US creditors in 1933, no permanent organization existed to negotiate settlements with defaulting debtors. The difficulty of rescheduling foreign bond issues relative to bank loans reflects the coordination problems of bondholders in negotiating settlements. Similar to the period after the Mexican crisis, the dispersion of ownership among thousands of creditors along with the lack of cross-default and sharing clauses inhibited the ability of bondholders to coordinate.

The conditionality imposed by bondholders' committees many times did not work as well as IMF conditionality. The commitments of governments were time inconsistent. For example, in 1895 foreign investors in Guatemalan bonds were to be given a determined portion of export duties. After the default settlement, however, the government arbitrarily reduced the duty by two-thirds. Similarly, the Brazilian government repeatedly renegotiated existing agreements during the 1930s. Debtors would agree to the conditions placed on them by creditors to gain an agreement for a reduction in debt payments. After obtaining the agreement it was no longer in their interest to carry out these conditions. Institutions such as the IMF, which lend conditional on certain government actions, have a role in helping debtors to make a credible commitment to adjust and gives incentives for the actual implementation of these commitments.

Limited US government involvement, although occasionally considering the status of the country's debt when extending Eximbank loans, contrasts with the growing involvement of governments and multilateral institutions during the 1980s. Similar to the United Kingdom in the early years after independence, the US government placed a higher priority on increasing trade with these countries during the 1930s than on payment of Latin American debts to US creditors.

Sanctions on defaulting countries appear to be limited during the period and even when capital flows resumed after WWII. Recent studies have claimed that the heavy defaulters of the 1930s grew faster and did not receive different treatment in access to world capital markets even after WW II. These findings could be interpreted to imply that it would have been better for the Argentine government to default in the 1930s and for Latin American governments to default during the 1980s. The import-substitution industrialization (ISI) policies pursued in the 1930s, however, are not likely to have been as effective during the 1980s as the benefits of ISI appear to have run their course by the this time.

Import Substitution and
Adjustment of the 1950s and 1960s

The period after WWII witnessed two new actors, multinational companies and government creditors, replacing bondholders as the largest creditors to the region. During the 1950s, multinational companies provided a greater degree of freedom for policy makers but also created some tension in allowing foreigners to control domestic production. Official bilateral and multilateral lending in the 1960s reflected the priorities of governments, imposing a high degree of conditionality on the use of credit. Since this lending was usually on fixed terms and at lower interest rates, however, the cost and risk of interest rate changes were reduced.

Most Latin American countries came to rely on private direct investments by multinationals, who were drawn to Latin America because of ISI policies such as protected domestic markets. During 1946–48 private US capital flows to Latin America amounted to 84% of total inflows from the US, falling slightly to 73% during 1949–55 and 70% during 1956–61. As foreign direct investors were satisfied with protected markets, various other incentives offered and the possibility of repatriating profits, they made few other demands on the policy profile of the region's countries.

ISI policies of the 1950s were unorthodox in that they implied substantial government interference with market forces. They were viewed in an unfavorable light by most governments of the industrial centers (especially the United States) and by the major Bretton Woods institutions (World Bank and IMF), who were the main sources of international capital. ISI policies included protection, overvalued exchange rates, various types of price controls and subsidies and the creation of new and expansion of already established state enterprises.

In the 1960s many Latin American countries found it necessary to cope with some of the excesses of ISI. Multinationals were replaced by official and multilateral loans, which imposed constraints on their use. The risks of these funds however, were reduced by the fact they were more likely to be at fixed interest rates and longer term, lowering the interest rate risk. Official capital flowed to the region through bilateral loans of the US aid agency (USAID), through the creation of the Inter-American Development Bank (IDB), which relied mainly on US funding, and through a change in the policies of the World Bank, where the United States had a major influence.

There was also a change in the attitude of the US government spurred on by a concern over the impact of the Cuban revolution on the rest of Latin America. With the arrival of the Kennedy administration in 1961 the Alliance for Progress was created. It resulted in the pledge of substantial sums of official capital flows to Latin America which was supposed to be linked to structural reforms and contained few references to US private investments. In the latter 1960s the Alliance became more conservative, stressing the need ". . . to foster economic growth and be neutral on social reform, to protect US private investment . . . "

During 1961–65 public inflows accounted for 60% of total external financing, falling to 40% in 1966–70. US bilateral aid accounted for 36.7% in the former period and 23.6% in the latter. One of the principal conditions linked to this increase in official flows was for governments to develop programs to improve the region's distribution of income.

Multilateral loans from the World Bank and Inter-American Development Bank were usually tied to specific investment projects reflecting priorities of the institutions. In the 1950s, 50% of World Bank lending was for power projects and transportation with little going to agriculture or social projects, reflecting the emphasis on industrialization. It is noteworthy that in the 1960s the bulk of lending by official bilateral and multilateral organizations went to the transportation, telecommunications, and energy sectors, which were mainly in the hands of state enterprises. This was a period in which the privatization paradigm had not yet become dominant in the US government and international multilateral aid institutions. During the 1970s, the priorities of the World Bank shifted toward agriculture, health and education projects. At times, they were also conditioned on clearing up defaulted loans from the 1930s while during the 1960s the provision of USAID loans was frequently linked to agreements with the IMF.

Commercial Bank Lending
and the 1970s

The 1970s was a period of freedom from explicit constraints on the use of external capital as private debt from commercial banks replaced equity and official sources as the leading provider of capital inflows. This greater freedom however, was accompanied by reduced risk sharing relative to equity and official long term fixed rate debt flows in the previous period. Floating rate lending with shorter maturities transferred more of the risk to debtors. In addition, coordination mechanisms improved for creditors over the prior era of bond flows with innovations such as loan syndication and the growing involvement of the IMF, enhancing their ability to enforce penalties on defaulting debtors.

The surge in foreign capital flows during the 1970s resulted from the role of commercial banks in recycling the oil surpluses of OPEC countries. The negative *ex-post* real interest rates were very attractive relative to equity finance, with these loans being given at relatively small spreads over LIBOR, ranging from 0.9% to 1.8%, during 1972–80.

Developing countries showed a preference for commercial bank loans over official and multilateral lending because of the freedom with which the funds could be used and the large quantities available. This preference for greater independence also led to a decline in foreign direct investment in favor of commercial bank lending. Few constraints were placed on macroeconomic policy and the use of funds compared to the strict conditionality placed on funds from official and multilateral sources in the 1960s. Bank loans were rarely restricted to specific projects and the use of these loans was not monitored to the extent of official loans. As a result, these loans allowed developing countries to maintain greater autonomy over domestic policy decisions. Commercial banks did not have certain development goals in mind when deciding whether to issue new loans with the more important criteria being whether the loan would be repaid rather than the direct impact on economic development. In contrast to bilateral and some multilateral lending of the 1960s, banks were more concerned about the stability of the government than influencing the political orientation of the government.

During the course of the 1970s, the proportion of debt financed at floating interest rates increased and maturities were shortened as more debt was being financed privately than publicly. The average maturity of debt declined from 20.4 years in 1970 to 14.2 years by 1982 while private loans with shorter maturities became an increasing proportion of this debt and had an average maturity of 8.2 years in 1983. The proportion of debt at floating interest rates increased from 16% in 1974 to 43% in 1983.

Commercial bank loans placed more of the interest rate and commercial risk on the borrower than official credit because the loans were usually at higher interest rates and had shorter maturities with floating interest rates. Since debt payments are greater in times of high international interest rates, debt finance is more likely to force the country into accepting the conditionality of the IMF. With equity finance, dividend payments and profit remittances are likely to be lower during periods of low growth so the eventual impact on government autonomy under debt finance may be larger than with equity finance. The ability of banks to coordinate however, helped to restructure and roll over loans more easily when debt servicing difficulties arose, reducing the risk of outright default.

The coordination mechanisms between private creditors and the growing involvement of the IMF helped creditors to impose penalties. The innovation of sovereign loan syndication helped commercial banks to enforce international debt contracts. Cross-default clauses specified that defaults on an individual loan would result in the default of all bank loans. Therefore, the ability to service an individual project became less important than the overall level of debt. These clauses constrained the ability of borrowers to default selectively. The punishment of defaulting on any project would be amplified by its linkage to all other bank loans.

Implicitly these flows imposed the same conditions as IMF credit in times of balance of payments difficulty because of the frequent requirement by commercial banks of obtaining IMF agreements before providing more funds. IMF resources were small in magnitude until the late 1970s. The conditionality of the IMF however, had been important beyond the magnitude of the flows since the

1960s in the 1970s, commercial banks began to use the approval of the IMF before providing new lending. The constraints of the IMF on the autonomy of policy makers depended on the availability and diversity of funds from other sources. Even the small sums of money provided by the IMF could impose significant policy constraints when other sources were unwilling to lend. The ability of countries to avoid the need for IMF loans such as Brazil in the 1970s and in the early 1990s allowed the government greater autonomy.

The Debt Crisis of the 1980s

The growing coordination among government and private actors during the 1980s reduced the risk of outright default but resulted in greater constraints being placed on Latin American policy makers. An important aspect of this period, in contrast to the interwar period and the 19th century is the greater activism of multilateral institutions and governments of creditor countries. The growing intervention of these institutions shifted the prior situation of two party negotiations between developing country debtors and private creditors into a three party negotiation between debtors, private creditors and official creditors. This relationship between multilateral institutions and creditors now assumed greater importance on the ultimate conditionality placed on the developing economies.

During the 1980s the increasing use by the IMF of upper credit tranche lending with greater conditionality restricted the independence of government decision making. Official debt expanded gradually, while the real value of debt to commercial banks remained stable. During 1982–90, the real value of developing countries debt to the official creditors increased from $115 billion in 1982 to $251 billion by 1990 while the value of debt to commercial banks declined from $278 billion to $200 billion. The potential uses and conditions of multilateral lending also changed during the 1980s. The World Bank introduced structural adjustment loans in 1981 to provide foreign exchange to help policy reforms and restructuring during balance of payments difficulties. These loans were in contrast to prior World Bank lending directed for specific projects.

The growing activism and coordinating mechanism of the IMF during the 1980s had benefits and costs for Latin America. The IMF reduced the costs and risks of rapid adjustments by reducing the probability of a rapid withdrawal of funds. Sovereign bank lending was concentrated in a relatively small number of banks. If debt servicing difficulties arose the government could negotiate a rescheduling of the debt payments with most of the creditors, reducing the free-rider problem of some creditors refusing to roll over the loans. It may have been in the interest of all banks to provide additional money, but a coordinating mechanism was needed to prevent individual banks from receiving payment on their individual loans. The IMF helped to internalize this externality, although in theory if the debtor were solvent a private investor could do the same.

IMF conditionality also provided these countries with a method to credibly commit to the constraints imposed, as new loans were dependent on the implementation of IMF stabilization plans. Without the existence of the IMF, new loans from banks may not have been forthcoming because of the inability of domestic policy makers to credibly commit to adjustment after an agreement with private creditors. Debtors could signal a commitment by accepting the IMF program.

The role of the IMF in organizing creditors also allowed creditors to impose greater conditionality on debtors and may have slowed down the eventual settlement. If a debtor was insolvent, it may have been easier to strike an agreement with creditors when the IMF was not active in organizing creditors. The constraints imposed by bondholders' committees or commercial banks were not as stringent as those imposed by governments or multilateral institutions. The only punishment available to private creditors would be the refusal of additional capital flows and the strength of this threat would depend on the likelihood of the renewal of flows. The unique nature of multilateral institutions derives from the long-term relationships with debtor countries along with their special role in signaling creditworthiness to other creditors. This gives the IMF greater power to impose conditionality than private creditors. Since IMF approval was often a necessary condition for additional funds to be provided by commercial banks, usually to service interest and amortization on existing debt, the conditions of the IMF were leveraged to become the conditions of all bank and IMF flows. In the 1930s, this lack of a coordinating mechanism reduced the ability of creditors to impose such conditions.

The conditionality placed on governments by the IMF could theoretically be carried out by private organizations, as bondholder committees have done historically. Politically imposing these constraints, however, is something private sector banks or governments in developing countries prefer to avoid.

Portfolio Flows in the 1990s

The composition of foreign capital inflows since 1990 has shifted from debt to equity, official to private sources and to securitized flows from commercial bank loans in the 1970s. These changes reflect the growing importance of pension and mutual funds as providers of external capital. The growth of equity inflows helps to diversify the risk of investments while other forms of portfolio inflows such as short-term debt add additional risks. The riskiness of these portfolio inflows is enhanced by the lack of coordination among widely dispersed bondholders and the reduced ability of official and multilateral institutions to coordinate the actions of creditors.

The importance of portfolio flows to Latin America peaked during 1993 with portfolio equity and bonds reaching 39.6% and 33.0% of total capital inflows respectively. This is in contrast to less than 5% of the total during the 1980s for both sources combined. Net commercial bank lending was negative during 1993, in contrast to 54% of total net flows in 1980 while direct investment increased slightly to 25.4% in 1993 from 20.5% in 1980. Official sources declined in size and importance during the 1990s, falling to 8.7% of net flows during 1993, down from 54.2% in 1985.

Risks of Portfolio Flows Relative to
Traditional Forms of Capital Inflows

First, we examine the risks of portfolio vs. traditional forms of capital inflows such as bank loans and official flows. Second, we demonstrate that the traditional treatment of all forms of portfolio investment in one category is mistaken, especially in the case of short-term debt flows versus different types of portfolio equity.

The inability of creditors to coordinate their actions and shorter time horizon for evaluating portfolio allocations can impose additional risks on the domestic economy. As was the case prior to WWII, recent portfolio investments in government bonds and local stocks are held by thousands of investors without any method of coordinating a continuation of flows, even if this was desirable for the entire group. This increases the risk that a liquidity crisis will turn into a solvency crisis. As is the case in a bank run, the ability of the bank to meet depositors' demand for funds depends as much on confidence in the bank's ability to meet these demands as the actual solvency of the bank. Similarly, the government's ability to service a large short-term capital outflow is constrained by the potentially large magnitude of outflows and the lack of any coordinating mechanism among creditors.

Portfolio flows are also distinguished by the short time horizon for evaluating portfolio allocations. These investors continuously evaluate the government's performance and decide where to locate their capital more frequently than official agencies, banks or foreign direct investment. Thus, demands on the government for timely provision of information on macroeconomic indicators and central bank reserves becomes vital. Government actions which change expectations about future returns on investments can have dramatic consequences because of the rapidity and magnitude of the response, as illustrated by the aftermath of the 1994 Mexican peso crisis. Credibility about future economic policies, which drive expected returns and risk on investments, along with explicit and implicit guarantees for government bonds, exchange rates and bank deposit insurance assumes a more central role.

The lack of qualified majority voting and sharing clauses in current international bond agreements will tend to hold up the settlement of these claims when the debtor is unable to remain current on debt service. These problems are magnified by the lack of permanent bondholder committees to coordinate and represent creditors as in 19th century British bond finance in Latin America. The difficulty of restructuring debt contracts results in greater restructuring costs to the debtor for maintaining debt service payments.

In contrast, loans from the IMF or commercial banks do not have as immediate consequences if the confidence of creditors is shaken. Even if the country is not found to be adhering to the requirements of the program after its quarterly evaluation, existing loans will not be fully withdrawn on short notice. Similarly, bank loans are typically of longer term than the current maturity structure of many domestic government bonds. Therefore, it may take months for a crisis to fully develop instead of days. Finally, when evaluating foreign direct investment, companies look to the long-term expected return and risk of investments, reducing the likelihood of large scale movements in capital over a short period of time.

Risks of Different Forms of Portfolio Inflows

Private portfolio capital can be in the form of equity or debt, with different risk-sharing characteristics. Each form of portfolio inflow has different constraints and risks. Portfolio equity can be invested in closed-end or open-end country funds, ADRs or directly in the local equity market. Portfolio debt can be distinguished by its maturity structure, currency of denomination and whether the credit is from the government, banks or non-banks. The frequency of rollover influences whether a change in expectations will result in an capital outflow or a change in asset prices while implicit government guarantees on the banking system and exchange rates impact the perceived responsibilities of the government under repayment difficulties.

Short-term debt flows allow creditors to place greater conditionality and influence on its use because of the option to refuse rolling it over. Government obligations with short-term debt can be explicit in the form of government bonds or implicit in government guarantees on bank certificates of deposit. The problem that short-term debt increases a debtor's vulnurability to a crisis of confidence and self-fulfilling expectations has been stressed in the literature analyzing the Mexican crisis. The necessity to roll over the debt every month requires the continuous confidence of investors. Any government decision which affects foreign investors' confidence can result in a quick withdrawal of funds, requiring severe adjustments for the domestic economy.

A decrease in confidence for longer maturity inflows such as portfolio equity, foreign direct investment or Brady bonds is distinguished from short-term bond investment because a fall in demand will decrease asset prices, reducing the impact on capital outflows. The key difference is that shares of equity or long-term debt do not need to be rolled over. Since any seller must find a buyer, there will be no outflow of total capital from the equity or Brady bond market. An outflow of *foreign* capital may occur if new information impacts foreigners' expectations more negatively than domestic investors. Empirical evidence presented below shows however, that this was not the case during the Mexican crisis. These types of investment also reduce the dead-weight costs from renegotiating claims and the free-rider problems of short-term debt flows because equity does not need to be rolled over while the claims of equity holders under bankruptcy will be resolved in the domestic courts along with domestic creditors.

Portfolio equity investment also comes in many forms, with different implications for the recipients of capital. During the 1980s, the primary form of portfolio equity investment in Latin America was closed-end country funds. With these funds, a fixed number of shares is raised through an initial public offering. Shares are not able to be redeemed for the underlying asset, in contrast to open-end funds. When an individual investor sells his stake, the impact will be on the price of the closed-end fund in the US market. No foreign outflow occurs because the shares in the fund must be sold to another foreign investor, with the only drain on foreign exchange being dividend payments. If arbitrage is limited between the closed-end fund and the domestic market, the impact on the prices of domestic stocks may also be limited.

Since 1991, a large portion of portfolio equity investment has taken the form of purchases of individual Latin American stocks traded in the United States in the form of ADRs and equities listed in the local markets. These investments may be made through open-end mutual funds or directly by pension funds and individual investors. Most Latin American ADRs do not transfer voting rights in the companies to foreigners, allowing the domestic country to retain control of the company. Foreign investment in domestic stocks has been achieved without yielding control of the company by allowing different classes of shares. The class of voting shares may be restricted to domestic investors who remain in control with the majority of the market value of the company being held by foreign investors with little or no control. In contrast to the fixed number of shares with closed-end country funds, domestic stock inflows can be reversed by selling the equities. Therefore, the impact on the local market of shocks to foreign expectations about future returns is greater under direct purchases of domestic stocks and ADRs than with closed-end country funds.

Conclusion and Policy Implications

The proliferation of new forms of portfolio flows in recent years, in addition to capital from traditional sources, offers greater opportunities for emerging economies to increase economic growth but necessitates an understanding of the risks and constraints associated with these flows. One lesson from the past 200 years of capital flows to Latin America is that shocks to expectations about future economic prospects in Latin America will occur periodically and result in debt servicing problems. The composition of capital inflows will influence both the likelihood of such problems and the ability of policy makers to absorb these shocks effectively.

Werner Baer and Kent Hargis, "Forms of External Capital and Economic Development in Latin America: 1820–1997," *World Development* 25, no. 11 (November 1997): 1805–20.

22

External Debt and
Macroeconomic Performance in
Latin America and East Asia

JEFFREY D. SACHS

SINCE THE ONSET of the international debt crisis in the early 1980s, the dismal economic performance of the Latin American debtor countries has been frequently contrasted with the strong performance of their East Asian counterparts. Throughout East Asia, with the exception of the Philippines, the developing countries have maintained strong growth rates and low inflation. None but the Philippines has been forced to reschedule its foreign debt. On the other hand, throughout Latin America, with the partial exception of Colombia, national incomes have grown slowly or have declined, inflation has surged, and debtors have been forced to reschedule their outstanding debts.

Many analysts have already tackled the problem of explaining why Latin America's record is so poor compared with East Asia's. Each has pointed to different "lessons" to be learned. Some argue that the Asian record is better because the external shocks that hit the Asian countries in the early 1980s were less severe than those that buffeted Latin America. Others suggest that the Latin American countries simply overborrowed. Some analysts point to exchange rate management and the trade regime as being crucial. Supply-siders contend that the Asian economies have flourished under lower tax rates, and many other economists join them in arguing that the Asian economies have been market-oriented, while the Latin American economies have not.

The available empirical evidence can help to discriminate among these alternative views.

This report is divided into three sections. In the first, I examine some of the leading hypotheses concerning the Latin American—East Asian economic record and show the importance of export growth in explaining the differential performance of the two regions. In the second section. I speculate on some of the political developments that turned the Asian economies toward export promotion and the Latin American countries toward import substitution. The third section looks briefly at the current political economy of trade in Latin America to show how political paralysis is contributing to the continued economic paralysis.

Explanations for Performance in East Asia and Latin America

The debt crisis of the early 1980s was triggered by a combination of global economic events and domestic developments in the debtor countries. The best evidence for the contribution of global events is the simultaneous onset of the crisis in more than forty developing countries. The best evidence for the role of distinctively national developments is the success of many debtor countries in surmounting the external shocks without an emergency debt rescheduling. The Latin American countries rescheduled, while the East Asian countries, by and large, did not.

The Role of External Shocks

The simplest explanation for the differences in performance is that the global shocks hit the Latin American countries with greater force. Two possibilities are often raised: first, that the commodity terms of trade deteriorated more sharply in Latin America than in Asia, and, second, that the Latin American countries had a higher proportion of debt in variable interest rate loans, and thus felt the effect of rising interest rates sooner.

Based on GDP weights for 1975–80, the terms of trade actually rose in both regions, but less sharply in Latin America than in Asia. Clearly, the terms of trade do not well explain "success" and "failure" in handling external debt in the early 1980s, since three of the six crisis cases in Latin America enjoyed terms-of-trade gains, while two of the four successful adjusters in Asia had terms-of-trade declines. The improvement in Latin America is not surprising, in view of the fact that Mexico and Venezuela are major oil exporters, while Argentina and Peru also export oil (the terms of trade for all of these countries except Peru improved during 1979–83). In Asia, Indonesia is a major oil exporter. Although real oil prices fell in 1982–83, the decrease was not nearly as large as the increase of the preceding four years. Note that the terms-of-trade experience of Colombia was below the Latin American average.

The second external shock of this period was the sustained rise in U.S. interest rates that began at the end of 1979. Higher interest rates affected not only the costs of new borrowing, but also the interest charges on existing debt, since a significant fraction of LDC debt was contracted at variable interest rates. Typically, syndicated commercial bank loans tie interest payments to a short-term dollar rate, such as the London interbank offer rate (LIBOR) or the U.S. prime rate, on a quarterly or semiannual basis. The extent of borrowing at variable interest rates differs widely across debtor countries. It is much higher in Latin America than in Asia (with the exception of Korea), since a higher fraction of the Asian debt is nonbank borrowing, originating instead from official creditors such as export credit agencies of the developed countries.

To measure the interest rate shock as a proportion of GDP, I multiply the change in the real interest rate by a debt-GDP ratio taken as a fraction of GDP for the year 1980. The real interest rate shock is large and negative only for Brazil, Chile, and Korea.

The inescapable conclusion is that macroeconomic performance and the need to reschedule are not closely tied to the magnitude of the external shocks as a proportion of GDP. Argentina, Mexico, and Venezuela had positive (that is, beneficial) net shocks. Korea and Thailand, on the other hand, had very large negative shocks relative to GDP, but both maintained strong economic performance. Part of the answer to this puzzle, we shall see, is that in Latin America, the debt servicing burden became very large as a fraction of exports, though not necessarily large relative to GDP.

The Extent of Foreign Borrowing

It might be supposed that the Latin American debtors have suffered far more because they borrowed far more during the 1970s. Consider first the cumulative current account deficit for the various countries. In a given year, the current account deficit equals the increase in a country's net liabilities to foreigners, subject to an adjustment for capital gains and losses on preexisting stocks of assets and liabilities. The cumulative deficit for the decade should then approximately equal the increase in the country's net liabilities over the course of the decade. There is a large variation in the extent of net borrowing in both regions, and on average the Latin American countries borrowed only slightly more. The variation in net borrowing within each region, compared with the uniformity of results, is striking. In Latin America. Venezuela ran a cumulative current account surplus, and Argentina and Colombia were approximately in balance. The remaining countries ran sizable cumulative deficits. In Asia, Indonesia and Malaysia maintained approximate balance, while Korea ran up a larger proportionate deficit than did any of the other countries in Asia or Latin America. Thailand and the Philippines also ran large current account deficits in the 1970s. It is certainly hard to see a strong link between the size of a nation's current account deficit and whether it suffers a debt crisis.

The difference becomes much more significant only when debt is expressed as a percentage of exports. The higher ratio of debt to exports is most likely the critical factor in making Latin America so vulnerable to the external shocks of the early 1980s.

The contrast between the two regions becomes decisive when the debt service to export ratios are compared. The debt service measure is taken at its most comprehensive level: interest payments on debt of all maturities, plus amortization of principal on medium- and long-term debt, plus complete repayment of all short-term debt. The results are striking, in that in Latin America, debt servicing requirements exceeded total exports, on average, in the years 1980–83, while in Asia (with the notable exception of the Philippines), the debt servicing was well below the level of exports. The higher ratio in Latin America is due to a combination of factors already discussed: higher debt-export ratios; a higher concentration of debt in short maturities; and a higher effective interest rate on the debt, because of its concentration in variable interest rate bank claims rather than fixed interest rate official credits.

With debt servicing ratios above 100 percent, it was impossible for the Latin American countries to service their debts fully when new lending dropped off in 1982. Debt reschedulings became inevitable. The slowdown in lending itself resulted from several factors: concern over economic mismanagement in the debtor countries; tight monetary conditions in the creditor countries; and the self-fulfilling fragility of the Latin American debt structure in light of the extraordinary debt service ratios. When each lender recognizes that a country will be unable to service its debt if the other lenders stop making loans, a "panic" or "run" on the country becomes possible, as each lender attempts to take out its assets ahead of the other claimants. With debt service ratios in excess of 100 percent, it is easy to see how such a run can occur.

Trade Policies and Exchange Rate Management

Models of optimal borrowing show that capital-scarce developing countries can profitably borrow over the long term, but only if the borrowed resources are invested sufficiently in the tradable goods that ultimately will be used to service the accumulated foreign debt. Over time, as debt is accumulated, the price of tradable goods should rise relative to nontradable goods, to encourage the movement of resources into the tradable goods sectors. Moreover, investment in tradables should be in sectors that are profitable when outputs and inputs are evaluated at world prices, rather than tariff-distorted prices. Latin American economies have violated both dicta in recent years.

It is not easy to get good measures of the size of the tradables sectors over time. The typical recourse is simply to measure the extent of actual exports relative to total income to get an estimate for the growth of the tradables sector. Though admittedly imperfect, the data strongly indicate the rapid growth of exports relative to GDP in East Asia since 1965, compared with a fairly flat pattern in Latin America. In 1965, the Korean export-GDP share was only 9 percent, the Indonesian share 5 percent, evidence that the recent high openness of these countries is a development of the past two decades, rather than a fixed feature of the economies. By 1983, the large debtor countries in Latin America (Argentina, Brazil, and Mexico) had a significantly smaller export base relative to GDP than did the Asian countries.

Another rough indicator of the extent of the tradables sector can be gleaned from data that divide production and employment into agriculture, industry, and services. The tradables sector is often loosely equated with agriculture and industry, the nontradables sector with services. In the absence of extensive trade barriers, this division is plausible. The data suggest that the Latin American countries have a much larger service sector, and hence presumably a much larger nontraded goods sector, than do the Asian economies, and that the growth of the service sector since 1965 has been faster in Latin America (11 percentage points on a weighted average basis) than in East Asia (8 percentage points). It is important to remember, however, that these data likely understate the differences in the two regions by counting heavily protected Latin American industries as part of the tradables base of the economy.

The allocation of resources between tradables and nontradables depends on trade policies, exchange rate management, and aggregate demand management. In considering the relative contribution of each, it is important to work within a framework of at least three sectors: importables, exportables, and nontradables. The three-sector framework helps to guard against an unnecessary and incorrect simplification that is present in the standard two-sector (exportable and importable) model of international trade. In the two-sector model, all policies that protect the import-competing sector necessarily hurt the exporting sector. Protectionism is anti-export biased, since resources pulled into importables must come from exportables. In the three-sector framework, it is immediately evident that protectionist policies can go hand in hand with export-promoting policies if resources are drawn from nontradables into both the tradable sectors. In fact, the export-promotion policies of Korea, Japan, and to a lesser extent Indonesia have had this character: exports have grown rapidly at the same time that import-competing sectors have been protected. In Latin America, on the other hand, the more traditional anti-export bias of protectionism has been present. The combination of expansionary demand policies, protected import-competing sectors, and overvalued currencies has meant that both importables and nontradables have benefited at the expense of exportables. Since the history of the long-term trade policies in the two regions is well documented, exchange rate management dominates the discussion that follows.

Latin American currencies, measured at official parities, became overvalued (with the notable exception of Brazil's and Peru's) in the late 1970s and early 1980s, and Latin American countries have frequently allowed very large premiums to develop in the black market in the face of downward pressure on the official exchange rate. The largest real currency appreciation recorded is that of Argentina (36.9 percent), followed by Mexico, Chile, and Venezuela. Measured by relative consumer price indexes (CPIs), Brazil in fact had a hefty real depreciation, Peru a somewhat smaller one. In Asia, all countries except Indonesia maintained the real exchange rate within 10 percent of the 1976–78 values. Moreover, the Latin American countries have allowed large black market premiums to develop in recent years, particularly after the onset of the debt crisis, while the Asian countries have generally kept small the discrepancies between the official and black market rates.

There are several reasons for the real appreciation throughout Latin America, but I suggest later that common political developments leading to such appreciations, and to their persistence for several years, are at work. In terms of proximate causes, it is necessary to distinguish between the two Southern Cone countries included in the table, Argentina and Chile, and the two major oil exporters, Mexico and Venezuela. The story in the Southern Cone is by now well known: Argentina, Chile, and Uruguay all embarked upon a path of disinflation, with a strong currency policy helping to reduce inflationary expectations. In Mexico, and in Venezuela to a lesser extent, the real appreciation resulted from oil-induced increases in domestic spending that crowded out tradable goods sectors, à la the "Dutch disease."

It is worth noting that the Asian policy of maintaining the real exchange rate has been extended to encompass a basket of currencies, rather than focusing exclusively on the bilateral rate with the U.S. dollar. During the years when the

Bretton Woods system was in effect, and for several years after its demise, the Asian economies maintained fixed rates against the dollar. However, by 1978, all of the countries in the region were worried about the large fluctuation of the dollar vis-à-vis other industrial country currencies. In rapid succession, Thailand, Korea, Indonesia, and Malaysia all switched from a dollar peg to an exchange rate basket. In Latin America, on the other hand, no country adopted a basket. All continued to peg to the U.S. dollar, either at a fixed parity, as in Mexico, Venezuela, and Chile after 1979, or in a crawling peg, as in Argentina, Brazil, Colombia, and Peru. All suffered, to some extent inadvertently, when the dollar appreciated sharply after 1980.

A Summary

Of all the causes of poor Latin American economic performance considered so far, the most significant seem to be trade and exchange rate policies. Put simply, the Latin debt became burdensome both because of its structure (short maturities, variable interest rate) and because of insufficient exports available to service it. After a decade of rapid foreign borrowing, too many of Latin America's resources were in the nonexporting sector, or abroad. When a financial squeeze in the early 1980s caused banks to draw in their loans, the only way that the Latin countries could maintain debt servicing was through a recession and a sharp reduction in imports combined with debt reschedulings.

The Political Economy of Export-Led Growth

Certain key elements in political and economic organization can help to account for the differing exchange and trade regimes in Latin America and Asia.

Trade restrictions tend to shift income from the agricultural and mineral producing sectors toward the industrial and service sectors. Since the agricultural work force in most middle-income developing countries is typically between 30 percent and 50 percent of the total, and since agriculture and mining account for a quarter or more of domestic GDP in most cases, the political and economic effects of this particular income redistribution can be profound.

These distributional effects provide some clues as to why the Latin American countries have chosen to rely on an overvalued currency, a large service sector, and a small export sector, while the Asian economies have lived with the reverse. I believe that long-term differences in the balance of power between urban and rural interests help to account for much of the discrepancy. To a first approximation, the Latin American governments—whether civilian or military, right-wing or left-wing—find their most important constituencies among urban workers and capitalists. For decades, the agricultural sector has been relatively weak, though certainly not powerless, almost everywhere in Latin America, with peasants only loosely organized and, with some exceptions, large-scale agricultural interests unable to hold decisive sway. Moreover, political unrest is most dangerous in the cities, so that urban interests must be bought off first in difficult periods. Interestingly, the opposite seems to be true in most of East Asia. Governments there, whether Japanese colonial rulers before World War II or nationalist governments, have felt the pressing need to win support of, or at least to appease, the rural sector.

The rural-urban distinction is but one element in a very complicated picture. Ideology, foreign policy, and even national security considerations have also contributed to differences in policy, and, indeed, many distinctions across countries within Latin America and Asia make any overarching generalizations treacherous. Several qualifications are therefore in order. First, there is no historical inevitability to the relative influence of agricultural versus urban interests in the two regions. It is well known that up until the Great Depression, large rural landholders in Latin America provided the dominant political power within the ruling oligarchies. And, indeed, until the Great Depression, trade policies throughout Latin America were stringently liberal, in line with the class interests of the ruling oligarchs. The shift to import substitution and vigorous protection of domestic industries dates from the decline of the relative power of the agricultural sector during the Great Depression. Similarly, in Asia, countries such as Korea and Indonesia pursued an import-substitution policy complete with Latin American-style inflation rates during the 1950s. It is not that rural strength in Asia made an export-promoting strategy inevitable; rather, rural strength helped to tip the balance in that direction in the 1960s, when the East Asian countries began their export drives.

Second, countries within a region differ substantially in their urban-rural balance. Large agricultural interests, particularly in coffee, have remained powerful in Colombia, for example, and were a substantial political force behind Colombia's liberalization in the mid-1960s. Third, intellectual and ideological elements have played a significant role, along with strict economic interests, in defining the trade and exchange rate policies in Latin America and Asia. Dependency theory and opposition to U.S. involvement in local economies have contributed to the strength of protectionist sentiment throughout Latin America. The influence on Latin governments of the Prebisch hypothesis that agriculture and primary products were a losing long-term bet for economic growth also contributed to the formulation of the import-substitution policy.

Some very rough indicators suggest why the hypothesis of greater rural power in Asia is at least plausible. The population in Asia remains largely rural, while the Latin American population is overwhelmingly urban. This difference remains very strong even after controlling statistically for per capita incomes across countries. Korea, now highly urbanized, is the single Asian exception, but it is not in contradiction to the thesis that rural political power is a force for export-oriented trade policies. Korea's decisive devaluations and export-promotion policies were instituted during the five years after 1960, when Korean urban dwellers composed only 28 percent of the nation's total population. Also the Latin American countries are far more unionized than are their Asian counterparts. Since urban workers are a major interest group in favor of overvalued exchange rates, this difference in labor market organization certainly plays an important role in the political calculus.

To tie down the relationship of agricultural political power and export promotion would require a detailed country-by-country study, though an initial examination of the historical record in several countries lends credence to the hypothesis. In Argentina, for example, it is clear that the urban-based political power of Peron, combined with the political weakness of agriculture due to low world prices in the Great Depression, contributed to the decisive shift away from export promotion. (Up to the Great Depression, the agricultural interests had succeeded in maintaining free trade and a competitive exchange rate.)

While the Argentine pattern is familiar throughout Latin America, almost the opposite is true in Asia. In Malaysia, Indonesia, Korea. Taiwan, and Thailand, the governments look to the rural sector as an important element of support. The same was historically true in Japan. and even today, the ruling Liberal Democratic party must bow to agricultural interests in maintaining high domestic prices for food.

The link between rural influence and export promotion is only the first step in the development of a successful export program. Once export-promoting policies get under way, urban-industrial exporters become their own lobbyists and eventually become the dominant political force in favor of an undervalued exchange rate, with rural interests losing their relative influence. Clearly this process is under way in Korea, where an enormous concentration of export-oriented industrialists is a strong force with regard to the exchange rate and trade policy. On the other side, after decades of import substitution in Latin America, manufacturing exporters are so weak politically as to be unable to overturn a strong currency policy, even acting in conjunction with the rural sector. Thus, the political biases of the export-promotion or import-substitution regimes probably feed upon themselves over time, and make it increasingly difficult to change course.

Jeffrey D. Sachs, "External Debt and Macroeconomic Performance in Latin America and East Asia," *Brookings Papers on Economic Activity* 2 (1985): 523–64.

23

Inflows of Capital to Developing Countries in the 1990s

GUILLERMO A. CALVO

LEONARDO LEIDERMAN

CARMEN M. REINHART

Half a decade has passed since the resurgence of international capital flows to many developing countries. About $670 billion of foreign capital has flowed to developing countries in Asia and Latin America in the five years from 1990–94, as measured by the total balance on the capital account of these countries. This is about five times the $133 billion total of the previous five years, when there was a debt crisis and many of these countries had little or no access to international capital markets. Although there was a substantial decline in capital flows to developing countries in the immediate aftermath of Mexico's currency crisis in December 1994, in most cases capital inflows have resumed and by mid-1995 have been sustained at relatively high levels.

The recent surge in capital inflows was initially attributed to domestic developments, such as the sound policies and stronger economic performance of a handful of countries. Eventually, it became clear that the phenomenon was widespread, affecting countries with very diverse characteristics. This pattern suggested that global factors, like cyclical movements in interest rates, were especially important. Moreover, the pattern reflected a growing trend toward integration of world capital markets and globalization of investments.

Capital flows from rich to poor countries are worth studying for a number of reasons. Foreign capital can finance investment and stimulate economic growth, thus helping increase the standard of living in the developing world. Capital flows can increase welfare by enabling households to smooth out their consumption over time and achieve higher levels of consumption. Capital flows can help developed countries achieve a better international diversification of their portfolios and also provide support for pension funds and retirement accounts into the twenty-first century. However, large capital inflows can also have less desirable macroeconomic effects, including rapid monetary expansion, inflationary pressures, real exchange rate appreciation and widening current account deficits. Hence, a surge in inflows of the magnitudes seen in recent years may pose serious dilemmas and tradeoffs for economic policy, especially in the present environment of high capital mobility.

History has also shown that the global factors affecting foreign investment tend to have an important cyclical component, which has given rise to repeated booms and busts in capital inflows. For example, in Latin America, marked episodes of capital inflows during the 1920s and 1978–1981 were followed by major economic crises and capital outflows, such as in the 1930s and in the mid-1980s. The Mexico balance-of-payments crisis of December 1994 is but a recent example of this phenomenon and highlights the vulnerability of developing capital-importing countries to abrupt reversals; thus, an aim of policy is to reduce that vulnerability.

This chapter discusses the principal facts, developments and policies that characterize the current episode of capital inflows to Asia and Latin America. We begin by discussing the determinants of capital flows to developing countries, with emphasis on the causes behind the heavy inflow of the 1990s. We then discuss the macroeconomic effects of the inflows and whether a policy response might be useful. The final section draws some policy lessons from the recent experiences and discusses areas for future research.

Causes of the Capital Inflows

The factors that encourage or hinder international flows of capital can be categorized into those that are external to the economies receiving the flow and the factors internal to those economies. Several of these factors and trends interacted in the early 1990s to make the developing countries of Latin America and Asia fertile territory for the renewal of foreign lending.

First, there was a sustained decline in world interest rates. For example, short-term interest rates in the United States were declining steadily in the early 1990s, and by late 1992 they were at their lowest level since the early 1960s. Lower interest rates in the developed nations attracted investors to the high-investment yields and improving economic prospects of economies in Asia and Latin America. Given the high external debt burden of many of these countries, low world interest rates also appear to have improved the creditworthiness of debtor countries that borrow at these rates.

Surely enough, the tightening of monetary policy in the United States and the resulting rise in interest rates in early 1994 made investment in Asia and Latin America relatively less attractive. Higher interest rates quickly and markedly affected developing country debt prices. Indeed, the rise in U.S. rates also triggered marked corrections in several emerging stock markets.

Second, the early 1990s brought recessions to the United States, Japan and many countries of Europe. This swing of the international business cycle doubtless made profit opportunities in developing countries appear relatively more attractive. However, as the OECD economies move toward recovery in the mid-

1990s, this factor will become less important in generating capital flows to Latin America and Asia.

Third, there has been a trend toward international diversification of investments in major financial centers and toward growing integration of world capital markets. Increasing amounts of funds managed by life insurance companies and mutual funds have entered emerging markets. Regulatory changes in the United States and Europe have also made it easier for foreign firms to place their equity and bonds under more attractive conditions to investors.

Fourth, many heavily indebted countries made significant progress toward improving relations with external creditors. Other domestic policies that could be added to this list include the role played by debt-equity swaps in encouraging foreign direct investment.

Fifth, several countries began to adopt sound monetary and fiscal policies as well as market-oriented reforms that have included trade and capital market liberalization. For example, Bolivia, Chile and Mexico implemented major disinflation programs in the late 1980s, while Argentina, Brazil, Ecuador and Peru have done so during the early 1990s. An effective inflation stabilization program can reduce macroeconomic risks and stimulate capital inflows. A similar outcome could result from the introduction of institutional reforms, such as the liberalization of the domestic capital market and the opening of the trade account, and policies that result in credible increases in the rate of return on investment (such as tax credits).

Finally, a large shift in capital flows to one or two large countries in a region may generate externalities for the smaller neighboring countries. These are the so-called contagion effects. For example, it could be argued that Mexico's and Chile's re-entry into international capital markets in 1990 made investors more familiar and more willing to invest in other emerging markets in Latin America. Indeed, the more recent events suggest that the Mexican crisis of late 1994 tended to make the attitude of investors toward emerging markets more discriminating.

Within this mix of external and domestic factors, it seems likely that the external factors have been quite important in the first half of the 1990s.

While this discussion has stressed external developments, domestic factors also remain important in both the magnitude and the composition of inflows. Countries with sound domestic fundamentals attracted capital on a larger scale and with a higher proportion of long-term investment. As the cross-country evidence shows, there appears to be a strong link between economic fundamentals and foreign direct investment. An earlier literature on capital flight also documented this link.

Policy Management of Capital Inflows

Capital inflows to developing countries have often been seen as beneficial by all parties. For the capital-rich developed economies, such investments appear a desirable way of diversifying risk and investing in productive assets that will, in a few decades, fund the retirement of the baby-boom generation. For the relatively capital-poor developing countries, the flows can fund investment and promote economic growth. Perhaps just as valuable for a developing country, foreign investment can also come with experienced management, new technology and useful business skills.

At least in theory, a laissez-faire attitude toward capital flows may work perfectly well. But in reality, judging from the fact that many countries have tried to exercise some control over such inflows or their less-desirable side effects, there is apparently a perceived cost to a strategy of no intervention.

Several possible consequences of capital inflows are of special concern to policymakers. The capital inflows can lead to inflationary pressures, especially when they are monetized. Since an inflow of capital also implies a higher demand for a nation's currency, it often means an appreciating exchange rate, which may widen the trade deficit to uncomfortable levels. If a nation's banking system has difficulty handling the capital flows, there is some risk of financial destabilization and even banking crises. Overall, in a world of high capital mobility, where capital inflows can depart just as rapidly as they arrived, there is a genuine risk that their effects on inflation, the exchange rate and the financial sector can lead to severe macroeconomic instability. The experience of Mexico in the aftermath of December 1994 is a vivid illustration of these potential problems and especially of the sharp contraction in economic activity that can follow sudden reversals of capital flows. Such concerns have often led the authorities to react to the inflows by implementing a variety of policy measures.

Monetary Policy: Sterilization and Regulation

Sterilization has been, by far, the most popular policy response to capital inflows in both Latin America and Asia. This policy aims at insulating the money supply and/or the exchange rate from the effect of the capital inflows; the intent is to mitigate inflationary pressures, the real exchange rate appreciation, and avoid the loss of control over the domestic money stock.

However, it is not clear that this policy can provide a lasting solution, and it can be costly. Presumably, funds are being attracted into the country by the promise of higher expected interest rates. But if the capital inflow is sterilized, this will prevent the interest rate differential from narrowing, and may thus induce further capital inflows. In addition, since sterilization involves increasing the number of domestic bonds to offset the currency inflow, it results in an increase in public debt. Eventually, this policy could result in a rise in public debt so large as to undermine the credibility of policymakers, especially if the public begins expecting a partial repudiation of the debt—expectations that may well halt the inflows altogether.

Other costs are associated with sterilized intervention. If the central bank were simply to provide its own currency for purposes of foreign exchange without sterilization, it would allow the domestic money supply to increase. The central bank would also end up holding foreign currency, which it could invest in the bonds of the foreign country. However, after selling domestic bonds to sterilize the currency inflow, the central bank must then pay interest on those bonds. To the extent that the interest rate on domestic bonds is higher than that on foreign exchange reserves (which is the case for most developing countries), this entails costs. Annual estimates of these costs in Latin American countries range from 0.25 to 0.80 percent of GDP.

Sterilization can take other forms. For example, instead of reducing the money supply by selling bonds, the central bank could raise bank reserve requirements or increase the discount rate. Such steps may be especially relevant in those countries where capital inflows have taken the form of marked increases in local bank accounts. An increase in reserve requirements (an option used by Chile and Malaysia) lowers the capacity of banks to lend without the quasi-fiscal costs of sterilization. The regulatory side of monetary policy—that is, bank regulation and supervision—can also help, especially in dealing with the risk of macroeconomic destabilization. For example, regulations that limit the exposure of banks to the volatility in equity and real estate markets, as well as establishing risk-based capital requirements would be especially timely.

However, many of these policies are not without their costs. They may promote "disintermediation," which refers to new institutions that develop to bypass these regulations. Moreover, greater controls on banks amount to a reversal of the underlying trends of financial liberalization in developing countries.

Controlling Capital Inflows and Liberalizing Capital Outflows

Various countries, such as Chile and Colombia, have imposed taxes on short-term borrowing abroad with the intent of discouraging inflows that are thought to be particularly speculative. For example, Chile chose to tax inflows (in effect) by imposing a reserve requirement on international loans intermediated through the banking system. The main disadvantage of such a requirement is that capital flows may eventually be rerouted through other channels—for example, the over-invoicing of imports and under-invoicing of exports—which may reduce the authorities' control on the financial system. Less explicit capital controls have taken the form of "prudential regulation," usually of the domestic banking system. Countries such as Indonesia, Malaysia, the Philippines and Thailand have sought to curb banks' offshore borrowing (a capital inflow) or their foreign exchange exposure by imposing limits on these or tightening existing regulations.

Another response has been to soften the domestic impact of capital inflows by lowering the institutional barriers to capital outflows. However, to the extent that lifting restrictions on capital outflows is viewed as a positive step toward economic liberalization, it may increase the confidence of foreign investors and thus may stimulate capital inflows.

Fiscal Policy

As noted earlier, some countries reacted to the surge in capital inflows by tightening fiscal policy, usually via a cut in public expenditures. To the extent that nontradable goods often represent a sizable share of government expenditure, cutting government spending will reduce the demand for nontradables relative to the demand for tradable goods. This step makes nontradables able to buy less of the goods traded on world markets—which effectively means limiting the appreciation of the real exchange rate.

However, the effectiveness of fiscal policy is limited in this situation. Changes in legislation and sensitive political actions usually cannot be undertaken on short notice, which would often be needed to offset the effects of the capital inflows. Furthermore, optimal fiscal policy considerations suggest that taxes and expenditures be set to reflect long-term goals, rather than in response to what can be excessively volatile fluctuations in international capital markets.

Exchange Rate Policy

A final option for a capital-importing country is to let the nominal exchange rate appreciate in response to capital inflows. The main advantage of allowing greater exchange rate flexibility is that the appreciation in the real exchange rate is likely to occur through a change in the nominal exchange rate and not through higher inflation. Moreover, exchange rate flexibility might strengthen the degree of autonomy of domestic monetary policy precisely when the central bank's function as "lender of last resort" might be needed—for example, during a temporary subsequent reversal of capital inflows.

A disadvantage of a pure float is that it may be associated with high volatility in the real exchange rate. Massive and rapid capital inflows may induce such a steep and rapid exchange rate appreciation that it may damage the competitiveness of strategic sectors for economic growth, like nontraditional exports.

To reduce the risk of excessive fluctuations in the real exchange rate, several countries have adopted crawling exchange rate bands, which can be seen as an intermediate case between fixed and flexible exchange rates. In 1994, for example. Colombia joined Chile and Mexico in adopting a preannounced crawling exchange rate band. The mere existence of these bands did not eliminate pressures on the exchange rate regime; in fact, faced with persistent capital inflows, Chile and Colombia had to realign their bands in 1994 by officially appreciating their central parity exchange rates. As the Argentine case highlights, this tendency toward partial flexibility has not been across the board. Yet in many developing countries, there have been theoretical and practical arguments for moving to a more flexible exchange rate arrangement. Greater exchange rate flexibility, by introducing uncertainty, could discourage speculative short-term, cross-border flows. Further, increased exchange rate flexibility grants the monetary authorities a greater degree of autonomy in the conduct of domestic monetary policy and permits them to exercise more control over the monetary aggregates.

Concluding Remarks

There are some important lessons in macroeconomic management that emerge from the surge of capital inflows to Asia and Latin America in the first half of the 1990s.

Gauging by their economic performance and their ability to withstand the adverse side effects of the Mexican crisis, the countries that have been the most successful in managing capital flows (for example, Chile and Malaysia) have implemented a comprehensive policy package and not relied on a single instrument. At the outset of the surge in inflows, these countries reacted by treating the inflows as temporary and resisted a nominal exchange rate appreciation; the foreign exchange intervention was mostly sterilized. As the inflows persisted, sterilization efforts were scaled back and the domestic currency was allowed to appreciate. To moderate the extent of the real appreciation and prevent the economy from overheating, fiscal policy was tightened. To moderate the volume of the inflows and lengthen their maturities, exchange rate flexibility was increased and measures to curb inflows were implemented.

A less productive policy mix has consisted of persistent sterilized intervention (which keeps short-term interest rates comparatively high), heavy intervention in the foreign exchange market (which results in little short-run exchange rate uncertainty) and no controls on short-term capital movements. All of these policies have tended to provide especially strong incentives for short-term capital inflows. To a large extent, this policy mix characterized the Mexican experience through most of the early 1990s. With the benefit of hindsight, it can be said that the severity of the Mexican crisis would have been lessened had the inflows (which became outflows) been smaller, had their maturity been longer and had the inflows been accompanied by a much smaller decline in domestic saving than that actually observed.

Guillermo A. Calvo, Leonardo Leiderman, and Carmen M. Reinhart, "Inflows of Capital to Developing Countries in the 1990s," *Journal of Economic Perspectives* 10, no. 2 (Spring 1996): 123–39.

24

Foreign Direct Investment in Developing Countries: Progress and Problems

JOEL BERGSMAN

XIAOFANG SHEN

Foreign direct investment (FDI) is playing a growing role in economic development. Unlike other forms of capital inflows, FDI almost always brings additional resources—technology, management know-how, and access to export markets—that are desperately needed in developing countries. Investors are exacting, however, when it comes to deciding which countries are the most desirable sites for investment, and the lion's share of FDI has been going to a handful of countries, mostly in East Asia and Latin America. In 1994, 11 countries accounted for about 76 percent of total FDI flows to the developing world.

Why East Asia and Latin America?

More and more developing countries have reduced barriers to FDI and improved their business climates. At the same time, multinational corporations are responding to increased competition by considering a broader range of locations for their facilities. These mutually reinforcing trends have combined with technological changes in communication, transportation, and production to make "the global marketplace" a reality for investment decisions. The days of producing shoddy, high-cost products for sale in local markets are passing; most foreign investors are interested only in sites where they can produce to international standards of quality and price.

This globalization means that the old distinction between export-oriented production and production destined for the local market is weakening and even disappearing. Countries that want to develop must offer good business conditions both for exporters and for production for local markets. The emphasis may differ, depending mainly on the size of the local market, but providing the combination is increasingly important. Countries in East Asia and Latin America have received the most FDI because they have adjusted their strategies to keep up with globalization.

Some of these countries initially based their development on exporting labor-intensive manufactured goods to the industrial countries. Recently, many have recognized that technological advances and intensified competition have increased the capital and skill intensity of production in many industries. This means that countries can no longer count on low labor costs alone but also need high-quality, productive labor to sustain their comparative advantages. Those that have succeeded in attracting FDI have focused on improving general education, industrial skill training, and labor and managerial discipline. Facilitating companies' efforts to upgrade technology has also been crucial in maintaining their competitive edge.

Companies interested in establishing facilities in emerging markets need access to quality supplies of parts, components, and supporting services. For manufacturing industries, especially, a major force driving success is a "flexible" system of intercorporate relations under which companies specialize in different stages of production, either upstream or downstream in a production chain, and cooperate closely with each other through networking and long-term buyer-supplier relationships. This type of system helps integrate foreign investment into host economies and allows the latter to derive more benefit from FDI through induced economic activities, the transfer of technology and management skills, and better access to export markets. But companies need great flexibility and highly developed skills to ensure "just-in-time" delivery of quality intermediate goods and services, without defects. Countries that have the conditions that facilitate these kinds of operations have become much more competitive in the eyes of foreign investors.

None of the countries that have attracted significant FDI inflows could have done so without sustained trade reform enabling them to keep up with the pressure of international competition. All have carried out substantial domestic economic reforms to encourage private sector development. Many have essentially succeeded in stabilizing the macroeconomic environment, reducing price distortions, deregulating investment procedures, and increasing general economic efficiency—getting the "fundamentals" right for *all* private investment, domestic and foreign.

What About Other Countries?

Many other developing countries have also embarked on reforms, addressing the same issues—fiscal and monetary imbalances, price distortions, bloated public enterprises, and unnecessary regulations, among others. But FDI has either not appeared or, if it has, still falls short of the amount desired. What is wrong?

One basic problem is that some countries possess few attractions for foreign investors. One traditional attraction of developing countries—cheap labor—is becoming less important in investment decisions. Economies at an early stage of industrialization do not offer the sophisticated providers of inputs—both goods and business services—that most foreign investors need to be competitive. Another factor that deters investment is poor economic performance—FDI tends to follow growth, not to lead it.

A closer look at the less successful countries, however, reveals that many that are potentially attractive to FDI simply have not carried their reforms far enough. Foreign investors do not come just because *some* progress has been made; to attract FDI, countries must have made enough progress to meet worldwide best-practice standards.

Obstacles to Entry

Many countries have liberalized entry policies over the past few years. They have relaxed restrictions on foreign ownership and entry in certain sectors, and they have also introduced "negative lists" to limit the types of investments that require screening and approval. In many countries, however, entry is still needlessly restricted and/or arbitrarily regulated—often because of pressure from domestic interest groups or from regulatory authorities with vested interests in screening.

Inadequate Legal Protection

Most governments have recognized the need for investment protection, and many have guaranteed equal treatment for foreign and national investments. An increasing number of countries have enacted laws forbidding expropriation or guaranteeing prompt and adequate compensation in the event of expropriation. In more and more countries, foreign investors have recourse to international arbitration for settling investment disputes.

Legal reforms are still far from adequate in most countries, however. In many cases, laws still implicitly allow expropriation of investors' property for arbitrary reasons. The very poor functioning of judicial systems in many countries calls into question the "prompt and adequate compensation" promised by law. Finally, investors are often required to exhaust domestic means for settling disputes before resorting to international arbitration. In the context of a weak domestic court system, this dramatically weakens investors' confidence.

Overvaluation and Restricted Access to Hard Currencies

Since the late 1980s, a growing number of developing countries have taken steps to liberalize their foreign exchange systems. Many have devalued their currencies, and some have allowed market determination of the exchange rate. In spite of considerable adjustments, however, many currencies are still overvalued, and extensive controls on exchange transactions are still seen as necessary. Moreover, foreign exchange liberalization in many countries has been accomplished by decree but not followed up by appropriate legislative steps, creating an atmosphere of uncertainty for investors.

Trade Barriers

In the past, many developing countries that had adopted an import-substitution strategy attracted FDI by offering investors a protected domestic market. Recognizing the importance of competing in global markets, most have now reduced protection and taken steps to promote exports. In too many instances, however, trade reforms have still not gone far enough. Some countries have reduced protection significantly, but still have too much to foster real competition at home or to provide an exchange rate that is conducive to exports. There is also a widespread problem in the developing world with customs services. Better trade policies may be negated by bureaucratic customs procedures and the obstructionist attitude of customs agents. Thus, imported capital equipment and other inputs do not arrive at production sites on time; drawback payments due to exporters are delayed for months or even years; and going through the multilayered clearance process is very costly.

Tax Distortions

To attract foreign investment, some countries use special investment incentives, including tax holidays, tax credits and exemptions, and reduction of duties. However, experience shows that such strategies have had little, if any, impact on most long-term investors. Tax holidays create distortions of tax regimes; they favor new investors and discriminate against existing ones—in some countries, they discriminate against domestic investors. The expiration of tax holidays causes sudden increases in tax burdens on companies. Moreover, these incentives are often granted through complex and bureaucratic administrative procedures that encourage corruption. A stable, automatic tax system with reasonable rates and without discretionary incentives is better both for investors and for the host country. Many countries have a long way to go to reach that goal.

Getting the Word Out

Investment promotion—persuading investors to come—has become widespread in recent years. More countries, however, need to have a carefully planned program of making the improvements achieved at home known to the world—not so much through expensive advertising supplements but rather through sophisticated, long-term public relations campaigns. Providing effective assistance to interested investors and businesslike follow-up, and helping existing investors to solve administrative problems are important parts of promotion that are too often neglected.

Role of Governments

For many countries that have not achieved the expected results, the problem is that reforms have been inadequate. Governments need to persevere with reforms already under way. Intensified global competition has put companies under greater pressure, and they are responding by investing only in the most favorable places. Countries should take this as a challenge rather than a threat if they want to win the battle for FDI.

Furthermore, policy liberalization alone may not increase competitiveness sufficiently. Economic opening is the necessary "stick" to force competition and shift resources to their most productive uses. Experience in many countries suggests that "carrots"—public support of efforts to make firms more efficient—are also urgently needed. For example, now that international investors have begun to be more interested in high productivity than in low labor costs, government assistance is needed to upgrade technology and labor skills. Access to information and technical services, general education, and specialized industrial and managerial training are more important than ever.

"Public support" does not mean, however, that governments should do, or even pay, for it all. To the contrary, many of the support services required by industries are best delivered by private institutions. Foreign investors themselves can provide assistance, motivated by their own business interests. Private companies not only benefit from such a supporting system but also can play a crucial role in the design and operation of it, and they must bear at least part of the cost.

The role of governments is thus becoming more complex. Governments can no longer act simply as monopolies providing certain services or goods, or even simply as regulators; their functions must include those of organizer, coordinator, assistant, and partner. To succeed, governments will need to change their orientation and acquire new skills. Commitment, creativity, and willingness to learn from mistakes are crucial assets that can lead to success.

Joel Bergsman and Xiaofang Shen, "Foreign Direct Investment in Developing Countries: Progress and Problems," *Finance and Development* 32, no. 4 (December 1995): 6–8.

25

The Political Economy of Foreign Direct Investment in Latin America

STEPHAN HAGGARD

The central focus of debate on the political economy of multinational corporations in Latin America in the last decade has centered on the insights of a "new
wave" of dependency theorists. This literature has explored in great empirical detail the complex relationships between foreign and local capital in Latin America.
The determinants of host-firm bargaining have also come in for closer scrutiny,
and although dependency theorists tend to overemphasize the structural constraints on host bargaining power, the focus on bargaining itself is an advance
over earlier dependency thinking. I argue, however, that the "new wave" remains
weak on the domestic politics of regulating foreign direct investment. By focusing on the external constraints on developing-country choice, the new wave fails
to theorize coherently about the way that domestic political forces shape public
policy toward foreign firms.

Local Firms in the "Triple Alliance"

Dependency writing was partly a reaction to the view held both by Communist
parties and modernization theorists that the local bourgeoisie constituted a "progressive" force for national development. Early *dependistas* considered industrial
interests weak, co-opted by agrarian elites, subservient to foreign capital, and
subject to the continual threat of denationalization. Peter Evans (1979) sought to
develop a more nuanced portrait, in which state, foreign, and local capital constituted a "triple alliance." As in any alliance, however, interests overlapped incom-
pletely; the motives of the three parties were a mixture of cooperative and competitive impulses. National firms used their political access to the government
and superior knowledge of the local market to defend their positions. Managers
of state-owned enterprises had their own institutional interests in expansion,

while political elites sought to balance the advantages of foreign investment against the claims of nationalism.

This picture in itself was highly indeterminate. It offered few clues about the market position and political interests of the private sector within the triple alliance in any particular case.

The reason for this failure, and a central problem in the new wave literature in general, is the lack of explicitly comparative analysis that would identify the political role of the private sector in defining different investment regimes. Evans offered "dependent development" as a generalizable model of a certain set of late industrializers; as such, the concept is necessarily less useful in understanding national variations in the composition of the triple alliance.

Despite its many advantages, this sectoral focus omits three intermediate levels of analysis that are important for understanding the politics of regulation. First, a more internally differentiated view of the domestic private sector would identify those segments of business that are likely to be threatened by the entry of a multinational corporation, as opposed to those likely to gain from such entry. This differentiation would permit a theory of business interests vis-à-vis the multinational corporations. Second, there is a need to focus more squarely on the political organization of business through peak associations, links to political parties, and formal and informal political ties to the state itself, in short, to focus on the political capabilities of business in different national settings. Finally, foreign investment can easily become implicated in larger political and electoral conflicts. The conservative administration of Misael Pastrana Borrero in Colombia changed its public stance on foreign investment in order to blunt an electoral challenge. Such analysis provides the broader political context within which the domestic private sector operates in supporting or resisting the entry of foreign firms.

Analysis of this kind is likely to reveal a longer term and more fundamental process that is exactly the opposite of denationalization: the creation of local firms through industrial policies that either foster linkages to multinational corporations or seek to limit their dominance. Evans shows that a triple alliance of public, local, and foreign firms may be orchestrated by the state not only within a particular industry but even within a particular project. The state's role in class formation through the promotion of national firms remains a rich area for future research.

Multinational Corporations, Dependency, and Bargaining

The new dependency writing differs from the old in paying much greater attention to bargaining between host and firm. This literature holds that multinational corporations possess structural advantages that will skew bargaining outcomes in their favor.

What are the advantages held by the multinational corporations? The first stems from the imperfections and information asymmetries that characterize the markets in which multinational corporations operate. The new dependistas draw heavily on theories of foreign investment that emphasize market imperfections. These theories argue that the costs of overseas investment deter firms from going abroad unless they are offset by firm-specific advantages over local competitors, such as access to finance, technology, product differentiation, marketing capabilities, managerial skills, and economies of scale. These advantages not only give the multinational corporations power vis-à-vis local firms in the market but translate into bargaining power and the ability to set the agenda.

The second source of bargaining power is the sheer weight that multinational corporations carry in developing economies. The oligopolistic structure of the markets in which multinational corporations operate is reproduced in the host economy, giving multinational corporations a dominant position in a number of important sectors. Market structure gives multinational corporations collective or "structural" power over economic performance. Finally, multinational corporations exercise power not only because of their various assets and local position but because of their superior organizational capabilities and ability to evade close government monitoring.

Host bargaining power may be weaker in the manufacturing sector than it is in extractive industries. Extractive investments had several characteristics that weakened the host at the point of entry. Investments were extremely large and demanded that the firm adopt a long time horizon. This necessity allowed the investor to extract substantial guarantees and support for the project prior to committing resources. Once the investment was sunk, however, and host governments increased their capacity to manage standardized production processes, bargaining power shifted toward the host; that is to say, bargains became obsolescent. Even with relatively stable prices, income from such projects resembled a pure rent and was subject to continual and incremental renegotiation. Any increase in commodity prices provided a powerful incentive for the host to rewrite contracts. Costly investments thus became easy targets for regulation, indigenization, and nationalization.

The host-firm relationship differs considerably in import-substituting manufacturing industries. One author has offered the term *renewable bargains,* as opposed to *obsolescing bargains,* to characterize negotiations in manufacturing. The ability of the state to hold out the promise of access to the local market allows the host to exercise selectivity, particularly where the degree of competition among firms is high, the domestic market is large, and overall economic performance is promising. If the industry is a new one, no established clientele may exist to favor entry; if the industry is already established, domestic firms may view foreign entrants as a competitive threat. At the point of entry, therefore, the investor is weakest.

The bargaining relationship changes once manufacturing firms are established. Networks of suppliers, distributors, joint-venture partners, and consumers provide a tacit political base of support for the multinational corporations. Product differentiation, advertising, trademarks, and consumer loyalty all enhance the bargaining power of import-substituting firms over time by reducing the credibility of nationalization as an alternative. Manufacturing industries are also more likely to be characterized by ongoing technological change than are extractive industries. Any move to increase national control "will run the risk of severing the lifeline of new innovations."

Above all, the bargaining approach demands careful specification of the resources available to the host, including such intangibles as bargaining skill and tactics. Some elements of bargaining power in less-developed countries are likely to be structural, such as market size and level of income. Host bargaining power is also a function of the ability to exploit alternatives to the products and processes offered by any particular firm. It is now easily forgotten that the expansion of commercial lending initially increased host country independence. Foreign borrowing financed the development of both local private and state firms during the 1970s, with a corresponding decline in the relative position of foreign direct investment across the continent.

One of the most important factors in determining bargaining outcomes is the sophistication and administrative capability of the state. A study of Colombia shows that the regulation of foreign investment was tied to the broader development of planning capabilities. In controlling foreign investment in 1966 for balance of payments reasons, a new institutional machinery was created that developed an interest in research and information about multinationals' behavior, including such practices as transfer pricing. Thus, a dynamic approach to host-firm bargaining demands attention not only to changes in the industry but to learning and institutional development in the host country as well.

The politics, bargaining strategies, and economic effects of foreign investment can all vary depending on the type of investment. Two new forms of investment are of particular interest in this regard: "offshore" export-oriented manufacturing investment and investment in services.

The *maquila* or *maquiladora* industries of Mexico's Border Industrialization Program represent a particularly pure form of export-oriented enclave investment. Maquilas are located in free-trade zones, all output is exported, and most exports are intrafirm because the factories in Mexico are usually integrated into "production-sharing" arrangements with counterparts on the American side of the border. This international division of labor was encouraged by proximity, liberal investment regulations, government provision of infrastructure, and items in the U.S. tariff code that allow duty-free importing of parts and components sent abroad for processing. Similar export-oriented enclaves have now developed in Haiti, Colombia, and the Dominican Republic.

The maquilas have come in for a number of criticisms. Even their defenders admit that they exhibit few direct backward or forward linkages with the domestic economy. As a result, they are unlikely to provide much in the way of technology transfer, except perhaps through labor and management training. The generation of foreign-exchange earnings has been an important motive for establishing such zones, but gross foreign-exchange earnings are partly offset by the cost of imported inputs, and in Mexico, by the tendency for workers along the border to spend a share of their income in the United States.

Host bargaining power is constrained by obvious limits in these offshore processing sectors. In seeking to attract extractive and import-substituting investment, host countries hold some bargaining advantages through their control of natural resources and access to the domestic market. But in the case of offshore industries, the assets that hosts hold are geographical proximity to major markets (an advantage held by Mexico and the Caribbean countries) but above all else, cheap labor. Because this "advantage" is shared by most developing countries, host countries usually extend additional benefits to lure investors, including provision of infrastructure, tax breaks, and even assistance in organizing and controlling the work force. The relative power of the firm is further enhanced by the fact that offshore investments tend to be small in size and relatively mobile, exactly reversing the conditions that give rise to the obsolescing bargain in extractive industries.

A completely different set of policy issues has arisen around the growth in services investment. The term *services* has become somewhat of a catchall that covers sectors as diverse as telecommunications, information and data processing, banking, and insurance as well as retail services, fast-food chains, filmmaking, education, and health care.

Some of the policy issues in the services area closely parallel those in import-substituting manufacturing, such as the conflict between the gains from a relatively open policy toward foreign investment versus the loss of control implied by foreign ownership. It is often assumed that developing countries would be consumers of such services, but the more developed Latin American countries are well positioned to develop production capabilities in certain areas, such as software.

The blurring of the line between trade and investment is particularly visible in services. Foreign firms provide goods, services, or financing that constitute an effective form of control over the project but without holding a majority, or perhaps even any, equity stake. This outcome may occur through licensing agreements, management contracts, franchising, sales of turnkey plants, production sharing, and international subcontracting. These forms of investment have crucial implications for bargaining relations between the host countries and firms. When a foreign company participates as an investor, it shares with its host-country partner an interest in maximizing the project's returns. Conflicts may arise over externalities and how profits or losses are shared, but an underlying common interest remains. When an investment project represents a sales operation, however, the foreign company's interest lies in maximizing profits on sales; the supplier's interest in the future profitability of the investment becomes secondary. Obviously, the host has the diametrically composed interest of minimizing the cost of purchased services and inputs.

Conclusion:
Alternative Approaches to the
Study of Foreign Direct Investment

Where do we go from here in advancing a political economy of foreign direct investment?

One alternative would be to "bring the firm back in." Even the most sophisticated of the new wave dependency theorists have followed neoclassical theory in treating the multinational corporation as a unified rational actor instead of adopting a behavioral approach to the firm that analyzes internal decision processes under conditions of uncertainty.

An alternative approach to the political economy of foreign investment, and one I have attempted to advance throughout this essay, would be to place it more squarely in the context of national development strategies. The dependency approach served as an important corrective to a previous generation of scholarship that ignored international constraints. Yet in doing so, it exaggerated the "external-internal" distinction. Recent work in international political economy and comparative politics, as well as open-economy macroeconomics, has shown that "external" constraints are closely connected with the policy regimes that govern the nexus between domestic and international markets. These regimes include trade and exchange-rate policy as well as the regulations governing foreign direct investment and borrowing, all of which are the object of domestic coalitional and bureaucratic conflict. The "relative autonomy of the domestic level" can be recaptured by exploring the relationship between these national policy choices and patterns of foreign direct investment.

Stephan Haggard, "The Political Economy of Foreign Direct Investment in Latin America," *Latin American Research Review* 24, no. 1 (1989): 184–208.

Section VI

Political Institutions and Economic Policy

Politicians, business owners, voters, and other actors make choices within a context of political and social institutions, which affect their opportunities and the consequences of pursuing them. Definitions differ, but the term *institutions* usually denotes formal organizations such as bureaucracies and central banks, as well as rules that stipulate how actors should behave in various circumstances. Institutions may empower or constrain, but they are almost always objects of heated debate. How do institutions affect human behavior, and how are they chosen in the first place? The readings in this section address both questions using the analytical tools of modern political economy.

During the 1980s, many Latin American countries turned from authoritarianism to democracy, and scholars asked whether the new political regimes would impede economic policymaking. At the time, it was widely believed that authoritarian regimes could launch and sustain economic reforms more effectively than democratic ones, which were sensitive to protests against painful adjustments like slashing the government budget or devaluing the national currency. Geddes (reading 26) debunks this conventional wisdom about the advantages of authoritarianism. Either intentionally or inadvertently, advocates of the standard view selected cases that illustrated their point, instead of considering a representative set of democratic and authoritarian regimes. Geddes shows that the apparent relationship between authoritarianism and reforms disappears once we consider an unbiased sample. Her article deserves special attention because it demonstrates the kind of methodological rigor that is a centerpiece of modern political economy.

Perhaps the relationship between political institutions and economic policy is subtler than the conventional wisdom suggests, however. After all, democracies differ on many dimensions. Some democracies vest political power in a parliament, whereas others divide it between a president and a legislature. Political parties are stronger and more ideologically coherent in some countries (such as Chile) than in others (such as Brazil), and the degree of executive autonomy varies from one democracy to the next. Haggard (reading 27) considers how these diverse institutional structures affect economic policymaking and political stability. He argues that certain democratic institutions are more effective than others at resolving the dilemmas of collective action, distributive conflict, and short-sightedness. As Haggard notes, research on the relationship between institutions and economic performance remains in its infancy. The Latin American region presents many opportunities for exploring the relationships in greater depth.

In studying the consequences of institutions, scholars sometimes forget that institutions themselves are human creations and subject to change. How do political and economic actors select the institutions that will govern their lives? This question is receiving increasing attention in the academic literature. We might like to pretend that leaders are benevolent planners, who design institutions to solve social dilemmas in the most efficient way, but we know that decisionmakers sometimes have other objectives in mind. Like government policy, formal organizations and social rules can be objects of fierce political struggle. By illuminating the nature of the struggle, modern political economy can help explain the constellation of institutions that we observe.

Consider an important institution: the bureaucracy that implements policy on a daily basis. Bureaucracies throughout Latin America have been criticized as inefficient and corrupt. Why do such institutions persist and when do they change? Geddes (reading 28) draws attention to the self-interest of legislators and party leaders who want to remain in power and use the corrupt bureaucracy as a vehicle for delivering perks to key supporters. Privileged politicians, who enjoy control over the bureaucracy, tend to defend the status quo, whereas underprivileged politicians advocate reforms to level the playing field. According to Geddes, reform is most likely to occur when the two leading parties have approximately equal access to patronage, in which case corruption does not afford a decisive advantage to either side. She compares her predictions to the record of bureaucratic reform in Brazil, Chile, Colombia, Uruguay, and Venezuela.

Next consider the central bank, which exercises power through its control over money and banking. Governments establish most central banks, but some enjoy more independence than others. In recent years, economists have argued that an independent central bank can keep inflation in check by preventing politicians from stimulating the economy. If so, why would self-interested politicians cede their power to a central bank? The final pair of articles addresses this interesting puzzle. Maxfield (reading 29) claims that politicians pursue central bank independence to increase their credibility with foreign investors. Boylan (reading 30) takes a different approach: Conservative politicians use central bank independence to tie the hands of left-wing successors. She cites the example of Chile, where the conservative administration increased the power of the central bank just prior to leaving office in an effort to constrain more liberal successors who might have been tempted to inflate the economy. For Maxfield, the stimulus for central bank independence is external and reflects the needs of foreign investors; Boylan, on the other hand, locates the sources of independence in domestic politics. Despite their differences, both authors recognize that institutions arise from a clash of political interests.

26

Challenging the Conventional Wisdom

BARBARA GEDDES

Until recently, it was widely accepted that democracies—especially fragile, unin-stitutionalized new democracies—have difficulty carrying out economic liberal-ization because its costs make it unpopular and hence politically suicidal to elected officials. Consequently, it was argued, authoritarian governments should be more capable of initiating and sustaining major economic reforms. A corol-lary to this claim is that the "best," in the sense of most decisive, economic reform strategy prescribes economic liberalization prior to political liberalization, as in the Chilean model.

In this essay, I assess the evidence on which the conventional wisdom about the relationship between regime type and economic reform was based; examine the implicit theory that made the conventional wisdom plausible, despite the absence of strong supporting evidence; and suggest a revision of that theory that empha-sizes the importance of government actors, their interests, and their incentives for explaining differences in the extent and success of economic liberalization in various political settings.

Prior to the debt crisis that began in 1982, the easy availability of foreign re-sources (mostly in the form of loans) made it possible for developing countries to sustain a set of policies, often called inward-oriented or import-substitution in-dustrialization, that routinely led to budget and trade deficits. Two elements of this general policy strategy, followed by many countries, created intense pressures to liberalize after the precipitous drop in foreign funding: heavy state spending and overvalued exchange rates. Heavy state spending coupled with an inadequate tax base led to large budget deficits. Overvalued exchange rates, which encour-aged imports and discouraged exports, led to trade imbalances. These budget and trade imbalances had been sustained prior to the debt crisis by the inflow of for-eign money. The debt crisis made the continuation of these policies impossible.

But economic liberalization—that is, exchange-rate reform, reductions in state spending and state intervention in the economy, decreased protection for domes-tic industry, and the like—is unpopular. Exchange-rate reform leads to higher prices for imports, including fuel, basic consumption items for the urban popular sector, and inputs for domestic manufacturing. Decreases in state spending lead to reductions in essential health and welfare services, food and fuel subsidies, employment and state-sector wages (which affect private-sector wages), investment in production and infrastructure, and maintenance of everything from roads to schools. Lower levels of protection for domestic industry lead to downward pressure on wages as well as bankruptcies and downsizing, and hence to increased unemployment. Economic theory and the experience of early liberalizers suggest that many of these costs are transitional. Yet transitional costs can and often do last long enough to be politically consequential, even devastating. In other words, the basic situation facing the governments of developing countries is one of very strong pressures to liberalize, both from the international economy and from international financial institutions, accompanied by strong domestic resistance to liberalization because of its short-run costs.

Assessing the Evidence

Given the immediate pain that economic liberalization inflicts, early observers expected authoritarian countries to have an advantage when it came to adopting these policies, for they would find it easier to ignore the complaints of groups hurt by reforms. Evidence that appeared to support a relationship between regime type and likelihood of economic liberalization came from some of the earliest liberalizers, especially Chile, South Korea, Taiwan, Mexico, and Ghana. Many of the studies of these cases are classic examples of what social scientists call "selection on the dependent variable": cases were chosen for examination because they had experienced the outcome the analyst sought to explain—in this instance, economic liberalization. The flaw in this research design is that the failure to examine cases that do not exhibit the "right" outcome lures analysts into identifying any plausible characteristics shared by the selected cases as causes of the outcome. Conclusions reached in this way are often wrong because unexamined cases may also have the traits the analyst has identified as causes.

When an unbiased sample is used, the evidence supporting a causal link between regime type and likelihood of economic liberalization is weak. Table 1 shows the liberalization efforts, by regime type, of governments in Latin America and the newly democratic parts of Southern Europe in 1976 (shortly after the initiation of radical liberalization by the Pinochet regime in Chile). In these cases, no connection between liberalization and authoritarianism is apparent. It might be argued that this is not a fair test, that no one would expect the smaller, less developed Latin American countries to liberalize. But even if we limit our attention to the bureaucratic-authoritarian regimes that announced their intention to modify their economies radically, there is still only one success in four: Chile. Elites in Argentina, Brazil, and Uruguay either did not want to liberalize or could not.

Table 2 shows which of these countries had, by the end of 1982, initiated policies that eventually led to substantial liberalization. Again, no strong evidence supports the conventional wisdom. Table 3 presents the situation in 1992, when every country had taken initial steps toward changing its economic strategy. Once again, the data fail to show a clear relationship between regime type and progress toward a market-oriented economy.

TABLE 26.1   Liberalization Efforts, by Regime Type, 1976

Regime Type	Yes	Ambiguous	No
Democratic		Colombia Portugal Spain	Costa Rica Greece Venezuela
Authoritarian	Chile	Argentina Brazil Uruguay	Bolivia Ecuador El Salvador Guatemala Honduras Mexico Nicaragua Panama Paraguay Peru

TABLE 26.2   Liberalization Efforts, by Regime Type, 1982

Regime Type	Yes	Ambiguous	No
Democratic	Costa Rica Portugal Spain	Colombia Ecuador Peru	Costa Rica Venezuela
Transitional			Boliva Honduras
Authoritarian	Chile Mexico	Brazil	Argentina El Salvador Guatemala Nicaragua Panama Paraguay Uruguay

Evidence from most other parts of the world is also weak. In Africa, Ghana has been the only conspicuously successful liberalizer out of a large number of authoritarian and single-party regimes. It is too early to tell what governments in the newly emerging multiparty regimes will do, but in Zambia there has been some movement toward greater market orientation since the 1991 electoral defeat of the party dominant since independence. In Eastern Europe, economic liberalization has gone furthest in two of the most democratic countries, Poland

TABLE 26.3 Degree of Liberalization Success, by Regime Type, 1992

Regime Type During Reform	Dramatic	Limited
Democratic	Argentina	Brazil
	Bolivia	Costa Rica
	Portugal	Ecuador
	Spain	Greece
		Nicaragua
		Uruguay
		Venezuela
Partially democratic*		El Salvador
		Guatemala
		Honduras
		Panama
		Paraguay
Authoritarian	Chile	Peru
	Mexico	

*Countries are considered partially democratic if (1) in spite of the existence of elections, the military still exercised veto power over policies; (2) a transition to democracy was in progress, but the first fully competitive national elections had not yet been held (Paraguay); or (3) the president, though previously elected, had been placed in power by U.S. invasion and was not perceived as legitimate by a substantial part of the population (Panama).

and the Czech Republic. The transition to capitalism has faced the stiffest resistance in precisely those parts of Eastern Europe and the former Soviet Union where the political system has changed the least and the old communist *apparat* has maintained its hold on the central government.

Only in Asia does authoritarianism appear conducive to economic liberalization. South Korea and Taiwan were early—though far from complete—liberalizers, while in India, the most stably democratic country in the region, liberalization came late and is still contested. China's astonishingly high recent growth rates have been achieved through partial economic liberalization guided by an authoritarian regime. Even in Asia, however, the evidence is not entirely one-sided. Liberalization has gone further in more-or-less democratic Thailand than in authoritarian Indonesia. Authoritarian basket cases such as Laos remain. And India's liberalization, though late, seems likely to be far-reaching and irreversible.

The bottom line, then, is that although some authoritarian governments have carried out successful transitions to more market-oriented economies, there is little evidence that authoritarianism as such increases the likelihood of such transitions.

Evidence to support the notion that carrying out economic liberalization prior to political liberalization involves less risk of chaos or derailment of the reform process is even flimsier. Of the early authoritarian liberalizers, only Chile and South Korea have become relatively democratic. Taiwan has made significant strides toward democracy, while Ghana, although it has begun the process of democratization, still has a long way to go. Mexico has, as of this writing, changed little. And there is no assurance of a democratic future for China. Only one democratic government attempting economic liberalization has broken down—Peru, where insurgency was as much to blame as economic crisis. In contrast, several transitions to multiparty politics in Africa have been helped along by the costs of efforts to liberalize and the inability of authoritarian governments to manage economic crisis. In short, the strategy prescribing economic liberalization prior to political liberalization is risky because most authoritarian governments fail to liberalize their economies and because those that do carry out successful economic reform find that success reduces the short-term demand for democracy.

Misleading Paradigms

Given the fragility of the evidence for it, why did the conventional wisdom emerge in the first place, and why did it remain unchallenged for so long? Sloppy methodological practices and the natural lag between events and scholarship are part of the answer. But three paradigms also converged to hinder understanding: pluralist theory, which nobody admits to, but which nevertheless underlies many arguments; traditional Marxism; and what we might call the standard economist's view of politics. What these three paradigms share is 1) a focus on interest groups or classes, without consideration of the ways in which political arrangements (except for authoritarianism) affect whether or not interests are politically influential; 2) a focus on material interests to the exclusion of other kinds of interests; and 3) a failure to think in any but the most abstract way about states or governments and the people who serve in them.

The focus on societal interests characteristic of pluralist theory, Marxism, and economic determinism led analysts to expect that the main impediment to liberalization would be the opposition of societal groups most immediately hurt by it. We are used to thinking about the costs of adjustment in terms of private interests and the punishment that they can inflict on political incumbents blamed for unpopular policies.

Expectations about the course of reform went something like this: Liberalization will be costly at least in the short run to the urban popular sector, especially organized labor. Labor will respond with strikes, demonstrations, and votes against the politicians who initiate adjustment policies. Consequently, elected politicians will not want to take the risk of initiating unpopular policies, or, if they do, they will lose the next election and these policies will be reversed. So democracies will not adjust. The unspoken assumptions that underlie such expectations can be traced to pluralist theory: politicians' careers depend on pleasing constituents; if large and well-organized groups of constituents are hurt by policies, they will be able to force the government to protect their interests. Economic crisis, caused either by liberalization itself or by the postponement of reform, will lead to political crisis, instability, and hence an increased probability of democratic breakdown. Authoritarian governments will be more likely to liberalize because they do not depend for their survival on competitive elections and can repress other manifestations of discontent.

This view sounds plausible; where is it wrong? Why did analysts fail to predict successful liberalization by democratic governments? Why did they fail to predict democratic stability in the face of severe economic crisis?

Some argue that the costs of liberalization are not as high as early observers assumed; this is probably true in specific cases. In the typical case, however, the costs to the urban popular sector are fairly high for several years. The puzzle from the standpoint of traditional theories, then, lies not in the governments' *ability* to initiate policies leading to real-wage declines, but in their *willingness* to do so and thus risk punishment at the polls or in the streets.

It is sometimes argued that governments had no choice and that wages were in many cases declining prior to structural adjustment. Both these statements are true, but wages declined faster immediately after the initiation of reforms. And although governments had little choice but to undertake some form of economic adjustment, they did have control over details, including the ability to make side payments to loser groups or otherwise redistribute the costs of adjustment. In a few countries, such as Spain, government efforts to mitigate the costs have been substantial and apparently politically important. In most, however, such efforts have lasted only a short time and have been largely ineffective. The question that needs to be answered, then, is why governments wholly or partly dependent on popular support were willing to impose high costs on labor.

The Ineffectiveness of Popular Opposition

The answer begins with the observation that, contrary to expectations, labor has not been able to translate its opposition to adjustment policies into credible threats to punish the initiators of adjustment. Labor has not lacked the capacity to mount opposition; there have been numerous strikes and demonstrations. But this opposition has not routinely led to threats of regime breakdown, the defeat of incumbents at the polls, or the wholesale abandonment of market-oriented policies. In just a few cases (Zambia, Senegal, and Venezuela) has popular opposition threatened regime survival. Such opposition has actually proved more destabilizing in less democratic settings (e.g., Zambia under Kaunda) than in more.

In some countries (most notably Uruguay and Brazil), popular opposition did block privatization and cuts in state spending through normal democratic political processes. But other parts of the reform package, especially trade and exchange-rate policies, have been sustained. In many countries, various elements of the standard package have been slowed down or abandoned, but the wholesale abandonment of the policies has been rare. The policy shifts in Peru beginning in 1985 and in Zambia in 1987 may come the closest to constituting reversals of liberalization policies. Even in these cases, governments were once again attempting substantial adjustment within five years.

Governments that have imposed the costs associated with adjustment have of course paid an electoral price for it. In 1988, the Institutional Revolutionary Party

(PRI) in Mexico might have lost a presidential election for the first time in its history had the votes been counted fairly.

Electoral costs, however, have not been as heavy as many predicted they would be. The party that initiated cuts in working-class income has been defeated in less than half the cases examined. This proportion does not seem larger than would be expected in any sample of elections in similar countries. In the rest, initiating governments won at least one election after the imposition of reforms. Furthermore, where initiating governments have been defeated, major policy reversals have not generally followed. In other words, working-class opposition to adjustment has resulted in neither systematic defeats for incumbent politicians nor the wholesale abandonment of reform policies.

The conclusion I would draw from these experiences is that organized labor by itself is not powerful enough to hinder adjustment or protect itself from bearing substantial costs. It needs the support of the rest of the urban sector. Labor can be isolated from the majority of the urban popular sector in numerous ways, depending on local circumstances and the political skills of leaders. In Argentina, lowered inflation was so widely welcomed that President Carlos Menem and his policies have maintained substantial support in spite of other costs. In Spain, the expectation of entering the Common Market increased tolerance for short-run costs. In Turkey, lowering tariffs on selected mass-consumption items (cigarettes, certain foods) just before elections helped to keep voters' minds off other costs. In all these cases, initiating governments won at least one election after the beginning of adjustment.

There seem to be two more general explanations for the political ineffectiveness of working-class opposition. First, unemployment and economic crisis decrease labor bargaining power and hence activism and political influence. Second, democratic politicians have more autonomy from societal interests than old theories gave them credit for. In my view, both are correct. Labor was never as powerful as the bureaucratic-authoritarian model implied; its influence, where it had influence, depended on particular institutional and historical circumstances that are not extremely common in the developing world. Labor is even less powerful now because the economic crisis has increased the labor surplus in many countries, and thus decreased labor's bargaining power.

The Interests of Government Actors

If urban workers cannot, in most cases, derail liberalization policies, who can? In many countries the biggest, and certainly the most articulate and politically influential, losers from the transition to a more market-oriented economy are government officials, ruling-party cadres, cronies of rulers, and the close allies of all three. These are groups whose ability to make effective demands does not decline as regimes become less democratic, which explains why many authoritarian governments have had difficulty liberalizing their economies. The failure of scholars to pay attention to the interests of government officials and members of ruling parties has, in my view, distorted ideas about the costs of adjustment.

If we want to understand better the politics of economic liberalization, we need to start by thinking in a careful and concrete way about the state. Liberalization involves the creation by a set of state officials of a new regulatory regime. To understand why a certain outcome occurs in one place and not another, we need to think about *who* the people are who make policies, what *their* interests are, and what *shapes* those interests. It is often assumed that politicians can best pursue their own interests by representing their constituents. If this assumption is correct, there is no need to examine the "black box" of the state: one can simply extrapolate from societal interests to policy outcomes. Where, however, we have reason to believe that the political process is more complicated than that posited by the simplest versions of democratic theory, we cannot ignore the actors and interests located within the state.

An examination of some cases in which popular opposition did successfully halt or at least dramatically slow adjustment efforts (Zambia, Senegal, and Venezuela) supports the contention that actors whose resource base lies in the government itself exert crucial influence over the sustainability of reform. In all three cases, the big losers from reform included ruling-party cadres and virtually the entire urban sector, not just the formal-sector working class.

In these three countries, party activists articulated and mobilized public discontent. Policies were criticized within party organizations and in party-controlled newspapers, and party activists played an important role in organizing opposition demonstrations. The reforms in these three countries, though not especially radical in comparative perspective, affected a broad range of the urban population. In Venezuela and Zambia, consumption subsidies were reduced at about the same time that trade and exchange-rate liberalization was carried out. Because subsidies in these two countries had been especially large and extensive, these cuts were felt deeply by many.

In all three countries, the content of the reforms provided the raw material for a broad, multiclass opposition to liberalization. Party activists, themselves opposed to the reforms for a combination of material and ideological reasons, were able to mold this opposition into compelling political pressure that forced the (probably temporary) abandonment of reforms in Zambia and Venezuela and caused significant backpedaling in Senegal.

These cases have two features in common: the parties that traditionally benefited from state intervention in the economy were still politically dominant at the time reforms were initiated; and the costs of reform, though not unusually high in comparative perspective, fell on a large part of the urban population (including party activists) rather than primarily on the urban working class.

Political Incumbency and Reform

In many countries, politicians, officials, and party activists along with their families, cronies, and client networks have customarily enjoyed many of the benefits of state intervention in the economy. They have monopolized the jobs in government and state enterprises, collected the rents created by import licensing and quotas, established many of the businesses that relied on government contracts, and benefited from subsidized credit. These material benefits have played a central role in building parties and maintaining party loyalties, and politicians have needed access to state resources in order to further their political careers. The factor that was left out of early discussions of liberalization, and that led to a failure to predict either the successful reforms carried out in democratic countries or which countries would have great difficulty in implementing reforms, was the effect of liberalization on incumbent politicians and their close allies.

Most reforms are initiated by executives who for one reason or another are not beholden to the party, faction, or group that has previously benefited from state intervention. A noted example is Socialist prime minister Felipe González in Spain, who, beginning in 1982, carried out extensive and successful liberalization and privatization. The state sector in Spain grew up during the Franco regime. The PSOE, outlawed under Franco, had received no benefits from state intervention. Liberalization thus did not pose the same threat to the material bases of party loyalty for the Spanish Socialists that it did for ruling parties in Venezuela and Zambia. In fact, privatization was politically attractive to the Socialists because it supplied a means of dislodging a substantial number of Franco loyalists from the bureaucracy.

Because the political benefits of state intervention tend to accrue to incumbents, political outsiders can, in some circumstances, increase their own competitiveness by liberalizing. Outsiders can come to power as a result of regime change, though regime change is no guarantee of a break in the continuity of political personnel. Highly fragmented and fluid party systems, such as those in Brazil, Peru, and some countries in Eastern Europe, have very low barriers to the entry of outsiders, even at the presidential level (witness the election of Fernando Collor in Brazil and Alberto Fujimori in Peru, and the strong showing of Stanislaw Tymiński in Poland).

Politicians with some of the traits of outsiders can also come to power in highly institutionalized party systems as a consequence of the democratization of nominating procedures. In Latin America, where such democratization occurred in several countries during the 1980s, it enabled individuals to secure their parties' nominations despite opposition from established party bosses. As a result, César Gaviria in Colombia, Carlos Andrés Pérez in Venezuela, and Carlos Menem in Argentina, though nominated by established parties, were not beholden to major segments of the established party leadership. All three initiated more substantial liberalization than was supported by the leadership or rank and file of their parties.

Because of economic crisis, regime change, the party fluidity that sometimes results from regime change, and internal party democratization, the current era provides considerable opportunities for outsiders. Outsiders, however, sometimes fail to achieve what they want, precisely because they are outsiders. Executive-initiated liberalizations can be blocked by factions of the ruling party itself that have customarily relied on the state for political resources and can ally with opposition parties to mobilize popular opposition and derail reforms—as has happened in Venezuela. Opposition from politicians historically dependent on state resources is even more likely to be successful in stalling liberalization in cases where the chief executive, coming from a small or new party that has not traditionally shared in the spoils, does not share the old guard's interest in maintaining the status quo. Outsider presidents such as Fernando Collor in Brazil, Alberto Fujimori in Peru, and Oswaldo Hurtado in Ecuador initiated radical reforms, but after a brief honeymoon, opposition in the legislature, judiciary, and bureaucracy—all dominated by parties other than the president's—blocked further liberalization.

In other words, the interests of incumbent politicians are fairly good predictors of whether economic liberalization will be initiated and how far it will go. Reforms are costly, at least in the short run, to significant numbers of citizens. But whether the citizens hurt by reforms will be mobilized into effective political opposition depends at least in part on the availability of political leadership that can serve its own ends by blocking reform. This leadership is most likely to come from politicians and activists in established parties who have customarily enjoyed both material and political benefits from their access to the rents created by state intervention in the economy.

Opportunities for Dual Transition

What can we conclude from the above? First, all generalizations about the political feasibility of economic liberalization should be treated as tentative at this time. It is a peculiarity of political scientists that we spend much of our time explaining events that have not finished happening. The result is a tendency to overgeneralize the apparent lessons of the earliest occurrences. Second, at the present time there is no solid evidence that less democratic governments are more successful than more democratic governments at initiating or carrying out programs of economic adjustment. Third, one of the reasons that democratic governments have been able to carry out successful adjustments is that the urban working class, though hurt at least in the short run in most countries, has usually not proved capable of impeding adjustment, protecting itself from having to shoulder significant costs, or punishing the initiators of adjustment at the polls. Even in democracies, politicians and officials do not simply reflect the interests of their constituents; they pursue their own interests, which can sometimes be served only by policy choices costly to politically important constituents. Fourth, where the state has in the past intervened heavily in the economy, the benefits of intervention have generally accrued disproportionately to incumbent politicians, officials, and their support networks. As a result, the costs of liberalization fall heavily on politicians, officials, and their close allies. The costs of liberalization to politicians are lower, and consequently the probability of sustained reform is higher, when the national executive 1) comes from a party or faction previously excluded from enjoyment of the spoils of state intervention, and 2) enjoys the support of a working majority in the legislature and a disciplined party. Taken together, these observations point to situations in which democracy and economic liberalization, far from being contradictory goals, can be expected to reinforce one another.

Barbara Geddes, "Challenging the Conventional Wisdom," *Journal of Democracy* 5, no. 4 (October 1994): 104–18.

27

Democratic Institutions, Economic Policy, and Development

STEPHAN HAGGARD

The relationship between regime type and economic development has long been a theme in the political economy literature, but the question has gained new salience with the global wave of democratization. Most new democratic governments have come to office facing daunting problems of short-term economic adjustment and long-term growth. This conjuncture of economic crisis and regime change raises the question of how the promotion of democracy and development can be most effectively combined.

Cross-national empirical evidence on the relationship between regime type and economic performance remains highly contested. Recent surveys conclude that there is no strong relationship one way or another. There may well be a relationship between the protection of property rights and growth, but an established property rights regime should not be confused with democracy. There are also other features of political systems, such as their stability, that affect policy and growth but these should not be confused with democracy, either.

Even if there were evidence that democracies outperformed autocracies, we would still be interested in explaining the wide variation that exists *among* them. There are a handful of stable, developing country democracies (or semidemocracies) that have fared reasonably well in economic terms, including Costa Rica and Malaysia. There are other countries, such as India, where democratic rule has arguably contributed to sluggish, though not disastrous, performance. There are also a number of "populist" democratic governments, such as Peru under Alan Garcia, that pursued disastrous economic policies that ran directly counter to the interests of the constituents they purportedly served.

Research is beginning to explore the effects that variations in democratic institutions might have on economic policy and performance; this chapter provides an introduction to some of this literature.

The Political Barriers to
Economic Reform

Recent work in political economy emphasizes three general political problems that recur regardless of the particular reform in question: collective action dilemmas, distributive conflicts, and the related problems of time horizon and credibility.

Collective action problems arise to the extent that economic policy has properties of a public good. Take, for example, the problem of stabilizing a persistent inertial inflation in a setting with extensive indexation, as in Brazil. Although some financial groups might derive speculative profits from high and volatile inflation, most groups would gain from greater price stability. However, the cooperative behavior needed to stabilize the price level might prove unobtainable since the risks of accepting deindexation are substantial if others are not making similar and simultaneous sacrifices.

Collective action problems also arise *within* political institutions. For example, legislators have a collective interest in effective fiscal management, since it affects overall economic performance and thus their reputations as incumbents. But legislators also have electoral concerns that tempt them to seek particularistic benefits for their constituents; if all legislators succeed in this strategy, perhaps through logrolling, then suboptimal policy will result.

The distributive implications of economic reforms constitute a second political challenge. In the collective action model, all parties would prefer a cooperative outcome but are blocked from it by incentives to cheat. In a distributive model, policy reform is supported by winners and opposed by losers, and the outcome is given by the balance of political power between the respective coalitions. Trade reform, devaluation, and price liberalization provide examples. Though these measures might increase both aggregate social welfare and the income of specific groups, they also typically encounter opposition from, respectively, import-competing interests, the nontraded goods sector, and those with access to goods at controlled prices.

In theory, a reform that generates a net social gain should also be politically viable. If the gains can be used to compensate the groups experiencing losses, it can be shown that it is always possible to construct a minimum winning coalition for reform. Yet it is pious to assume that such compensatory mechanisms exist, and there are thus good reasons why "losers" may prevail. One classic problem is that the costs of reform tend to be concentrated, while benefits are diffuse, producing perverse organizational incentives. Losers are usually well organized, while prospective winners face daunting collective action problems. As Fernandez and Rodrik point out, additional difficulties are introduced if we assume uncertainty about the outcome of the policy. Not only are prospective winners likely to be poorly organized, they may not even know who they are.

Both the collective action and distributive approaches to reform assume that policy is the result of conflicts among contending social groups or their political representatives. A third set of related problems arises if we examine the time horizons of government decision makers. Again, politicians should be willing to undertake reforms that yield net social gains. Yet political constraints can lead the politician to discount future gains steeply, for example, because of impending elections or the fear of sparking demonstrations or riots. This does not mean politicians are irrational; it simply means that, given some set of institutional and political constraints, the time horizons over which they assess the political costs and benefits of reform may be "too short."

This final problem is closely related to problems of credibility and commitment that have been prominent in recent discussions of reform. Politicians may commit themselves to reform but may also have an interest in reneging on that commitment when political pressures mount. If actors are forward looking and can see that there is an incompatibility in the incentives of the politician, they will discount policy pronouncements, thereby reducing their effect.

The underlying assumption of the new institutionalist analysis is that institutions can either exacerbate or mute the three political dilemmas just outlined.

Parliamentary Versus
Presidential Rule

The most fundamental constitutional difference among democracies is between parliamentary and presidential systems of government. The debate over the relative merits of these two systems has been particularly intense in Latin America, where presidentialism has been held responsible not only for the region's economic failures but for its long-standing history of political instability as well.

Parliamentistas argue that the two core features of presidential systems—separate and independent election of the executive and legislature and fixed terms—pose significant difficulties for the stability and efficiency of democratic rule.

Separation of Powers

In parliamentary systems, at least in theory, there are clear lines of authority from voters, to ruling party or coalition, to cabinet, to bureaucracy. In presidential systems, by contrast, the lines of authority are complex and overlapping; rather than a clear division of powers, presidents and legislatures typically share them. As a result, there are more veto points over policy, particularly where legislative powers are further divided between two houses.

One result of this divided political authority is the tendency both to stalemates and to "bidding wars" between the branches. Executives with an independent electoral base and separate powers have fewer incentives to seek enduring coalitions, and independently elected legislators are less likely to cooperate for the purpose of making the president look good. This is true even when the president's own party holds a legislative majority and will be still more marked when executives are limited to a single term or when the president's agenda includes difficult adjustment measures. Divided government (when the president and the legislative majority are from different parties) further exacerbates these problems, as can be seen with the failures of American fiscal policy in the 1980s.

A second consequence of presidential rule is bureaucratic inefficiency. Presidents, who have a national constituency, have an interest in efficient administrative structures that can serve as an instrument for implementing their programmatic agendas. However, legislators in a presidential system are not in the business of creating effective government; they are in the business of making themselves popular and their jobs secure. They accomplish this by courting interest group backing and pursuing particularistic legislative concerns.

Moreover, in a presidential system with competing and overlapping centers of power, it is possible for legislators to protect their policies against future reversal by designing complicated rules that reduce the discretion of bureaucrats, such as decision criteria, procedures, timetables, personnel rules, and so forth. Given the independent institutional and electoral interests of legislators and the multiple veto points built into a system of divided powers, these structures become extremely difficult to eliminate once in place.

The separate electoral mandate for executives in a presidential system can complicate policy making in an additional way. In presidential systems with weak parties, direct elections open a clearer route for "outsiders" to gain executive power; where many candidates are in the race, there are also greater opportunities for leaders appealing to the extreme end of the political spectrum. If countries such as Brazil and Peru had parliamentary systems during the 1980s, it is unlikely that a Collor or Fujimori would have come to power or that leaders like Lula or Brizola would have been serious contenders for the Brazilian presidency. Because "outsiders" or "extremists" can come to power without the backing of broadly based party organizations, they are poorly positioned to develop the legislative support required to sustain economic reform programs.

In parliamentary regimes, executive and legislative authority are fused. This central institutional feature of parliamentarism not only eliminates the problem of executive-legislative stalemate but also can enhance party discipline. Particularly in majoritarian systems, backbenchers have strong incentives to cooperate with the party leadership and to maintain party discipline, if for no simpler reason than that the fall of the government could lead to the calling of new parliamentary elections. These arrangements have important implications for policy; political competition is structured to a greater degree around broad party programs than around the particularistic interests of individual legislators. Narrow interest groups, particularly geographically based ones, are less likely to have effective access to policy making. In such a system, it is also impossible for legislators to protect against future policy changes through complex and efficiency-reducing administrative engineering, since succeeding governments can undo the policies of their predecessors at will.

In parliamentary systems, executives are highly unlikely to be outsiders. Parliamentary leaders normally ascend to office as a result of extensive party and legislative experience. Moreover, since their tenure depends on their capacity to maintain legislative majorities, they must consult with supporters to retain those majorities, whether within their own parties or among coalition partners. For these reasons, they are also more likely to be able to forge coalitions to support their programs; this is taken by some to be a particular virtue of multiparty parliamentary systems.

Fixed Terms

A second cluster of defects in presidential systems arises from the existence of fixed terms. It is extremely difficult to change governments when the legislature, but more particularly the president, has lost political support and exhausted leadership potential. Presidentialism served to prolong crises in Brazil and Peru, for example, where presidents Sarney, Collor, and Garcia outstayed their effectiveness. In Bolivia and Argentina in the 1980s, lame duck presidents were forced to resign before the expiration of their terms. Changes of government would arguably have come earlier and more smoothly under parliamentary rule.

There are, however, reasons to doubt that parliamentarism per se is inherently superior to presidentialism for undertaking and sustaining economic reform; much depends on the nature of the party system. A parliamentary system is not necessarily more conducive to consultation with affected parties. Where parties rule by absolute majority in a parliamentary system, or where majority coalitions are cohesive, prime ministers can acquire greater discretionary latitude than presidents, who must necessarily negotiate with legislatures to achieve their objectives. The potential for wide swings in policy is therefore increased.

Executive-legislative stalemates are possible in parliamentary as well as presidential systems, though they naturally take a different form. Under parliamentary systems with proportional representation, fragmentation of the party system and patronage demands from party leaders can create dangerous stalemates not only in making policy but in the formation of governments. The few empirical studies of this issue—all focusing on European parliamentary systems—suggest that stabilization is more difficult as the number of parties in the governing coalition grows larger because of the increase in the number of side payments required. Turkey in the late 1970s stands out as an example of a parliamentary system in which economic policy making was incoherent because of the difficulty of negotiating compromises within coalitions and the instability of governments themselves.

The political upheavals in Japan and Italy in 1993 show that pork-barrel politics and corruption can flourish just as well in parliamentary systems as in presidential ones, particularly where there are strong incentives to dispense patronage. Though such systems do not appear to have slowed growth in those two cases, the costs of patronage are arguably higher in the developing world.

Haggard and Kaufman find no clear pattern differentiating presidential and parliamentary systems with respect to their capacity to manage the economy or undertake economic reform. Korea and Chile continued their high growth trajectories under presidential auspices, and the Philippines avoided the tragedies of a number of Latin American cases. In Colombia and Costa Rica, presidential regimes instituted moderate adjustment policies and maintained positive growth rates. On the other hand, all of the cases of developing-country hyperinflation in the 1980s (Argentina, Bolivia, Brazil, and Peru) occurred under presidential or mixed-presidential systems. Performance in the Dominican Republic was highly erratic. The Venezuelan regime did not address major structural problems until the end of the decade; when it did, it experienced the most profound political upheaval since the inception of its contemporary democratic structure in 1958 and, partly as a result, reversed policy course in the early 1990s.

Multiparty parliamentary regimes in Thailand and Turkey sustained adjustments undertaken by their authoritarian predecessors. But Thailand's political system was only semidemocratic for most of the 1980s, and its successful adjustment was, arguably, in spite of the parliamentary nature of its democratic rule. The military's reentry into politics in the early 1990s was partly in response to the growing incoherence and corruption of democratic rule. Turkey performed reasonably well through the mid–1980s, but fiscal policy deteriorated in the late 1980s and early 1990s as the political system became more competitive, and the country experienced a crisis in 1994.

Economic performance was relatively good in a number of the pure Westminster systems, in which parliamentary rule is coupled with plurality voting rules in single-member districts. But the strong record with respect to inflation management probably has less to do with parliamentarism than other British institutional inheritances, such as strong currency boards. Moreover, most of these cases were small island economies in the Caribbean that do not provide particularly enlightening comparisons for large, middle-income countries. Trinidad and Tobago is the largest of these, but its record is not encouraging; the country experienced profound policy drift and seven straight years of economic decline in the late 1980s.

India's economic performance is mixed. Growth was higher than in the past, but budget deficits and inflation increased as well. Moreover, the country showed disturbing signs of increasing ethnic and regional polarization. It could be argued that these forces have been contained by the country's strong parliamentary heritage. Yet it is just as plausible to argue that it was the dominance of the Congress Party and federalism, rather than parliamentarism per se, that mattered in this regard.

This review does not imply complete agnosticism on the question of the effects of parliamentary versus presidential rule. However, it suggests that the effects of this fundamental constitutional choice are contingent on other components of institutional design, particularly the party system.

The Structure of the Party System:
Fragmentation and Polarization

To understand the effects that party systems have on the initiation and consolidation of reform, it is important to consider the incentives facing individual politicians in more detail. Most incumbent politicians seek reelection and are, therefore, responsive to the interests of voters. Politicians' views of reform should thus reflect trends in public opinion among their constituents. They are likely to acquiesce to adjustment initiatives during honeymoons, oppose those elements of reform that cut against the interests of core constituents, and adopt more favorable views when—and if—the reforms yield results.

Party politicians, and particularly party leaders, must also respond to political pressures emanating from the competitive context in which they find themselves. The party system constitutes a critical determinant of politicians' behavior in this regard. First, politicians are engaged in a strategic interaction with adversaries; their positions with respect to reform and their willingness to compromise are a function not simply of their constituent base but also of the strategy and tactics of their political opponents. Second, party leaders must respond to competing factions, backbenchers, and organizational activists within their own ranks. How politicians respond to these pressures is a function of two features of the party system: the number and the ideological distribution of parties and the internal politics of party organization.

Alternative Party Systems:
Fragmentation and Polarization

A number of features of party systems are salient for understanding political behavior and resulting policy outcomes, but fragmentation and polarization have
received the most sustained attention. Fragmentation is typically defined by the
number of effective parties. Polarization is defined by the ideological distance between the extreme parties in the system. Fragmentation can be measured easily,
but it is notoriously difficult to gauge the extent of ideological distance among
parties, even in the advanced industrial states. The problem is compounded in
developing countries, where party cleavages do not always fall along a clear left-
right dimension. Several indicators to point to polarization, however. One is the
presence of left and populist parties that have historically mobilized followers
around anticapitalist or antioligarchic protests. It is also useful to consider the
strength of "movement parties" that exhibit the sectarian characteristics of a social movement and rest on strong solidaristic and exclusivist loyalties among
party activists; the Italian fascists constitute an historical example, as do the Peronists at several points in their history.

Nonpolarized party systems, by contrast, are characterized by a low level of ideological distance among parties, typically meaning that left and populist parties are
weak or nonexistent. Nonpolarized systems rest on "pragmatic" parties, in which
ties between leaders and followers are largely instrumental and rest on shared interests in obtaining political office rather than strong ideological commitments.

Fragmentation should create impediments to the coordination required both
to initiate and sustain policy changes. More cohesive systems, by contrast, generate the stable electoral and legislative support that is a prerequisite for consolidating economic reform. However, fragmentation alone says nothing about the underlying preferences of the contending political forces in the system or the extent
of cleavage among them. We expect that reform will be more difficult in polarized systems in which strong left, populist, and movement parties compete, both
because of their effects on partisan conflict and because of their influence on the
stance of interest groups, particularly the labor movement and the urban popular
sector, which includes lower-middle-class, white-collar workers and portions of
the informal sector.

The principal effect of fragmentation on the conduct of policy is the difficulty it
poses for coordination within the ruling coalition, between executive and legislative branches, and among levels of government. In parliamentary systems based
on proportional representation with high proportionality, a multiplicity of parties
increases the difficulty of forming and sustaining coalition governments. The division of cabinet posts among contending parties that is required to form such
coalitions can undermine the capacity of central authorities to undertake the coordinated implementation of reform programs; policy becomes a logroll. When
such governments are formed, small coalition partners can hold veto power over
policy decisions. Israeli politics exhibits these characteristics in the extreme.

Analogous problems can exist in presidential systems. Party fragmentation in
presidential systems compounds the chances that executives will become politically isolated and powerless to pursue their agenda. The incentives for small parties to cooperate with the government are weaker than in a parliamentary system,

since there is no ability to threaten early elections, and the temptations to legislative blackmail are correspondingly greater.

The effects of fragmentation on policy making will also depend on whether the system is simultaneously polarized. This can be seen by comparing economic policy and performance in Thailand and Brazil. Thailand in the late 1980s had a highly fragmented party system but showed no signs of polarization. In the absence of strong left or populist parties, the principal coordination problems centered on the struggle for pork. With multiple contenders and weak party organizations, there were few constraints on politicians in the competition for patronage and pork-barrel expenditures and limited incentives to cooperate around reforms that provide public goods.

Coordination becomes even more difficult when the centrifugal pressures in fragmented systems are compounded by strong ideological polarization or sectarian tendencies. Parties in such systems are more likely to engage in programmatic bidding wars, both to differentiate themselves from opponents and to maintain the allegiance of relatively narrow constituencies. For similar reasons, fragmented and polarized systems amplify the distributional demands coming from antiadjustment interest groups. These two consequences are particularly marked when there are splits among populist or left parties, which then compete among themselves for support of labor unions and other popular sector groups. This characteristic was particularly true of Peru during its first two posttransition governments.

The combination of polarization and fragmentation also affects economic management by exacerbating political business cycles. Not only do elections in such systems invite opportunistic behavior and encourage the delay of adjustment efforts, but the combination of an unstable and volatile party landscape with deep partisan antagonisms increases the uncertainty surrounding elections due to the potential for large policy swings between successive governments. Argentina, Bolivia, Brazil, and Peru all experienced profound economic collapse in the run-up to elections.

In cohesive party systems, competition is organized among a small number of large parties. At the time of its transition to democracy, the Philippines had probably the most cohesive party system among new developing country democracies; the transitional election was fought between two blocs, consisting of pro-Marcos and anti-Marcos forces. In subsequent elections, the weakness of party organizations and the tendency to personalism and fragmentation emerged more clearly, but these tendencies were constrained by the centripetal incentives associated with single-member electoral districts for the lower house. Chile, Korea, and Taiwan also showed low levels of fragmentation, as all three moved toward the formation of broad-based political blocs. Korea even evolved "past" a two-party system toward a dominant party model, along Japanese lines. Argentina and Uruguay were also relatively cohesive, although the Uruguayan case is complicated by institutionalized competition within the major parties, which had important implications for its adjustment efforts in the late 1980s and early 1990s. Turkey also constitutes an ambiguous case. At the time of the transitional election in 1983, the country had less than three effective parties, but this was the result of a military ban on full party participation. By the late 1980s, the Turkish party system had become both more fragmented and more polarized, which helps explain the growing incoherence of economic policy.

What are the effects of a cohesive party system with a low degree of polarization on the conduct of economic policy? First, we would expect politicians to crowd the center and to avoid strong programmatic appeals that would differentiate them sharply from their competitors. Where the median voter opposes reform, or where the party is captured by powerful interests, stalemate is certainly possible. Party leaders in cohesive, nonpolarized settings can be expected to resist reforms when these threaten patronage opportunities or remove protection from core constituents. If there are strong interest group and electoral forces arrayed against reform, then a cohesive, nonpolarized system would militate against radical market-oriented reforms in favor of a more incremental approach.

But broad-based, catchall parties also have advantages with respect to initiating and sustaining reform. Given the tendency for such parties to move toward the center, we would expect cohesive, nonpolarized systems to generate strong organized support for the initiation of reform in crisis situations in which voters are disaffected with the policy status quo. In opposition, catchall parties will naturally seek to discredit the policies of the government. But when things are going well, they are less likely to press for the wholesale reversal of government initiatives; when things are going badly, they are less likely than leftist or movement parties to gravitate toward radical, polarizing solutions or to back strikes, demonstrations, and protests that complicate the ability of governments to act.

A small number of large parties also has a moderating influence on the way interests are aggregated. In countries with cohesive party systems, interest groups are forced to operate in an encompassing coalition, in which diverse interests are represented and among which compromises must be struck. Unlike both fragmented and polarized systems, politicians operating in such systems are not as closely linked to, or dependent on, specific economic interests. This has the effect both of facilitating the organization of support and of diffusing opposition.

Given these incentives, the combination of a cohesive yet polarized system is unlikely. There are fewer opportunities for strongly ideological or movement parties to operate in a system with a small number of parties; most cohesive systems are not polarized. As we would also expect, the left and movement parties that have resurfaced in more cohesive systems have had strong incentives to move toward the center. The exception that proves the rule is Turkey, which did become more polarized over time. However, this was partly the result of lowering the barriers to political entry and allowing more parties to compete; the system became more polarized as it became more fragmented.

Chile and Argentina do combine a low level of fragmentation with the presence of parties with strong populist and socialist legacies. By around 1990, both the Chilean socialists and the Peronists, once highly sectarian, had taken on many properties of pragmatic catchall parties. When compared to movement parties in more fragmented systems, those in cohesive systems have a strong incentive to broaden their appeal and deemphasize traditional solidarities.

The behavior of left and movement parties operating in a cohesive party system depends on whether these parties are in or out of power. Incentives for left and populist parties to resist reform are strongest when they are in the political opposition and adjustments are initiated by their rivals. Movement parties in opposition are much more likely than catchall parties to launch a "principled" opposition to adjustment initiatives, with broad appeals to egalitarian and nationalist values. They are also more inclined to back these appeals with support for labor activism and social protest.

The case of Argentina demonstrates that this behavior has an important effect on the position of more moderate groups within both the government and opposition. Militant opposition by the Peronists increased the electoral risks of initiating reforms or of continuing their implementation, even when these seemed important for averting more severe economic difficulties. In short, cohesive but polarized party systems can come to resemble fragmented and polarized systems under some circumstances.

The policy orientation of left or populist parties can change substantially, however, if they are incorporated into the government; this observation may be important for understanding the politics of "reformed" communist parties in the former socialist countries. This outcome is much more likely to occur in consolidated, than in fragmented, systems. In fragmented systems, the movement of some left or populist groups toward the center is likely to be resisted by other factions that can gain through militant appeals to narrow constituencies. Consolidated systems, by contrast, provide opportunities for left or populist parties to gain office by extending their appeal beyond their core constituencies and demonstrating their capacity for moderation; there is space to move toward the center. Left parties in power have an additional advantage in cohesive systems: their links with organized labor and other groups disadvantaged by reform may actually make it easier for them to gain trust and to negotiate compensatory agreements that permit reform to move forward.

Internal Party Organization

At several points in the foregoing discussion, issues of intraparty organization have necessarily entered into the analysis. For example, in discussing the parliamentary-presidential debate, it was noted that legislators in a presidential system have a tendency toward particularism. However, this might be due to the lack of party discipline rather than presidentialism per se. How precisely do the incentive structures *within* parties affect the propensity to provide public goods and coherent economic policy?

The key variable is the relative strength of the party leadership vis-à-vis the individual politician. Where party leaderships are strong, there is greater prospect of enforcing programmatic discipline on followers and less likelihood that programs will be dominated by geographic or other constituent interests. Party strength is likely to be reflected not only in intraparty organization but also in the design of legislative institutions themselves. Strong parties are more likely to favor rules and institutions that further buttress party discipline, such as strong oversight or control committees, extensive agenda-setting and committee assignment powers for party leaders, and weak policy committees.

The strength of the party leadership depends on the extent to which electoral rules encourage politicians to cultivate a personal reputation. Where politicians have incentives to cultivate the personal vote, they are more likely to develop narrow constituent bases of support and to press for particularistic policies at the expense of party platforms.

A number of interrelated rules affect the extent to which party control is centralized. First, party leaders must control access to the ballot and the order in which candidates are elected. Such control, exercised through closed-list rules on nomination procedures, allow party leaders to screen out undesirable mavericks. For those with secure positions on the party list, closed lists may encourage complacency. However, they are also likely to encourage loyalty to the party platform if one exists because a politician's position on the ballot is determined by the party leadership. A more open and decentralized nomination procedure weakens party control. In an open-list system, the electorate effectively orders the ballot. Open lists allow entrants to free-ride on the party label while simultaneously encouraging them to curry a personal reputation for the provision of particularistic goods.

A closely related feature of the electoral system that determines politicians' behavior is whether they are competing against members of their own party. In some systems with multimember districts, members of the same party are in competition with each other. As the size of the district increases, and the individual politician is competing with more members both of the opposition and her own party, this competition becomes more fierce. Of course, the party label is of no use in competition with members of one's own party; the only way to conduct such rivalry is by stressing personal traits that differentiate the candidate. In effect, politicians are encouraged to pursue a "niche" strategy. These strategies might be subtly ideological: politicians from the same party may emphasize different aspects of the party platform. Nonetheless, it is usually easier to secure niche support on the basis of instrumental promises to followers and the provision of personal services than it is by standing up for the public good.

A third feature of the electoral system is whether voters choose parties or candidates. If voters choose parties, then the politician has little incentive to differentiate himself from the party platform; his fate rises or falls with the party's. If the voter chooses individual candidates, there are, again, incentives to cultivate a personal vote.

Fourth is the control of campaign finance. Where individual politicians have responsibility for raising their own campaign money and, consequently, control their own purses, there is an incentive to cultivate a personal reputation. Donors in such settings typically provide candidates with money for the purpose of realizing particular objectives.

It is important to underscore that centralized control is certainly not a guarantee of good economic policy. Centralized parties might well have ideological platforms that are hostile to economic reform. The distribution of private goods is also of use to politicians even in a centralized system. Party leaders still have an interest in maintaining the loyalty of both legislators and voters and will use patronage and pork to that end. Venezuela, for example, has highly centralized party institutions, but they have been riddled with corruption and patronage.

However, the distribution of private goods through centralized monitoring mechanisms, either the party's or the legislature's, may have a salutary effect in the reform process. The distribution of a certain amount of patronage and pork provides a mechanism for building support, including among previously excluded groups, and of partially compensating losers. The key issue is guaranteeing that pork is distributed in a relatively efficient way. One way of achieving this is through electoral reforms that reduce intraparty competition, such as the formation of single-member districts. However, control may also be exercised by delegating greater authority to the executive.

The Constitution of Executive Authority

A centralized executive authority plays a pivotal role in overcoming the collective action problems and distributive conflicts associated with the initiation of comprehensive economic reforms. In the early phase of a reform, key decisions about the design of policy and the political and legislative strategy are usually taken by the president or prime minister on the basis of counsel from a hand-picked team of advisers. The executive's ability to act aggressively is partly a function of conjunctural factors. In democratic systems, honeymoons provide new governments with the opportunity to take new initiatives. Economic conditions can also generate strong pressures for policy change and a willingness to expand the discretionary authority of the executive.

In addition to these conjunctural determinants of executive power, institutions have also been explicitly designed either to buttress central authority or to insulate decision making from political interference. In analyzing the powers of the executive, it is important to distinguish between those powers that belong to the executive by constitutional right and those that are explicitly delegated. In presidential systems, the former typically include a veto (of varying scope and with differing provisions for legislative override) that provides some check on legislative power. Presidential authority also typically includes certain legislative or decree powers that grant presidents more direct control over the policy agenda. These powers can be extremely important for the conduct of economic policy. In Korea, the president introduces the budget, and the legislature has no power to increase spending; it may only shift expenditures between categories and reduce spending. In Brazil, presidential authority to issue "urgent" laws was used by the Collor administration to initiate reform legislation, though not always successfully.

These powers must be distinguished from those that are explicitly delegated to the executive by the legislature. Prime ministers and their cabinets in parliamentary systems are typically quite powerful; they can legislate more or less at will. However, this power results from their backing by a majority in parliament, either of the dominant party or a coalition. Similarly, in presidential systems, legislators may delegate quite substantial decree powers to the president on a temporary basis. Such powers were important in the initiation of reforms in Argentina and Peru but would not have been possible without ultimate congressional backing.

Another feature of the executive that can have important implications for the conduct of economic policy is the delegation of decision-making authority to specialized agencies *within* the executive. Such delegation can substantially alter the political calculus, and even the very organization, of interest groups. Perhaps the best-known examples are the creation of independent central banking institutions and quasi-judicial structures for the adjudication of certain trade policy issues. In both cases, the establishment of independent agencies limits the access of groups to decision making or alters the way in which they exercise influence. The establishment of quasi-judicial procedures for the management of unfair trade practices may provide access for aggrieved parties with protectionist intent, yet they are also demand that petitioners demonstrate that their cases are in conformity with statute. Such a process differs fundamentally from a lobbying relationship with a legislator.

Though constitutional arrangements and processes of delegation can strengthen the hand of the executive by expanding the discretionary power to initiate policy or by insulating decision making from short-term political pressures, such mechanisms do not necessarily provide an effective basis for policy coordination and the management of distributive conflict over the long run. To the contrary, strong executive discretion can weaken the incentives for party, legislative, and interest group leaders to support policy initiatives. Legislators with limited influence over policy are likely to distance themselves from the chief executive, particularly during times of economic distress; this is especially true in presidential systems and where parties are weak.

Efforts to insulate decision making can also backfire. The purpose of such institutional arrangements is to offset threats from the opposition to policy continuity and coherence, particularly in countries with long histories of polarization and social conflict over economic issues. However, as both Turkey and Thailand demonstrate, an insulated executive is not sufficient to prevent opposition to reform as barriers to political contestation fall, and it may itself become the focus of the opposition. To the extent that both executive power and the insulation of agencies are the result of delegation, both can be reversed—though only at some cost. Such processes of delegation may run particular risks in weakly institutionalized democracies. Take for example the recent tendency in Latin America for legislators to grant executives substantial powers for the purpose of undertaking economic reform measures. First, it is not clear that the decisions taken under such conditions are necessarily optimal or even politically sustainable, since they avoid consultation with affected parties. Second, there is also the question of whether they will lead to a plebiscitarian political style and the atrophy of representative institutions.

Nonetheless, the process of delegation is central in all democratic systems; modern democracy would be impossible without it. Thus, the issue is not whether or not to delegate but how delegation can be structured to maximize both efficiency and accountability. This is probably the area of institutional design where outside donors can have the greatest influence. The transition to the market involves the creation of new, or the strengthening of old, regulatory institutions: from rules and laws governing industrial relations, to environmental agencies, to the oversight of financial markets. There are two competing conceptions of how such institutions can be strengthened and given more independence. One is to increase their capacity. This technocratic strategy has some merit. By increasing salaries, attracting high-quality personnel, and injecting greater expertise through training, agencies gain political weight. The foreign link itself constitutes an important resource.

The record of the recent past suggests that such a technocratic strategy is inadequate by itself. For agencies to sustain themselves over time, they must also build on bases of constituent support. For example, recent research on central banks reveals that these institutions gain "independence" not through statute but by maintaining close relationships with those politicians and interest groups favorable to the conduct of stable monetary policy. The task for institutional design is therefore to consider how new policy-making bodies can enfranchise and strengthen the hand of proreform groups that have previously been underrepresented not only within the party system more broadly but also within the state itself.

Conclusions

Research on the relationship between institutions and economic policy and performance is in its infancy, and it is thus important to retain caution and humility when drawing policy implications. It is dangerous to think that all political barriers to effective economic reform and governance can be overcome through institutional engineering. Moreover, institutional design itself is not exogenous to politics. Nonetheless, this survey suggests some findings that may be useful for those involved in the design and reform of institutions.

It is, first, important to underscore some general analytic principles. Most analyses of economic policy focus on the distribution of underlying preferences or the organization of interest groups. I argue, by contrast, that the organization of interests and their influence is contingent on institutions, as are the incentives facing the politicians who constitute the ultimate decision makers with respect to economic reform.

Given a particular distribution of interests, what institutions are conducive to economic reform? This depends to a certain extent on the distinction between initiating and consolidating reform. The initiation of reform is facilitated by institutions that expand executive discretion. In presidential systems, these include constitutionally entrenched or delegated powers. In parliamentary systems, executive power is tied directly to the structure of the party system. Rules that limit the number of parties also limit the need for coalitions and, thus, expand executive independence.

A central theme of this chapter is the importance of building bases of support for reform over the longer run; the key issue is how such support is organized. One solution is corporatism. However, it is not clear that such a solution is likely in most developing countries—nor, if it were feasible, whether it would be desirable to bypass fragile democratic institutions through direct corporatist bargaining.

I place particular attention on the interaction between basic constitutional choices—presidential versus parliamentary rule—and the party system. In a democratic system, parties serve as the key link between politicians and constituents, and the party system establishes the incentives for partisan competition. Electoral rules that provide low barriers to political entry encourage the fragmentation and polarization of the political system, factors that make coordination difficult. These problems are compounded by incentives to politicians to cultivate the personal vote and, thus, particularistic policies.

It is again worth emphasizing that institutions are not the end of the story; preferences matter. Getting the institutions right, however, increases the likelihood that reform will succeed and, thus, that underlying political preferences will shift in a proreform direction.

Stephan Haggard, "Democratic Institutions, Economic Policy, and Development," in *Institutions and Economic Development: Growth and Governance in Less-Developed and Post-Socialist Countries*, ed. Christopher Clague (Baltimore: Johns Hopkins University Press, 1997): 121–49.

28

A Game Theoretic Model of Reform in Latin American Democracies

BARBARA GEDDES

Bureaucratic inefficiency, patronage-induced overstaffing, and outright corruption retard economic development and reduce public well-being in developing countries. They prevent governments from effectively carrying out the economic plans to which they devote so much official attention, and deprive citizens of government services to which they are legally entitled.

The costs associated with bureaucratic deficiencies are widely recognized. Nevertheless, the initiation of reforms has proved difficult. In this essay I explain why reforms that are widely regarded as necessary and desirable often face such severe obstacles to their initiation. The explanation lies in the interests of the politicians who must make the decisions that would promote or impede reform. The heart of the argument is that these individuals frequently face a choice between actions that serve their individual political interests and actions that would improve the long-run welfare of their societies and that when this happens, individual interests generally prevail. Reforms only occur in political circumstances that render the individual interests of the politicians who must initiate them consistent with the collective interest in reform.

The analysis focuses on one type of reform, the introduction of merit-based hiring for civil servants. This aspect of reform was selected for emphasis because the many administrative reform packages proposed during recent decades nearly always include it; because rules for merit-based hiring, unlike other kinds of reform, vary only moderately from country to country; and because the effects of laws requiring recruitment by exam are relatively easy to assess. Meritocratic recruitment is not always the most important aspect of administrative reform; but it is always at least moderately important, and it is the easiest element of reform to "measure" and compare across nations.

I analyze the legislative struggle over reform in South American democracies, of which some have initiated reforms, and some have not. The choice of this set of cases holds roughly constant several variables that are often mentioned as possible causes of honesty and competence in government: culture, colonial institutional structure, and level of economic development. At the same time, it preserves sufficient variance in contemporary political institutions and reform outcomes to allow the testing of hypotheses.

The Need for Reform

Demand for reform in Latin America resulted from widespread recognition that the traditional use of government resources for partisan purposes had led to excesses. In Uruguay during the 1950s and 1960s, for example, so large a fraction of the budgets of many government agencies went for wages to pay patronage appointees that there were no funds left for operating expenses.

In spite of widespread support, however, reforms have occurred only slowly and sporadically. Two groups have opposed reform: those who have found in bureaucratic jobs a "refuge from which to make a last-ditch stand for their right to a quiet, incompetent existence" and elected politicians and party activists. The opposition of employees who gained their jobs through patronage reflects the expected costs of reform to them. But perhaps less obviously, administrative reform is also costly to the politicians who must enact it. Traditionally, jobs in the bureaucracy and the multitude of contracts, subsidies, exceptions, and other scarce values distributed by bureaucrats have served as important electoral resources. Politicians and officials have been able to trade help in acquiring these resources for support.

Administrative reform threatens to eliminate these political resources. Reforms that introduce merit as the main criterion for hiring and promotion decrease the ability of politicians and party leaders to reward supporters with jobs.

The cost of administrative reform to politicians and party activists is thus clear. Under certain circumstances, however, administrative reform may also provide them with benefits. If the national economy improves as a result of increasing the competence of officials and the effectiveness of their decisions, incumbent politicians and their party can claim credit for it in the next election. Moreover, politicians and their party may gain support from voters who favor reform. Politicians may gain a sense of satisfaction from having helped provide the country with more honest and competent administration. A final possibility is that as the electorate grows, politicians and party leaders will prefer to switch from offering private goods in exchange for support to offering public goods, because, in a mass electorate, public goods cost politicians less per voter reached.

To explain why reforms have occurred at some times and places but not others, then, one must answer the question, Under what circumstances will the benefits of reform outweigh the costs to the politicians who must at least acquiesce in passing them?

The Interests of Legislators
and Party Leaders

Whether politicians will initiate administrative reform depends on the incentives they confront. Only if the individual aspirations for power, status, wealth, or policy change on the part of political activists and politicians can be furthered by the provision of reforms will they be provided.

The interests of elected officials in Latin America resemble the interests of politicians elsewhere. They want to be re-elected, and they prefer some policies over others. Without doing them too much of an injustice, we can assume that for most politicians most of the time, the desire to be elected takes precedence over policy preferences. For some, the desire for office and its perquisites truly overwhelms their commitment to particular policies. Others may want to be elected only in order to enact preferred policies; but if they fail to be elected, they lose their chance of influencing policy outcomes. Thus, even for the public-spirited, the preference for election will be strong, since election grants the opportunity to achieve other preferences. This is not to deny that for some politicians, ideological commitments outweigh the desire to be elected. The electoral process, however, tends to weed out such individuals; they are elected less frequently than those who consider winning of paramount importance. No politician in competition with others engaged in trading jobs and favors for votes can afford unilaterally to eschew reliance on patronage.

If this pattern of incentives were the whole story, there would never be any reason for legislators to approve administrative reform. Each individual who relies on patronage is better off, no matter what others do and whether the game is repeated or not. If for any reason, however, legislators place a positive value on reform—if, for example, they think supporting reform would sway the votes of a small number of middle-class idealists or improve their standing by a tiny increment with party leaders—they might in some circumstances vote for reform.

Consider four scenarios. First, members of both parties vote against reform, so that neither can claim credit and neither is hurt by the other's claiming credit. The reform fails since neither large party voted for it and members of both parties continue to rely on patronage during election campaigns. Second, both parties vote for reform. Since both voted for it, the electoral advantage of voting for it cancels out. The reform passes and neither party can rely on patronage during future campaigns. Third, the majority party voted in favor of reform and the minority party voted against. The reform passes so neither party can use patronage in future campaigns; and the majority party reaps a small electoral advantage, at the expense of the minority party from voting for reform. Finally, the majority party votes against reform and the minority votes in favor. The reform fails to pass so both parties continue to distribute patronage. The minority party gains a small amount of credit at the majority's expense for its vote for reform. So, if the two parties have approximately equal access to patronage resources, the majority party will vote for reform, and it will pass.

To reiterate, in an election, all candidates can be expected to rely on patronage. Members of a party disadvantaged by the distribution of patronage resources, however, would be better off if the merit system were imposed on everyone. Thus, they always have an incentive to support reform in the legislature. Giving up the use of patronage would make them better off as long as everyone else also gave it up. As many observers have noted, the reform issue generally appeals to the "outs" in politics.

Where patronage is equally distributed and politicians can gain even a small amount from a vote for reform, members of both parties have reason to vote for it. In this situation, patronage conveys no relative advantage, but voting for reform may improve electoral chances. Consequently, political interest dictates the passage of reform.

Spoils will be outlawed in democracies when two conditions are met, namely, that the benefits of patronage are approximately evenly distributed among the larger parties, and legislators have some small incentive to vote for reform.

Such reforms may turn out to be fragile if access to patronage again becomes one-sided, a subject to which I will return below. For now, let us look in more detail at how the game-theoretic prediction fares when confronted with evidence from the Latin American democracies.

The Effect of the Distribution
of Patronage on Reform

In this section I shall test the predictions derived from the game-theoretic model on the universe of Latin American countries that have experienced 15 or more years of consecutive competitive democracy since 1930: Brazil, Chile, Colombia, Uruguay, and Venezuela. Costa Rica was excluded because its legislators cannot be immediately reelected, so that the simplifying assumptions about the interests of legislators used here could not be expected to apply to them.

Colombia

Competition between the Liberal and Conservative parties for control of government and the spoils associated with control has structured all of Colombia's modern history. Until 1958, transfers of power from one party to the other were accompanied by large-scale turnovers of personnel and partisan violence. Public welfare suffered from the inefficiency of a bureaucracy composed of patronage appointments as well as from periodic outbreaks of violence. As early as the 1920s, critics identified the parties' excessive reliance on patronage as one of the pathologies of Colombian life. Reforms have been undertaken, however, only during two time periods, both of which correspond to periods of approximate equality between the two parties.

Colombia's first experiments with merit-oriented administrative reforms occurred during the presidency of Enrique Olaya Herrera (1930–34). The Olaya administration marked the first electoral victory of the Liberal party in the twentieth century. Olaya won by a slim margin, and the reformist Liberals' hold on government during his first two years was tenuous. Several administrative reforms were passed at this time, the most important of which aimed at improving the performance of the Ministry of Public Works and other agencies responsible for the construction and maintenance of railroads and highways.

By 1934 the Liberals had consolidated their electoral dominance, and Alfonso López won the presidency easily. He continued many of the new economic policies of Olaya but permitted the reassertion of partisan considerations in hiring. The Olaya administration's merit-based reforms quietly disappeared during the Liberal hegemony of 1934–46.

Colombia's next attempt to establish merit as the basis for recruitment to the civil service occurred in 1958. At that time, each of the major parties controlled exactly half of the legislature and half of the available administrative appointments. This was due to a pact—the National Front—between the Liberal and Conservative parties that established parity between the two traditional rivals in the national legislature, in departmental (i.e., state) legislatures, in municipal councils, and in administrative appointments. This pact, designed to end a decade of repression and partisan violence in which more than 200 thousand people had been killed, was scheduled to remain in effect for 16 years. Each party would receive 50% of the seats in legislatures and councils. The presidency was to alternate between the two parties. A career civil service was proposed as a means of removing key jobs from partisan control, and other administrative jobs were to be distributed equally between supporters of the two parties. In short, the pact established an equal sharing of power and patronage, regardless of electoral outcomes for 16 years.

The pact called for the creation of a merit-based career civil service, but presidential and legislative action were required to initiate it. Individual legislators facing this decision about whether to forego a portion of customary patronage would have to consider the electoral costs and benefits associated with patronage. By law, each party could claim an equal share of patronage. Nevertheless, no individual legislator could afford to eschew the use of patronage unilaterally.

Two factors contributed to making a vote for reform more attractive than it might otherwise have been. The first was the interest of all politicians in reestablishing a democratic system, which depended on ending partisan violence. Administrative reform was expected to help end the violence by providing a fair means of distributing jobs and also by contributing to better quality economic policy. Leaders in both parties had committed themselves to agreements, including complicated parity arrangements as well as civil service reform, as a way of reducing the violence and reestablishing a competitive political system. Thus, party elites had managed to forge an enforceable cooperative solution to the prisoner's dilemma of unrestrained party competition. The career interests of high-level party leaders in reestablishing the competitive electoral system explain their support for the pact. Legislators' second reason for voting for reform was the expectation that it would affect future placement on electoral lists. Party leaders in Colombia at that time could influence legislators' decisions with special effectiveness because of party cohesion and a closed list proportional representation system. Although the proliferation of factions within Colombia's two major parties during the pact subsequently reduced the influence of party leaders over legislators, in 1958 both parties were still relatively cohesive.

Evidence from the Colombian case is thus completely consistent with the model. Reform occurred when access to patronage was distributed equally. Party discipline enforced by the closed list system provided legislators with an additional incentive to vote for reform.

Uruguay

In Uruguay, the career civil service was first mandated by the 1934 constitution. This constitution legalized a pact between two factions of the traditional dominant parties, the *terrista* faction of the Colorado party and the *herrerista* faction of the National, or Blanco, party.

Uruguay has historically had a two-party system within which multiple factions have independent legal status and run their own lists of candidates in elections, thus creating a de facto multiparty system. Prior to the reform, Gabriel Terra, head of the *terrista* faction, had been elected president on the Colorado ticket. In the face of severe economic distress caused by the Depression and an apparently insurmountable policy immobilism caused by Uruguay's collegial executive and powerful but factionalized legislature, Terra staged a coup d'état in 1933. Luís Alberto Herrera, caudillo of the most important Blanco party faction at the time, collaborated with Terra; and the two faction leaders entered into a pact to share government offices, excluding other factions of both parties.

The sitting legislature was dismissed. Terra and Herrera chose a Deliberative Assembly of 99 members made up of approximately equal numbers of Colorado supporters of Terra and Blanco supporters of Herrera to act as a provisional legislature. They in turn elected a Constituent Assembly made up of Terra and Herrera supporters. The resulting constitution institutionalized the pact by mandating minority representation in the president's Council of Ministers and the equal division of Senate seats between the most-voted lists of the two most-voted parties. The division of the Senate assured these two factions equal control of appointments of all important administrative positions, the boards of directors of state enterprises, Supreme Court justices, and members of the Accounts Tribunal. At the same time, it excluded other factions from access to spoils. In effect, it transformed what had been a de facto multiparty system into a two-party system with approximately equal access to patronage for both parties.

Traditionally, the Colorado party had attracted more electoral support and controlled more patronage than had the Blancos. More popular parties usually have access to more patronage, but the pact resulted in an equal division of patronage in spite of electoral inequality. In this setting, the Constituent Assembly was able to agree to establish a career civil service, which would remove some appointments from the discretion of party activists. As in Colombia, the closed list system provided faction leaders with incentives they could deploy to affect the votes of members of the Constituent Assembly.

This brief period of relative equality between two factions was unique in Uruguayan history. The two parties achieved approximate equality in electoral strength in 1962 and 1971, but the largest factions within each party remained unequal. No legislation passed to enforce the principle of meritocratic hiring in practice. Legislative and constitutional additions to the civil service law after the 1930s generally focused on providing job security, vacations, grievance procedures, and so on. In other words, later additions to the civil service laws were designed to benefit well-organized civil servants and thus contribute to electoral gains for legislators—not to require further sacrifice of electoral interests.

Venezuela

At the beginning of the democratic period in Venezuela, administrative reform seemed to be supported by everyone. Excessive corruption had helped discredit the dictator, Marcos Pérez Jiménez; and administrative reform was widely seen as needed, both to reduce corruption and to improve the state's ability to use oil revenues to foster development and increase social welfare. President Rómulo Betancourt expressed strong support for reform, foreign experts were hired to help formulate a reform and train Venezuelans to implement it, and a reform agency attached to the presidency was created.

The agency completed its draft plan for civil service reform in 1960, and the president submitted it to Congress. The president had a coalition majority in Congress. Since party discipline in Venezuela is strong (in part because of party leaders' control of electoral lists), prospects for reform should have been good. Nevertheless, the civil service reform bill was never reported out of committee.

It continued, moreover, to languish in Congress throughout the Betancourt presidency and through that of his successor, Raúl Leoni. Venezuelan observers note that despite flamboyant public statements supporting reform, neither president really pushed the bill. Throughout this period, the party Acción Democrática (AD) controlled the presidency and a strong plurality in Congress. The AD leaders had much more to lose from giving up patronage than leaders of the other parties.

In 1968 Rafael Caldera of the Social Christian party (COPEI) was elected president with 28.9% of the vote, as compared with the AD-led coalition vote of 28.1%. In the legislature, the vote was split between the two largest parties, with 25.8% for AD and 24.2% for COPEI. The civil service reform was brought forward for consideration in Congress again, revised to make it congruent with recent constitutional and institutional changes, and passed in 1970 with support from both AD and COPEI. Thus, Venezuela's first merit-based civil service law also passed during a period of temporary equality between parties.

Brazil

Getúlio Vargas established a career civil service in Brazil during the dictatorship of 1937–45. The reform had made a fair amount of headway in imposing merit as the criterion for hiring and promotion by the time Vargas was overthrown in 1945. But after the return to democracy, earlier reforms were to a considerable extent undermined.

From the establishment of democracy until the military coup in 1964, the distribution of electoral strength and patronage in Brazil was quite unequal. The country had a multiparty system with open list proportional representation in the lower house and a majoritarian system in the Senate. The three most important parties were the Partido Social Democrático (PSD, a traditional, conservative party despite its name), the Partido Trabalhista Brasileiro (PTB, the Labor party), and the União Democrática Nacional (UDN, a middle-class reformist party). The PSD and PTB had developed from the traditional and labor wings of the political machine created by Vargas during the dictatorship. They were entrenched in the government bureaucracy prior to Vargas's overthrow, and their patronage resources remained impressive throughout the democratic period. In spite of apparently important ideological differences, the PSD and PTB formed frequent electoral alliances. The UDN, in contrast, developed in opposition to the Vargas political machine. Over the years it achieved some access to patronage as a result of entering coalitions and winning some elections, but it never equaled the other parties.

During the 1950s and 1960s, as economic development became the most important goal of the Brazilian government, concern about administrative reform reached new levels. Presidents Getúlio Vargas (during his second administration), Juscelino Kubitschek, and Jânio Quadros all proposed reforms. Public demand for reform, as expressed in the press and in answers to survey questions, was widespread. For example, a 1964 survey asked, "Which one of these do you think our country needs most: an honest government without corruption; a government that gets things done; a fair distribution of wealth; national unity; or individual freedom?" Even though the income distribution in Brazil was one of the most skewed in the world, 62% of those who answered chose "an honest government without corruption." The second-most-frequent choice was "a government that gets things done." When asked to agree or disagree with the statement, "The only really important problem in Brazil is the problem of lack of character and honesty," only 15% of those who had an opinion disagreed. When asked the most important reason for their party preference, 44% mentioned honesty first, more than twice as many as mentioned party program or past record.

Even in the face of such expressions of public opinion, however, legislators making the decision whether or not to vote for reform had to take into account the costs and benefits associated with patronage. Members of the UDN would have been better off if they had been able to pass a reform. Under these circumstances, it is not surprising that the UDN espoused "the struggle against the forces that have been dominant for many years of administrative corruption" in platforms, campaigns, and speeches. Individual members of the party could still improve their chances of being elected, however, by relying on promises of patronage during the campaign.

Members of the UDN behaved as would be expected, given the costs and benefits they faced. Most members relied on patronage and deals in electoral campaigns but advocated the passage of reform bills in Congress. This stance, though rational, left them vulnerable to charges of hypocrisy from both idealists within the party and opponents outside.

In contrast, PSD and PTB legislators had no reason to vote for reform and every reason to continue relying on patronage during electoral campaigns. During the democratic period, the career civil service remained on the books; but control over new hiring returned, for the most part, to the realm of patronage. Congress reduced the status and powers of the Departamento Administrativo de Servico Público (DASP), the agency in charge of enforcing civil service laws. During much of the democratic period, exams were not held and appointments were made in the temporary and extranumerary (i.e., outside the merit system) categories of employment. The dividing line between merit-based career and noncareer civil servants was blurred by the passage of laws conferring career civil service status and perquisites on "temporary" employees who had not taken the exam but who had spent five years or more in public employment.

Reform laws were proposed at various times; but only two kinds of civil service laws made it through Congress: those which granted benefits to civil servants and thus involved no electoral cost to legislators and those which extended meritocratic norms into agencies controlled by one particular party and thus involved gains rather than costs for the majority of legislators. In the realm of granting benefits, Congress increased the wages of civil servants and passed several laws granting job security and higher status to unclassified employees.

The one exception to the overall decline in the merit-based civil service during the democratic period occurred when Congress extended the merit system to cover the social security institutes. Thousands of jobs in these institutes had been used during the second Vargas and Kubitschek presidencies to reward the presidents' Labor party (PTB) coalition partner. Hiring in the institutes had, in effect, been turned over to Labor party activists. By voting to include the institutes in the merit system, members of Congress from other parties could decrease the resources available to the Labor party without incurring any cost themselves. Given the unusual circumstance of the existence of a group of agencies dominated by one particular party, the vote for reform did not depend on parity in the legislature.

Chile

During its long history of democracy, Chile never passed a comprehensive civil service reform. It had no civil service commission and no uniform system of recruitment and promotion. It did have some requirements for entry, such as completion of the tenth grade; but even these were violated in practice. Each agency controlled its own recruitment system. As a result, some agencies were highly professionalized, others extremely politicized.

The Chilean party system was far more fragmented than those of the other countries discussed. Traditionally, the Radical party had greatest access to patronage. Radical party dominance began to decline in the early 1950s, but no conjuncture occurred that gave approximately equal patronage to the largest parties in Congress.

Two characteristics of the Chilean democratic system further decreased the likelihood of passing a reform: the open list system of proportional representation initiated in 1958 and the fragmented party system. It might appear at first that in a fragmented party system such as Chile's, in which the "dominant" party often receives only 20%–30% of the vote in legislative elections, several smaller parties could band together to pass reforms that would deprive the largest party of its disproportionate access to patronage. In this way, a group of smaller parties with less access to patronage could improve their ability to compete against the party with the closest ties to the bureaucracy.

In an open list system, however, incumbents' interest in maintaining their advantage over competitors in their own parties outweighs their interest in depriving members of other parties of access to patronage resources. In open list systems, the candidate's place on the party list is determined by the vote the candidate receives. In other words, a candidate runs not only against candidates from other parties but also against other candidates from his or her own party.

Patronage thus becomes an even more valuable resource to the candidates who have access to it. Candidates can distinguish themselves from the candidates of other parties on the basis of programmatic appeals, offers of public goods, and ideology; but attention to casework and the distribution of private goods are among the few ways of distinguishing themselves from other candidates in the same party. Incumbents have a great advantage over other candidates in terms of their ability to distribute favors. Consequently, incumbents of all parties in an open list proportional representation system can be expected to be especially reluctant to give up patronage.

Had Chilean party leaders had an interest in reducing reliance on patronage, they might have succeeded in overcoming incumbents' reluctance to vote for reform. Despite the open list system, Chilean party leaders (in contrast to Brazilian) have substantial influence over the political careers of legislators. They influence them through control over who achieves a place on the list, whose name appears at the top of the ballot (and thus receives a disproportionate share of the votes of the unsophisticated), and who receives cabinet appointments, often a stepping-stone to executive office. Given the unequal distribution of patronage among parties and the importance of patronage to the organizational survival of parties, however, party leaders had no interest in reform.

The fragmented party system necessitated government by coalition. Agreements on the distribution of spoils among coalition partners held these coalitions together. Even if the president's party had been willing to make an agreement with the opposition to eschew patronage, it could not have done so because disintegration of its governing coalition would almost certainly have followed. Such an agreement with the opposition would, in effect, constitute defection in the ongoing cooperative game between the president and his coalition partners; and he could expect to be punished by loss of support for defection.

Given the fragmented party system, unequal access to patronage, open list proportional representation, and the need for coalitions in order to govern, the game-theoretic approach would predict no civil service reform in Chile; and none occurred. With regard to the occurrence or nonoccurrence of an initial reform, then, game-theoretic predictions seem to be consistent with events in all the countries examined.

———————

Barbara Geddes, "A Game Theoretic Model of Reform in Latin American Decmocracies," *American Political Science Review* 85, no. 2 (June 1991): 371–92.

29

International Capital Flows and the Politics of Central Bank Independence

SYLVIA MAXFIELD

Countries ranging from Eritrea to Malta, France, Kazahkstan, New Zealand, England, and Chile have recently approved, or contemplated, new central bank legislation. Between 1990 and 1995 at least thirty countries, spanning five continents, legislated increases in the statutory independence of their central banks. This represents a rate of increase in central bank independence many times greater than in any other decade since World War II.

Recent trends have spurred research on why and when government politicians delegate authority to central banks. Central banks have great potential to influence national economies. Why would government politicians give up control over the economy, especially when economic performance influences political popularity? Most answers to this question assume a political economy isolated from its international context. In a world of global financial markets, however, this assumption is false. In most developing countries national and international financial circumstances are inseparable.

The wave of central bank reform during the 1990s in countries all over the globe lends credibility to the argument that global financial forces are at work. The 1990s witnessed a wave of increase in legal central bank independence because government leaders were trying to attract and retain capital.

Actual central bank independence in middle-income developing countries varies with a country's need for credit and investment, as perceived by government politicians. Politicians try to signal their country's creditworthiness by ceding central bank discretion and recognizing central bank authority. International financial asset holders should be more willing, ceteris paribus, to invest in countries with independent central banks for two reasons. First, investors expect central banks with discretion and authority to help keep national economic policy on a stable, consistent course. Therefore central bank independence increases the extent to which international investors can predict their relative returns. International investors view the costs politicians pay to reverse central bank independence as a partial guarantee of stable, consistent economic policy.

Central bank independence may also increase the confidence of some international investors in a second way. Concerned about host-country policies that threaten anticipated returns, international investors may believe that their ability to influence policy is greater the more independent the central bank is from the executive branch. Foreign investors read central bank independence as a signal of the strength of domestic proponents of sound monetary policy, both within the government and among domestic social groups, with whom the investors might implicitly or explicitly ally in an effort to influence policy.

Obviously politicians' use of central bank independence to signal creditworthiness in middle-income developing countries will rise with the objective need for international financial resources measured through the balance of payments. Objective balance of payments conditions equal, three other factors increase the likelihood that the need for international financial resources will lead politicians to increase central bank discretion and government recognition of central bank authority. The expected responsiveness of investors partially guides politicians' use of central bank independence to increase creditworthiness. If the global supply of financial resources vastly exceeds demand, as in the 1970s, costly efforts to signal creditworthiness will be foolish. Furthermore, not all international investors will be equally responsive to central bank independence; investor responsiveness varies by asset type (foreign direct investment, international bank loans, foreign bonds, foreign equity shares). Politicians' use of central bank independence to increase creditworthiness also rises with more extensive financial liberalization for the host country and longer effective time horizons and tenure security for its leaders. Subsequent sections explain these mechanisms in turn.

The Effectiveness of
Signaling Creditworthiness

Politicians seek creditworthiness in the eyes of international investors to improve the quantity and price of financial resources offered to their country. The effectiveness of efforts to increase creditworthiness will vary with the predominant form of international financial intermediation.

We consider four types of international investors: foreign direct investors, equity investors, international bank lenders, and purchasers of foreign government bonds.

Foreign Direct Investment

Foreign direct investors should not be very responsive to changes in the general macroeconomic policy environment, which is what change in central bank independence signals. Foreign direct investments cannot be quickly liquidated, although they can be abandoned. Foreign direct investors will find their influence over policy limited once they have invested in physical plant. They should be most sensitive to changes in the regulatory environment for foreign corporations, in sectoral policies, and in trade restrictions. Foreign direct investors have a physical presence in the host country. Generally speaking, they are closer to local information sources and have less need than arm's length investors to rely on signals of policy direction that are more easily observed from afar, such as central bank independence. If the policy environment changes, foreign direct investors are likely to lobby to try to protect their sunk costs. Their responsiveness to signaling via change in central bank authority should be low.

Foreign Equity Shares

International equity investment involves no time commitment. International equity investments are very fungible compared with foreign direct investments. They are usually more liquid than commercial bank loans. Yet the decision to divest at any given moment can be expensive, because returns vary and risk is shared by investor and borrower. International equity investors are fairly responsive to changes in the policy environment and have more need to rely on signals of change in the policy environment than do foreign direct investors. Yet their responsiveness to central bank independence should only be moderate because, as already noted, they are more concerned with sectoral than with overall macroeconomic policy.

Debt: International Bank Loans

Commercial bank lending involves relatively few actors with relatively homogeneous interests; syndications (formal groups of international banks) may specify terms of seniority and subordination for individual member institutions. As a comparatively small group often facing large exposure, commercial bank lenders can afford to be less responsive to market signals than equity or government bondholders. In other words, moral hazard operates in the case of bank lending. The promise of home government support induces greater risk-taking than market conditions warrant. Typically international banks facing borrower country default receive third-party assistance for efforts to secure the promise of repayment as debt is rescheduled. Through the organization of market or government actors or multilateral intervention, "conditionality" is applied. International or multilateral organizations make loans or loan-term renegotiation conditional on borrower governments' committing themselves to a particular set of policies.

To the extent they feel a need to respond to market signals, bank lenders should be concerned with the overall macroeconomic policy environment signaled by central bank independence. International bank lenders are more likely than international equity investors to have a local presence. Local information could be channeled through correspondent banks in the borrowing country or, in some cases, through branches or subsidiaries operating in the country. Yet this local presence generally does not generate information used by loan officers to the extent expected. This gives greater weight to the need for signals about the macroeconomic policy environment, such as central bank independence, that can be observed from abroad.

Despite this paucity of local information and a concern with the macroeconomic policy environment, the likelihood of market actor or third party intervention and the relatively low liquidity of secondary loan markets both lower international banks' responsiveness to market signals, such as central bank independence.

Debt: Foreign Government Bonds

On the far end of the responsiveness continuum from foreign direct investors lie investors in foreign government bonds. As financial assets, the specificity of bonds and bank loans is a function of market demand. In the post-World War II era there was virtually no international demand for government bonds issued by developing countries until the 1980s. The market boomed in the 1990s. In contrast, demand for repackaged and resold international bank loans was virtually nonexistent in the 1980s; it revived slightly in the 1990s.

Holders of foreign government bonds must respond to market signals because there is no comfort in numbers. International bondholders are much more numerous than international bank lenders. The likelihood of home government intervention or of successful organized action to pressure issuing governments for policy change is low.

International government bondholders should be especially concerned with macroeconomic conditions and have no special advantage in obtaining local information; they look for signals of the future policy environment. Other things equal, holders of foreign government securities are more likely than any other international investors to be responsive to central bank independence as a signal of creditworthiness. The signals the market relies on may change as time proves them more or less accurate. But in the early 1990s the conventional wisdom was that inflation induced by a government's deficit spending was less likely to the extent that the government relinquished the prerogative for unlimited borrowing from the central bank. The more authority the central bank had in determining interest rates and money supply growth, went the average mutual fund manager's thinking, the less likely these policy instruments were to be used by politicians in accord with their electoral concerns, rather than to further the goal of price stability.

So, other things equal, trying to signal credit-worthiness via central bank independence should be least effective when foreign direct investment is the predominant form of "north-south" capital flow and most effective when the predominant form is investment in developing country government bonds. One important determinant of the effectiveness of signaling cuts across asset type. The relationship of the global supply and demand for international resources shapes the need for capital-scarce countries to compete for capital. If global capital supply greatly exceeds demand, as it did in the 1970s, the need to signal creditworthiness is lower.

Politicians' Tenure Security

National leaders' tenure security will also affect the decision to pursue creditworthiness.

The rule for developing countries between 1945 and 1990 is that national leaders insecure in their positions are likely to want to maintain policy flexibility because it provides greater potential for vote-buying and because the benefits of creditworthiness may accrue for the succeeding leadership. Rising economic literacy in developing countries could reduce this rule's general applicability if electorates understand and value the role of the politician-central bank relationship in sustaining capital flows. For example, Carlos Menem's reelection as president of Argentina in 1995 depended in part on convincing voters that he would be able to sustain a credible commitment to investors. He pursued somewhat expansionary fiscal policy, but did not contemplate encroaching on the central bank or eliminating the currency board. Partisanship is likely to become necessary in explaining the impact of tenure security as democracy becomes institutionalized in developing countries. One can then expect a rise over time in the number of instances in which tenure insecurity leads politicians to increase central bank independence in order to protect gains threatened by electoral successors.

Sylvia Maxfield, "International Capital Flows and the Politics of Central Bank Independence," excerpt from *Gatekeepers of Growth: The International Political Economy of Central Banking in Developing Countries* (Princeton, NJ: Princeton University Press, 1997): 3–4, 35–49.

30

Preemptive Strike: Central Bank Reform in Chile's Transition from Authoritarian Rule

In recent years research on central bank autonomy in the advanced industrial countries has mushroomed under the umbrella of the literature on "credibility." This literature argues that governments create autonomous central banks in order to "tie their own hands." Models build from the premise that all politicians have the ability to use surprise inflation in order to generate short-term gains in output. Even when governments pledge their commitment to macroeconomic stability, domestic economic agents know that politicians will always be tempted to inflate in order to improve their electoral fortunes. Because private agents build these expectations into their wage contracts, the net result is an inflationary spiral with no corresponding gains in employment.

In order to solve this "commitment" problem, governments take monetary policy out of their own hands and place it in the control of independent central banks. Precisely because the central bank does not have to respond to voters' interests, it is thought to be more likely to pursue policies conducive to macroeconomic stability. In sum, according to the literature on credibility, central bank autonomy enables governments to commit credibly to low inflation, and society is left unambiguously better off.

The credibility hypothesis has become the received wisdom in political science as well as economics. Its influence has been particularly strong on a small but growing body of literature that attempts to explain the recent trend towards central bank reform in developing countries. Maxfield, for example, argues that the governments of developing countries make their central banks autonomous in order to shore up their credibility with their foreign creditors and investors.

Despite the widespread currency of credibility-based reasoning within economics and political science, it needs to be nuanced in three ways with a more distinctly political orientation. First, the empirical evidence is not convincing.

Developing countries face severe external constraints that make them vulnerable to the whims of the international economy. If these international economic pressures were the sole determinant of central bank independence, then virtually all developing countries would have autonomous central banks. However, they do not. Even in the face of strong economic pressures to delegate authority over monetary policy, some governments clearly find it advantageous to maintain political control over the central bank.

Second, while the underlying premise of the literature on credibility assumes that all politicians have the same incentives to inflate, partisan theories of political economy have long argued precisely the opposite. They suggest that parties of the left and right, for example, differ systematically over the mix of inflation and unemployment they prefer. Early variants of partisan theories were discredited for their assumption of a permanently exploitable Phillips curve (the trade-off between low inflation and low unemployment). Recent theoretical work has demonstrated, however, that in the wake of uncertainty surrounding elections politicians can capitalize upon a short-run Phillips curve to manipulate the economy temporarily to their advantage, whether towards low inflation in the case of the right or low unemployment in the case of the left. To the extent that central bank autonomy augments the costs of generating short-term expansionary cycles, parties of the left are likely to view it as a liability.

Third, the assumption of the literature on credibility that central bank reform is necessarily cost free is questionable. While a growing body of research demonstrates an empirical association between central bank independence and low inflation, the jury is still out on the effect of autonomy on other long-run macroeconomic outcomes such as growth, deficits, and unemployment. Recent empirical work suggests that central bank autonomy may actually increase the short-term trade-off between output and inflation. If the effects of central bank autonomy on these other macroeconomic variables are unknown or indeed adverse, then left-leaning politicians have yet another reason to be wary of autonomy.

In light of these theoretical and empirical considerations, central bank autonomy may shift from being an issue of valence to one of positions. Rather than something that all actors welcome equally, central bank autonomy might instead be perceived as benefiting those actors who prefer low inflation and disadvantaging those who favor more political control of the economy. Viewed from this more political perspective, we can at least cast doubt on the claim that governments choose central bank autonomy exclusively to tie their own hands. Rather, it seems at least plausible to suggest that central bank autonomy might also serve as a means through which conservative governments seek to tie the hands of their successors.

While earlier work also underscored the effect of tenure insecurity on central bank autonomy, the argument presented in this article differs. Unlike these earlier accounts, which maintain that the logic of "replacement risk" should hold regardless of the macroeconomic preferences of the party in power, I contend that only conservative politicians have incentives to limit the flexibility of monetary policy in the future.

It is quite possible that regime change might enhance the central bank's value as a strategic instrument, as inflation-averse authoritarian elites adopt central bank reforms as a means of insuring against the threat and uncertainty of democracy itself.

Central Bank Autonomy in the Transition from Authoritarian Rule

Transitions and Turnover: The Insulation Incentive

An anticipated turnover in power may prompt politicians to use institutional reform to protect their interests. A change of regime drastically increases this "insulation incentive." It is precisely at the moment of the transition that authoritarian elites realize that they will not rule indefinitely, and unlike their counterparts in first world democracies, who can expect to return to power someday, they may well be experiencing their last "hurrah." In this heightened climate of threat, the authoritarians have an incentive to think about how the onset of democracy is likely to affect their interests in the future. As previously marginalized groups gain a voice in the political arena under democracy, the potential for a radical change in policy must increase.

In "normal" times, we would not expect authoritarian regimes to delegate authority to protect their interests. First, the nature of hierarchy is such that the creation of an independent agency is inevitably characterized by "principal-agent" problems. Even under the most carefully monitored circumstances some degree of slippage inevitably occurs. Second, the authoritarians also know that, once established, rules create expectations in the minds of other actors. It becomes quite costly for governments to violate such rules without incurring the wrath of their partners in exchange.

Aware of these problems of political control and the binding nature of rules, the authoritarians should be reluctant to cede authority to an independent agency unless they have no better alternative. However, if they face losing power, insulation becomes strategically desirable as a way to protect those arenas of policy that they care about most. They can deny their opponents a substantial niche of power under the new regime, thereby constraining future rulers to move within a set of preexisting policy parameters.

Just how much insulation is enough depends on two factors. First, it is likely to be affected by the intensity of threat or the extent to which the preferences of exiting authoritarian elites and incoming democrats are expected to diverge. Where preference incongruities are marked, officeholders have a more powerful incentive to cement their interests in an institutional form. The degree of insulation then depends on the proximity of threat, or the relative imminence of the transition to democracy. Where the authoritarians believe that they will never lose power, or only in the distant future, they are unlikely to insulate at all. Conversely, if they face an imminent threat of democracy, they are likely to respond with a highly insulated institution. In sum, the incentives to insulate are expected to be stronger, the greater the expected policy distance is between the authoritarians and the democrats, and the closer the onset of democratization is.

A Model: Actors, Interests,
and the Demand for Autonomy

This hypothesis can be tested in central bank reform. It is necessary first to understand who the likely holders of power under democracy are, what they want, and why they might be threatening to outgoing authoritarian elites. In this model, the "democrats" are the political parties of the democratic opposition around whom the democratizing coalition clusters once the transition is underway. Regardless of their ideological stripe, we can expect opposition politicians to care about their prospects for election. This electoral motive influences the sorts of economic policies that they are likely to endorse.

As a general rule, we should expect the democrats to favor policies that enable them to use the economy for political ends, ranging in scale from modest forms of intervention to more extreme populist measures. The onset of elections following authoritarian rule provides incentives for newly elected politicians to choose policies that benefit social groups who recently obtained a voice in the political arena. They are thus more likely than politicians in established democracies to resort to deficit spending and expansionary policies. Because the new powerholders are more vulnerable to the risk of being overthrown, they are also more likely to use macroeconomic policy to buy public support. Finally, incoming democrats also have incentives to pursue policies that curry favor with a very specific segment of the economy: "sheltered" sectors with high asset specificity (import competing industries and nontradables). Because these less competitive sectors tend to be more labor intensive, they constitute a natural target for office-seeking politicians of all political persuasions, who can be expected to favor the sorts of subsidies and credits that they prefer.

Thus, newly empowered democratic leaders have incentives to favor a more interventionist economic agenda that may be at odds with macroeconomic stability. Naturally, there will be variation; not all democrats will be equally motivated to intervene in the economy to the same extent. But even where the democrats are not rabid populists, we can still safely say that politicians in emergent democracies are likely to want greater flexibility over the economy in the short term so as to appeal to different constituencies.

To be sure, this "democratic" economic scenario does not always constitute a threat to outgoing authoritarian elites. The extent of threat depends on the economic policy preferences of the authoritarians, which in this model are determined by the interests of dominant economic actors (capital). The model posits two types of authoritarian regimes. For those authoritarian regimes that cater to the interests of sheltered and asset-specific capital, those in power have no reason to fear the future in a strictly economic sense. Because their constituents are the direct beneficiaries of the increased spending and preferential credit policies associated with democracy, these interventionist authoritarian regimes have no incentive to limit the central bank's ability to monetize government deficits and act as a development bank. But in a set of important cases the preferred policies of the authoritarians will not mirror those of the democrats. These authoritarian regimes cater to a different type of capital, predominant in the "exposed" and non-asset-specific sectors of the economy (financial capital, foreign capital, and tradables). For these market-oriented authoritarian regimes that value macro-economic stability, economic openness, and financial liberalization, the specter of intervention inherent in democratization constitutes a strong threat. Accordingly, the creation of an autonomous central bank should be a very attractive strategy. Because an autonomous central bank views credit policy through the lens of macroeconomic management, it is likely to resist policies that result in excess spending, loose monetary policy, and high inflation. By establishing a monetary regime where such populist economic alternatives are virtually off the agenda, conservative authoritarian regimes can thus set up powerful constraints over the types of policies that governments can pursue in the future.

The degree of autonomy afforded the central bank will vary on a continuum according to the intensity of the democratic threat (as indicated by the sectoral support base of the authoritarian regime and the democrats' economic agenda) and the proximity of this threat (as measured by the relative strength of the incoming opposition). Neither of these variables is sufficient in and of itself for the establishment of central bank autonomy. Rather, both conditions must be present.

Explaining Institutional Persistence

A final theoretical puzzle remains. If central bank autonomy runs so obviously counter to the interests of the democrats, why do they not simply repeal it once they are elected to office?

The answer is rooted in the concept of "reputation." While I questioned earlier the universality of reputation-based arguments as the sole cause of central bank autonomy, they play a crucial role in explaining its persistence. Once established, an autonomous central bank acquires tremendous reputational value in the eyes of international creditors and investors as a symbol of commitment to macroeconomic stability. Regardless of their policy preferences, new governments are thus loath to tamper with autonomy. They risk a massive outflow of foreign capital, with disastrous consequences for the economy. While incoming governments may not like an institution that denies them short-term flexibility over the economy, the instantaneous costs associated with central bank autonomy are sufficiently dramatic—and politically salient—to make this point moot.

Chile is a good example of a transition to democracy in which central bank reform occurred. Because of the central bank's pivotal role in ensuring—or imposing—the basic pillars of Chile's much-touted economic model, it is a particularly worthy candidate through which to trace the course of the authoritarians' institutional legacy.

The 1989 Chilean Central Bank Reform

Reform Timing: Questioning the Logic of Credibility

When the Chilean government of General Augusto Pinochet enacted legislation granting autonomy to its central bank in December 1989, the official rationale was twofold. In light of Chile's inflationary history under democracy, central bank autonomy would aid in preserving a climate of macroeconomic stability. By making the effects of fiscal deficits transparent, an autonomous central bank would "sound the alarms . . . at this nonlegal tax called inflation." In addition to this more conventional credibility-based explanation, the reform was also justified on legal grounds: the 1980 Chilean political constitution had called for an organic constitutional law to establish an autonomous central bank.

There is, however, good reason to question both of these avowed motives. The original idea for central bank reform actually dates back to the mid 1970s, when the "Chicago boys" first attempted to make the central bank autonomous. But despite explicit pressures for central bank reform by the Chicago economic team and the powerful financial conglomerates they represented, the initiative encountered considerable resistance from Pinochet's political and legal advisors, who dismissed it as "politically inconvenient."

Economic explanations of the reform's timing appear even more suspect with respect to the period after 1980. If the constitution stipulated a legal mandate for this reform as early as 1980, why did the regime wait nine years to implement it? The government claimed that the reform initiative was stymied by the 1982 economic crisis, in which the combination of recession, a highly indebted private sector, and the abrupt termination of external credit erupted into a financial crisis of massive proportions. But even if the 1982 crisis temporarily derailed Chile's central bank reform, why could the government not have acted sooner?

Nor does it seem likely that international economic pressures played a predominant role in influencing the timing of autonomy legislation. By 1989, when the reform was finally undertaken, Chile failed to meet any of Maxfield's conditions for when central bank autonomy is likely to be employed as a signaling device to the international community. If anything, the government was most in need of such external creditworthiness just after the 1982 crisis, when central bank reform would have been an obvious means through which the regime might have bolstered its flagging international image.

In sum, if economic credibility had been the issue, there were any number of junctures in the seventeen-year span of the Pinochet regime when the government had sufficient economic incentives to make the central bank autonomous. The fact that the government chose to wait until 1989 suggests that its motive and timing were not strictly economic, but also political.

Reform Motive: Transition, Fear, and the Drive to Insulate

Prior to 1988 there was no incentive for central bank reform precisely because Pinochet himself enjoyed a tremendous amount of power and security that enabled him to defend the neoliberal model and those interests behind it with impunity. First, his position as president of the republic invested him with numerous powers that placed him at the center of the political system. Second, because he was also the head of the armed forces, the professional loyalty and subordination of the military reinforced his political leadership. Finally, the 1980 constitution provided legal legitimacy for the regime by institutionalizing this extraordinary concentration of power through 1988 and by establishing mechanisms for the passage from a military to a "protected democracy" after 1989.

The only potential source of uncertainty in this iron hold on power was a popular plebiscite to be held in 1988 in which the electorate could choose between allowing Pinochet to continue to rule Chile for another eight-year term and holding a popular election to select a new president. Economic prosperity together with Pinochet's megalomania made it impossible for the government to imagine that it would lose the plebiscite. The vote was seen simply as a legitimating mechanism for maintaining power until the end of the century. This confidence exploded overnight when, to the surprise of many, voters opposed eight more years of authoritarian rule by a margin of 55 percent to 43 percent.

Above all, the victory of the opposition was an unequivocal indication that democracy was not only inevitable, but also imminent. The only remaining question was who would replace Pinochet: a right-wing government that could be expected to continue his programmatic agenda, or the center-left coalition that had united to bring about his downfall in the plebiscite. The results of the plebiscite suggested the latter. The government and its powerful business allies had sufficient reason to worry about how this probability would affect their interests in the future. After seventeen years in which they had enjoyed free rein to impose their policy preferences at will, the authoritarians could not take a chance. If they wanted to take action to protect these interests, they would have to move quickly.

Imminent Threat, Ironclad Response: The 1989 Chilean Central Bank Reform

The military government used its final year and a half in power to entrench the central pillars of its authoritarian project. In addition to passing a series of laws to constrain incoming democratic governments in the political and military spheres, the government also set about cementing a market-oriented bias within the economy. Prominent among these laws was a constitutional law to grant autonomy to the central bank. The last-minute nature of the reform is reflected in the fact that the bill was not passed in the legislature until October 10, 1989, and did not go into effect until December 10, 1989, just four days before the presidential elections.

The fact that the regime waited until it had been defeated in the plebiscite in order to ratify the central bank reform lends plausibility to the argument that its timing was dictated by political reasons. For, if this reform had been a purely technical initiative, the logical strategy would have been to sign the law into practice prior to the plebiscite so as to have an institutional guarantee regardless of who won the referendum. Instead, the government waited until it was absolutely sure that it would lose power. This timing suggests that it was not going to move ahead with the central bank reform unless it was absolutely necessary, particularly given the "inconvenience" of having an autonomous central bank during the year prior to an election.

The magnitude and proximity of the democratic threat perceived by Chile's outgoing authoritarian regime were reflected in the institution that it created. By formal measures the Chilean central bank is widely considered to be one of the most autonomous in the developing world.

The Reform in Retrospect:
Explaining Institutional Persistence

In light of the considerable controversy that erupted over the reform when it was announced, why did the democrats not attempt to overturn or at the very least modify the legislation upon assuming office?

Important constraints that made reversal of the central bank legislation unlikely were the nature and extent of Chile's integration into the international economy. During the early 1990s portfolio investment flooded Chilean financial markets, representing almost 20 percent of all capital inflows, and rising as high as 26 percent in 1993. In light of this highly liquid economy, it seems unlikely that incoming governments would have jeopardized Chile's relationship with foreign capital. Aylwin's administration knew that, because international markets viewed it with skepticism, the danger of substantial capital flight at the slightest signal of economic problems was a strong possibility. Indeed, the democrats had only to look at the experiences of Venezuela and Mexico in 1994 to remind themselves of the costs involved in sudden, unpredictable swings in policy.

Governments in Chile's incipient democracy have thus been forced to live with this essentially coercive economic institution. The considerable ideological affinity between the central bank and the executive during Chile's first two democratic administrations does not alter the essentially imposed nature of this reform. Were a populist government to lock horns with a conservative central bank board in the future, politicians would quickly discover that in many respects their economic policy choices had already been made for them.

Delia M. Boylan, "Preemptive Strike: Central Bank Reform in Chile's Transition from Authoritarian Rule," *Comparative Politics* 30, no. 4 (July 1998): 443–62.

Section VII

Social and Economic Issues

As Latin America begins a new millennium, policy attention has turned to what many analysts call a "second generation" of reforms. The term builds from the notion that most countries have accomplished the fundamental tasks of achieving macroeconomic balance and freeing markets, and now attention should turn to refining market institutions and addressing social issues. Whether the "first generation" is truly over is debatable—after all, Latin America continues to suffer from the occasional recurrence of currency crises, populist leaders, and botched adjustments. Still, there is widespread agreement among both scholars and policymakers that long-overdue issues of income inequality, gender discrimination, and environmental integrity should finally be on the analytical and policy table.

There is, however, less agreement about what governments and societies should do about these challenges. Some worry that the move toward privatization and market forces if unchecked will exacerbate socioeconomic inequity and accelerate environmental damage; from this camp comes the argument that it is time to temper the market with new programs and regulations. Others worry that government intervention will simply create new opportunities for rent-seeking in a region that has just shaken loose from the worst aspects of "predatory" states; respecting market mechanisms is of special concern to governments eager to maintain credibility in international financial circles. Caught between pressures for change and confusion about the appropriate tools, governments have often done little—and the underlying problems have simmered.

Although modern political economy shares the normative concerns about socioeconomic equity, environmental protection, and gender equality, it tends to focus more on *why* regressive policies result from current political arrangements and *what* the impact of these inequities may be on economic performance itself. The answers to these questions can help to design new decisionmaking structures and offer a broad rationale for more egalitarian approaches.

From a political economy perspective, the twisting of public policy to serve particular distributional ends is no surprise: The interplay of class and sectoral interests helps determine government choice. Indeed, only a small portion of Latin America's current inequality can be attributed to traditional straightforward economic logic (that is, the Kuznets-style explanation that distribution necessarily worsens in the initial stages of development because the scarcity of capital relative to the need for growth will produce high rates of return). Rather, inequality of income stems primarily from the holding of land in too few hands, an educational system that neglects mass primary instruction but subsidizes university education, and a segmented financial system that fails to lend to the poor (InterAmerican Development Bank, reading 31).

What are the consequences of such maldistribution? The traditional argument is that shifting income upward will at least lead to increased savings, investment, and growth. Yet the empirical evidence for this proposition is weak and there are many reasons to expect the opposite effect: A poor distribution of income can produce social conflict and macroeconomic instability, and inequity can negatively affect public support for, and individual investment in, human capital formation (UNCTAD, reading 32).

This analysis of the distribution-growth nexus is quite typical of one element of modern political economy analysis: Causality between two key variables runs both ways in complex fashion. Such an approach is also characteristic of Palmer's work on gender (reading 33). Women likely suffered more as the adjustment policies of the 1980s and early 1990s displaced costs, including health care, from the state to the family. However, gender differences in market outcomes and policy treatment might themselves affect growth: Bias in credit markets can impede the expansion of female-owned enterprises, and cutbacks in social infrastructure (such as health systems and child care) can reduce women's participation in the workplace.

The two-way analysis of causality is also present in the examination of environmental decisionmaking by Kaimowitz and Kyle and Cunha (readings 34 and 35). The latter authors suggest that one key reason for environmental abuse in the Amazon is straightforward: Because land is seemingly abundant (due to distorted market signals), it is overused. Kaimowitz argues that activism could rectify the problem but notes that the relative power of international nongovernmental organizations, direct economic interests, and social justice movements to affect environmental decisionmaking is itself dependent on the impacts of economic policies, such as export promotion.

Fully addressing the problem requires a return to the issues of inequality. After all, market failures around the environment tend to be worsened by the high levels of poverty and a maldistribution of income: Poorer individuals and poorer societies are likely to be constrained from investing in environmentally sensitive technology, and the same inequality that can impede healthy growth can also derail environmental consensus. Breaking the cycle of stagnation and environmental degradation will therefore require a new politics and a new public policy approach, especially the linkage of the environment and social justice.

The systematic approach used in the articles in this section—an analysis that links market failures, political challenges, and policy opportunities—is characteristic of the modern political economy approach. Authors have deployed this framework on other key topics, including the role of racial minorities and indigenous peoples in Latin America, the emergence of nongovernmental organizations as social actors, and the construction and impact of transnational migrant communities. As Latin America grapples with both the time-worn issues of growth and distribution, and the more contemporary problems of macroeconomic stability, gender and racial equity, environmental integrity, and migration, modern political economy will be increasingly useful for both analysis and policy prescription.

31

Facing Up to
Inequality in Latin America

INTERAMERICAN DEVELOPMENT BANK

Introduction

On average, the countries of Latin America suffer from the greatest income inequality in the world. True, there are some countries, such as Costa Rica, Jamaica and Uruguay, where inequality is relatively low by regional standards. But the region also has the countries with the widest income gaps in the world: in Brazil and Guatemala, the top 10 percent of the population amass almost 50 percent of national income, while the bottom 50 percent scrape up little more than 10 percent. More importantly, the problem shows no obvious signs of improvement. Our best measures indicate that income distribution improved in the 1970s, worsened considerably in the 1980s and has remained stagnant at high levels in the 1990s. Even these variations are small relative to the high overall level of income inequality. Thus, income inequality appears to be an enduring phenomenon with deep long-run causes.

Addressing income inequality in the region is important for social and political as well as economic reasons. Inequality contributes not only to high rates of poverty, but also to social tension and political disaffection. When only a few can feast on the fruits of economic progress, social stress tears at the fabric of society and political support wanes for the policies that underpin that progress. The issue is on the table in most countries of the region. Despite relatively little evidence, and many unsatisfactory explanations, income distribution is an issue impassioned by strong opinions. This study attempts to assemble the available evidence on inequality, expand it with special statistical information, and use it systematically to test a wide range of potential explanations and remedies.

Surveying the Evidence

Much of the region's inequality is associated with large wage differentials. In other words, it results not only from differences between owners of capital and workers, but from a divergence of incomes among workers. Large wage differentials reflect, among other factors, unequal distribution of the quantity and quality of schooling. The inequality in wages also reflects gender differences, gaps between formal and informal employment and between rural and urban incomes, and other forms of labor market segmentation that are exacerbated by current labor legislation.

Much of Latin America's inequality relates to the difference between the top 10 percent of the population and the rest. While in the United States families in the top decile have an average per capita income about 60 percent higher than those in the ninth decile, in Latin America they earn about 160 percent more. The top earners in Latin America are mainly employees and professionals who receive very high returns for their education and experience.

Much of this gap between the top 10 percent and the rest reflects the region's slow and unequal progress in improving the level and quality of schooling. The second richest 10 percent of the population has three fewer years of education, and those in the bottom 30 percent have almost seven years less. Moreover, differences in schooling are transmitted from one generation to the next through the family. Human capital is, after all, a family affair. It involves an inter-generational transfer of resources, as parents limit their own consumption to pay for the education of their children, who go on to enjoy the benefits of their accumulated human capital in the future labor market. This transfer of educational attainment from one generation to the next has led many to fault the educational systems, which do carry part of the blame. But families also make decisions and choices that affect the educational attainment and welfare of their children.

Families play many roles in the complex relationships that sustain income inequality. They mitigate the effects of high inequality by sharing resources, often across generations. They also play a role in determining how many of their members should try to find work, how many children to have, and how much education to give them. Many of these decisions are influenced by relative prices in the economy, particularly wages.

A very important relative price in these choices is the return to a woman's work in the market. As this expected wage rises, more women tend to participate in the labor force. Under these circumstances, families also tend to have fewer children, and the children they do have complete more years of school. But this wage is not the same for everyone. Unskilled women can expect much lower earnings than their counterparts from higher-income families, since they have less education and because they are more likely to find informal than formal sector jobs. Furthermore, these wages will vary across countries, depending on the structure of each economy and trends in its particular labor market. Each country's particular economic structure generates differences—some large, some small—in the relative prices faced by different families, which in turn cause variations in the amount of human capital each family will accumulate. From this point of view, educational attainment is not only the consequence of education policy but also reflects wage patterns in the labor market, family choices about working and having children, and other factors that vary across countries. Two couples with similar characteristics who live in different countries of the region can be expected to make very different choices about education, work and children. Furthermore, the income inequality they and their children will face varies by about a factor of three from one country to the next. Hence, inequality only partially reflects personal characteristics and family choices; it also reflects important elements of the economic environment where people live.

It is precisely this economic environment that we have tried to piece together in this study. Our tentative diagnosis is that the malady of income inequality in Latin America reflects both growing pains typical of developing societies and congenital features peculiar to the region. This combination has exacted a high toll from the socioeconomic health of many countries in recent years. But there is hope. Latin America is expected to eventually outgrow the transitional income inequality that often accompanies the early stages of development. And countries can choose policy remedies capable of turning their inherent liabilities into important assets.

More Than a Transition

Economic development is a long process whose fruits may seem forbidden for large segments of developing societies. In fact, the somewhat perverse relationship between income distribution and the initial stages of development is at once unsettling and accepted. It has long been suspected that economic development worsens income distribution, at least in its early stages. After all, societies do not move as a whole along the development curve. On the contrary, certain development trends—education, for instance—give some individuals and groups an advantage over others, advancing them more quickly along the curve and introducing a source of inequality. After a certain point, the relationship between development and equality is a win-win situation, but until then, results can be frustrating at best.

Stage of Development

We have identified five development trends in particular whose effects on inequality follow just such a tortuous path: capital accumulation, urbanization, formalization of the workforce, education, and the demographic transition. In each case, Latin American countries are either close to or on the crest of the development wave, suffering the transitional effects of greater inequality but poised for the long-term rewards.

Economic development is, to a large extent, the story of accumulating capital. In its early stages, capital tends to be very scarce, so its returns are very high. Initially, at low levels of capital accumulation, the share of national income going to profits is high. However, when enough capital has eventually been accumulated, the returns and the profit shares tend to decline. As a middle income region, Latin America is probably at a point in terms of capital accumulation where profit shares are still very high and will tend to decline as the development process continues and expands the capital stock.

A second characteristic of development is increasing urbanization. In underdeveloped societies, most people live in rural areas and most people are poor. Weak product and labor markets, lack of infrastructure and inadequate health and education services are just a few of the factors affecting poverty in rural areas. From this poor but generally equal baseline, a country urbanizes. But since incomes are higher and grow faster in the cities, the urbanization process will contribute to gradually increasing inequality. Near the end of the process, when most workers have made the transition to the urban sector, the rural-urban earnings gap will affect only a small fraction of the population, and its effect on the country's income inequality will thus be small. In Latin America, the rapid urbanization of the past four decades has, in most countries, contributed to rising inequality. But now that most Latin Americans are already city dwellers, the natural increase in the share of the population in urban areas will tend to reduce inequality in the future.

As an economy develops, it also becomes more formalized. Incomes in the formal sector tend to outstrip those of the informal sector, introducing a similar source of inequality in the initial stages of this process. But differences in hourly income among formal sector workers of similar characteristics are much narrower than those among workers in the informal sector. This means that, once a large share of the workforce is incorporated into the formal sector, inequality tends to decline.

A more educated society is also a more developed one. However, at low levels of development, most people have little or no education, and the absence of educational differences keeps income inequality low. As countries establish and expand their educational systems, new cohorts attain higher levels of education and earning potential, while uneducated cohorts are left behind. This inter-cohort inequality is accompanied by unequal attainment within each cohort; those in areas (generally urban) with more schools enjoy more and better education than individuals of the same age in less privileged areas. Once again, Latin America is at a stage where inter-cohort educational inequality is still very high, while intra-cohort inequality has been falling. Over time, this should lead to less inequality overall.

Finally, the development process is marked by a demographic transition. As countries move from high to low fertility and mortality rates, a very powerful set of changes is unleashed. In the first phase, mortality declines but fertility remains high. More children survive to adulthood, the average age of the population is low, and much of the potential labor force is engaged in caring and raising children. In this context, educational progress is hampered by the large number of children relative to the low number of working adults. Families frequently need to depend on a single wage earner, limiting resources to improve the education of children. However, in almost every Latin American country today, fertility rates are on the decline, families are having fewer children, and women, in particular, are participating in the labor market in growing numbers. With more earners and fewer children, families can concentrate their resources on fewer children, helping them attain ever higher levels of education. Rates of population growth are still very high in some Latin American countries, but as this pressure recedes, income concentration will decline.

We will show how these five trends are closely inter-related. A large factor in diminishing family size is related to a rise in women's earning potential in the labor market. As women become more educated, they tend to have fewer children, participate more in the job market, and demand more education for their children. More education also means better access to those types of employment that offer higher wages and more security. More capital per worker means a higher value for women's work in the labor force. In urban areas, this process proceeds more quickly than in rural areas. Hence, the five trends interact in a reinforcing manner. They are not specific to Latin America, but clearly they are at work in the region and explain a substantial part of its high level of income inequality. Although it may be little solace for those riding in the last cars of the development train, most of Latin America appears to be turning the corner; as these trends continue, they should provide a basis to reduce income inequality in the future, as long as the adequate economic and social policies are in place.

However, our analysis suggests that inequality in Latin America is only partially explained as a hapless moment on the development time line. Only about one-third of the gap in income inequality between Latin America and the industrial countries can be attributed to the region's stage of development vis-à-vis these five trends. Obviously, there is more to the story than a simple transition.

Endowments

Having found only part of the answer in the process, we turned to the characteristics and location of the region itself. What is it in the make-up of Latin America or in its particular history that makes it more unequal than other regions of the world? Important clues can be found in the region's geography and in its endowments of land and natural resources. Overall, tropical countries, especially when their economies are intensive in land and mineral resources, tend to be more unequal. The strong statistical relationship reflects a combination of factors whose relative importance is still under discussion. In more land-intensive countries, more of national income accrues to land, an asset whose ownership tends to be more concentrated than other assets such as human capital. At the same time, tropical land and the crops it supports offer larger economies of scale under more adverse climatic conditions with less technological innovation than temperate lands. The result has been relatively low labor productivity in tropical areas, which has depressed the wage level for unskilled labor across sectors and over time. All told, while temperate lands historically have promoted family-run farms and institutions aimed at fostering cooperation, the larger economies of scale and harsh labor conditions typical of tropical lands have generated plantation agriculture and promoted slavery. This in turn has promoted vertical relationships, hierarchies and class divisions rather than the horizontal linkages that build social capital and contribute to development and equity. Hence, while part of Latin America's inequality may have been inherited from its colonial past, this past itself may have been shaped by its geography and resource endowments.

Another intervening factor is the capital-intensive nature of the region's natural resources. Mineral resources and agricultural crops are capital intensive and act as capital sinks. They suck up scarce capital in the economy while offering few employment opportunities, thus making capital more scarce and labor more abundant for other activities. The low return to labor in tropical farming is thus reinforced by the region's exploitation of its natural resources.

Another factor that contributes to inequality is Latin America's history of volatility. Economic instability is strongly related to inequality. It slows the development process by limiting the accumulation of capital, interfering in the ability of families to educate their children, and adversely affecting productivity. Moreover, weaker groups in society are less able to cope with volatility and become even worse off.

Hence, natural resources and volatility make inequality a more serious problem. The transitional stories are played out against this permanent backdrop, adding another layer of complications. If natural resources keep the wages of unskilled workers low, demographic and educational transitions are slowed. Inequality may increase distrust and make political agreement more difficult, preventing societies from reigning in the distributive pressures that interfere with fiscal prudence, which is the key to overcoming volatility.

Globalization can also affect the process of becoming more equitable societies. It has been argued that globalization drives down the price of unskilled labor, as populous countries such as China and India supply increasing proportions of goods that are labor-intensive. Globalization increases the relative price of Latin America's abundant natural resources to the detriment of labor, promotes technological changes that increase the returns to skilled workers, and limits the ability of governments to tax the now more mobile capital.

These challenges, to whatever extent they exist, provide even further justification for a development strategy that emphasizes the accumulation of skills and the use of the natural resource base in order to avoid competing in sectors dependent only on low wages for unskilled labor.

It Takes More Than Time

Many of the forces that keep inequality high will prove temporary, especially if the development process deepens. Over the long term, there are no tradeoffs between development and equality. Still, neither development nor equality are matters of destiny. It takes more than time to overcome income inequality and to advance a country along the development curve. This is particularly true in Latin America, where transitional concerns are superimposed on very special regional handicaps. For this reason, the third part of this study looks at policies aimed at furthering the five key development trends, promoting their mutual reinforcement, and converting the region's characteristic impediments to equitable growth into viable assets for reconciling development and equality.

The Demographic Window of Opportunity

Latin America is peeking through a unique window of opportunity in its demographic transition. Since fertility is falling, the proportion of people of working age is rising faster than the number of children. The decline in fertility also means that more adult women will be working. Thus, there will be fewer students per worker, making it easier to finance a better educational system. But while this trend will persist for many decades, eventually it will be overtaken by the rise in the proportion of elderly people. Still, in most of Latin America over the next two decades, the declining ratio of children to workers will be more important financially than the rising ratio of retired to active workers. This leaves two decades to accelerate the development process. Not only should this allow Latin America to finance improvements in education, but it should also allow it to raise its savings ratio, as today's workers make provisions for their old age. Therefore, it is of the utmost importance that the region adopt fully funded pension systems. This will make it clear for the present generation how much must be set aside to provide for old age. If they simply pay as they go, they will be transferring the costs of old age onto the generation of their children, who will face far less favorable demographic trends. A fully funded pension system would generate over the next few decades a major stock of savings that could be used to accelerate the development process, so that pensions could be paid out of increased wealth and not increased taxation of the next generation. If, in addition, the social security system generates claims not only on the government but also on the broader economy, as the Bolivian capitalization program does, it will expand the constituency with a vested interest in market-oriented policies.

A Social Context for Human Capital Accumulation

The demographic and educational transition must also be hastened so that families gradually become smaller and more educated. To this end, female participation in the labor force must be facilitated to provide the incentives for smaller families and generate the resources for higher educational attainment. One line of action is to increase the productivity of housework by improving access to water, electricity and telecommunications so that appliances and information can be used in order to save time. Better urban transport will allow easier access to jobs and more time at home. More child care and longer school days and school years, although basically aimed at improving the quality of education, will also cut down on the need for women to be at home taking care of the children. Better preventive health will make for fewer days lost to children's illness. More flexible labor codes will allow women to overcome many of the limitations that currently prevent them from entering the formal sector. It is also important to reduce the cost and increase the benefits of sending children to school and keeping them there, especially through the secondary level. In this respect, school lunch programs and subsidies for books, uniforms and transportation can reduce the out-of-pocket expenses of keeping children in school. Better quality education will raise the returns to schooling and hence the incentives to forgo work.

Educating Everyone

Educational inequality within each income level is coming down as educational attainment improves. Overall inequality is still high because of the widening gap between the educational attainment of more-educated younger cohorts and older ones. This process will continue to cause a significant amount of measured inequality. However, this can be seen as a positive trend, since it ultimately means that children are becoming more educated than the previous generation.

For most countries in the region, universalizing elementary education is a fait accomplis. In a few, such as Brazil, Honduras and Guatemala, it remains a problem. For the others, the challenge now is to improve the quality of primary education and to universalize secondary education. This would increase returns to education and reduce the inefficiency of school repetition and dropouts. Better quality education may mean lengthening the school day and year, and therefore have the secondary effect of increasing female labor force participation.

The biggest educational differences today are related to secondary education. The poor drop out soon after primary school while the rich go on to higher education. Moving quickly in the direction of universal secondary education would upgrade the labor force, increase the incomes of the great majority, enlarge the pool of potential university students, and promote a different, more humanistic and capital-intensive kind of development process.

Inequality in Latin America is unusually concentrated in the top decile, which in part reflects the relatively high returns to higher education and the fact that relatively few people get that far. Moreover, returns to higher education in most countries have been rising in recent years with the recovery of growth. The market is giving clear signals that it needs more of this type of education. Consequently, any changes in higher education policy should not imply a reduction in the supply of graduates. Rather, policies should support better targeting of subsidies to higher education so as to use the resources to increase overall supply.

Finally, the governance structure of educational systems must be improved in order to align what societies seek from those systems with the incentives that providers have. This implies moving away from centralized monopoly provisioning by increasing school autonomy, empowering citizens with information, voice and choice, and making budgetary resources follow outputs, and not inputs.

Opening up the Labor Market

There is significant labor market segmentation in Latin America and it is an important contributor to inequality. Controlling for other observable factors such as education, experience and hours worked, rural workers make nearly 30 percent less than urban workers, urban formal workers make about 20 percent more than their informal counterparts, and within the informal sector women make a quarter less than men. In part, this reflects imperfections in the markets for products and for capital, as well as women's need for greater flexibility. But there is also increasing evidence that these income differentials reflect the rigidities caused by regulations regarding formal employment. These regulations were designed to protect workers from the greater power of employers and from labor market risks. They include restrictions to temporary or part-time work, extra hours, and high costs of firing. However, current legislation tends to protect prime-age urban formal male workers but restrict opportunities to other groups. Hence, initiatives to make labor market protection less discriminatory must be considered. These may include a more socialized solution to unemployment risk by substituting current severance payment schemes with contributory individual savings and credit accounts. Also worth considering is greater flexibility in the working day, fewer restrictions on temporary or part-time contracts, and a socialization of the cost of maternal leave to facilitate formal female employment.

In order to expand the social security system to workers outside the formal sector, a basic noncontributory pillar paid for by general taxation is needed. This will expand the system and reduce the current reliance on payroll taxes, which negatively impact on formal employment.

Expanding Financial Markets

A poor functioning capital market tends to generate high returns to the lucky few with access to capital, but opportunities lost for those with abilities and ideas but no access to financing. Taxi drivers need not have enough capital to cover the full value of a car—they simply need to have access to credit at a reasonable rate. The same goes for many other activities. However, financial markets are underdeveloped in Latin America and the blame goes beyond the region's history of inflation and financial instability. Weak institutions to support the credit market are also at fault. Credit is a relationship based not only on an assessment of the borrower's ability to repay, but also on his or her willingness to do so. It is efficient for markets to price credit according to the borrower's ability to repay because this ability reflects the economic risks involved. Willingness to repay is different because it essentially reflects the availability of institutional arrangements that allow a person to commit to repay. Such arrangements must be provided by society and cannot be created by individuals. If these arrangements are not present, lenders will inefficiently restrict worthy customers from credit because they are unsure about their intentions to repay. Collateral, credit bureaus, creditor rights and group lending are mechanisms to deal with this problem that are sorely lacking in much of the region. Inadequate land titling is also an obstacle that limits not only access to credit but also mobilization of savings. In particular, rural land tenure and informal urban dwellings are assets that could be used as collateral but lack proper legal titles. A deeper credit market would increase the availability of capital to both the formal and informal sector, causing productivity to increase and boosting the incomes of the groups currently excluded.

Managing Natural Resources

Latin America's natural resource endowment of minerals and (especially tropical) land is strongly associated with its inequality, although there are policies that could alter this relationship. In general, restricting the development of natural resource-intensive sectors seems inefficient—there must be something better to do than to blame one's own good fortune. However, it can also be argued that tax exemptions and other incentives to exploit scarce natural resources are inefficient because they imply giving away, at below its opportunity cost, resources that are scarce and often nonrenewable. This would accentuate the capital sink characteristics of the natural resource sector with its negative distributive implications. Also, the natural resource sector tends to produce unstable revenues. Tax structures should not transfer all these risks onto the government so that the perceived risk by private investors is artificially lowered. The government should also adequately manage the risks involved in the revenues generated by this sector so that they do not increase the overall volatility of the economy.

Using the Distributive Power of Fiscal Policy

Given Latin America's high level of inequality, how much can fiscal policy contribute to redistributing unequal revenues generated by the economy? If the government were to appropriate a larger share of national income and distribute it more equally, would that not improve income distribution? Latin America has a long history of attempting to make the tax structure more progressive. In doing so, it has severely limited its tax capacity, cutting down the resources the government can appropriate to promote its social agenda and maintain macroeconomic balance. It is much easier to achieve progressive spending than progressive taxation. After all, the top decile of the population uses neither the health nor basic education services provided by the government. Latin America has been able to collect more revenue from a relatively flat income tax than it used to collect from rapidly rising marginal tax rates. Value-added taxes with a broad base and few exceptions perform far better than those that exclude goods in order to make them more progressive. In this context, tax systems in the region would be far more progressive if collection were improved. The best way to improve the distributive power of fiscal policy would be to make tax administration more efficient and evasion more difficult by adopting simple tax structures.

Conclusions

Latin America is very unequal in its distribution of income and wealth. While this report helps us to understand why, there is still much to be learned about the underlying causes of inequality. The complicated multidimensional story of the region's stage of development, plus a discussion of its bittersweet natural endowments, suggests that the causes of inequality are deep and complex. They are not simply the consequence of denying political representation to the majority and therefore ignoring the issue. On the contrary, Latin America has in fact been largely democratic for most of this century, and in keeping with the democratic tradition its governments have tried to cater to the median voter. This voter is far from the top of the income scale and, contrary to rhetoric, far from ignored. Government after government in Latin America has tried to appeal to this majority with policies they promised would achieve redistribution.

And that's the irony of it all. Latin American governments have tried hard to mitigate the unequal outcomes that economies tend to generate. They have long committed their countries to universal education and health care. Often their policy repertoire has been cluttered with large public enterprises, massive subsidy schemes, unmanageable progressive taxation, restrictive labor legislation, multiple exchange rates and price controls. This is the stuff of which Latin American populism has been made—populism directed not to the elite but to the vast majority of the people, the median voter. All these efforts were conceived as means of spreading the wealth and protecting the poor; most achieved very much the opposite. Clearly, the problem is less related to a lack of trying and more to a lack of effectiveness in the strategies and instruments adopted.

To break the stalemate in progress in this area, a deeper understanding is needed of the processes that have made Latin America unequal and of the dynamics that may usher in a more equitable region. Not only should equity be a goal in itself, but without it the region will fail to achieve sustainable development. To further the development process, broad support is needed for successful policies, yet this will be hard to achieve if the benefits of development are not widely shared.

Latin America has overcome difficult hurdles in the past decade. It has brought down inflation and begun to grow again. A hidden benefit of this effort is that it allows societies to think more about their long-term problems. Inequality has plagued the region for a long time and will take quite a while to quell. The first step is to increase understanding of its causes in order to be more successful in attempts to achieve equity.

———

Interamerican Development Bank, *Facing Up to Inequality in Latin America: Report on Economic and Social Progress in Latin America, 1998–1999* (Washington: IADB, 1998): introduction.

32

Income Distribution, Capital Accumulation, and Growth

UNITED NATIONS CONFERENCE ON

TRADE AND DEVELOPMENT (UNCTAD)

This article examines the effects of income distribution on capital accumulation and growth. It concentrates on various channels through which personal and functional income distributions influence savings, investment, and growth.

The next two sections examine how inequality in income distribution can slow accumulation and growth, concentrating on various channels of influence. First, it is shown that inequality can trigger political and social pressures that may eventually undermine incentives to save and invest. Second, it can reduce the average skill level of the labor force by making it harder for the poor to finance their education and that of their children.

The proposition is then examined that unequal income distribution is essential for rapid accumulation and growth because the rich save and invest a greater proportion of their income than the poor. It is shown that, while the rich may indeed save and invest proportionately more than the poor, the same degree of inequality among countries is often associated with different rates of accumulation, or that a given rate of accumulation is compatible with lower or higher inequality. Thus, accelerating growth does not necessarily require a greater concentration of income in the hands of the rich.

The relationship between inequality and accumulation is greatly influenced by the extent to which profits are saved and invested. An examination of sources of capital accumulation shows that corporate profits are often the principal source of investment in industry, while the contribution of voluntary household savings to productive investment is relatively small. However, the extent to which profits are saved and reinvested varies considerably among countries. It is argued that high retention and reinvestment of profits foster accumulation and growth at minimal inequality in terms of personal income distribution. What distinguishes East Asian newly industrializing economies (NIEs) from other developing countries is not so much an exceptionally high rate of household savings as a considerably higher propensity of corporations to save and invest profits.

298

The Political Economy of
Distribution and Growth

Recent work has concentrated mainly on two possible channels through which greater inequality can reduce incentives for accumulation and growth. The first is through the impact of inequality on social and political instability, and on instability of investment. Income inequality and polarization can lead to social discontent, demand for radical changes, political violence, and attempts at an unconstitutional seizure of power. In particular, the absence or weakening of a relatively well-off middle class can be a major factor contributing to sociopolitical instability, which has an adverse effect on investment and growth. The interaction among income distribution, instability, and growth may threaten to set off a vicious circle whereby greater inequality leads to increased instability and reduced growth, which in turn can lead to still greater instability. Consequently, successful redistribution policies could promote growth by reducing social and political instability, provided, of course, that they do not introduce other impediments to accumulation and technical progress.

Placing social and political instability at the center of the analysis of the link between income distribution and investment provides an important insight into how social and economic phenomena interact. However, the link between inequality and political instability is not a mechanical one. History shows that in most societies there is at any moment in time a notion of a socially acceptable distribution of income, and hence of inequality, which is widely regarded as legitimate. It reflects a long history of class bargains and struggles over income distribution specific to each society. In other words, the degree of socially acceptable income inequality varies among societies. Although this notion of what is acceptable changes over time as the balance of power among different classes shifts, at any particular moment it sets a limit to the extent to which income distribution and inequality can be changed in either direction without causing serious socio-political dislocations. Thus, just as a sharp deterioration in income distribution often leads to serious socio-political instability and even to a social revolution, there are also socio-political limits to policies of progressive income redistribution.

The question of legitimacy also relates to specific types and sources of income. Some sources of income are almost everywhere considered illegitimate (e.g., the profits of heroin dealers). Some are legally tolerated in some countries but not in others (e.g., interest on loans). Some are permitted by law, but may not be acceptable to all (e.g., lottery winnings). There is a whole spectrum of what might be called "legitimacy weightings" attached to different types of income. A rise in the "aggregate legitimacy index" can also cause social and political turmoil, as recently seen in some Central European countries.

The fundamental problem is, thus, that there are two sorts of income inequality, one unacceptable (illegitimate) and the other acceptable (legitimate), and any existing pattern of income distribution embodies both, in proportions that are hard to analyze statistically. To the extent that the inequality of income distribution reflects legitimate inequalities, it is compatible with socio-political stability.

It follows that instability would be greater where high inequality is accompanied by widespread poverty, because in that case the legitimacy of the measured inequality would be lower. Thus, social unrest and political instability can be expected to be less pronounced in economies where a given income inequality is associated with relatively high average-per-capita incomes and a relatively low level of poverty. For instance, the United States has as high a Gini coefficient as a number of poor countries, but does not have the political instability of many of the latter. Moreover, people often find higher inequality more tolerable if incomes are rising and poverty is diminishing. Thus, inequality does not necessarily lead to greater socio-political instability, unless it is associated with widespread poverty. By the same token, a relatively equitable income distribution may result in instability if the average level of income is low and poverty is wide-spread. Finally, the impact of inequality on socio-political instability and growth may vary with the nature of the political system.

These various factors shaping the effect of income distribution on political instability differ considerably from one country to another. There is some evidence of a positive correlation between income inequality and the degree of political instability, and between political instability and investment, suggesting that income inequality is harmful to growth. It appears that socio-political instability exerts a greater influence on growth than the nature of the political regime itself, and that transition from dictatorships to democracy is often, but not always, associated with increased instability and less growth. However, it cannot be deduced simply from this correlation whether it is political instability that leads to slow growth or slow growth that leads to political instability. Moreover, not all studies linking political stability to growth find a significant relationship between the two.

Another link between growth and income inequality is through government intervention. It is often argued that a highly skewed pattern of income distribution can generate significant social and political pressure on governments to pursue redistributive policies. Such policies can introduce serious distortions and lead to a reduction in the after-tax return on capital, thereby impeding accumulation and growth. Such outcomes can be expected to emerge more easily in democratic societies, where the poor may vote in favor of redistributive taxes that reduce incentives to invest. However, governments that are more autocratic may also be subject to similar social and political influences.

It is also argued that government intervention is linked to unequal asset distribution as well. Because of imperfections in capital markets, people cannot borrow against their future earnings to finance long-term investment, and they have thus to rely on their own resources, including assets that provide collateral for loans. Unequal asset distribution can generate political pressures on governments to intervene in capital markets, leading to distortions in the allocation of resources and thereby reducing investment and growth.

Political pressures arising from highly unequal income distribution can indeed lead to populist policies that harm investment and growth through their effects on macroeconomic stability or the return on investment. However, such pressures do not necessarily give rise to harmful intervention. For instance, if they lead to policies of taxing the rich to provide better public education, they may both reduce inequality and promote faster growth. Similarly, they could lead to government transfers that may help reduce criminal activities, thereby alleviating social tensions and instability, and stimulating investment and growth. There is indeed some evidence of a positive relationship between government transfers and growth. It is therefore possible that growth may be low in more unequal societies because they redistribute less, not because they redistribute more.

Indeed, income inequality does not always lead to redistributive policies in favor of the poor. For instance, in most of those developing countries where income distribution is highly unequal, taxation is also regressive, suggesting that the link between corrective policy action and income distribution is not automatic. In the same vein, redistributive policies are not always associated with large inequalities; for instance, despite a relatively high degree of equality in income distribution, Japan effectively pursued redistributive policies in the form of concessional lending and technical support in favor of small producers both in industrial and in rural sectors in the post-war era, which helped accelerate growth.

While various political pressures generated by income inequality may adversely influence investment and growth, the considerations above suggest that the link between inequality and growth is a highly complex one. That is perhaps why empirical studies of the subject covering a number of countries have failed to demonstrate any robust relationship. In most studies either the two are found to be unrelated, or the relationship loses its significance when other variables are included. Even where an inverse relationship is found, the impact of inequality on growth is rather small. Nor is it possible to generalize about how different political systems influence the relationship between inequality and growth.

Distribution, Education, and Skill Acquisition

Distribution and Education

Another influence of income distribution on growth is through its effect on human capital formation. The degree of educational attainment has come to be considered a crucial determinant of a country's stock of human capital, as well as of an individual's earnings capacity. Income distribution exerts an important influence on school enrollment, since the financial situation of individuals is an important determinant of their capacity to invest in education. Family income has a direct impact on that capacity because people make most of their investments in education when they are young. Families that are better off financially can more easily finance the education of their children to more advanced levels; they also tend to have lower fertility and fewer children to educate. One part of this investment consists of the direct cost of education, such as tuition fees and the cost of textbooks and other teaching materials. The other, and more important part, is the opportunity cost in the form of current earnings that the family unit forgoes. The two-way causality between income levels and investment in education points to the possibility that families on the lower rungs of the income ladder, dependent on subsistence earnings, may be caught in a low-education and low-income trap since they cannot afford to forgo current income and invest in education.

Similarly, the distribution of wealth has a significant effect on investment in education because bequests allow current income forgone and the cost of education to be covered. The initial distribution of wealth can also have long-term effects since investment in education allows the wealthy to obtain better-paid jobs and to bequeath more to future generations. Moreover, wealthy individuals may form a club that provides private education with a bias toward advanced education for a few rather than basic education for all. Education also provides them with greater exit options by equipping them with skills that enable them to obtain more remunerative employment abroad. Hence, the manner in which society stratifies largely determines who has access to education, what skills are accumulated, and, therefore, the future distribution of income and wealth. Initial inequality in income and wealth distribution can create a low-skill-low-income trap for the poor, while for richer families these variables are constantly on the increase. The combination of low skills and low income also tends to be perpetuated since differences in socio-economic status between families in which children are raised lead to differences in their achievements as students. Consequently, groups or neighborhoods in deep poverty have great difficulties in overcoming their initial circumstances because their state of poverty tends to be self-perpetuating.

In linking asset distribution and investment in education, recent work has emphasized the role of assets (noted above) in providing collateral for loans. While there is some evidence that land ownership is a determinant of educational attainment, and that there is a negative correlation between the degree of inequality in initial land distribution and subsequent growth, the precise mechanism linking the two is not clear. In this view, the relationship between land distribution and growth should be especially strong in low-income countries, but this is not always the case. The fact that a number of developing countries with egalitarian land distribution have experienced slow growth (e.g. India, Islamic Republic of Iran, Mali, the Philippines, Senegal, and Uganda) suggests that the link between asset distribution and growth depends on a host of other factors, including incentives for individuals to invest in skill acquisition and the provision of public education. More importantly, it does not appear that using land as collateral for educational loans is a common practice in developing countries. Commercial banks are usually unwilling to extend credits to small farmers since farmland is a difficult collateral to handle. It is usually specialized state-owned banks that fulfill this role, but the credits they extend are rarely for purposes other than agricultural activities. It is therefore more likely that land ownership influences investment in education as a source of income rather than as a collateral for credits.

The argument that an individual's or family's capacity to invest in education depends on their own incomes and assets assumes that there is no provision of free education or of public credit schemes to cover the costs involved. The provision of government finance for education is required because the value to society of investment in skill acquisition exceeds its value to the individual; it creates positive externalities that are not captured by the individual concerned. As already noted, educational subsidies for the poor are one of best redistributive policies because they not only help attain greater equality but also promote growth.

Employment, Investment, and Skill Acquisition

Investment in education depends not only on the ability of the individual to afford the costs involved but also on the incentive to do so. The incentive is there if the future flow of income can be expected to rise in consequence. That in turn depends on wage differentials between better-educated and less-educated labor and on the probability of finding employment that adequately rewards the skills achieved. In order for higher wages for better-educated labor to provide an adequate incentive for investment in education, the wage differential should be large enough to compensate for the costs incurred throughout the investment period. There is strong evidence of such a differential in developing countries. Moreover, the differential seems to widen as educational levels increase; the difference between the wages of workers with secondary and primary education tends to exceed that between workers with primary education and those with no schooling.

The probability of finding employment compatible with increased skills arising from investment in education, and also the extent of wage differentials between better- and less-educated labor, depend very much on the demand for skilled labor. But in many developing countries, lack of such demand and widespread unemployment among labor with primary or secondary education, or employment of such labor in low-paid jobs not commensurate with their education and skills, is as important an impediment to an individual's or family's investment in education as ability to afford it.

On the other hand, too fast an expansion of the educated labor force out of line with industrial growth can also be problematic. The high level of education in the early 1960s in the Republic of Korea is often remarked on, but it has also been reported that in 1964, when per-capita income there was about $100 and one in every 289 citizens was in college, college graduates were competing for jobs as municipal street sweepers despite a tradition against manual labor. A major policy goal of the government in the early 1960s was to reduce college enrollments by a third. Unemployment has also been important among secondary-school leavers in Malaysia.

Demand for skilled labor depends very much on the level of technological development reached and rises at a pace determined by the speed with which the economy moves up the technology ladder. Since the latter depends on the rate of capital accumulation, investment and technological change are the two most important determinants of the demand for skilled labor. Thus, rapid accumulation and technological change stimulate investment in education by creating high-wage jobs and thereby the ability to finance such investment.

Moreover, capital accumulation, technological upgrading, and job creation play a key role in raising the quantity and quality of skilled labor by allowing workers to acquire and develop skills through on-the-job training and learning by doing. From the viewpoint of workers, incentives to enroll in industrial training programs are similar to those for schooling. At the same time, the training may benefit employers by developing specialized job-related skills and raising productivity. The acquisition of such skills is a benefit to society as a whole; they can be transferred to other firms or industries while their costs are firm-specific. If skilled labor is attracted by higher wages elsewhere in the economy or abroad, the firm will need to match these levels in order to retain it, thereby incurring additional costs. That is why firms may be reluctant to undertake costly training. One way to overcome this problem is through the public provision of training facilities. A direct subsidy to a firm, linked to the labor force and skill formation, often provides a better alternative.

It is sometimes argued that foreign direct investment (FDI) may also be an important means of skill acquisition because the skill content of production associated with it tends to be higher than that of domestic production. However, the extent to which these benefits spill over to the local economy depends on how strong the linkages are between transnational corporations (TNCs) and domestic producers and on indigenous capabilities to allow such linkages to develop. Indeed, evidence suggests that positive and significant spillovers occur only when the capability and technology gaps between domestic and foreign firms are moderate. In countries where such linkages are lacking, there are significant skill and wage differentials between foreign and domestic enterprises.

Training and learning by doing during an individual's career are important aspects of human capital formation. For jobs requiring moderate levels of skill, they can indeed be much more effective than providing basic education. In most developing countries, skills acquired through apprenticeship in artisan workshops are often considered superior to those resulting from primary and even secondary education. Thus, the fact that individuals from poor families cannot invest much in formal schooling does not always mean that they are totally excluded from skill acquisition. At higher levels of technology, post-school skill acquisition through learning by doing and training is often an integral part of an individual's skill level, and much training in manual and managerial skills is of an on-the-job nature. General training provided by schools improves adaptability and learning capacity and is an essential complement to on-the-job industrial learning; it is especially vital to an agenda of technological upgrading. However, its contribution to industrialization depends crucially on capital accumulation and job creation.

Educational attainment is a necessary but not a sufficient condition for skill-intensive production. All countries with a high share of skill-intensive exports also have a relatively high educational attainment, while the evidence for countries such as Argentina, Chile, Peru, and Uruguay suggests that relatively high educational attainment does not automatically translate into skill-intensive exports. These countries have educational attainments as high as East Asian NIEs, but their skill intensity is much lower. By contrast, Brazil and Tunisia have lower educational attainment than those NIEs, but their skill intensity is considerably higher. Almost all countries where high educational attainment has translated into skill-intensive exports are those that have sustained a rapid pace of capital accumulation, technological upgrading, and productivity growth over many decades, most notably the East Asian NIEs.

These considerations strongly suggest that even when greater equality in income or wealth distribution does succeed in stimulating greater investment in education, it will not necessarily also create sufficient skilled jobs to reward the expectations of all who have so invested. Whether that goal can be reached depends on the pace of accumulation and technical progress. Since investment in physical assets plays a crucial role in stimulating demand for education and the supply of job-related skills, the impact of income distribution on the acquisition of education and skills depends very much on its effect on capital accumulation.

Personal and Functional
Income Distribution and Accumulation

Notwithstanding significant differences among countries, a relatively large share of national income in capitalist societies accrues to a relatively small minority. It is, therefore, primarily the spending behavior of this minority that determines savings and accumulation. This is particularly true for developing countries, where incomes of a large majority of the population are barely sufficient to meet their basic needs. Such spending behavior provides the basis for the view in mainstream economic analysis that there is a trade-off between income equality and growth because the rich have a higher savings ratio than the poor. This view is consistent with various formulations of private savings behavior.

However, unlike the standard analysis of the relation between savings and the incomes of rich and poor, an approach different from that of the classical tradition focuses on the functional distribution of income, that is, between rents, profits, and wages. Each functional type of income is defined as the income source of a particular class: Landowners earn rents, capitalists earn profits, and workers earn wages. In this analysis, the propensity to save out of profits is greater than the propensity to save out of wages, so that a redistribution of income in favor of profits would raise aggregate savings at any given level of income.

The idea that capitalists save a higher proportion of their profits than workers save out of wages was used by Keynes to justify the working of the capitalist system of the nineteenth century in Europe and North America. He described the system thus:

> Europe was so organized socially and economically as to secure the maximum accumulation of capital. While there was some continuous improvement in the daily conditions of life of the mass of population, society was so framed as to throw a great part of the increased income into the control of the class least likely to consume it. . . . Herein lay, in fact, the main justification of the capitalist system. If the rich had spent their new wealth on their own enjoyments, the world would long ago have found such a regime intolerable.

In this view, therefore, inequality is an essential feature of the accumulation and growth process in the capitalist system. Investment provides social as well as economic justification for the concentration of an important part of national income as profits in the hands of a small minority. It indeed acts as a social tax on profits that restricts their use for personal consumption of the capitalists, and thus makes for lesser inequality in consumption than income. Thus, unlike the "social instability view" discussed in the previous section, here social cohesion and stability depend not so much on the distribution of income as on the way the rich dispose of their incomes. Inequality can be tolerated if it is associated with accumulation and "continuous improvement in the daily condition of the mass of population."

However, higher propensity to save from profits than from wages does not necessarily imply that aggregate savings and investment rise with inequality in personal income distribution. Although some empirical studies find a positive correlation between income inequality and aggregate savings, these results are not robust to different specifications and for different country groups. A recent study using the "high-quality" distribution data for 52 countries finds no support for the hypothesis that income inequality affects aggregate savings, either in developing or in industrialized countries.

United Nations Conference on Trade and Development, "Income Distribution, Capital Accumulation, and Growth," *Challenge* 41, no. 2 (March/April 1998): 61–80.

33

Public Finance from a Gender Perspective

INGRID PALMER

Introduction

This paper explores ways to incorporate gender in some major areas of macro
policy concern. Gender issues in macroeconomic policy can be approached in
two ways. One is to focus on the different outcomes of policy for men and
women and on changes that are required to bring about gender equality. The
other is to examine the implications that gender relations and disparities hold for
macroeconomic analysis and policy options. It is the latter that provides the primary orientation of this paper. If gender equality figures strongly in this paper it
is because of its crucial importance to the macroeconomists' goal of efficient and
sustainable growth.

Ultimately macroeconomists are the guardians of external and internal economic balances. Prosperity may be possible in the short-term while ignoring imbalances, but the shocks to the economy from subsequent debt repayments and
import restrictions, as well as the corrosive uncertainty and adverse distributional effects of inflation, are in very few people's interests in the long term. Such
imbalances have to be addressed sooner or later by monetary and fiscal policies.

The main macro policy instruments for managing the external balance are the
exchange rate and foreign trade restrictions. In the last decade and a half the ma-
nipulation of these instruments has been in the direction of devaluing and freeing the one and reducing the other, with the objective of making production of
exports more profitable and purchases of imports more costly. Such liberalization of trade and payments places domestic producers in open competition with
international producers. Therefore, in addition to promoting external balance,
devaluation and liberalization start the process of adjustment by eliminating distortions in factor and product markets.

Internal balance (between demand and supply of domestic resources) is managed by operating on the amount of effective demand through public expenditure and taxation; and influencing the price of borrowing via interest rates. The

new competitive economic efficiency has been accompanied by adverse externalities in the form of worsening unemployment and poverty.

There are good reasons for believing that women have suffered more than men
from the adverse impact of adjustment policies in many countries of Latin America and Africa. Judging from the available literature, the outcome of SAPs for the
majority of poor women seems to have been a serious reduction in their capabilities for leading healthy stress free lives.

The change in policy stance to fiscal restraint and an open competitive economy has had the effect in many cases of shifting costs from the state to women.
Health service and local infrastructural cutbacks have made social reproduction
more difficult, with women substituting more of their labor to cover the deficit of
state provision. In many places urban unemployment had risen as old industries
have declined while new ones have not grown strongly enough. The new urban
poverty has forced many women into greater participation in the labor force for
extremely low remuneration. Lack of public provision, and rigidity of the gender
division of labor in social reproduction has combined to jeopardize standards of
childcare, health and family welfare.

Many rural areas have experienced greater incentives to export primary products. The extra effort required to increase such exports has interacted with
gender-typing of tasks leading to greater increases in work for women than for
men. In addition, this was often in addition to a more onerous burden of social
reproduction work. New production incentives have tended to give male heads of
household reason to appropriate and redirect household resources, including
women's labor. The forced redeployment of resources to production of export
cash crops would not only have added to the stress on women but could have led
to long-term social costs in the form of disinvestment in the health and education of children. Any exacerbation of gender asymmetries of rights and obligations would worsen allocative inefficiency and raise long-term social costs. An
important reason for these consequences lies in biased and absent markets; and
the intensification of the distortions caused by market bias and market absence
through ill-judged cuts in public expenditure.

Biased and Absent Markets

There are two aspects to market bias: inequalities of access to and of participation
in markets. Access is obviously weaker for those who live at a distance from markets and who are denied the use of competitively priced transport. Access is also
limited by inconvenient trading hours and imperfect availability of information.
There may be severe social obstacles or outright prohibition to market entry facing certain categories of individuals. Privilege and power can affect the degree of
exclusion. Poor men suffer from biases in access too, but poor women are likely
to suffer much more, not just because of their greater poverty but because of
women's much greater immobility, due to family and social obstacles.

Once in a market, transaction costs are incurred in making sales and purchases. A supplier's standing is determined by contacts, reputation, credibility
and acceptance. Where a supplier is unable to go to market on a regular basis and
deals only with small quantities, weak reputation and credibility can affect the

price. Formal buying institutions may accept only consignments of a certain minimum size or accept smaller quantities but at lower unit prices. Again all poor people experience these biases, but women more so. Women with young children are the most disadvantaged.

The markets for purchasers of factors of production, particularly credit, should be of at least as much concern for policy makers, as this is the stage at which entrepreneurs can be blocked completely regardless of their efficiency in production. Purchasers of raw materials may face similar cost-incurring biases in availability of transport and information, and requirements for minimum size quantities and regularity of exchange, as suppliers in product markets. Underlying access to all other factors is the need for credit of one kind or another. In addition to class-based determinants of access there is gender discrimination in the formal credit market which either raises transaction costs to women enormously or simply blocks women's access to formal sector credit and obliges them to face interest rates several times higher in the informal credit market. The official image of women as poor credit risks, though changing in the face of overwhelming evidence to the contrary, is still an obstacle to women's equal access to cheap credit.

Many of the goods policy makers wish to see produced in larger quantities, to earn foreign exchange or to hold domestic food prices down, may be produced by women; but gender factors add significantly to the transaction costs of a positive response. Criteria for economic efficiency suggest that structural interventions should be made to eliminate or counterbalance gender-based transaction costs, but this has been lost to sight in the emphasis on deregulation and liberalization.

Gender bias in the labor market is extensive. Much of its emanates from segmentation and gender-typing of jobs. There has been a sharp growth in numbers of women undertaking casual or part-time, home-based work under contract. These women are generally young and poorly educated. But wage disparities cannot always be explained by the existence of different productivities or tasks. Women systematically receive lower wages than men because of lower sociocultural values placed on women's work; and this means that women's labor is effectively subsidizing the return to other factors of production or the consumers of female labor-intensive products. Nor is this a small subsidy: women's wages tend to average only 66% of men's.

It is where markets are absent, however, that the greatest misallocation of women's resources occurs. Because of biology, many women spend part of their most active years pregnant and lactating. But it is because of gender, not biology, that most of the work of childcare is done by women. In as much as this extra work of women (the double day) reproduces the labor force at no obvious direct cost to the market-based economy, women provide a positive social externality, akin to a free public good. Like the provision of a defence force, the provision of a labor force is supported by government inputs; in the case of labor, health and education services. But, unlike a defence force, the major input underpinning the provision of a labor force comes from a socially determined labor tax on private resources, paid by women in the hours they spend in social reproduction work for children (and for adult men and other family members). The labor force is, in effect, a part-free public good largely funded in a sharply regressive way.

If the conditions of the reproduction of the labor force become too arduous, something has to "give," usually the health, strength and skills of part of the labor force. It is difficult to see how productivity improvements in the tasks of social reproduction can be achieved without state intervention through targeted public investment.

Aside from childcare, markets can also be absent from the production and consumption of a range of other goods and services. Among the poor, particularly in rural areas, there is much self-provisioning of the essentials of life: water, fuel, food, health care, cleaning and sanitation. Almost all this work is done by women. The time it takes varies with environmental and economic endowments, proximity to markets and sociocultural background. It is reasonable to assume that allocative principles of a kind are followed, dominated by prioritization of essential use-values. To the extent that these use-values provide the essentials of life which are not available to women in accessible markets, the work involved is a fixed overhead from which time cannot be subtracted however "profitable" the production of market-oriented nonessentials may be.

There is clearly a huge social opportunity cost to continuing with so much of women's labor time locked up in low-productivity social reproduction and self-provisioning work, outside the processes that mobilize investment in increasing productivity. Insofar as stabilization and structural adjustment programs lead to cuts in public expenditure, which increase the time women have to spend in social reproduction and self-provisioning, then they increase the misallocation of resources. Such cutbacks worsen the problem of biased and absent markets; as do cutbacks in the provision of the kind of infrastructure which reduces transaction costs and facilitates access to markets for women.

Growth with Gender Equity— A New Approach to Public Finance

Fortunately a space is opening up for a new approach which could combine gender equity and growth, through an emphasis on public finance which supports and is complementary to women's economic activities. This approach can take as its starting point the discussion in international organizations of a "new growth theory" which emphasizes long-run public investments in education, health, infrastructure and market access. This theory emphasizes the complementarity of efficiency and equity, with the state investing in services that support and "crowd-in" private sector responses in order to achieve this. This opens up a space for issues of gender equity to be discussed in the context of public investment to support women's access to remunerative work, even though the "new growth theory" does not itself refer to gender. The Economic Commission for Latin America has advocated a similar approach which emphasizes the interdependence of growth and equity. It calls for an "integrated approach" of combining social and economic policies which would strengthen areas of complementarity and reduce areas of tradeoff between equity and growth. The prescription rests on strategic intervention in diffusion of appropriate technology, the modernization of basic infrastructure, and the active development of well-functioning markets, especially those of capital and labor.

It has to be recognized that the new growth theory with its stress on investment in human resources and infrastructure so as to socialize important positive externalities requires a great deal of public investment, which has to be balanced by raising revenue. Balancing public finances, however, is only the outer aggregate framework. Sources of revenue can themselves be patterned to emphasize this same strategy of growth which rests on complementarities between efficiency and equity. Moreover, expenditures can be targeted on certain strategic capacities, and the effectiveness of those targeted allocations can be improved. There is no reason to assume that fiscal stringencies must worsen gender relativities.

For instance, the exemption of a range of essentials can turn a value-added tax (VAT) into a modestly progressive tax. Since men and women partly purchase and produce different things, VAT can also be used as a policy instrument to advance gender equity. User charges can be highly regressive as they constitute a tax on services which were formerly often free at the point of delivery. Moreover, they frequently exacerbate discrimination against girls with respect to provision of health care and education. One way to mitigate this is to apply user charges to services where gender disparities would not be significantly worsened by attaching a price tag. Thus user charges for university education or for specific curative health services might not add to discrimination against women and girls as much as would user charges on primary and secondary education and on primary and maternal health care.

In addition agricultural research could be redirected to produce an agricultural technology which address the needs of female as well as male farmers and which is designed with recognition of the gender divisions of labor and management.

Put through a gender lens, all public revenues and expenditures can become better focused, with consequent benefit in the form of both gender equity and allocative efficiency.

Labor Markets,
Social Reproduction and Public Finance

Public finance is also critical to the development of a well-functioning labor market. A well-functioning labor market is one that fosters the development of productivity growth and new comparative advantage. This is not the same as one in which labor is cheap, or wages rapidly change to clear the market. Rather, it is a labor market that has low entry barriers, is not divided by rigid segmentation, is free from discrimination, and facilitates increases in the quality of labor. A set of well-designed taxes and expenditures is the basis for such a market: and good design requires a gender analysis, since entry barriers, segmentation and discrimination are organized along gender (as well as other) lines.

A major cause of gender inequality and resource misallocation in the labor market is women's individualized burden of social reproduction. To impose the cost of maternity leave on individual employers is a recipe for discrimination against female employees. It also creates distortions of markets by imposing what is in effect a production tax on some enterprises but not others. Serious consideration should be given to "socializing" the cost of maternity leave to neutralize its effect. The way to do this is to levy a tax on all enterprises, regardless of the ratio of men to women among their employees. Another suggestion is instead of a payroll tax (which would be anti-employment), a tax of a percentage of value added (which would be anti-capital). In the same way, vouchers for childcare could be funded. The argument is that it is the society as a whole that should fund the "free public good" of a labor force. In return, the society benefits by enabling women to pursue economic opportunities which previously were impossible because of prohibitive private costs attached to social reproduction.

Maternity leave and childcare benefits could also be extended to those in self-employment. For women in non-market work, however, such measures are not immediately relevant. Here, public provision of water, sanitation, electrification, commuter transportation, and health services help to socialize the costs of producing a labor force, and release women's time for income-earning.

A well-organized and regulated labor market, in which labor is able to move to where it can be most efficiently employed from the point of view of long-run dynamic efficiency offers dividends to the whole economy. It therefore pays society to invest collectively in that development through social security insurance. Social security minimizes transaction costs for the individual and internalizes the cost of negative externalities. For instance, new labor market entrants, mobile workers, or those reentering after sickness or unemployment need to be able to afford some waiting time to gain knowledge of the market and to find the appropriate employment. A security provision makes available bridging finance. In short, social security provision brings order to the labor market and helps to price human resources efficiently.

But in all too many cases, accessing social insurance itself presents additional transaction costs for women. It is particularly difficult for the majority of women who do not enjoy regular employment status with a large-scale employer. The Self-Employed Women's Association (SEWA) in India, however, has developed group social security schemes among women in the unprotected labor market and in self-employment. Governments could promote similar group social security schemes among unprotected women. With some subsidy SEWA-type initiatives could spread quickly.

Conclusion

We have seen that the new growth theory emphasizes public investment in infrastructure and human resources. This approach is still in its early days as far as policy is concerned; but this means that there are opportunities to make gender analysis central to it from the start instead of trying to add gender later.

Ingrid Palmer, "Public Finance from a Gender Perspective," *World Development* 23, no. 11 (November 1995): 1981–86.

34

The Political Economy of Environmental Policy Reform in Latin America

DAVID KAIMOWITZ

Introduction

Latin America faces serious environmental problems, including deforestation, pollution from industry, mining and motor vehicles, soil and pasture degradation, siltation of dams and waterways, misuse of pesticides, and contamination of water supplies by human wastes. These problems threaten both the natural resources on which the region's economy depends and the quality of life of its citizens.

To solve these problems requires changes in property rights, trade and finance policies, taxes and subsidies, public investment, and regulatory mechanisms, as well as private initiatives aimed at modifying people's attitudes and behaviour, generating new technologies and market opportunities, and achieving popular participation in environmental initiatives. Whether these changes can be made, however, will depend largely on the relative power of the groups favouring and opposing them, how compatible they are with the prevalent models of economic development (or feasible alternatives), and each country's institutional capacity to implement them.

A priori, there is every reason to be pessimistic. The beneficiaries of environmental improvements are often dispersed groups of relatively powerless people, for whom "the environment" is only one concern. Well-organized, powerful groups have a vested interest in environmentally destructive activities and much to gain by continuing their current behaviour. The current economic strategies of many Latin American countries depend heavily on activities associated with high levels of pollution or resource depletion. Moreover, in general, the Latin American governments have limited capacity to implement environmental policies, and nongovernmental organizations (NGOs) and local community groups, while doing valuable work, have been unable to completely fill the gap.

Nevertheless, despite the obstacles to overcoming environmental problems, there have also been some notable successes. Deforestation in the Brazilian Amazon has fallen sharply since 1987, thanks, in part, to the elimination of fiscal incentives for livestock. Strong regulatory measures in Mexico City have reduced air pollution in the last few years. The expansion of Costa Rica's protected areas, combined with fiscal incentives for reforestation, have largely reversed the decline in forest area in that country. Vegetable growers and exporters in Guatemala have eliminated the use of certain toxic pesticides and improved their fumigation practices as a result of stricter control of pesticide residues on vegetables imported into the USA. Recognition of Indian land rights in several countries has helped protect large areas from deforestation. Environmental movements in Mexico, Nicaragua and Venezuela have succeeded in halting the construction of a nuclear power plant in Patzcuaro, Mexico, the granting of a large lumber concession in north-eastern Nicaragua, and the Trans-Amazon car rally between Venezuela and Brazil.

The question is why these initiatives have been successful, while many others have not. This article hopes to begin to answer that question by analysing three key aspects: 1) the strengths and weaknesses of different types of groups which have promoted environmentally friendly policies; 2) the degree to which the region's current emphasis on export promotion, trade liberalization, and reduced public sector participation in the economy is compatible with different environmental policies; and 3) the relationship between the type of political regime in each country and the opportunities for environmental improvements. Through this analysis, it seeks to lay the framework for identifying possible alliances, substantive proposals, and institutional arrangements which can form the basis for successful environmental reform.

Strengths and Weaknesses of Different Groups Concerned with the Environment

At least seven distinct groups have promoted concern for the environment in Latin America: i) developed country organizations, such as governments, multilateral banks, international organizations, and NGOs; ii) middle class environmental organizations; iii) entrepreneurs involved in "green" businesses; iv) farmers and communities affected by pollution; v) indigenous communities; vi) professional environmentalists; and vii) political parties and social movements concerned with social justice. Some of these groups have a direct material motivation for their involvement, while for others cultural or ideological factors are more important. The following section examines both the potential and the limitations of these different groups for solving environmental problems.

Developed Country Organizations

Recent concern about the environment in the region has been largely inspired by political, economic and intellectual influence from the USA and Europe. These influences, in turn, have their origin in the environmental movements of those countries, which entered into maturity in the 1970s and 1980s.

The initial interest of developed country environmental organizations in Third World issues can be traced to two broad concerns: wildlife protection and population control. Conservation groups such as the World Wildlife Fund (WWF) and the International Union for the Conservation of Nature (IUCN) have been involved for decades with international efforts to protect animal and plant species from extinction. With the negotiations for the Convention on International Trade in Endangered Species (CITES) in the early 1970s, these organizations expanded their efforts and were joined by other groups. Around the same time, Paul Erlich published his best-selling book *The Population Bomb* (1968) sparking widespread public concern with population growth. Since most of that growth was concentrated in the Third World, those countries came under closest scrutiny.

In the 1980s, the size and strength of the US and European environmental organizations and their interest in Third World issues grew dramatically. International NGOs such as Friends of the Earth, Greenpeace, IUCN and WWF became more prominent and most major US environmental organizations, including the National Audubon Society, National Wildlife Federation and the Sierra Club, became involved in international issues such as climate change and loss of biological diversity. New international networks were created for climate change, rainforests, toxic wastes and pesticides.

Developed country environmental organizations have influenced policy in Latin America through various mechanisms. NGOs such as Greenpeace, the Rainforest Action Network, and the Pesticide Action Network have organized international campaigns to put pressure on Latin American governments to prohibit the importation of toxic wastes and banned pesticides, cancel lumber concessions, eliminate incentives to deforest, and create national parks and extractive reserves. The powerful Green Parties and caucuses in Germany and Scandinavia have successfully pressured their governments to include environmental issues in their foreign policy agendas. Environmental organizations in the USA achieved significant changes in American foreign aid policies by bringing a law suit against the Agency for International Development (AID) for not considering the environmental impact of its actions. In the mid-1980s, a coalition of major American environmental organizations launched a successful campaign pressuring the World Bank to focus more on environmental issues and stop financing projects which harm the environment. Most major environmental organizations have lobbyists who seek to influence the US Congress and European parliaments regarding funding for natural resource projects, international environmental agreements, policies towards multilateral banks, and trade agreements.

The pressure from environmental organizations has led bilateral and multilateral agencies to increase funding for projects dealing with forest management, protected areas, water quality and sanitation, soil conservation, watershed protection, and institution building for environmental agencies. The World Bank and the Inter-american Development Bank (IDB) have created large internal environmental divisions and it has become more difficult to get foreign loans for road and settlement projects in the humid tropics. On at least two occasions (the pressure on Brazil to curb deforestation in the Amazon and the inclusion of the environment as a topic in the negotiations of the North American Free Trade Agreement), there has been explicit environmental conditionality, requiring Latin American governments to adopt certain environmental policies in order to secure loans or gain access to developed country markets. There are also a growing number of trade restrictions in developed countries limiting the importation of wild animals, tropical lumber, non-degradable packaging materials and foods containing pesticide residues.

International NGOs also operate directly in Latin American countries and finance the activities of local environmental organizations. Organizations such as Conservation International, the Nature Conservancy, IUCN, Rodale and WWF have Latin American offices and operate projects focusing on national park management. Several of them have been involved in 'debt for nature' swaps in Bolivia, Costa Rica, Ecuador and the Dominican Republic, allowing them to obtain local currency funds for conservation activities by agreeing to purchase highly-discounted government debts. Many traditional international private voluntary organizations now promote projects related to soil conservation, pesticide management and environmental education. Greenpeace and the World Resources Institute (WRI) provide technical assistance and advice to Latin American environmental organizations and several communications networks tie Northern and Southern NGOs together through electronic mail. This increased collaboration has been reflected in the International Forum of NGOs and Social Movements at UNCED, in international co-ordination around trade negotiations, and in the negotiations related to the Biodiversity Convention and other international agreements.

Influences from the developed world have helped to make environmental issues more visible in Latin America, to finance Latin American environmentalists and natural resource projects, and to bring about specific policy reforms such as the elimination of subsidies for livestock in the Brazilian Amazon, greater restrictions on pesticides, and the creation of new environmental ministries. On the other hand, they have had little impact on the underlying causes of environmental degradation such as poverty, the short-term time horizons of Latin American societies, the region's heavy dependence on environmentally degrading activities, and the limited capacity of Latin American governments to regulate resource use.

The Urban Middle Class

Environmental movements in the developed countries form part of what are now called the 'new social movements'. The social bases of these movements are middle-class professionals and young people with a certain degree of education, who join the movements not so much to receive direct material benefits but rather to express their frustration with government and modern society and their desire for an identity and greater opportunities for participation.

Similar social movements also exist in Latin America, particularly in large urban centres such as Caracas, Mexico City, Rio de Janeiro, Santiago and São Paulo. In Brazil, for example, the country with the strongest environmental movement, of approximately 700 environmental organizations operating in 1989, 90 per cent were located in the prosperous south-east, with over 100 in the city of São Paulo alone. These groups concentrate on protecting ecosystems such as the Atlantic

Forests, the Amazon and the watersheds of Paraná, and on offering environmental education. They were also heavily involved in lobbying to include environmental considerations in the 1988 Brazilian constitution and in the preparations for UNCED. In 1986, São Paulo elected its first congressman on an environmental platform and around the same time the 'Green Party' achieved 8 per cent of the votes in the gubernatorial race in Rio de Janeiro. In both cases the basic constituency was largely middle-class professionals. Similarly, in Chile middle class environmentalists have brought national attention to the plight of that country's native forests and were influential in the debates surrounding the recently adopted 'Law of the Environment'.

In addition to organized environmental movements, a much broader universe of middle class public opinion is also sensitive to the environmentalist messages transmitted by the mass media. These groups' interest in the environment tends to centre around urban pollution, food safety, traffic congestion, and some widely publicized symbols of the destruction of nature, such as deforestation in the Amazon, threats to well-known animal and tree species, and the indigenous peoples' struggle for land. Their concerns have been strong enough to oblige practically all of Latin America's political parties to incorporate environmental planks into their political platforms. They have also led governments in countries such as Chile and Mexico to take concrete measures to reduce air pollution in their capital cities.

On the other hand, the middle classes' concern for the environment is sporadic and based more on images than on a clear understanding of the problems and their underlying causes. Middle class public opinion responds emotionally to the environmental symbols of popular culture and the mass media, but has proven difficult to sustain and to translate into effective action; this is reflected in rapid shifts in survey responses about environmental issues in public opinion polls. This hinders the consolidation of stable organizations that can maintain pressure for reform over time.

Groups Motivated by Direct Material Interests

At least four groups have strong direct material interests in solving environmental problems: companies and farmers focused on so-called 'green markets', producers and communities affected by critical pollution problems, indigenous communities, and professional environmentalists.

A growing number of companies and small farmers are looking to take advantage of new opportunities offered by the markets for organic foods, ecotourism, recyclable containers and products from sustainably managed forests. Small farmers' organizations in Mexico, Central America and Bolivia are heavily involved in the production and export of organic cacao, coffee and sesame. Ecotourism is a multi-million dollar business in Costa Rica, Ecuador, and Mexico. There has also been a proliferation of 'green labels', which supposedly justify higher consumer prices for goods produced through environmentally sound processes. All these groups have a direct interest in promoting environmental awareness, since it helps expand their markets, and in some places they have begun to organize themselves into federations or chambers of commerce. In addition, many companies who sell traditional products now use ecological messages or symbols in their advertising because market research indicates that this will increase their sales. These companies' advertisements are often misleading but they also help maintain public attention on the environment.

At the other extreme are producers and communities with major pollution and resource degradation problems which directly affect their livelihoods. These include fishermen affected by water pollution, rubber tappers, Brazil nut gatherers and small-scale lumber producers threatened by forest destruction, communities affected by nuclear power plants, toxic waste dumps and other types of waste, agricultural workers poisoned by toxic pesticides, and farmers harmed by pollution from the mining or petroleum industry. These groups have started to protest and to put their grievances under the national spotlight.

Indigenous peoples' struggle to protect their traditional land rights has received considerable public support, in part because these groups are perceived as living in harmony with their surrounding environment (Hurtado and Sánchez, 1992). The efforts of these groups to defend their territories are critical to their survival as peoples. The most well-known struggles are those of the Yanomami Indians in the Brazilian Amazon and the Mayan Indians of Chiapas, but indigenous movements for land rights with environmental undertones have also been important in Bolivia, Ecuador, Panama and Venezuela.

Finally, there are many people directly employed in environmental organizations and agencies who have an evident interest in maintaining public support for 'the environment'. Most Latin American countries now have a number of public agencies, NGOs with professional staff, and foreign-financed projects focused on environmental issues, as well as university professors and journalists working on these topics. This group is not large, but it exercises significant influence because its members tend to be opinion-makers and have frequent access to the media. Scientists have played a particularly important role since their research findings have lent greater credibility to environmentalists' claims regarding environmental destruction.

None of the four groups just mentioned is currently a major force in Latin American societies, but all are growing rapidly. With the exception of the academics and professional environmentalists, their presence tends to be local. By themselves, they probably lack sufficient force to spur deep reforms, but they have helped keep the subject of the environment in the public eye and have achieved concrete results in specific cases.

Movements for Social Justice

In 1990, an estimated 240 million Latin Americans lived in poverty. The main concern of these people is to achieve a dignified standard of living for themselves and their children.

Given Latin America's massive poverty, linking environmental problems with the struggle for social justice is the only way to make environmental issues relevant to most people. Without this convergence, some environmental reforms may still take place, but they would be élite reforms, lacking the benefits of wide and democratic popular participation. As long as environmental concerns are associated in the public's mind with wildlife protection, biodiversity, the ozone layer and global climate change, they are unlikely to win the attention of the majority of Latin Americans, who live on the edge of survival. There are other issues, however, such as access to safe water supplies and firewood, soil conservation on marginal lands, safety from pesticide poisoning, protection from other toxic chemicals in the work place, and reproductive rights, that could potentially appeal to such groups.

In recent years, left-wing and centre-left organizations in Latin America have paid more attention to the environment. The Brazilian PT has a strong environmentalist current and weaker environmental caucuses exist in most of the other parties mentioned above. Many grassroots organizations and NGOs associated with 'the left' have also taken interest in the environment. These groups perceive that concern for the environment has the potential to win almost universal support, as did peace in the past, and by addressing environmental issues they might be able to broaden their appeal beyond the sectors directly involved in specific struggles for social justice to public opinion as a whole. Their intuition tells them that the environment constitutes a weak point in the neoliberal paradigm, to which they are opposed, and thus a critique of neoliberal environmental policy lends itself to more general questioning of neoliberal thought.

At the same time, there is reason to doubt the depth of the Latin American left's commitment to the environment. Although almost every party gives at least rhetorical support to environmental issues, parties such as the PRD in Mexico, the FMLN in El Salvador, and the Sandinista Front in Nicaragua have shown little real interest in 'green issues'. For some Latin American leftists, environmentalism is a superficial fad imported from the developed world. They argue, with some reason, that many conservationists are more concerned with animals and plants than with people. There seems to be much greater support for environmental causes among the middle class supporters of left-wing parties than among their poorer constituencies or party bureaucrats. Certain trade unions are afraid that environmental restrictions will limit job opportunities. Furthermore, it is relatively easy to be an environmentalist from the opposition. It is not so clear that leftist movements will give high priority to environmental issues once they acquire governmental responsibilities.

Patterns of Economic Development
and Opportunities for
Environmental Policy Reform

Policies which affect what the Latin American economies produce, how they produce it, and what they consume also largely determine the impact which these societies have on their environment. In recent years, these policies have emphasized export promotion, foreign trade liberalization, fiscal austerity, privatization and reduced government intervention in the domestic economy. To the extent that such policies are compatible with improvements in environmental conditions, these improvements will be easier to achieve, and vice versa. It is possible to identify some situations where such compatibility exists, but easier to find cases where it does not.

Resource Exploitation as a Source of Competitiveness

Over the past twenty years, Latin America has become less competitive in international markets. Between 1950 and 1970, its share in world exports dropped from 11 per cent to 6 per cent, and by 1990 it had plunged to 4 per cent. To maintain even this low level of world market share, the region depends disproportionately on exports of non-renewable resources, goods manufactured by polluting industries, and agricultural commodities produced using unsustainable production systems.

Approximately one third of Latin America's exports come from petroleum and other non-renewable mining products. Another third come from agricultural exports, a major percentage of which are made up of fruits, flowers, vegetables and cotton, grown using high levels of pesticides, and of products such as beef and timber, often associated with deforestation. Compared with industrial production worldwide, Latin America has more than its share of polluting industries, such as oil refineries, chemical plants, steel and iron foundries and cement, glass and paper factories. In contrast, the region has a small share in the international markets for services, high-tech industries (such as microelectronics and biotechnology), and other sectors that exert less pressure on natural resources.

Policies which promote exports based on perceived comparative advantages, without taking into account their environmental impacts, are likely to further this dependence. Thus, the recent growth of high value exports in Chile and Costa Rica has been associated with a rapid rise in pesticide use, despite marginal efforts aimed at integrated pest management and safe pesticide use. Trade liberalization between Mexico and the United States has led to a concentration of heavily polluting industries on Mexico's northern border; promotion of shrimp farming in Ecuador and Honduras has had a devastating impact on the mangroves, and Chile's export-oriented policies have led to massive investments in heavily-polluting paper mills.

Occasionally, export promotion policies and changes in international markets can lead to environmental improvements. In Costa Rica, for example, rapid growth in tourism and forest plantations has tended to strengthen the political forces in favour of nature conservation and reforestation, while stagnation in the beef and extractive lumber industries has diminished the pressure to clear primary forests. One major beneficiary of export promotion activities in El Salvador is coffee, which provides most of the forest cover and fuelwood in that country, as well as other positive environmental attributes. The expansion of forest plantations in Chile has reduced erosion on large areas of land. Such cases, however, are relatively exceptional.

In contrast to the developed countries, most environmental problems in Latin America are more closely associated with production than with consumption. Thus, the groups affected by the necessary reforms are often a small number of powerful businesses, which tend to be less dispersed and have greater political capacity to oppose the reforms than do consumers in the industrialized countries. The region's heavy dependence on activities that degrade natural resources and on maintaining low taxes and wages in order to be competitive on world markets further strengthens the power of those groups.

The Effects of Other Recent Economic Policies

In addition to promoting a structure of exports which, on balance, favours highly-polluting activities and natural resource depletion, recent economic policies in Latin America have also affected the environment in other ways, both positive and negative.

On the positive side, real exchange rate devaluations designed to promote exports and reduced public credit subsidies associated with fiscal austerity and financial market liberalization, have tended to raise the real price of pesticides and lower their use. Thus, for example, in both Nicaragua and Honduras pesticide imports fell by over 40 per cent after major devaluations in the late 1980s. Increases in water and electricity rates and the establishment of private water rights have favoured more efficient use of water for irrigation and energy. The substitution of agricultural price supports by direct payments to farmers in Mexico, in connection with the North American Free Trade Agreement, has theoretically reduced the incentives to use agrochemicals and to grow annual crops on marginal lands. Similarly, fiscal austerity was among the principal reasons for eliminating livestock subsidies in Brazil.

On the other hand, at the same time that Latin American governments are promoting fruit, vegetable and flower exports which require massive use of agrochemicals, they have reduced their support for basic foodstuff production by small farmers, who typically have more diversified production systems, which are less dependent on agrochemicals. Macroeconomic and trade policies which discriminate against small-scale food production in El Salvador, for example, have promoted rural to urban migration and more extensive production systems, and these, in turn, have led to a falling water table in the San Salvador aquifer and greater soil erosion and siltation of hydroelectric plants. Small farm production on hillsides and the humid tropical lowlands has its own associated environmental problems, such as erosion and deforestation, but there is no reason to believe that reduced government support for small farmers is likely to alleviate those problems.

It has often been acknowledged that, at least in the short run, structural adjustment and fiscal stabilization policies tend to increase poverty, since they restrict aggregate demand, eliminate government subsidies, reduce public employment, and shift relative prices in favour of tradable goods and against real wages. Although it has proven difficult to trace the ultimate effects of these changes, increases in poverty can have numerous negative environmental impacts.

Tariff reductions and the elimination of import restrictions often lead to greater air pollution as a result of increased automobile imports and to more use of toxic pesticides. In Costa Rica, for example, where more than 70 per cent of air pollution in the San Jose Metropolitan area comes from vehicles, the total number of vehicles more than doubled between 1984 and 1994 thanks to import tax reductions in the 1980s; relaxation of pesticide registration requirements to facilitate intraregional Central American trade has allowed more highly toxic pesticides onto the market. Privatization of the electrical industry has tended to favour petroleum-based energy over renewable sources, since it is much more difficult for private investors to raise the capital for a large hydroelectric or geothermic plant than for smaller petroleum-based generators. Amongst public sector utilities, it has also diminished both the interest in and resources available for watershed management in the areas which they still control, as well as reducing their incentive to promote energy conservation. Liberalization of financial markets has been associated with rapid rises in real interest rates. These, in turn, discourage long-term productive investments in forestry, watershed management, perennial crops, and pasture improvements.

Finally, the decline in government resources and authority associated with recent economic policies has made it more difficult than ever for the public sector to monitor and regulate natural resource use, invest in research and extension focused on 'green' technologies, subsidize activities such as reforestation, soil conservation, and conservation of genetic resources, and establish land and forestry tenure regimes which discourage deforestation and favour more environmentally sound production systems based on agroecological principles. Despite a proliferation in recent years of new environmental legislation, ministries, agencies and projects, there are few signs of improvement in the *ésprit de corps* of public employees, government budgets for on-the-ground environmental activities, the quantity and quality of personnel working in public sector environmental programmes, or salaries for poorly paid civil servants. Many national parks exist only on paper since governments lack the resources to manage and staff the parks and compensate former land-owners for the loss of their access to the lands. Similarly, new forestry and pesticide regulations are often irrelevant because governments have no capacity to enforce them.

Environmental Implications of the Type of Government Regime

The final aspect of relevance to our analysis requires an examination of the factors which affect the relative power of different interest groups and government bureaucracies, and of how the levels of democracy and decentralization influence the outcomes of environmental struggles.

Competition for Control over the State

In addition to the groups promoting environmental reform discussed above, various other groups both within and outside government also influence public policies affecting the environment. To the extent that government policy is driven by mining companies, polluting industries, banana plantations, large ranchers, lumber companies, agrochemical corporations, and others dependent on polluting activities and natural resource exploitation, much higher levels of social mobilization are likely to be required to achieve positive environmental reforms. Similarly, because of the negative implications already mentioned of many economic policies currently favoured by international financial agencies, greater influence on public policy by these agencies may also hinder substantive environmental reform.

In this regard, government policy-makers and bureaucrats who have some degree of autonomy from pressures by individual businessmen or business federations seem more likely to be willing and/or able to make decisions which negatively affect specific corporate interests for the sake of broader concerns. Governments are likely to be more autonomous in countries where: a) the economy is sufficiently large to ensure that no specific group has enough individual power to heavily influence national policy; b) business groups are weak or fragmented; c) senior government officials have pursued careers in the public sector rather than in the private sector; d) government enterprises have substantial economic resources of their own; and e) major social upheavals have forced business groups to make room for participation by other sectors. Thus, it was probably easier for the Salinas administration in a large country like Mexico—which has undergone a profound social revolution, has an economically powerful public sector, and whose senior servants have traditionally been life-long bureaucrats—to take the controversial decision of closing a major petroleum refinery in Mexico City in order to reduce air pollution, than it would have been for the government of Honduras to take decisive action to eliminate misuse of pesticides on the banana plantations. Similarly, it was probably easier for Brazilian government officials to eliminate livestock subsidies in the Amazon than it would be for the government of Ecuador to control environmental destruction by the mining industry.

Democracy and Decentralization

There is some evidence that democracy favours effective solutions to environmental problems. Under democratic governments there are greater opportunities for environmental movements to develop without being repressed, fewer restrictions on NGOs and local organizations engaged in environmental projects, and more openness to negotiated solutions of policy disputes. Thus, it is no coincidence that Costa Rica, Nicaragua and Panama, countries with strong democratic undercurrents, have been more successful in developing promising alternatives to their forestry problems than have El Salvador, Guatemala and Honduras, where governments have been more authoritarian. Similarly, there have been (slightly) more environmental policy reforms in Brazil and Chile under the current democratic governments than under their military predecessors.

On the other hand, democratic elections, in and of themselves, do not guarantee strong environmental policies. Despite the fact that every country in Latin America now holds regular elections, many have made little substantive progress on environmental issues. Even under democratically elected governments, interest groups associated with economically destructive activities can be quite powerful and environmental movements may be weak.

In the same way, decentralization of decision-making and of resources sometimes favours environmental initiatives and sometimes hinders them. Since many groups which promote environmental policy reforms and engage in environmental activities operate at a local level, decision-making at this level favours their participation. Moreover, without the active local participation and support fostered by decentralization, many national policies are almost impossible to implement. Decentralization may make it easier to take advantage of local knowledge regarding natural resources and their management and, under certain circumstances, community management of forests and other natural resources can be the most effective alternative for safeguarding these resources.

At the same time, local and provincial governments and other decentralized structures are easily susceptible to influence by local élites involved in environmentally destructive activities. In many agricultural frontier areas, for example, the mayors are large ranchers, owners of lumber companies, or mine owners, who often use their influence to support road construction into forest areas, oppose national parks and indigenous land rights, or seek greater support for livestock. In areas where there are large plantations or mines, the companies which own them often dominate the nearby local governments. In other cases, local government officials have been corrupted by petty bribes or have simply been unwilling to enforce environmental regulations when that involves people they have known all their lives.

Conclusions

Concern for the environment has grown measurably in Latin America over the last fifteen years, and has brought together a wide variety of social forces with different interests and motivations.

In specific instances, where it has been possible to put together coalitions focused on a particular policy reform, or where the changes involved have not threatened powerful entrenched interests, environmental problems have been successfully addressed. Nevertheless, three major problems have limited the possibility of more general progress: 1) the difficulties involved in linking environmental issues with concerns for social justice; 2) the current emphasis in Latin America on economic policies which weaken the public sector and promote exports based on the exploitation of natural resources and cheap labour; and 3) the considerable influence over the region's governments of economic groups involved in deforestation and polluting activities and of international financial institutions.

Ultimately, the continued growth of Latin America's environmental movements and their ability to achieve major reforms depend on the ability to link— conceptually, programmatically and organizationally—concern for the environment with the issue of social justice. To go beyond partial, piecemeal environmental reforms whose overall impact is minor or short-lived, requires broad alliances between the urban middle class, poor urban neighbourhoods, farmers, and indigenous communities. But uniting the diverse factions, constituencies and interests concerned with the environment and social justice around a coherent alternative programme will be no easy task.

David Kaimowitz, "The Political Economy of Environmental Policy Reform in Latin America," *Development and Change* 27, no. 3 (July 1996): 433–52.

35

National Factor Markets and the Macroeconomic Context for Environmental Destruction in the Brazilian Amazon

STEVEN C. KYLE

AERCIO S. CUNHA

This paper argues that understanding the causes of environmental degradation in the Amazon requires an evaluation not only of economic conditions *within* the region, but also of the links between the regional and national economies. The dependence on national markets for determination of factor and output prices combines with existing technology and resource availability to produce the cycle of destruction seen in the area. The next section discusses important aspects of regional and national factor markets. This is followed by an analysis of the interrelationship between these and the pattern of development in the region. Finally, policy implications and recommendations are presented.

A Neoclassical Hypothesis: Unbalanced Factor Proportions

Predatory occupation such as that in the Amazon Basin is neither new nor peculiar to that region. Rather, it is the result of extension into the area of the familiar pattern of agricultural expansion at the extensive margin that has characterized the growth of Brazilian agriculture since the sixteenth century. What makes the Amazon different is an ecosystem that is more fragile than that of most other places, a pace of occupation more intense than in other areas and an especially adverse macroeconomic environment in the 1980s. In the Amazon, it takes only three to four years for the consequences of improper use of the soil to become apparent compared to decades in places with a less fragile environment, although the underlying reasons for resource and environmental destruction are in many ways the same. An exacerbating factor is the extreme austerity, instability and lack of investment that have characterized Brazil over the past decade.

Expansion of agriculture at the extensive margin is a consequence of economic conditions resulting from an abundance of land and scarcity of almost every other complementary factor—the most important of which are labour and capital. In this sense, it is a problem of unbalanced factor proportions, which result in extremely low cost for private use of resources and so do not provide incentives for conservation. Producers are induced to economize on the use of scarce factors by substituting them with the more abundant one. Or, in terms of the problem's duality, the producers' objective is to maximize returns to labour and capital, which can be accomplished through the extensive use of land. Given the technology, the fact that land is abundant (and cheap) is what accounts for its being extensively and carelessly used.

An added difficulty is that technological innovations, if and when they come about, will tend to reflect and therefore reinforce rather than change relative factor scarcities. The direction of technological change which is most beneficial in the light of environmental considerations is, unfortunately, not that which is most likely to be induced by relative factor endowments and prices in the Amazon. Current production technologies make extensive use of abundant land, and use relatively little labour. In order to avoid the destructive consequences of this production technology, it is necessary to promote technological change, with a much higher man-land ratio.

It has been shown that the nature of economic activities and technological innovation to be expected in such a land-abundant situation are of a land-*using* nature; i.e. left to its own devices, the market will not promote land-saving technological innovations since land availability is not a constraint to individuals at the micro-level. It is tempting to suppose that the government could improve on this situation due to its ability to take a more macro view in the context of a more long-term strategy. Unfortunately, it is more likely that government-conducted research will not fare any better. Public research agencies, such as the Empresa Brasileirá de Pesquisa Agropecuária (EMBRAPA), calculate the return to research resources using relative factor prices generated by the imbalanced endowment which causes the problem in the first place. The technology which EMBRAPA is likely to produce will favour the intensive use of the cheaper factor. Unless the government adjusts its research objectives, expansion of Amazonian agriculture will continue in its historic pattern.

Specifically, there are two choices facing policy-makers interested in promoting a more environmentally sensitive outcome to Amazonian occupation. First, they can try to alter the apparent relative factor prices by, for example, limiting the land allotted to each farm. Second, rather than relying on market mechanisms, they can actively promote research into the types of technologies needed. This is likely to produce better results for several reasons. One is that markets cannot be depended on to function as desired in the relatively primitive conditions of the Amazon. Second is the fact that the prevailing extractive mode of development gives little incentive to individuals to invest in the needed research. Finally, individual innovators are likely to produce changes on an incremental basis starting from the technological base they already possess while what is desired involves a relatively radical break with past techniques. So it is important for government not just to be aware of the nature of the 'mismatch' between technology and resource base—it must also actively promote alternatives.

Rather than take the route of promoting the correct type of technical change to redress the imbalance between endowments of land and other factors, Brazilian policy has consistently pursued the shorter path of subsidizing capital and stimulating migration to relieve local labour scarcity. Nothing has been done to restrict the amount of land owned or operated by single producers. On the contrary, policies have stimulated demand for land by making ownership not only a condition of eligibility for government programmes but also by making the size of the benefits directly proportional to the area owned. This type of policy has helped give Brazil one of the highest indices of land concentration in the world; it has also ensured that farmers face an imbalanced ratio of land to capital and labour for a long period.

The important policy question is whether Brazil should allow this process to continue by acquiescing in the use of the Amazonian frontier for agricultural expansion at the extensive margin, or whether the country should instead take steps to actually promote growth at the intensive margin. The thesis proposed by this study is that nothing short of a radical change in the pattern of agricultural growth inside and outside the Amazon can have any impact on the pattern of destruction seen in that region.

Development with Abundance of Natural Resources

The discussion in the previous section indicates that it is no surprise that a region with an abundance of natural resources and a shortage of almost everything else bases its development on intensive exploitation of its only abundant factor. However, that exploitation should go to such extremes as to become self-defeating is more difficult to explain. Agricultural expansion has been the goal of most Amazonian occupation projects and, so far, the main cause of deforestation.

Labour Markets on the Open Frontier

A typical farm in an Amazon settlement project has 100 ha and a cattle ranch at least 3000 ha. In either case, 50 per cent of the available area may legally be cleared, the remaining 50 per cent being left as forest reserve. However, a typical settler, with the limited means at his disposal, can work little more than 1 or 2 ha per year. Similarly, cattle ranchers depend heavily on labour to clear and maintain the 1500 plus ha allowed for pasture. Such labour, by and large, is not available, so that prospective ranchers often acquire land already cleared from failed settlements in order to establish themselves, instead of bringing in workers from other parts of the country. Even then, the shortage of labour makes upkeep difficult so that both small settlers and large ranchers have far more land than they can use productively.

At going wage rates it is very difficult to attract workers to the Amazon. The low-value product of labour effectively sets a ceiling on wages, thus limiting employment. The problem is not that labour is not available but that the demand for labour is too limited.

In the open Amazon frontier, workers have the possibility of off-farm income such as hunting, gathering and subsistence production of foodstuffs. For this reason, the opportunity cost of farm employment, or workers' reservation wage, may be quite high. The labour supply curve would thus be located to the left and above the one that would prevail if the frontier were 'closed'. Open access to natural resources effectively reduces the supply of labour. With both demand and supply restricted, non-existence of market equilibrium is a possibility (if not in the aggregate, at least locally). In this sense, what appears as labour 'shortage' has less to do with demographic dynamics than with the non-existence of equilibrium in the labour market.

Capital and Investment

Capital scarcity for agricultural production is probably as acute as that of labour in the Amazon. In relation to the size of the area opened to settlement, few physical resources (equipment, cattle, etc.) have been brought in, due either to the poverty of immigrants or failure to invest on the part of landowners and entrepreneurs. Capital scarcity can also result from failure to generate an economic surplus or from failure to reinvest locally. In the latter case the region would be exporting capital, a not unlikely hypothesis in the present case.

Working capital is also scarce; credit is not available or, more precisely, given the level of risk, prospective borrowers cannot afford the interest rate required to induce lenders to come forth with money. Shortage of capital can also be understood as incapacity to wait. For example, waiting for tree crops to grow, for cattle herds to reproduce, for timber prices to rise or for research to produce results implies relatively long-term investment. This means that future income flows are heavily discounted and that producers take a short-term outlook. Real interest rates have been high and volatile in Brazil, often above 30 per cent per year, due mainly to central government actions with respect to fiscal and monetary policy and debt management. Credit for periods longer than one year must normally be obtained via administrative allocation; long-term capital markets are thin or non-existent. Inadequate infrastructure can increase marketing costs and reduce the economic value of goods and take economic stimulus out of conservation. Finally, because capital is mobile, a shortage of capital is equivalent to inability to compete for capital with other regions.

This discussion indicates that capital markets may be facing a problem of non-existence of equilibrium similar to that of labour. Because of lack of infrastructure, very high marketing costs, complete absence of 'economies of concentration', lack of proven production technology and high risk, the rate of return to agricultural investments in the region is likely to be low. Likewise, the region's inability to attract private voluntary savings and to retain locally generated surpluses accounts for the small supply of investible resources, but also serves as evidence of the relative attraction of alternative investments.

Scarcity of labour and capital is but a symptom of the economic unworthiness of projects undertaken in the Amazon. Government support for regional development through funding of unsound projects has not attracted labour or capital on a permanent basis, hence the strong reliance on natural resources. A corollary to this conclusion is that the starting point of a programme to stimulate resource-saving practices is to stop throwing money into projects which are not economically viable. The challenge of Amazon development is not to channel resources into the region but to keep capital and labour from fleeing from it.

Policy Implications

What can be done to reverse the trend of reckless exploitation of Amazon resources and to promote sustainable development in the region? The main goal of Amazon policy should be to break the pattern of agricultural expansion at the extensive margin and to stimulate modernization in the Amazon and elsewhere.

To change the pattern of agricultural growth from extensive to intensive margin, it is recommended, first, that the process of 'closing' the agricultural frontier be accelerated. Problems of surplus population and unemployment can be more cheaply and effectively dealt with in their place of origin. Escape valves may be convenient but in the case of the Amazon are not effective. Second, the conditions which account for the speculative demand for land should be eliminated. Measures should include elimination of subsidies to agricultural credit and inputs, an end to agricultural tax breaks, introduction of a more effective land tax and, to stimulate agricultural production, a policy of high agricultural prices through a more aggressive commercial policy both externally and domestically (real devaluation of the exchange rate, investments in marketing infrastructure, food subsidy programmes to low-income classes). Third, it is important to conduct research on tropical agricultural production, on evaluation of the Amazon resource base and on the environmental impact of possible development projects. Unless more information is gained about the region's resources and about the dynamics of its ecosystem, no rational development strategy can be formulated.

Steven C. Kyle and Aercio S. Cunha, "National Factor Markets and the Macroeconomic Context for Environmental Destruction in the Brazilian Amazon," *Development and Change* 23, no. 1 (January 1992): 7–33.

Acknowledgments

H.W. Arndt, "The Origins of Structuralism," World Development 13, no. 2 (1985): 151–59.

Anne O. Krueger, "Government Failures in Development," *Journal of Economic Perspectives* 4, no. 3 (Summer 1990): 9–23.

John Williamson, "What Washington Means by Policy Reform," in *Latin American Adjustment: How Much Has Happened?* ed. John Williamson (Washington, DC: Institute for International Economics, 1990): 7–20.

Brian Levy, "How Can States Foster Markets?" *Finance and Development* 34, no. 3 (September 1997): 21–23.

Sanjay Pradhan, "Improving the State's Institutional Capability," *Finance and Development* 34, no. 3 (September 1997): 24–27.

Jeffry A. Frieden, "The Method of Analysis: Modern Political Economy," excerpt from *Debt, Development and Democracy: Modern Political Economy and Latin America, 1965–1985* (Princeton, NJ: Princeton University Press, 1991): 15–41.

Alberto Alesina, "Political Models of Macroeconomic Policy and Fiscal Reforms," in *Voting for Reform: Democracy, Political Liberalization and Economic Adjustment*, eds. Stephan Haggard and Steven B. Webb (New York: Oxford University Press, 1994): 37–60.

Dani Rodrik, "Understanding Economic Policy Reform," *Journal of Economic Literature* 34, no. 1 (March 1996): 9–41.

Stephan Haggard and Steven B. Webb, "What Do We Know about the Political Economy of Economic Policy Reform?" *World Bank Research Observer* 8, no. 2 (July 1993): 143–68.

Barbara Geddes, "Uses and Limitations of Rational Choice," in *Latin America in Comparative Perspective: New Approaches to Methods and Analysis*, ed. Peter H. Smith (Boulder, CO: Westview Press, 1995): 81–108.

John H. Coatsworth, "Obstacles to Economic Growth in Nineteenth-Century Mexico," *American Historical Review* 83, no. 1 (February 1978): 80–100

Nathaniel H. Leff, "Economic Retardation in Nineteenth-Century Brazil," *Economic History Review* 25, no. 3 (August 1972): 489–507.

Stanley L. Engerman and Kenneth L. Sokoloff, "Factor Endowments, Institutions, and Differential Paths of Growth Among New World Economies," in Stephen Haber, ed., *How Latin America Fell Behind: Essays on the Economic Histories of Brazil and Mexico* (Stanford: Stanford University Press, 1997): 260–304.

Rory Miller, "Latin American Manufacturing and the First World War: An Exploratory Essay," *World Development* 9, no. 8 (August 1981): 707–16.

Carlos F. Diaz Alejandro, "Latin America in the 1930s," in *Latin America in the 1930s: The Role of the Periphery in World Crisis*, ed. Rosemary Thorp (London: MacMillan, 1984): 17–49.

Eliana Cardoso and Ann Helwege, "Import Substitution Industrialization," in *Latin America's Economy: Diversity, Trends, and Conflicts* (Cambridge, MA: MIT Press, 1992): 84–103.

James E. Mahon, Jr. "Was Latin America Too Rich to Prosper? Structural and Political Obstacles to Export-Led Industrial Growth," *Journal of Development Studies* 28, no. 2 (January 1992): 241–63.

Rudiger Dornbusch, "The Case for Trade Liberalization in Developing Countries," *Journal of Economic Perspectives* 6, no. 1 (Winter 1992): 69–85.

Manuel Pastor and Carol Wise, "The Origins and Sustainability of Mexico's Free Trade Policy," *International Organization* 48, no. 3 (Summer 1994): 459–89.

Luigi Manzetti, "The Political Economy of MERCOSUR," *Journal of Interamerican Studies and World Affairs* 35, no. 4 (Winter 1993): 101–41.

Werner Baer and Kent Hargis, "Forms of External Capital and Economic Development in Latin America: 1820–1997," *World Development* 25, no. 11 (November 1997): 1805–20

Jeffrey D. Sachs, "External Debt and Macroeconomic Performance in Latin America and East Asia," *Brookings Papers on Economic Activity* 2 (1985): 523–64.

Guillermo A. Calvo, Leonardo Leiderman, and Carmen M. Reinhart, "Inflows of Capital to Developing Countries in the 1990s," *Journal of Economic Perspectives* 10, no. 2 (Spring 1996): 123–39.

Joel Bergsman and Xiaofang Shen, "Foreign Direct Investment in Developing Countries: Progress and Problems," *Finance and Development* 32, no. 4 (December 1995): 6–8.

Stephan Haggard, "The Political Economy of Foreign Direct Investment in Latin America," *Latin American Research Review* 24, no. 1 (1989): 184–208.

Barbara Geddes, "Challenging the Conventional Wisdom," *Journal of Democracy* 5, no. 4 (October 1994): 104–118.

Stephan Haggard, "Democratic Institutions, Economic Policy, and Development," in *Institutions and Economic Development: Growth and Governance in Less-Developed and Post-Socialist Countries*, ed. Christopher Clague (Baltimore: Johns Hopkins University Press, 1997): 121–49.

Barbara Geddes, "A Game Theoretic Model of Reform in Latin American Democracies," *American Political Science Review* 85, no. 2 (June 1991): 371–92.

Sylvia Maxfield, "International Capital Flows and the Politics of Central Bank Independence," excerpt from *Gatekeepers of Growth: The International Political Economy of Central Banking in Developing Countries* (Princeton, NJ: Princeton University Press, 1997): 3–4, 35–49.

Delia M. Boylan, "Preemptive Strike: Central Bank Reform in Chile's Transition from Authoritarian Rule," *Comparative Politics* 30, no. 4 (July 1998): 443–62.

Interamerican Development Bank, *Facing Up to Inequality in Latin America: Report on Economic and Social Progress in Latin America, 1998–1999* (Washington: IADB, 1998): introduction.

United Nations Conference on Trade and Development, "Income Distribution, Capital Accumulation, and Growth," *Challenge* 41, no. 2 (March/April 1998): 61–80.

Ingrid Palmer, "Public Finance from a Gender Perspective," *World Development* 23, no. 11 (November 1995): 1981–86.

David Kaimowitz, "The Political Economy of Environmental Policy Reform in Latin America," *Development and Change* 27, no. 3 (July 1996): 433–452.

Steven C. Kyle and Aercio S. Cunha, "National Factor Markets and the Macroeconomic Context for Environmental Destruction in the Brazilian Amazon," *Development and Change* 23, no. 1 (January 1992): 7–33.

Index

CPSIA information can be obtained at www.ICGtesting.com
Printed in the USA
LVOW06s0456270314

379080LV00002B/117/P